British Policy in South-East Europe
in the Second World War

STUDIES IN RUSSIAN AND EAST EUROPEAN HISTORY

Phyllis Auty and Richard Clogg (*editors*)
British Policy towards Wartime Resistance in Yugoslavia and Greece

Elisabeth Barker
British Policy in South-East Europe in the Second World War

Richard Clogg (*editor*)
The Movement for Greek Independence, 1770–1821

Olga Crisp
Studies in the Russian Economy before 1914

D. G. Kirby (*editor*)
Finland and Russia, 1808–1920: Documents

Martin McCauley (*editor*)
The Russian Revolution and the Soviet State, 1917–1921: Documents

Further titles in preparation

British Policy in
South-East Europe
in the Second World War

ELISABETH BARKER

BOOKS
10 East 53d St., New York 10022
(a division of Harper & Row Publishers, Inc.)

First published 1976 by
THE MACMILLAN PRESS LTD
London and Basingstoke

Published in the U.S.A. 1976 by
HARPER & ROW PUBLISHERS, INC.
BARNES & NOBLE IMPORT DIVISION

I S B N 0-06-490301-x

Printed in Great Britain

Contents

Foreword

First, what this book is not. It is *not* a history of South-East Europe in the Second World War. Nor is it even a comprehensive record of British policies (or lack of policy) in the area; space does not permit. It aims rather to provide the essential materials and pointers for an understanding of British dealings with South-East Europe. Even then, for the period after April 1941, it gives a good deal less space to Greece and Yugoslavia than their importance to Britain would merit. This is because so much has already been written, in the way of authoritative first-hand records, about British relations with these two countries; so this book merely tries to set out the broad lines of the story, as far as possible on a comparative basis, adding here and there fresh material when it offered itself. Proportionately more space has been given to the countries about which less has already been written – Rumania, Bulgaria, Hungary and Albania. Turkey only comes into the story in so far as its policy directly influenced British relations with the area.

Why South-East Europe? The area was treated as a convenient and in some ways logical unit of concern by the British Middle East and Mediterranean Commands, by the Special Operations Executive, and by the Political Warfare Executive. In the Foreign Office, Hungary belonged to the Central Department and the other countries to the Southern Department, but efforts were fairly often made to look at the area as a whole, for instance when British representatives from South-East Europe were summoned to London in April 1941.

My main sources have been the official documents now available in the Public Record Office. They reveal a great deal even though some documents – how many, and how important, it is hard to tell – are still withheld. The volume is enormous and I am grateful to the staff of the P.R.O. for the help they gave me when I got hopelessly lost. Extracts are published by permission of the Controller of H.M. Stationery Office. Maps 2–5 and 7–9, from J. F. Horrabin's *Atlas History of the Second World War* (London: Thomas Nelson & Sons Ltd, 1946), are republished by permission.

I have tried to round out this source with the first-hand records of those who took part in events, whether British or non-British, but I make no claim to have read them all, and I have not attempted a serious study of German documents since that seemed outside my brief. But I have made a particular effort to find indications of the attitude and actions of the Communist parties of South-East Europe, in so far as these were relevant to Britain.

Where I have been especially lucky is in the extremely generous help given by individuals who played some part in events. In my 'note on sources' (page 269), I have particularly mentioned George Taylor, Bickham Sweet-Escott, Ivor Porter, Lázló Veress and Professor W. J. M. Mackenzie, and to them I am particularly grateful. Among others whom I should like to thank for information or pointers to the interpretation of events are Sir Fitzroy Maclean, the Hon. C. M. Woodhouse, Sir Alexander Glen, Colonel W. S. Bailey (now, to my sorrow, dead), Sir John Henniker-Major, Sir Eric Berthoud, Dr C. A. Macartney, General Veress de Dalnok and Sir Frank Roberts. Bojan Dimitrov of the Macedonian Ministry of Information in Skopje gave me useful books and documentation on the Macedonian question, and I should like to thank him; so, too, Sir William Deakin for encouraging me to undertake the book and Krsto Cviić for keeping up my spirits while I was writing it and lending me important books which I could not get otherwise.

Finally, a word of self-defence. It may be said that it is irrelevant or unfair to quote the bad-tempered or despairing outbursts or scrawls of exhausted and overburdened ministers or senior officials as valid historical evidence. It seems to me that they can reveal more about the way in which courses of action (or inaction) were actually adopted (or drifted into) than the formal policy papers, often composed after the event to justify (or throw a decent veil over) actions already taken or at least begun, for the benefit of Cabinet colleagues or Allied governments.

PART ONE

A FOOTHOLD
WON AND LOST

MAP 1. South-East Europe, August 1939

1   The Eve of War

The British were sucked into involvement in South-East Europe in 1939 unwillingly, almost unthinkingly. Their eyes were fixed elsewhere: on the German threat to Poland, which might destroy the European power balance, and on the Italian threat in the Mediterranean against the sea route to the Middle East and India. South-East Europe was a shadowy no-man's-land lying between the German thrust in the east and the Italian thrust in the south.

For the British, Turkey was an area of important strategic interest, a bulwark guarding their position in the Middle East against German, Italian (or Russian) ambitions. But 'the Balkans', with the doubtful exception of Greece, was a murky place, economically and socially backward and politically unstable, full of feuds, intrigues, plots, hidden danger and sudden death. Its kings were slightly ridiculous, its leaders clamoured for foreign help but rejected foreign advice. 'Typically Balkan', a phrase dear to the Foreign Office, meant some peculiarly tortuous and shady manoeuvre. The Hungarian landed aristocrats and gentry might be more civilised but were equally turbulent and trouble-some.

The wisest thing was therefore to keep out. Unfortunately neither Hitler nor Mussolini was willing to keep out. Both were determined to move into South-East Europe, at times in rivalry, at times in collusion. In consequence the British found themselves entering the Second World War bound by promises not only to Poland – the immediate target of German aggression – but also to two South-East European countries, Greece and Rumania.

By unilateral guarantees of April 1939 the British, along with the French, undertook to give these two countries 'all the support in their power' in the event of a clear threat to their independence which they themselves 'considered it vital to resist with their national forces'.[1] That a British government – in particular the government of Neville Chamberlain – should have taken on such commitments to intervene on the European continent was surprising, all the more in that the two countries lay at the extreme limits of Europe, much more remote than Czechoslovakia, the 'far-away country' which a year earlier had been placed firmly outside the sphere of British interest.

But the decision to accept entanglement in the Balkans was not the outcome of serious political or military planning. It was a hastily improvised reaction to the moves made by Hitler and Mussolini in the spring of 1939 and followed on the heels of the equally improvised decision to guarantee Poland, announced on 31 March, and undertaken, in Chamberlain's words, to avoid being taken by surprise 'by some sudden coup or swoop'.[2] The guarantee to Greece was a panic response by Britain to the Italian invasion of Albania on 8 April; it was more understandable than the guarantee to Rumania since it could be seen as serving the requirements of traditional naval strategy in the Mediterranean. The guarantee to Rumania was a response to the spate of rumours, following Hitler's march into Prague, about impending German attack on Poland or Rumania. But the British would not have moved so quickly if their hand had not been forced by their French allies. The Chamberlain government agreed with the French that there was a real threat to Rumania, but thought that the best answer was to create a four-power group of France, Britain, Poland and Rumania, which could perhaps be extended to Turkey and Greece and even Bulgaria; at the very least Poland and Turkey could perhaps be persuaded to commit themselves to defend Rumania.

This would have been a slow, hard slog. The Polish Foreign Minister, Colonel Joseph Beck, who visited London at the beginning of April, withstood polite pressures from the Foreign Secretary, Lord Halifax, and from Chamberlain himself for Poland to make some commitment to defend Rumania;[3] he wished to avoid annoying Hitler unnecessarily, hoping to keep the door open for a deal. The Rumanians stated the position frankly. When their Minister in London, Virgil Tilea, saw Halifax on 7 April, he made it clear that the British plan for a four-power group would be likely to provoke Germany, adding that the Poles were afraid of anything that looked like the encirclement of Germany.[4]

However, Chamberlain and Halifax intended to go on trying for a four-power group. But then on 12 April the French ambassador presented Halifax with the text of a proposed French declaration of 'an immediate guarantee to Rumania'. Halifax argued against such haste: 'if we give Rumania an unconditional guarantee we throw away the lever which we have for bringing Poland and Turkey into a wider arrangement'.[5] The Permanent Under-Secretary at the Foreign Office, Sir Alexander Cadogan, recorded in his diary what happened to the French proposal: 'got H. to go over to see P.M. about 7.30, and latter strongly against . . . H. turned up at 9.30 and we drafted telegram to Paris protesting.' But the next day the French ambassador produced a 'reasoned exposé' of French views, and they were unanswerable'. Cadogan sent a record of them to the Cabinet, and was later sent for himself: 'they had agreed to the Rumanian guarantee!' he noted, with obvious surprise.[6] So the unilateral guarantees to Rumania and Greece were announced simultaneously in London and Paris.

Unanswerable the French arguments may have been; the fact remained that in military terms it was about as hard for the Western allies to help an isolated Rumania as to help an isolated Poland; the guarantee was therefore singularly unconvincing unless – failing Poland – either the Soviet Union or Turkey or both could be persuaded to reinforce it. So Britain immediately asked Turkey to guarantee Rumania; in return, Britain would guarantee Turkey.[7] But the Turks were much too canny to swallow the bait; instead, they made an interim agreement with Britain on 12 May to co-operate in the Mediterranean area, and went so far as to say that it was also necessary to ensure the establishment of stability in the Balkans. Britain and Turkey then started negotiations for a treaty, into which the French were brought in July; but these had still not been concluded when the Second World War broke out. Meanwhile, the efforts of Britain and France to reach political or military agreement with the Soviet Union had failed, largely because the Poles and Rumanians, like the Baltic States, did not want to give the Russians any excuse for sending troops into their territory. But this in no way affected the validity of the British–French guarantees, even if it made them virtually useless.

So Britain, along with France, entered the war committed to the defence, not only of Poland, but of two South-East European countries, without possessing the military means of fulfilling these commitments. For Greece, given British sea power, the outlook was a little less gloomy than for Rumania. Yet even to Greece it was hard for Britain to give effective help unless Italy were benevolently neutral – and it was clearly against Italian aggression that the British guarantee was directed.

As things began, so they went on. The story of Britain's relations with South-East Europe during the Second World War was for the most part a story of last-minute improvisation and the undertaking of commitments without the resources to fulfil them. Policies, if that is the right name for them, were largely dictated by negative outside factors: first fear of annoying Mussolini, then fear of provoking Hitler prematurely, after that fear of irritating Stalin; there was later the wish to avoid trouble with nagging exiled governments. Positive policies, when committed to paper, were often documents designed to justify or defend actions already taken for urgent short-term reasons, against attack by critics or opponents either inside the British War Cabinet or within the anti-Hitler alliance.

There were occasional successes and many instances of extraordinary personal courage, persistence and achievement by individuals; but inevitably more failures. Yet on balance the British readiness to tackle the impossible or try to solve the insoluble, regardless of the hard facts of military, economic or political power, contributed something to the defeat of the Axis – even if very little to serve British national interests in the narrower sense.

HITLER'S ASSETS: TRADE AND FRONTIER REVISION

One of Hitler's great assets was that the western allies had left South-East Europe a virtual power vacuum. After the First World War the British had left it to the French to organise the area politically through the Little Entente group of anti-revisionist States, until this collapsed following Hitler's march into Austria. Thereafter the British and French left it to the Germans to organise and exploit the area economically. When Cadogan tried to sum up the moral to be drawn from the aftermath of the Munich crisis, in October 1938, he wrote: 'we must cut our losses in central and eastern Europe – let Germany, if she can, find there her "Lebensraum" and establish herself, if she can, as a powerful economic unit.'[8]

This economic disinterest extended even to Greece and Turkey, although they were regarded as Mediterranean rather than South-East European countries. In the same minute, Cadogan wrote: 'the Mediterranean area is a direct interest of ours, being the highway to our eastern possessions and Dominions, and we should do everything we can to maintain the best relations with, and give such assistance as may be possible to, Turkey and Greece.'[9] But when it came to actually buying Greek and Turkish tobacco, the government found it useless to try to change the tastes of the British smoker. In the month after the British guarantee to Greece, the Chancellor of the Exchequer, Sir John Simon, wrote:

> I have always recognised that it is most unfortunate from our point of view that Greece and Turkey depend economically to so large an extent on their export of Tobacco to Germany and that the best way in which we could help those countries economically would be by creating a permanent market for Oriental tobacco in the United Kingdom. We have however always felt that this would be attended by very great difficulties . . . Our main desire was to find some means of making it clear to the Greek Government that we attached a very real value to their preserving their independence.

But now that Britain had given Greece a guarantee, the Chancellor argued that it was possible to abandon 'the attempt to market increased quantities of Oriental tobacco in this country'. 'Surely,' he concluded, 'the immense commitment we have now entered into is worth something.'[10] The Greeks were, of course, not asked whether they would rather have a market for their tobacco or a diplomatic promise.

Other countries in the area had even less chance of economic favours from Britain. A typical reaction was Cadogan's diary entry in October 1938: 'George Lloyd[11] at 6.30 about Roumania. Says we *must at once* buy 600,000 tons of Rumanian wheat. But we don't want the damned stuff – and the question is – are we going to declare economic war on

Germany? (No one can pretend that it is a commercial proposition).'[12] Ex-enemy and potentially pro-Axis countries such as Bulgaria and Hungary could expect still less sympathy.

Germany was therefore quite free to get an economic stranglehold on South-East Europe, without British opposition. Hitler also had a powerful political weapon which the British dared not use – or rather, if they tried to grasp it, they soon found it too hot to hold. Hitler had established Germany as the great revisionist power, destined to right the wrongs said to have been committed by the Treaties of Versailles, Trianon and Neuilly, together with other real or imaginary wrongs for which the victors of the First World War could be held responsible. This gave him an almost irresistible power to seduce or bribe Hungary and Bulgaria with slices of territory which they had once held, and to terrorise countries which feared the loss of territory, particularly Rumania. Such bribes could overcome – at least for a time – the moral scruples even of a man with such a high reputation for honour and decency as the Hungarian Count Pál Teleki, since the recovery of national territory could be seen as the highest of all imperatives – though Teleki's suicide suggested that in the last resort he found this moral theorem unconvincing.

Possibly King Boris of Bulgaria did too, in the end, though, in spite of many rumours, his premature death was probably due to natural causes, not suicide.

The British did not like the role of defender of the status quo and always felt that it had somehow been unfairly forced upon them by the unashamedly anti-revisionist French. During Chamberlain's appeasement period, Halifax made it dangerously clear to Hitler that all that worried England was that any frontier alterations should come about peacefully without 'far-reaching disturbance'.[13] Hitler's annexation of Austria and break-up of Czechoslovakia soon followed.

When in 1939 the British plunged into their commitments in South-East Europe, they were soon drawn into the game of territorial grab, and were soon in trouble. Their guarantee to Rumania angered the Hungarians who, thanks to Hitler, had recovered a slice of Slovakia and Ruthenia, and were now eager to get back Transylvania from the Rumanians. The British guarantee to Rumania placed a new barrier in their way. It was also an obstacle to Bulgaria which had its own claim on Rumania for part at least of the Dobruja.

Early in July the Rumanian Foreign Minister, Grigore Gafencu, told the British Minister that he was worried about 'the encouragement which Hungarian or Bulgarian irridentism is now receiving from the Axis Powers'; he thought this 'part of a general plan to exert pressure on Rumania so as to weaken her'.[14] In London the Hungarian Minister called attention to the 'important territorial problems existing between Hungary and Rumania in consequence of the unjust conditions of the Treaty of Trianon', adding that their solution would 'clarify by peaceful means the present poisoned atmosphere of Europe'. Anxious to encourage the Hungarians to stay neutral in the war now clearly looming, the Foreign Office rashly suggested to the Rumanians that the British might reply to the Hungarians that they had 'no wish to close their minds to the existence of this issue', but were 'convinced that territorial questions cannot in the present strained atmosphere be profitably discussed'. But the Rumanians reacted so violently that the British hastily withdrew their suggestion and promised that no reply would *ever* be sent to Hungary without previous consultation with Rumania.[15]

Over Bulgarian claims Rumanian feelings were milder. As the British Minister in Bucharest, Sir Reginald Hoare, remarked: 'Transylvania is an infinitely more sensitive spot than the Dobruja.'[16] So the British could, from April 1939 on, express cautious sympathy for the idea of the Rumanian Foreign Minister Gafencu about making concessions to Bulgaria, of a half-way sort.[17] But the British dared not display their sympathy publicly and so earned little good will from the Bulgarians.

South-East Europe was littered with many other territorial or national disputes which were potential weapons in Hitler's hands – the Bulgarian claims against Greece for an Aegean outlet and against Yugoslavia for Macedonia and the Tsaribrod area, the Hungarian claim against Yugoslavia for the Bačka, perhaps even Croatia and Fiume; the Greek claim against Albania for the territory known as Northern Epirus or even the whole country, to say nothing of Yugoslav claims against Italy for the Trieste region, or Italy's reported offer to partition Albania with Yugoslavia, recounted by the Yugoslav Prince Regent Paul to Halifax in July 1939.[18] There were also Yugoslavia's rather vague aspirations to control of Salonika, exploited by Hitler in 1941. All these were well fitted to serve as explosive charges for destructive purposes in Hitler's hands. They could only be obstacles to the British in their early efforts to build up some sort of defensive dam against Hitler and Mussolini in South-East Europe.

So the British went to war, whatever their inner reservations, in the guise of an anti-revisionist power. As Chamberlain said, announcing the guarantees to Greece and Rumania: 'His Majesty's Government attach the greatest importance to the avoidance of disturbance by force or threats of force of the status quo in the Mediterranean and the Balkan Peninsula.'[19]

This too was how they were seen by the country which was later to play so powerful a part in the area – the Soviet Union. In the mid-1930s most Europeans would have regarded the Soviet Union – in spite of its aspirations to world revolution – as a defender of the European status quo against Hitler. But Hitler's bloodless gains in 1939 did not only frighten Stalin but also tempted him to thoughts of future Russian pickings. The Soviet–German agreement and secret protocol of August 1939 whetted his appetite still more sharply. Stalin later told Sir Stafford Cripps[20] that during the pre-war negotiations with Britain and France the Soviet Union had wanted to change the old equilibrium in Europe, for which these two countries stood, but they had wanted to preserve it. On the other hand Germany had wanted to change the equilibrium and 'this common desire' had created a basis for the rapprochement with Germany.[21]

Hitler's technique of bribery therefore worked well with Stalin – up to the point when Stalin became, in Hitler's eyes, too greedy. But the British, even after they became Stalin's allies, refused to give him the public formal recognition he wanted for Soviet claims in the Baltic States, Eastern Poland, Bessarabia and Bukovina – a scruple which delayed the conclusions of an Anglo-Soviet treaty by several months and made Stalin even more suspicious of Britain's motives. Hitler's encouragement of Soviet ambitions was a sort of delayed-action time-bomb in Britain's path.

BRITAIN'S ASSETS IN SOUTH-EAST EUROPE

Even if the British were at a disadvantage in the game of territorial grab, there were other political weapons. They had some friends and admirers in the small governing elites which were to be found in the South-East European countries, perched more or less precariously on top of rickety social structures based on a mass of poor peasants and a few industrial workers, with a very small middle class in between. (Hungary, with its rather more developed industry and past member-ship of the Habsburg empire, had a more developed middle class; the same was true of Greece, with its big shipping and trading interests.) The pro-British elements were to be found both inside the govern-ments in power and in the 'democratic' oppositions, particularly the peasant parties.

The reasons for pro-British feeling were various. The British (on the whole) were gentlemen. Hitler (on the whole) was not. The British succeeded with some justification in taking up a superior moral position to Hitler. British diplomats could lecture South-East European foreign ministers, prime ministers, even heads of State, like a senior prefect reproving some grubby small boy caught out in some particularly squalid lapse from the school code of behaviour, and they often got away with it. Churchill could impose on others his own personal con-viction that neutrality was a form of delinquency and that concessions to Hitler were a sin against the higher morality.

In Greece, Yugoslavia and Rumania, there were friendly memories of alliance in the First World War. Kings and Regents had a suitable respect for the British royal family, in some cases ties of personal affection. King George VI was asked by the Foreign Office to send

letters of encouragement or warning to King George II of Greece, the
Prince Regent of Yugoslavia and King Boris of Bulgaria – even a
signed photograph and a verbal message to the Regent of Hungary.
Only King Carol of Rumania was excluded from the royal correspondence, not for political reasons, but presumably because he was
living openly with his mistress, Madame Lupescu, while his wife,
Queen Helen, lived in Florence.

(While, however, the Foreign Office made full use of royal contacts
so long as kings or regents were in power, it is not true – though
often believed – that they tried, as a matter of principle, to keep
monarchs on their thrones or restore them once they had gone into
exile. Churchill, himself a devoted believer in monarchy on both
historical and sentimental grounds, once minuted: 'I know how marked
is the Foreign Office prejudice against all Kings.'[22] This was a deliberate taunt; yet of all the kings who fled from South-East Europe,
King George II was the only one whom the Foreign Office – and
Churchill – tried really seriously to put back on his throne; efforts on
behalf of King Peter of Yugoslavia appear in retrospect as a peculiarly
lengthy and elaborate face-saving device.)

For the pro-British elements, encouragement came from the old
legend of Britain's invincibility. In the black summer of 1940 the new
legend of Hitler's irresistible force became far more potent, but after
his invasion of Russia it soon began to fade, and pro-British feelings
were reinforced among the upper and middle classes of South-East
Europe – even among some of the peasants – by the new fear of Soviet
domination and social upheaval.

One odd aspect of the war in South-East Europe was that although
a potentially revolutionary situation existed there, neither Hitler nor
Stalin – nor, less surprisingly, the British – tried seriously to use revolution as a war weapon. Hitler's experience of the Rumanian Iron
Guard – some of whom had real revolutionary aims while others were
a revolutionary rabble – was an unpleasant one, and for military
reasons he ultimately backed the socially conservative General Ion
Antonescu against them. Moscow was happy to use the Communists
of Bulgaria or Rumania for purposes of pro-Soviet propaganda or
occasional strikes, demonstrations or sabotage, but not for anything
more serious. Its enthusiasm for the Greek Communists was half-
hearted, and that not only for reasons of Anglo-Soviet good relations.
In Yugoslavia, the Communist Tito stepped out of line and created
his own revolution regardless of Moscow. It was a freak of the prag-
matism or opportunism of the British that it should have been they
who worked most closely with the Communist-led revolutionary
movements in South-East Europe.

At the outbreak of war, however, British 'ruling circles' were strongly
anti-Communist and deeply suspicious of the Soviet Union.

2 Salonika Front or Balkan Bloc?

When war broke out, the Western allies had, in theory, the choice between political and military action in South-East Europe. The British, anxious to avoid irritating Mussolini and doubting the practical possibility of military action, favoured political efforts to get the South-East European countries to bury their national quarrels and join together in a Balkan bloc strong enough to withstand German pressures. This was to be based on the Balkan Entente of 1934, and seemed a possible way of giving reality to the guarantees to Rumania and Greece.[1] It also was favoured by the Rumanian Foreign Minister, who during the summer of 1939 received some encouragement from the Turks.[2] On the outbreak of war Halifax told the War Cabinet that his policy was 'a neutral Balkan bloc', adding that Bulgaria was 'the key to the Balkans'.[3] This policy quickly acquired short-term tactical merit as a means of heading the French off the idea of a Salonika front.

The Balkan Entente had been formed by Rumania, Yugoslavia, Greece and Turkey to keep Bulgaria in order and prevent it, if necessary by force, from pressing its territorial claims against the four. Inevitably the Bulgarians disliked it as the British Minister in Sofia, George Rendel, wrote later: 'it represented to the Bulgarians the prison warder far more than the friendly policeman.'[4] Hitler's success in the field of treaty revision naturally encouraged hopes in the Bulgarians of recovering at least the southern Dobruja from Rumania. Gafencu, and some other Rumanians, would perhaps have been ready to concede at least a promise of its eventual return, as the price of securing Bulgarian adherence to a Balkan bloc: Halifax spoke hopefully of this possibility in October.[5] But the difficulty was that if Rumania made any concession to Bulgaria, this would open the way to territorial demands from Russia and – even worse – from Hungary.

In January 1940 Mihai Antonescu – then a minor Rumanian politician – visited Rome, and canvassed the idea that in return for a Hungarian promise of non-aggression, Rumania might cede to Hungary a strip of territory 20 to 40 km. wide known as the Szatmar–Arad strip as well as Temesvar; but the Hungarians preferred to hold out for a much bigger gain and turned down the idea when it was put to

them by the Italians.[6] At home, Gafencu found his way blocked by
the powerful opposition leader, Iuliu Maniu, of the National Peasant
Party, who was campaigning early in 1940 against any form of territorial concession.[7]

When the Balkan Entente met in Belgrade in February 1940, Gafencu
had come to a dead end; he was willing to admit that the Bulgarian
claim to southern Dobruja was good, but it could not be dealt with
before a general peace settlement because to deal with it at once would
greatly strengthen Soviet and Hungarian claims against Rumania.[8]
This meant there was little hope of Rumania – or Turkey – drawing
Bulgaria into the Balkan Entente. Nevertheless, Halifax took a dog-
gedly optimistic view of the Belgrade meeting: the four countries, he
wrote to Lord Chatfield, the Minister for Defence Co-ordination, 'to a
greater extent than ever before feel that they sink or swim together',
and had decided to renew the Entente for seven years. (It had in fact
met for the last time.) Above all, Halifax wrote, the Balkan Entente
governments had decided to hold staff talks, to prepare for mutual
defence.[9] As late as April 1940, General Ioannis Metaxas, the Greek
Prime Minister, was forecasting that these Balkan staff talks were about
to begin.[10]

Bulgaria, while staying aloof from the Balkan Entente, displayed
restraint. The Foreign Minister told a Belgrade newspaper: 'we shall
do nothing until the end of the war which would make the situation of
our neighbours difficult.' He also spoke of Bulgaria as 'a loyal member
of the Balkan family of nations.[11] Halifax could therefore, without too
much exaggeration, present a memorandum to the War Cabinet on
29 April: 'up till now we have with a fair amount of success been able
to constitute and maintain a front in the Balkans in opposition to
German pressure and penetration. Based on Turkey this front has included Yugoslavia, Rumania, Bulgaria and Greece, with Hungary as
a weakly-held outpost. Bulgaria has always been a weak point in the
line, but even here we have succeeded in recent months in definitely
strengthening our position . . .'[12]

But Germany's victories in the West quickly shattered this fragile
Balkan structure, for which British diplomats – especially in Sofia – had
worked so hard. On 10 May, the Southern Department of the Foreign
Office minuted: 'there are for the present *no* Balkan Entente staff
conversations . . . If things go not too badly for us in the West, the
Yugoslavs may pluck up courage and take part . . .' On 18 June however the Minister in Belgrade, Ronald Campbell,[13] advised 'great discretion' in working for Balkan solidarity: 'an active and above all open
intervention is dangerous and any clear attempt at hustling harmful . . .'

In reality, British hopes of a 'neutral Balkan bloc' were destroyed by
the fall of France, which led to Rumania's loss of large territories to

Russia, Hungary and Bulgaria and its denunciation of the Balkan Entente and the British guarantee. The British turned to trying to form a defensive alliance of four, three or even two countries; this hope was finally killed in April 1941.

The British plan for a 'Balkan bloc' was undermined from the start by the territorial disputes of the area, even more seriously by Britain's lack of military strength to back up its diplomacy. After it collapsed, the British turned to the idea of confederation as the solution for South-East Europe's post-war problems – an idea equally doomed to failure, because Stalin thought otherwise.

A SALONIKA FRONT?

From the first days of the war, the Chamberlain government was involved in argument with the French over the question of a front in South-East Europe. It was a dispute which Churchill, taking over the French role, later carried on with the Americans and Russians.

The immediate problem was to find somewhere to hit Germany other than the western front. Britain and France agreed fully that they were not yet militarily prepared for action in the west. But the British did not think they were prepared for action in the south-east either; they wanted for the time being to concentrate on Economic Warfare – it usually appeared with capital letters at that period – against Germany. The French, less phlegmatic and more directly threatened by Germany, felt the need for some sort of military action, if only to ensure political stability and keep up morale at home.

The idea of a Salonika front had obvious attractions, reviving memories of the 1914–18 war and the final victorious campaign under French leadership which took French armies across the Danube into central Europe. (British memories were rather of fustration, sickness and long periods of boredom; when victory came the British turned east to the Straits, leaving the French to sweep north.) In 1939 the Daladier government sent General Maxime Weygand to Syria. He was famous as one of the great military leaders of the 1914–18 war and as the man who in 1920 had helped the Poles in their historic stand against the Bolshevik armies; more recently he had involved himself in French politics, on the far right, and so was a potential threat to Daladier.[14] A famous and ambitious French general who could pull strings in Paris, holding a command in a traditional British area of interest, the Middle East, was certain to worry the British; and he did.

Five days after Britain declared war, Halifax told the War Cabinet that he was going to tell the French that 'in the period until Italy made clear her intentions, H.M.G. hoped that the French government would not authorise action in the Balkans by the French military authorities such as had been discussed between the French and British military authorities prior to the outbreak of the war, when it had been assumed that Italy would take sides with Germany'. Halifax then presented his alternative of 'a neutral Balkan bloc'.[15] But there were doubts whether diplomatic pressure would be enough to restrain the French: three days later Chamberlain told the War Cabinet that he was going to Paris, partly to discuss with Daladier the attitude of the Allies towards Italy and 'the plans believed to be entertained by General Weygand for action in the Balkans'.[16]

The Foreign Office fear was that apart from other drawbacks, an Allied military move might provoke Mussolini to enter the war; and not only Chamberlain, who had perhaps not lost all hope that Mussolini might turn out to be a gentleman, but even more the British military leaders had every reason to want to keep Italy neutral for reasons of Mediterranean strategy. On 14 September the War Cabinet considered a Foreign Office memorandum, which concluded: 'a neutral, and a fortiori friendly Italy seems more valuable to us than a Balkans forced by us into belligerency. And the two are almost certainly incompatible.' But Churchill, then First Lord of the Admiralty, looked further ahead to a possible German move against Rumania: in that case 'we should do everything possible to marshal Yugoslavia, Greece, Turkey, Bulgaria and Rumania against the German threat'.[17]

On 20 September the War Cabinet was told that the Chiefs of Staff still felt 'considerable apprehensions' about Weygand's activities in the Balkans. The British Ambassador was 'to urge upon the French government the need for the utmost caution'.[18] Nevertheless at a Supreme War Council meeting a day later Daladier stressed 'the importance of maintaining an Eastern Front' and said that some tangible evidence of Allied intention to help the Balkans, 'such as the despatch of a force to Salonika or Istanbul', would have a very steadying effect; he asked for a very early decision. Chamberlain stalled.[19]

Anglo-French staff talks produced an outward show of agreement. The Chief of Naval Staff told the War Cabinet on 6 October that 'one of our main objects in our discussions with the French had been to convince them of the unsoundness of their project of an expedition to Salonika. In this we had been successful.' The conclusion had been that only in the case of a German attack in South-East Europe, with Italy neutral, would a limited Allied defensive force be landed in Salonika, and then only if Greece asked for it and Italy agreed.[20] (Oddly, this was the first time Greece's wishes had been taken into account.)

So far, so good. But in late November the British learned that Weygand was expected back in Paris with 'rather far-reaching ideas for staff conversations with the various Balkan countries'.[21] Simultaneously the British Chiefs of Staff, in a 'Report on the Strategic Situation in South-East Europe and the activities of General Weygand',[22] concluded that Weygand had 'gone beyond the policy which had been agreed between H.M.G. and the French government'. In the War Cabinet on 30 November Halifax insisted that Weygand should be 'dissuaded' from disturbing 'the present equilibrium'. Churchill however hoped that British views 'would be conveyed in terms consonant with the respect due to so distinguished a person as General Weygand', adding that he himself thought that the Balkans were gradually veering towards the Allies; if Greece, Rumania and Yugoslavia were to come in on our side, it was even possible that Italy might too.[23]

It soon became obvious that the French did not really share British views on the need for Italian neutrality. Early in December Lord Chatfield, the Minister for Co-ordination of Defence, told the War Cabinet that the French were thinking of a Balkan expedition even if Italy should be hostile.[24] The Cabinet continued to feel that the 'dominant consideration' was that even preparations for the Balkans should in no way antagonise Italy.[25]

At a meeting of the Supreme War Council on 19 December, the French soft-pedalled the need for early Allied intervention but pressed for building up a 'Balkan front' of the South-East European countries by diplomatic action and supplies of war materials. Chamberlain again talked of the danger of 'unfortunate reactions in Italy'. The French could not see the need for consulting Italy but conceded that the British Ambassador should informally approach the Italians. The British, in return, conceded that the French should carry on secret staff contacts with Yugoslavia and Rumania; they were nervous about contacts with Greece, as a country about which Mussolini was likely to be 'particularly susceptible'.[26]

The French by this time were clearly irked by British stalling, and wanted action, or at least the show of action. Before the British ambassador had got to the point of approaching the Italian government, the French ambassador nipped in ahead and saw Count Galeazzo Ciano on Christmas Eve, informing him that France and Britain had decided they could not stand aside when 'Germany and the U.S.S.R.' committed aggression against Rumania. They therefore wanted to take certain preliminary measures so that their forces in Syria and elsewhere in the Middle East should not arrive too late. They did not want to arouse Italian suspicions, indeed they hoped for Italian co-operation. Ciano replied coolly, saying that Italy would not disinterest herself from the Balkans and that he would report to the Duce.[27] The French move naturally piqued the British. When the British ambassador finally saw Ciano early in January, he was merely told that Mussolini was not ready to talk.[28]

By this time, rumours of the Anglo-French dispute over the Salonika front were beginning to cause a stir in South-East Europe and beyond. Weygand had at first found the Yugoslavs eager to co-operate. When he was in Paris in December 1939, he told the Yugoslav Minister there that it was necessary to prepare a base at Salonika and that five divisions were needed for the purpose.[29] Also in December a French staff officer from Paris visited Belgrade for 'unofficial' talks with the Yugoslav General Staff.[30] But the Prince Regent Paul told the newly arrived British Minister, Ronald Campbell, on 31 December that he had heard that the French were very keen on a Salonika front and that the British government opposed it. This he thought very wise since the French had only three divisions in Syria, whereas the Germans had perhaps 48 available for operations in the Balkans.[31]

What Prince Paul particularly disliked was not the confidential staff talks so much as the fact that the French were 'trumpeting the project in the press, giving Germany full warning for preparing countermeasures'.[32] Soon after the British Minister in Sofia noted that 'reports of Allied intentions to create a Balkan front, based on speculation as to the objects which have led to the creation of General Weygand's army, are very general in the Balkans'.[33] In Bulgaria such rumours caused gloom since it seemed obvious that if the western Allies wanted to go to Rumania's rescue via Salonika, they would march across Bulgaria. The British Minister, George Rendel,[34] wrote later: 'it is ... no exaggeration to say that during the first six months of the war the Bulgarians genuinely believed that their neutrality was less likely to be violated by Germany than by the Allies.'[35]

On 11 January Moscow radio added its voice, attacking the plans of the 'Anglo-French coalition' for a southern front in the Balkans: 'as soon as General Weygand's troops start to disembark in Salonika, Germany would not stand idle ... German mechanized troops will be able to occupy the whole of northern Yugoslavia up to Belgrade before the French and British are on the scene.'[36]

Only in Athens did there seem to be some liking for the Salonika front idea. When the British and French military attachés saw the Greek commander, General Alexander Papagos, early in January, he discussed the possible extension of the war to the Balkans, and according to the British account 'gave the impression that he definitely considered himself and Greece as being our allies in all except the word'.[37] (After news of this reached London, British military attachés in South-East Europe were warned not to take part in the French contacts with the Balkan General Staffs.)

Between the British and French military leaders, the argument became bitter. The Chiefs of Staff discovered that Weygand was now signing himself 'Commander in Chief of the East Mediterranean Theatre of Operations'; they insisted that there could be no question of their accepting as a *fait accompli* the position which Weygand was apparently trying to build up for himself, and they would be against British forces serving under a French commander in a part of the world which they regarded as a predominantly British interest.[38] Four months later they were still worrying about 'a curious misapprehension' that Weygand had been appointed 'Generalissimo of the Allied Forces in the Near and Middle East'.[39]

The British hoped, vainly, that hard military facts would restrain the French. On 19 January the Chiefs of Staff approved an aide memoire which argued that 'a minimum force of some 20 to 24 Allied divisions' would be needed to cover Salonika and prevent enemy penetration past Salonika. The Greeks had offered to supply 10 Greek divisions – an offer which the British did not accept at its face value – and this meant that, since any available British forces would have to be earmarked for defence of Turkey, the French would have to provide 10 to 14 divisions; and the British did not think the French could provide them.[40] In any case the British felt they had a power of veto since, as the Chiefs of Staff pointed out, French ability to land forces depended on the British producing the necessary ships.[41]

The French belief that it might even be possible to defeat Germany on its own soil by means of an advance 'through Yugoslavia, Croatia and Austria'[42] was partly based on the belief that Greeks, Serbs and other South-East Europeans would rally to the Allies and fight with them, so that with 'a limited expenditure of Allied forces' it might be possible to develop an offensive operation, 'possibly on a decisive scale'.[43] This was just the kind of idea that Churchill cherished – but not Halifax, who wrote on 16 February: 'until we dispose of greater strength . . . I doubt our being able to count . . . on the cooperation of those Balkan States who will be directly exposed to attack or intimidation by Germany, i.e. Yugoslavia, Rumania, Hungary and Bulgaria . . . It all comes down to the old point, that in the Balkans we must cut our coat according to our cloth.'[44] Halifax returned to the charge in late March: 'stalemate in the West affects the French position and morale more than our own . . . Paris therefore will be searching for some way out of the deadlock . . . South-east Europe will certainly be one of their suggestions.' But, Halifax argued, the main object of the South-East European countries was to remain out of the war and to retain their independence; the Allies would therefore lose a great deal if they brought war to South-East Europe 'unless – and this is the crucial point – their military action in the Balkans can be overwhelmingly successful and decisive'. And, he clearly meant, it could not.[45]

At this time the British learnt of yet another project of Weygand's, for an air-borne expedition to Rumania. This was disclosed to Wing Cdr. Lord Forbes, the British Air Attaché in Bucharest, when he saw Weygand in Beirut at the end of March. Weygand claimed that the French Air Commander in Chief had promised him as many aircraft as he needed; he had sent a staff officer to Rumania to discuss the plan, which had at first 'been received with terror' by the Rumanian

General Staff, though Weygand thought they would accept it in the end. The Rumanians were to provide exclusive use of 'a large number of aerodromes' and the aim would be to hold the line of the Carpathians.[46] When the British made enquiries about this plan in Paris, they were told that Forbes must have misunderstood Weygand.[47] Obviously he had not.

In their secret staff talks in Greece and Yugoslavia, however, the French continued to report success. They said that the Greek General Staff were showing great good will. French officers from Syria had been authorised to inspect Greek aerodromes and agreement had been given for creation of Allied supply dumps. The Greek Chief of General Staff, they said, was willing to allow French troops to land at Salonika before Greek concentrations were complete. The French also reported that the Yugoslav General Staff had handed over a first instalment of information on communications and transport and had promised information on aerodromes.[48]

The British Chiefs of Staff, however, though they agreed to continued French staff contacts with Yugoslavia, Rumania and Greece, insisted that 'on no account should the Balkan States be given grounds for believing that the Allies wish to disturb their neutrality'.[49] When British diplomatic representatives met in London in April – the meeting was Halifax's substitute for military action – they gave rather pessimistic estimates of the willingness of the South-East European countries to resist Germany.

Military disaster in Scandinavia in April did not quench French enthusiasm for a Salonika front, but it strengthened British opposition. As late as 23 April the French were planning – with reluctant British agreement – to make a démarche to the Greek government about sending a force to Salonika. Four days later however the Chiefs of Staff told the War Cabinet that the experience of Scandinavia confirmed that it was quite out of the question to land troops unless there were adequate air defences, and anti-aircraft guns and aircraft were not available for Salonika. If the French could produce them, well and good, 'otherwise we would have to make it quite clear . . . that the idea of an expedition must be ruled out'.[50] By 6 May Pierson Dixon[51] could minute: 'the Salonika project now having been suppressed, there is less danger of the French alarming the Greeks', and on 13 May John Nicholls minuted: 'the Salonika project, for which the French were pressing, is not going to materialize owing to the opposition of our General Staff.'[52]

So the British won in the end, and the French, overwhelmed in the west, summoned Weygand home to try to save the situation; he eventually aligned himself with Marshal Pétain. In part, British resistance to a Salonika front stemmed from jealousy of Weygand; much more, from distrust of what looked like total lack of realism or serious planning on the French side. Above all, it stemmed from determination to concentrate all resources – such as they were – on the fundamental British aims of safeguarding the Mediterranean sea route, defending Egypt and defending the Straits; everything else was secondary.

Yet, hostile and sceptical as the British were at the time, the idea of a Balkan front and a drive against Germany from South-East Europe lived on, especially in Churchill's mind, as a seductive alternative to more orthodox strategies, alarming and shocking the Americans as it had once alarmed and shocked the British. In South-East Europe itself, the myth of a Salonika front – or of an air-borne expedition to Rumania or Hungary – lived on, influencing Yugoslav military leaders in 1940 and 1941 and Mihajlović and Tito thereafter, as also the Rumanians and Hungarians in 1943 and 1944. It was also a ghost that haunted Hitler throughout the war; he could not forget that, as he once said, 'Salonika had been the beginning of Germany's defeat last time.'[53]

SETTING THE BALKANS ALIGHT

The imminent collapse of France in June produced a last-minute change of heart in the British military experts, who decided that it was in the Allied interest to 'set the Balkans alight'. The Joint Planning Committee considered the need to help France by 'an anti-Axis flare-up in the Balkans' and argued on 4 June that 'in the possible event of a complete collapse of France, while the Balkans were still neutral, we feel that the last chance of ever bringing in the Balkans on our side would have vanished'. Therefore British policy should be 'to encourage Balkans intervention on our side in the event of war with Italy'.[54] Meanwhile the French Minister in Sofia was telling his British colleague that they must 'set alight' the Balkans, while in Belgrade the French were encouraging the Yugoslavs to attack the Italians in Albania.[55] But there was no response. In the Foreign Office, Nicholls minuted on 15 June: 'it seems very doubtful whether we shall be able to do anything whatever to set the Balkans alight.'[56]

France fell. Early in July the Chiefs of Staff told the Foreign Office that 'there is now little hope of our being able to influence the Balkan situation one way or the other'; the important thing, however, was that Germany and Russia should be on opposite sides in any Balkan conflict.[57]

The Foreign Office then told its representatives in the South-East European capitals that their first object must be 'to exploit conditions which are likely to embroil Russia and Germany in the Balkans'.[58]

3 Britain, Russia and South-East Europe, 1939–41

'Embroiling' Russia and Germany over South-East Europe seemed at first an ill-starred undertaking, given Stalin's apparent determination to avoid war at any price; and there is no evidence that any British machinations in the area influenced Hitler's decision to attack Russia. 'Embroilment' was in fact only one of a series of widely differing policies which Britain followed towards Russia up till June 1941.

On the outbreak of war, there was a natural feeling of disillusionment and suspicion in Britain towards the Soviet Union, caused by the collapse of the Anglo-French-Soviet talks in the summer of 1939 and the Soviet-German Pact of August. Yet Chamberlain had still not lost hope of reaching an understanding with the Russians and detaching them from Germany.

This was shown in the War Cabinet discussions on the negotiations for a British-French-Turkish treaty, which in September and October 1939 became entangled with negotiations between Turkey and Russia for a mutual aid pact. The Anglo-French-Turkish conversations during the summer had been troublesome since the Turks pitched their price high. However on 18 September Halifax told the Cabinet that it should be possible to get a treaty if Britain increased its proposed credit for war materials from £10m. to £21m.[1] Time pressed: the Turkish Foreign Minister, Sükrü Sarajoglu, was off to Moscow and Halifax wanted him to sign the treaty with Britain and France first, since this might 'strengthen his hand in his discussions with the Soviet government'.[2] Sarajoglu postponed his departure to Moscow so that agreement could be reached on the political side of the treaty, which under Protocol II specifically exempted the Turks from taking any action which might result in war with Russia – a point on which they had been very insistent.[3] The Turks then demanded a further £4m. – which, Halifax said, was 'a heavy price, but . . . not too heavy . . . to pay for Turkish neutrality'.[4] The Anglo-French-Turkish treaty was initialled on 28 September, but its signature was delayed until Sarajoglu came back from Moscow.[5]

So for the British, much depended on the Turkish-Soviet talks. Behind the scenes, the Germans were putting heavy pressure on Stalin and Molotov to use the bait of a Turkish-Soviet pact to detach Turkey from the Western allies, if possible to stop Turkey signing the Anglo-French-Turkish treaty, also to get Turkey to close the Straits completely.

On 4 October Halifax told the War Cabinet that Stalin was pressing Sarajoglu 'very strongly' to get the Anglo-French-Turkish treaty watered down, as his price for a Turkish-Soviet pact. In particular Stalin wanted a provision that if the Soviet Union became engaged in war with Britain and France, the entire three-power treaty would be suspended for the period of the war.[6] This demand caused anxious heart-searchings in the War Cabinet on 4 and 6 October: was the treaty worth having at such a price? One view was that to accept the watering-down of the treaty would be to suffer a serious diplomatic defeat and would make it still more difficult to fulfil the guarantees to Rumania and Greece. On the other hand, Britain had an interest in better Turkish-Soviet relations.

Chamberlain came down firmly in favour of concessions to Stalin. By accepting the Soviet demands, it would be possible to secure not only the signature of the French-British-Turkish treaty but also the signature of a Turkish-Soviet Pact. 'The world would thus see,' Chamberlain said, 'Great Britain, France, Turkey and the U.S.S.R. entering into agreements either with one another or with one another's concurrence, and would thus be enabled to judge the hollowness of Germany's boast of an alliance with the U.S.S.R.' This argument did not sound very convincing, but it persuaded the Cabinet to accept the Soviet demands.[7]

In the event, British heart-searchings proved unnecessary. The Germans overdid their pressure on Stalin and Stalin overdid his pressure on the Turks. On 18 October Halifax reported that the Turkish-Soviet talks had broken down over two demands which the Russians had reiterated three times though Sarajoglu had twice rejected them – that Protocol II, or the 'Suspense Clause' of the Anglo-French-Turkish treaty should apply in the case of Germany as well as the Soviet Union, and that Turkey should immediately close the Straits to non-Black Sea Powers. Sarajoglu was leaving Moscow and the Turks wanted to sign the treaty with Britain and France as soon as possible – though great secrecy was to be preserved 'until M. Sarajoglu had safely left Soviet territory'.[8]

The treaty was signed the next day. It was a welcome success for the British. Nevertheless, Halifax commented that the Turkish break with the Soviet Union put an end, for the time being, to British hopes of building, through Turkey, a bridge to the Soviet government; and he surmised that in the background there might be some secret German-Soviet arrangement over the Balkans.[9]

The Russians showed no gratitude for Chamberlain's willingness to meet Soviet wishes. When the British ambassador in Moscow, Sir William Seeds, was paying a farewell call in December, Molotov complained that Britain, 'by its acts all over the world', was unfriendly to

Russia; he refused to believe that over the Anglo-French-Turkish Treaty the British had tried to meet Soviet demands: since Sarajoglu's Moscow visit, he said, Soviet-Turkish relations had deteriorated, 'which showed what we had been up to'. Seeds could only repeat that the British had sincerely hoped that better Soviet-Turkish and Anglo-Turkish relations 'would work to the mutual advantage and better understanding between all three countries'.[10]

Britain's would-be friendliness towards the Soviet Union was badly shaken when the Russians attacked Finland at the end of November. The French had in any case always been more bellicose towards Moscow than the British. On 7 December the War Cabinet discussed the apparent willingness of the French to launch an expedition in the Balkans against the Russians as well as the Germans, but was told that it would be in the British interest to avoid open hostilities with the Soviet Union if possible: the Russians had designs on Iran, Iraq and Afghanistan which they could exploit to our serious disadvantage.[11]

Nevertheless, Soviet reverses in Finland produced an atmosphere of anti-Soviet euphoria among British diplomats and others in South-East Europe. Sir Reginald Hoare, the pleasantly eccentric but normally sceptical British Minister in Bucharest, was not immune to it. He wrote to the Foreign Office urging that the British guarantee to Rumania should at once be extended to cover attack by Russia as well as Germany – this was something the British government had steadily refused to do, from April 1939 onwards – and suggesting that the Allies should 'take steps to prove to the world that Russia is indeed a colossus with feet of clay . . . These steps, as I see the matter, can only be military action (e.g. against the vital oilfields of the Caucasus) and a counter-revolution or even chaos inside Russia.' 'If we do not meet Stalinism in the gate,' he added, 'we are going to lose the peace . . . If we beat Stalin, we need have no fear of Germany, which will in due course collapse.'[12]

Hoare's letter met a mixed reception in the Foreign Office. Fitzroy Maclean,[13] who had just spent three years in Russia, commented: 'it is not at present our intention to declare war on the Soviet Union, for we have nothing to gain by so doing . . . It is however quite possible that sooner or later the moment will arise when our interests will best be served by an open conflict with the Soviet Union . . .'[14] But a senior official, Laurence Collier, was more sceptical: ' . . . I suppose it is natural for diplomats in countries adjacent to the Soviet Union . . . to regard Stalin as a greater menace than Hitler, but I am convinced that it is *not* true, and that to say that 'if we beat Stalin, we need have no fear of Germany' is, to speak frankly, nonsense!'[15]

The French plan for bombing the Soviet oilfields with long-range bombers drawn from Tunisia was seriously examined by the British early in 1940. The Chiefs of Staff were dubious; apart from other drawbacks of war against Russia, they held that the spread of the war to the Balkans would be to Britain's disadvantage. But Maclean prepared a paper in which he concluded that 'the risk involved would not . . . appear to be necessarily as great as the Chiefs of Staff . . . seem at first sight to suggest'.[16]

Halifax himself remained decidedly cautious. He told the Turkish ambassador in mid-February that 'we were not disposed to declare war upon Russia, but, at the same time, were not disposed to be deterred from any action that might suggest itself to us for fear that Russia would declare war on us'. The Turkish ambassador agreed: he felt that nothing would give the Germans greater pleasure than that the British should declare war on Russia.[17] The Turks themselves remained quite determined not to get involved in any anti-Russian activity. When Weygand suggested to them that 'something should be dropped on Russian territory out of aeroplanes' – the British ambassador was not sure whether the something was propaganda agents or other human beings or merely pamphlets – the Turks refused absolutely.[18]

In March 1940 the replacement of Daladier by Paul Reynaud led to a fresh wave of French pressure for action in far-away places. Reynaud proposed formally that the Allies should send warships into the Black Sea to stop the passage of Russian oil and other supplies to Germany. This idea had strong appeal for the First Sea Lord, Churchill, who had put it to the War Cabinet in October 1939 and again backed it on 27 March: 'two or three submarines would not only interrupt the Russian oil traffic in that sea, but would have a terrifying moral effect on Russia'. He suggested that Halifax should get the Turks to co-operate.[19] Halifax knew this was hopeless; as Cadogan had minuted: 'in the matter of the Straits we are not free agents . . . It is most unlikely that Turkey, if non-belligerent, will tear up the Montreux Convention for our convenience.'[20] This was a hard fact which Churchill, then and later, found it difficult to accept.

Reynaud also raised at highest level the plan for bombing Soviet oil-fields, with or without war against Russia. But Halifax told the War Cabinet that the Turks would oppose any activity likely to provoke the Russians.[21] The War Cabinet decided that the British should 'indicate' at the next Supreme War Council that they were willing to prepare detailed plans for bombing Baku 'without however committing ourselves to this operation'.[22]

It is hard to tell how seriously the British – or the French – really took the Baku project. But the enormous amount of paper-work undertaken in Paris, London, Egypt and Syria must have provided tempting fodder for spies. When Molotov made a major policy speech on 29 March, he hinted that he knew a good deal: 'we must . . . watch certain suspicious activities, particularly the concentrations of the Eastern Army of the Western Powers, commanded by General

Weygand, in Syria and other neighbouring countries. We must be vigilant against any attempts to use these troops for a purpose hostile to the Soviet Union. The danger of playing with fire should be apparent to these countries . . .'

When Halifax held his meeting of British diplomatic representatives from South-East Europe in early April the Baku project was mentioned but, in effect, quietly shelved. Sir William Seeds, who had just retired from his post as ambassador in Moscow, threw doubts on the project: first, the effect would not be decisive; second, 'it would be difficult to justify to public opinion in this country, if not in France, an unprovoked aggression on the Soviet Union' – a forthright argument seldom heard at that time. Halifax concluded that 'on the whole it would be better to postpone the Baku project for the moment and to reconsider it in the autumn'.[23]

In practical terms the Baku project was dead. But it lived on to serve German propaganda and poison Russian minds. When a few months later Sir Stafford Cripps, the ambassador in Moscow, suggested to the Foreign Office a fresh effort to win over the Soviet Union, he said that Britain would, among other things, have to 'guarantee that [Russia] will not be attacked from the south from Iran and Turkey and especially that Baku will not be attacked from these countries by us or any of our allies'.[24] At almost the same moment Ribbentrop was writing to Stalin that the captured secret papers of the French General Staff showed that it was only German victories in the West that had saved the Soviet oil centre of Baku from British attack.[25]

The German victories in the west inevitably changed the attitudes of both Britain and Russia towards South-East Europe, and to each other. Stalin's first thought was to acquire compensation in the east for Germany's enormous gains in Western Europe, and to use the fall of France as the moment to take over the Baltic States and, soon after, to annex Bessarabia and northern Bukovina from the Rumanians. This last move did not please the Germans: in August 1939 Ribbentrop had virtually promised Molotov a free hand over Bessarabia but Bukovina had not been part of the bargain, and in 1940 the Germans did not want any disturbance in Rumania which would damage its economic contribution to the German war effort. The Russians had to limit their immediate claim to northern Bukovina, instead of the whole territory, before the Germans would 'advise' the Rumanians to yield peacefully.

The British, on their side, gave up thoughts of bombing Baku or opening a Salonika front, and turned to a search for better relations with Russia – perhaps an understanding over South-East Europe. The first British move was made before the fall of France, in mid-June, when Britain was trying to back the French in their last desperate efforts to seek help in the most unlikely quarters. In support of a move by the newly arived French ambassador, Cripps saw Molotov on 14

June and said British policy was to maintain the independence of the Balkan States against German and Italian aggression; he believed that Britain 'had common cause with the U.S.S.R. who might assist in bringing the Balkan countries together for this purpose'. Molotov immediately seized on this innocent phrase and twisted it to his own purposes: he 'expressed interest' in what he called Cripps's 'formal suggestion' about a Balkan bloc.[26]

Molotov then followed this up with an official denial through the Soviet news agency TASS of 'a report' that fresh steps were being undertaken 'under the direction of the U.S.S.R.' to conclude a stronger anti-aggression pact between Rumania, Yugoslavia and Turkey with the object of resisting German and Italian expansion in the east.[27] This was presumably issued first, to place it on public record that some such proposal had been made to the Soviet Union, next, to appear virtuous in German eyes by claiming to have rejected it.

Undeterred, Cripps pressed on. On 17 June he telegraphed: 'in critical situation which has now arisen desirability of inducing Soviet government to adopt a policy of co-operation with Great Britain is clearly greater than ever.'[28] On Fitzroy Maclean's suggestion,[29] the Foreign Office decided that the best thing would be to send Stalin a personal message from Churchill through Cripps. The message proposed Anglo-Soviet consultation in face of the prospect of a German 'hege-mony over the Continent' and declared that Britain and Russia, lying at the extremities of Europe, were in a 'special position' to resist this.[30] Cripps was instructed not to give Stalin 'the impression that we are running after him', and not to discuss Soviet claims on Bessarabia.[31]

On 1 July Cripps delivered the message to Stalin. During a long conversation Stalin – according to Cripps's full account – raised the question of a Balkan bloc, asserting that Cripps had proposed to Molotov the creation of such a bloc 'under the aegis of Russia'. Stalin then said that Russia had no desire to rule the Balkans and that such a policy would be 'incorrect and very dangerous' for the U.S.S.R. Cripps replied that 'his reference to the Balkans seemed to have been misunderstood: he had certainly not suggested that the U.S.S.R. should rule the Balkans'. What he had really suggested was that 'without a lead . . . by some major and neighbouring Power who desired to bring these countries together, it would be difficult to ensure any stabilisation in the Balkans'. Russia and Turkey, Cripps added, might be able to do this. Stalin repeated that the Soviet Union had 'no wish to assume the role of super-arbitrator or to get embroiled in the Balkans'. He then turned to Turkey and said it was wrong for the Straits to be under the absolute control of one power, which might abuse it. Cripps replied that Britain might be able to 'encourage' the Turks to come to some agreement in the matter; this Stalin promptly accepted.[32]

The Cripps-Stalin talk had no immediate result. Throughout July the Foreign Office tried cautiously to 'encourage' the Turks to make some concession over the Straits, as Cripps had proposed; but they came to the conclusion that 'there was no basis for agreement between Russia and Turkey in regard to the Straits, which was the subject in which M. Stalin was most interested'. The Turks had made it quite plain that they would not give up their special position under the Montreux Convention, and the Foreign Office bore in mind 'the very great importance of not giving the Turkish government the impression that we were prepared to sell their vital interests to the Russians in our own interest'.[33] By mid-August Cripps concluded that 'it is beyond question that there is not the slightest chance at the present time of producing any kind of rupture in German-Soviet relations'.[34]

But in October, impelled by many signs of coming Axis action in South-East Europe, Cripps made a fresh effort: the Foreign Office authorised him to propose Anglo-Soviet consultation on the post-war settlement, but to keep off any question of recognition of Soviet claims to territories such as Bessarabia and Bukovina.[35] The approach failed; Molotov was otherwise engaged, in arranging a visit to Berlin, to be followed later by a visit by Stalin himself.[36]

The curious exchanges between Cripps and the Soviet leaders over a special Soviet role in the Balkans may perhaps have had more effect than was immediately visible. Stalin and Molotov, by twisting Cripps's words into a British offer of Soviet leadership, may have hoped to strengthen their own bargaining position and elicit an even better counter-bid from the Germans. When Molotov told the German ambassador about the Stalin–Cripps interview, he completely ignored Cripps' explanation of his real meaning and quoted him as saying that 'the British government was of the opinion that unification and leadership of the Balkan countries for the task of maintaining the status quo was rightly the task of the Soviet Union . . . this important mission could be carried out only by the Soviet Union'.[37]

Molotov's Berlin visit in November 1940 was the turning-point in Soviet-German relations and led to Hitler's final decision to attack Russia. The visit failed because Hitler offered too little and Molotov asked for too much: for southern as well as the northern Bukovina; for German agreement to a mutual aid pact between Russia and Bulgaria, which was to be recognised as part of the Soviet security zone; and not merely for revision of the Montreux Convention but for Soviet land bases on the Bosphorus, if necessary acquired with German military help.[38] Between Molotov's Berlin visit and the final statement of Soviet demands, the details of the latest British approach to Moscow were leaked to the press. Halifax told the War Cabinet that the leakage certainly came from the Soviet side.[39] The Cabinet then decided that it would not be worth while making any further advances to the Russians for the present.[40]

It was therefore clear that Cripps's approaches in Moscow had at least encouraged Stalin to overestimate his own bargaining-power, raising his price so high that Hitler called off the deal, preferring war. So the British had, rather unexpectedly, succeeded in doing something to 'embroil' Russia and Germany.

Puzzled by Hitler's failure to respond to their demands and increasingly worried about the German advance into the Balkans, the Soviet government made a series of moves during the early months of 1941 which had the effect of irritating Hitler without deflecting him from his determination to take over South-East Europe. It issued a series of statements, in the oblique form of denials of foreign press reports, intended to convey Soviet displeasure at German plans to move troops into Bulgaria (12 January); at the Bulgarian-Turkish non-aggression pact (22 February); and at the Bulgarian government's agreement to the entry of German troops (3 March). Finally there was the Soviet action in signing a non-aggression pact with Yugoslavia (though not, as the Yugoslavs had hoped, a military pact) on 5 April, on the eve of the German invasion. (See p. 104 below.)

Although Britain and Russia by this time had an obvious common interest in opposing the German advance into South-East Europe, all these Soviet moves were made without any consultation with the British. They did nothing to stop Hitler, but they certainly puzzled him. At the end of April he asked the German ambassador in Moscow, Count F. W. Schulenberg, what the devil had possessed the Russians to conclude a pact with Yugoslavia. The ambassador replied that it was solely a matter of 'the declaration of Russian interests in the Balkans', adding that 'Russia had done something each time that we undertook anything in the Balkans'.[41]

On one move only was there consultation and even co-operation between Russia and Britain – the Soviet statement of 25 March that if Turkey were obliged to go to war in self-defence, it would count on the complete understanding and neutrality of the Soviet Union. This was the outcome of a great deal of hard work by Cripps in Moscow; an answering Turkish declaration equally resulted from British labours. But these reciprocal assurances were not enough to persuade the mistrustful and cautious Turks to join Britain, Greece and Yugoslavia in fighting the Germans. They remained aloof during the Balkan campaign of 1941 – as did the Russians too.

4 Economic War, Sabotage and Subversion, 1939-41

When in February 1940 General Weygand was urging the need for military action in South-East Europe, he asked what the alternative was: 'were we merely going to wait and let the Economic War do its work?'[1] For the British the answer was 'yes', if only because they thought it the only form of war then open to the Western Allies. In March Weygand was again complaining that the Allies had adopted the wrong strategy in not 'carrying the war to the Balkans'; the Foreign Office commented: 'but with what?'[2]

In 1939 the British were filled with optimism about economic war as a deadly weapon, and saw South-East Europe as a crucial source of oil, foodstuffs and minerals essential for the German war effort. They hoped to cut off these supplies by various means, ranging from pre-emptive purchases – buying up those products most vital to Germany – to sabotage and air attack.

There were many difficulties. The South-East European countries started the war as neutrals and therefore had to be treated with some circumspection – or so at least the Foreign Office thought. Hugh Gaitskill, then working at the Ministry of Economic Warfare, said bitterly: 'the Foreign Office won't let us bully them and the Treasury won't let us bribe them'.[3] Sabotage in neutral countries presented special problems and was inevitably disliked by British diplomats trying to cultivate the friendliest relations with the governments in power. Lord Hankey, as Minister in special charge of oil questions, said just after the fall of France that the reason why major sabotage schemes had so far failed lay in the reluctance of the Foreign Office to authorise them, or at any rate to authorise them until too late.[4] There was no decision at the top whether the diplomats or the economic warriors should have higher priority.

Another difficulty was that before the war Britain had displayed almost total lack of interest in trading with South-East Europe, even when this was urgently necessary to counter German economic penetration. Some people in fact continued to regard this penetration as natural and right. As late as April 1940 Sir Nevile Henderson, former Ambassador in Berlin, said in London that from a British viewpoint Eastern Europe was 'a very ungetatable proposition': Germany had a preponderant part to play there, and if she were to confine herself to legitimate aims no one in Britain could object.[5] Any British effort to step up trade suddenly was therefore bound to be regarded with suspicion by the countries concerned and strongly opposed by the Germans, who were determined to keep poachers out of their private preserve.

The Germans had one special advantage. All the South-East European countries, terrified of Germany or Russia or rapacious neighbours, desperately wanted arms: the Germans could supply them, the British could not. The British would have been far more successful in economic warfare if they had been able to supply arms, especially anti-aircraft and anti-tank guns. In January 1940 the Minister for Defence Co-ordination, Lord Chatfield, wrote of a Rumanian request for these weapons: 'the Rumanians are being rather troublesome and inclined not only to give the Germans more oil than is desirable but to prevent us from exporting Rumanian oil for our own purposes . . . If there was anything we could offer Rumania we could use it as a lever to make her accept our demands about oil.'[6] But the British needed everything available for themselves – or for the Turks, their new-found and privileged allies. This put British diplomats in an awkward position. From Bucharest Sir Reginald Hoare wrote: 'it would rather stick in my gizzard to do anything really disagreeable to the Rumanians in the matter of oil when she is providing that oil in return for the armaments which we and the French fail to supply'.[7]

In May 1940 Cadogan received a report that all the Balkan Ministers in London were complaining of British slowness in supplying arms, and that a Yugoslav Military Mission had left England 'with nothing accomplished and the worst possible impression'. 'If we had any goods to sell,' Cadogan wrote, 'the transactions would go through quick enough. But we have to haver and procrastinate to hide the emptiness of the shop.'[8]

For the Germans, things were different. The British Air Attaché in Belgrade and Sofia wrote in January 1940 that Germany's main aims were to get as much food and raw materials as possible from the Danubian basin and the Balkans, and to exchange these goods for armaments: 'the Germans are known to have a large surplus of armaments . . . partly made up of Czechoslovak and Polish loot and partly – where aircraft are concerned – of German types becoming obsolescent for use in a war against the great powers. There is not one Balkan country (including Greece) to which Germany is not at this moment supplying aircraft.' Bulgaria, which had no air force at all, had been 'obligingly supplied . . . with a complete second-hand outfit from Czechoslovakia and Poland'.[9] In Bucharest, Eric Berthoud[10] wrote that the Rumanians had to sell oil to Germany to pay for vitally required armaments which only the Germans could supply, largely out of captured Polish equipment and deliveries from Czech armaments factories.[11]

The Germans had a still stronger weapon – fear. The South-East European governments believed that if the Germans could not get what they wanted by other means, they would use force. In February 1940, the British Minister in Belgrade, Ronald I. Campbell,[12] wrote of Yugoslav anxiety about 'a German attack on the Balkans being provoked by Allied efforts to prevent or hinder exports'. In the Foreign Office, the Southern Department minuted that this raised a question of 'fundamental importance' and suggested that British policy should be to carry out pre-emptive purchases sufficient to 'hamper the Germans at every turn', but insufficient to provoke a German attack – though it was extremely doubtful if this was possible.[13]

There was yet another British weakness. The new war-time organisations were usually under-staffed; they lacked experience and tended to fight one another, though more often they fought the orthodox-minded permanent bodies such as the Foreign Office, Treasury and permanent Secret Intelligence Service (also known as M.I.6 or 'C'). There was not only the Ministry of Economic Warfare itself. There was Section D, originated when, after Hitler's annexation of Austria in March 1938, the Chief of the S.I.S. recruited Major Laurence Grand to start planning for secret activities with special reference to Rumanian oil and Swedish iron ore; Section D remained nominally part of the S.I.S. until the late summer of 1940. Then there was M.I.(R), set up towards the end of 1938 within the War Office to plan irregular warfare; its boundaries with Section D were ill-defined. In the autumn of 1940 the two were eventually merged in S.O.E. under the Minister of Economic Warfare, Hugh Dalton. In the early months of the war both found themselves working in competition with the Director of Naval Intelligence and the Director of Military Intelligence. The outcome was inevitably confusion, amateurishness and in some cases indiscretion, together with plenty of mutual back-biting – all weaknesses in the British effort to fight an economic war in South-East Europe.

CONVENTIONAL ECONOMIC WARFARE: PROBLEMS OF PRE-EMPTIVE PURCHASE

Conventional economic warfare – mainly pre-emptive purchasing – was the responsibility of the M.E.W., with the Foreign Office, Treasury and Ministry of Food all taking a keen interest; where oil was concerned the Committee on Preventing Oil from reaching Germany (the P.O.G. Committee) was set up by the War Cabinet in October 1939 under Lord Hankey, Minister without Portfolio.[14]

In November 1939 the M.E.W. decided to send a mission to South-East Europe, under a representative of the Ministry of Food, to look into possibilities of buying up foodstuffs.[15] After visiting Rumania, Bulgaria, Hungary and Yugoslavia, the mission reported that Germany most needed maize, oilseeds and oilcake, bran, fat pigs and lard. The National Banks were holding large balances of German Marks against which no German goods had been delivered. Yugoslavia was less afraid than the others of German or Russian aggression, but the whole Bulgarian scene was overcast by fear. The mission concluded that there was only one way to stop Germany getting goods from the Balkans 'and that is to buy them ourselves'.[16]

But there were obstacles. When Chamberlain told the House of Commons on 2 April that one 'weapon in our armoury' was that of purchase, he added: 'it is obviously out of the question to purchase the entire exportable surplus of Germany's neighbours'.[17] The Treasury fulfilled its traditional role of keeping a tight hold on the purse-strings. In April 1940 the first Minister of Economic Warfare, Ronald Cross,[18] wrote a pleading letter to the Chancellor of the Exchequer, Sir John Simon: 'I think there is no reason to doubt the importance of doing everything that we can to keep Germany short of fats ... I am convinced that if we could prevent Germany from importing fats and feeding stuffs, it would be impossible for her to contemplate another winter of war ... Unfortunately, owing to the objections raised by the Treasury ... we have been able up to the present to do very little.' In the Foreign Office C. E. Shuckburgh[19] minuted on this: 'the attitude of the Treasury hitherto has been so obstructive that practically no pre-emptive purchases have been possible'.[20]

The M.E.W. was also interested in buying up minerals from South-East Europe. On 2 April Chamberlain told the House of Commons that allied purchases in the area had been on a large scale. The most important purchases of minerals had in fact been made in Yugoslavia; but the official British economic war historian, W. N. Medlicott, later estimated that 'except ... in the case of chrome, it did not appear that German purchasing programmes had been thwarted to any extent'.[21] Some effort was also made to buy up mining options, and in April 1940 the M.E.W. asked the Treasury for the modest sums of £1,000 each for Rumania and Bulgaria and £5,000 for Yugoslavia, for this purpose; the work was to be done through the Selection Trust and Chester Beatty, who was co-operating whole-heartedly with the government in economic warfare, whether or not his own mining interests were damaged thereby.[22] The Treasury grudgingly agreed, adding 'we don't want to encumber ourselves with a lot of second-rate chrome properties at enhanced prices'.[23] In the case of Bulgaria, anyhow, there was little danger: the prospectors soon told Chester Beatty that the Germans had already got hold of the only chrome worth having and that British chances of getting any chrome of value were close to zero.[24]

To give a more acceptable face to British pre-emptive purchasing and to concentrate British bargaining power, the government had decided in December 1939 to create the United Kingdom Commercial

Corporation, which came into being in the following spring with Charles Hambro[25] and Frank Nixon[26] as directors and Lord Glenconner as a high-powered representative in South-East Europe. From Sofia, Rendel[27] reported that the Bulgarians suspected that the Corporation's activities were purely anti-German, and pleaded that it should work to 'establish normal trade relations on a permanent basis'.[28] This was clearly not its purpose. As the Foreign Office informed Washington, where there were fears of unfair trade competition, the U.K.C.C. was to have the monopoly of supplying Hungary, Greece, Yugoslavia, Rumania and Bulgaria with raw materials such as tin, rubber, jute, cotton, tea and coffee, and was to use this monopoly to exercise maximum bargaining power for extracting from those countries commodities which it was essential to deny to Germany, such as oil-seeds. Its object was 'purely political'.[29] But the U.K.C.C. failed to make Bulgaria sell soya beans to Britain instead of Germany, in spite of its capacity to cut off tin and rubber.[30] In October 1940, with the Germans moving into Rumania and the Bulgarian police starting petty persecution of U.K.C.C. officials, the Corporation withdrew from Rumania and Bulgaria. Hambro and Glenconner were absorbed in S.O.E.

From then on Britain had to rely on such contraband control as could be exerted without naval access to the Black Sea (much desired by Churchill but denied by Turkey). In March 1941 Dalton, now Minister of Economic Warfare, told the House of Commons that except for Greece and Turkey, where Britain was doing its utmost to meet war or civilian needs, Britain's policy was to let no imports through its controls into South-East Europe, where there was a risk of important goods falling into enemy hands. Britain also expected importing countries to show their 'independence' by exporting to Britain goods which the British wanted to keep out of Germany's hands.[31]

CONVENTIONAL ECONOMIC WARFARE: RUMANIAN OIL

The most important economic target of all was Rumanian oil, and there pre-emptive purchasing was attempted, as well as less conventional methods. In 1939 Rumanian oil exports totalled 3.5m. tons and the British believed that Rumanian oil was essential to the German war machine. When in April 1939 Chamberlain was discussing the proposed guarantee to Rumania, he said that it seemed 'a vital spot because of her immense resources . . . If Germany obtained control of Rumania's oil and wheat . . . this would mean a great accession of strength to Germany and a weakening of the other side.'[32]

On paper the western allies were in a strong position. A large sector of the Rumanian oil industry, accounting for around three-quarters of production and exports, was controlled by British and French capital.[33] Moreover until the fall of France there was an avowedly pro-western government in Bucharest with Grigore Gafencu as Foreign Minister; and King Carol himself, though far more anti-Russian than anti-German and liable to rapid change of front, could at that time be regarded as pro-western. So it did not sound ridiculous when the Chancellor of the Exchequer told the War Cabinet on 16 September that 'satisfactory arrangements' had been made for 'the purchase of all available oil supplies' by Shell. Shell was under contract to export Rumanian oil to Germany, but would limit sales as far as possible.[34] (Shell was Anglo-Dutch with over half the shares in Dutch hands.)

In practice, things were not so simple. In March 1939 the Rumanians had concluded a commercial agreement with Germany by which they undertook to export to Germany 25 per cent of their production of key commodities. Moreover, after the destruction of Poland, even though they did not have a common frontier with Germany, they were frightened of the Germans and doubted the value of the Anglo-French guarantees. They were also natural bargainers.

On 8 December Hankey told the War Cabinet that the Rumanians were now 'raising difficulties' over oil and were proposing to apply a quota system to all countries.[35] This meant they were not going to risk German anger by falling in with the British plan for buying up Rumanian oil in such quantities as to cut oil to Germany to a trickle; during December they concluded a quota agreement with Germany providing for monthly oil exports of 130,000 tons.[36] They also started making it hard for the British to get export licences for oil.[37] The Rumanian Minister in London, Virgil Tilea, at first told the Foreign Office that under the quota system Britain and France were to have 'equality' with Germany: between them they were to get 1.9m. tons of oil a year.[38] But a few days later Tilea said that Rumania would refuse to sell to Britain unless its demands for an arms credit and arms supplies were met.[39] This was regarded by the British as 'bluff' and long haggling started over arms credits, with the British trying out their own counter-bluff.[40]

In spite of these British-Rumanian difficulties, German-Rumanian trade negotiations in March 1940 did not go well.[41] When the newly-appointed German economic plenipotentiary, Hermann Neubacher, a forceful personality, paid his first call on King Carol, he was snubbed when he urged him to bring pressure to bear on western oil companies to sell 'some quantity' to Germany.[42]

From such things, the British took comfort. In mid-March the War Cabinet took note that Germany's main anxiety in the field of raw materials was probably the inadequacy of its oil supplies.[43] But in his lightning campaigns in the west between April and June 1940, Hitler showed little sign of this 'inadequacy'. Thereafter the fall of France, Italy's entry into the war and Rumania's adherence to the Axis resulted – as Berthoud commented later – in the 'collapse of the British and

French petroleum buying policies'.[44] However, Berthoud also pointed out that the German-Rumanian quota agreement had not been fulfilled. In the 12 months starting 1.10.39 actual deliveries fell short by nearly 400,000 tons. This result, Berthoud wrote, was 'not unsatisfactory'.[45] But it fell far short of the wild hopes of the War Cabinet in September 1939.

UNCONVENTIONAL ECONOMIC WARFARE: THE GOELAND
SHIPPING COMPANY

In March 1939, there was a meeting of Halifax, the Chief of the S.I.S., and Major Grand to discuss 'with special urgency' the Rumanian oil question. One result was that Section D was told to make an effort to get the Danube oil barges out of German hands and take them down the river and, if necessary, remove them. George Taylor of Section D then approached the Anglo-Danubian Transport Corporation which had an office in London under a Rumanian manager who was anxious that his son should acquire a British passport and was a connoisseur of French poetry. Friendly relations were established, the Home Office was unusually pliant, the son got his naturalisation, the British (through Maurice Bridgeman)[46] acquired the assets of the Anglo-Danubian Corporation and therewith control of its barges.[47]

This was the background of a decision taken by the War Cabinet in the first few days of the war, that all available barges in Rumania should be chartered.[48] By the end of 1939, 148 vessels of various types had been chartered.[49] These included the 32 vessels of the Yugoslav Schultz fleet, secretly purchased in December 1939,[50] and the Belgian Danube fleet of 23 lighters and 3 tugs also bought in December 1939 for 7m. Belgian francs.[51]

During the autumn of 1939 proposals had been made that the British government should form a company to manage the whole operation, and the Goeland Company[52] held its first meeting on 1st February 1940.[53] It was managed in Rumania by William Harris-Burland. One of its most important achievements was the acquisition of the French fleet of 29 barges, 17 tankers, 3 grain barges and one tug, transferred to British ownership and control by a contract signed by the British and French naval attachés in Bucharest at the time of the fall of France (though dated 10 June 1940).[54]

By this device the French fleet was saved from German control when France fell. By June 1940 it was clear that the time had come to carry out the plans for evacuating the vessels which had been drawn up six months earlier.[55] About this time the British Minister in Bucharest received 'a very urgent hint' that the sooner British-controlled river craft were sent out of Rumania the better.[56] About 35 vessels got away with Rumanian permission; then King Carol, seeking to win the favour of the victorious Germans, seized a number of vessels including some French craft, placing them at the Germans' disposal.[57] But some escaped by various ways to Istanbul; and even after German troops entered Rumania, the British were still getting Danube craft out of the country.[58] In all about 75 vessels reached Istanbul.[59]

There – except for two tugs which reached Suez and one kept by S.O.E. Istanbul for their own purposes – they were immobilised by Turkey's strict interpretation of neutrality. The Vichy government, prompted by the Germans, brought a law-suit in the Turkish courts to gain possession of the former French vessels, clearly for the use of the Germans. When in 1941 a German attack on Turkey seemed likely, the British made plans to sink the lot.[60] But the Germans did not attack. The law suit dragged on and the Germans never got the vessels.

The orthodox-minded British Consul-General at Galatz, Russell Macrae, complained that the Goeland Company wasted hundreds of thousands of pounds on useless activities.[61] In fact its operations cost about £1m., and were financed by the purchase of Rumanian currency on the black market at extremely favourable rates, against transfers of sterling from London to Palestine.[62] The Company achieved real results, up till June 1940. Berthoud later estimated that on average the Germans did not get more than 80,000 tons of Rumanian oil a month during the first nine months of war 'owing primarily to their deficiency in transport'. Even after the fall of France, he added, the British action in acquiring oil barges and laying them up or removing them from the Danube continued to meet with some success.[63]

ECONOMIC WAR: DESTRUCTION, SABOTAGE, SUBVERSION

It was in the field of destruction and sabotage that the British showed lack of experience, though plenty of enterprise and enthusiasm, sometimes too much. In the case of Rumanian oil, both Section D and M.I.(R) were involved, and also the Director of Naval Intelligence. The oilfields had been destroyed by the British with Rumanian help in the 1914–18 war. In the summer of 1939 M.I.(R) drew up destruction plans. George Taylor, though belonging to Section D, not M.I.(R), took the plans to Bucharest and handed them over to the Rumanian General Staff, in the hope that the Rumanians would put them into practice in the event of German invasion. The Rumanians were friendly but both Taylor and the British Minister, Hoare, had the impression that they intended to shelve the plans.[64] However, once the war started, the British and French governments started discussions with the Rumanian government about compensation for the destruction of the oilfields, if it happened. The Chancellor of the Exchequer told the War Cabinet in November 1939 that agreement had been reached between Britain and France that payment would be on a 50–50 basis, with Britain advancing £1m. to the Rumanian government to cover 'preliminary expenses'.[65]

The British knew however that if the oilfields were to be destroyed efficiently, the Rumanians might need British help or even some form of British military intervention. The idea of sending a British expeditionary force was rejected.[66] But for over 6 months a body of Royal Engineers, under the wing of M.I.(R),[67] was standing by in the Middle East for a possible move by air to Rumania.[68] In April 1940 the Air Ministry was still concerned over 'the urgent transport from Egypt to Rumania of a company of Royal Engineers which is being kept in readiness to assist in the destruction of the oil wells in the event of Rumania being involved in war'.[69]

The Germans however were watching. As early as December 1939, according to the British Air Attaché in Bucharest, a German broadcast showed that 'the Germans are well acquainted with our oil destruction plan ... they disclosed the exact number of men involved'.[70] In any case, as the Foreign Office later put it, the British destruction plans seemed 'doomed to failure': 'when the time came the Rumanian authorities refused to act and put military guards round the wells and refineries to prevent any action by British agents.' These plans were of a highly secret nature but, the Foreign Office said, fell into German hands after the fall of France.[71]

A totally different plan for destroying the Rumanian oilfields quite independently of the Rumanians was considered by the British shortly before the war started, but was nipped in the bud. The Jewish leader, Chaim Weizmann, offered the services of the Jewish Agency to the British through Sir Robert Vansittart, then Diplomatic Adviser to the Foreign Office, who charged Section D with maintaining contact with the Jewish Agency. Simultaneously a Jewish Agency representative in Bucharest approached the British Legation, offering the use of the system of underground escape routes for Jews from Rumania. The consequence was a meeting in the Waldorf Hotel in London between Section D's representatives, including George Taylor, and Jewish Agency representatives including David Ben Gurion and Moshe Shertok (later Sharett) who put forward a plan for an attack on the oilfields by picked men from the inner core of the Jewish Hagana, who would make their own escape from Rumania afterwards: the condition was that Major Orde Wingate should lead the operation. When Section D asked the Chief of the Imperial General Staff, General Sir Edmund Ironside, whether he would release Wingate for the job, he was sympathetic but ultimately refused; Wingate himself was enthusiastic. The Foreign Office strongly opposed any such undertaking in a neutral country. The scheme died.[72]

In addition to destruction plans, there were also two or more other plans, for blocking the Danube. One was the special responsibility of

Julius Hanau, a South African who had served on the Salonika front
in the 1914–18 war and had then settled in Belgrade. He had been
recruited for Section D by Grand in June 1938, and he was later told
that it was a major British interest to block the Danube in the event
of war. There were three possibilities. One was to block the Greben
narrows by destroying the retaining wall. Hanau got preparations made
but the scheme misfired because an over-enthusiastic Yugoslav fired
an explosive charge prematurely in the autumn of 1939. Another was
to block the Kazan Gorge by blowing part of the over-hanging cliff
on the Yugoslav side into the Danube. Hanau and his agents got to
work but their activities were detected by the Germans in December
1939 and the Yugoslavs were compelled to conduct a not over-searching
enquiry. Hanau had to stop work; in April 1940 the Germans pressed
the Yugoslavs to expel him, but he did not actually leave until June.[73]

The third possibility was to block the Iron Gates by sinking cement-
filled barges in the narrows. Section D had originally considered this,
as had the French 5th Bureau. But the plan passed into the hands of
the Director of Naval Intelligence, Admiral Godfrey, and the Naval
Attaché in Bucharest and Belgrade, Captain Max Despard R.N., a
man of powerful personality with a gift for alarming and upsetting
British diplomats. (Hoare, in Bucharest, finally said in June 1940 that
he could not put up with him any longer. The Foreign Office commented: 'he is a man who is always liable to let his somewhat wild
enthusiasm run away with him . . . but he is unfortunately the apple
of the Admiralty's eye'.[74] Despard then made Belgrade his headquarters.)

In December 1939, as a result of a joint report from the British and
French 'naval authorities' in Bucharest, asking for 'experienced personnel' from England and possibly also British crews,[75] the D.N.I. sent
to Bucharest two R.N.V.R. officers on 'special service', Lt Michael
Henry Mason and Mr H. G. Minshall.[76] Minshall was given as cover
the title of Vice-Consul at Galatz, which deeply distressed the Consul-
General, Macrae, who disapproved of his carefree unorthodox activities, particularly a clash with the local police, in circumstances which
Macrae regarded as somewhat scandalous. More seriously, Macrae
brought a charge of lack of discretion and security: 'stories have been
broadcast of wholesale British schemes of sabotage against the interests
of the government with which we were on friendly terms ... The
fantastic posturing of some of the young men involved gave every
excuse for gossip if not for credence, particularly as some of the wildest
versions can be traced to the amateur Guy Fawkes themselves . . . I
am aware I am particularly prejudiced in this matter.'[77]

The Despard plan involved the use of British naval ratings. These
arrived in Braila – according to the disgruntled Macrae – 'thinly disguised', and 'threatened violence in a quite unnecessary quarrel with

the Port authorities'.[78] It was said that they were described on their
passports – all issued on the same day in Alexandria – as writers and
artists; they did their daily P.T. on deck.[79] They did not realise the
need for security on their way up the Danube in a flotilla of barges –
which was awkward for the Rumanian authorities, who had been
expected to turn a blind eye, but were compelled by the German
security men to take action. Suitably, 1 April was apparently the
day fixed for the operation. But the expedition never got beyond
Giurgiu. The crews went ashore for refreshment. When they got back
the barges were in the hands of the Rumanian police.

The Germans put out their version of the story on 8 April, declaring
that the attempt of British agents to block the Danube was a flagrant
violation of Rumanian neutrality: a number of British barges proceeding up the Danube had been found to be loaded with explosives, depth
charges, machine-guns and grenades, with '100 soldier specialists' on
board, commanded by five officers, all disguised as bargemen, and
piloted by 'an agent of the British Secret Service camouflaged as a
vice-consul'. (This seems to have been Minshall.) The aim, so the
Germans said, had been to block the Iron Gates by sinking the barges
and blowing up part of the dykes, and the arms had been intended to
protect the party in case of surprise; the plot had been uncovered by
the Germans who informed the Rumanians.[80] The embarrassed
Rumanian authorities did their best to play down the affair, saying
that all that had happened was that the Rumanian police discovered
a case of small arms on a British barge at Giurgiu.[81]

The incident caused great discomfort to the British and to the South-
East European governments. Prince Paul of Yugoslavia told Peter
Garran[82] of the British Legation that British activities on the Danube
were causing him grave preoccupation; British 'service people' were
once again engaged in 'hanky panky', preparing to blow up the
Danube; Gafencu had sent him a telegram about it. The game, Prince
Paul said, was not worth the candle: 'you will stop a few oil tankers
. . . but against that you will have the Balkans over-run by the German
Army. And if you feel that you must do it, then inform us officially,
so that we can mobilise; for if you act secretly like this and we are
caught unprepared, we shall just all be slaughtered.' A few over-zealous
members of the 'Intelligence Service', he added, should not be allowed
to commit an act of irreparable folly.[83]

The incident gave the Germans a useful handle. Already in March
they had asked the Hungarians for permission to police the Hungarian
sector of the Danube.[84] Now they proposed joint policing of the Danube
with German participation, and even a German armed flotilla, for
protection of the Iron Gates sector. At the meeting of British diplomatic
representatives in South-East Europe in London in mid-April, Owen
O'Malley,[85] the Minister in Budapest, said this proposal was very

dangerous, both for the effect it would have on the Danube States but also because it would make sabotage much more difficult and would facilitate the infiltration of German agents.[86] When O'Malley got back to Budapest he pressed the Hungarian Prime Minister, Count Pál Teleki, to reject any such scheme.[87] The Rumanians told friendly governments that Gafencu had categorically rejected the proposal.[88] Instead, the four Danube States, Rumania, Bulgaria, Yugoslavia and Hungary, announced on 18 April that they themselves would undertake the policing of their own sections of the Danube, adding that in future the transport of arms, munitions, explosives and heavy goods such as cement, stone and iron would be forbidden except under special permit.[89]

The Foreign Office summed up on 21 June: 'the unfortunate incident at Giurgiu . . . resulted in the seizing by the Rumanians of a large quantity of war material belonging to us and the drastic restriction of all our activities on the river.'[90]

Nevertheless there was one more British effort to block the Danube at the Iron Gates. In mid-May 1940 Churchill said that no action should be taken likely to precipitate the armed occupation of the river or an early German invasion of the Balkan States; all that should be done was to press on the Rumanian and Yugoslav governments the need for action.[91] In the autumn of 1940 Section D – now S.O.E. or S.O.2 – was authorised to approach the Yugoslav General Staff and urge them to take action in the case of German invasion. This produced little result; in February 1941 Campbell approached Prince Paul himself and as a result instructions were given to the General Staff who put S.O.2 representatives in touch with Yugoslav 'experts' before the end of the month. The main plan then discussed was the sinking of 16 or more barges in the narrows at the Iron Gates.

After the coup of 27 March 1941, S.O.2 had to start again with the new Chief of General Staff, while Campbell pressed the new Foreign Minister, Momčilo Ninčić. Two days before the German invasion, the Yugoslavs had 12 barges ready for action.[92]

George Taylor – then in Belgrade – received a telegram from S.O.E. in London: 'Minister and all high authorities know you realise fully that a successful blocking of Danube before it is too late would be the decisive factor for England in this war.'[93] On 5 April he received warning from London that 'the balloon is expected to go up tomorrow'.[94]

It did. But the actual operations were in Yugoslav, not British hands; the speed of the German advance and the suddenness of the Yugoslav military collapse made it impossible for S.O.E. to observe the results of the Yugoslavs' attempts to block the Danube. This placed Dalton in a very awkward position, when Churchill was pressing for information. (See p. 151.) The original estimate was that the Danube had been blocked for three months; a later estimate was six weeks. The most likely guess is between three and five weeks.[95] Certainly there was no noticeable drop in figures for Rumanian oil deliveries to Germany in April and May 1941.

ECONOMIC WAR AGAINST RUMANIAN OIL: NO BOMBING, NO SABOTAGE

Distinct from the British official plans for destruction of the Rumanian oilfields were lesser plans for sabotage. Originally these provided for action by the British themselves; a key figure in planning was the Bucharest representative of Section D, A. G. de Chastelain, Sales Manager of the Unirea Oil Company.[96] Just before France fell, the War Cabinet considered a paper by the Chiefs of Staff about plans for 'interference in Rumanian oil supplies to Germany by bribery and sabotage'; these had now been authorised.[97] The Treasury in fact approved the sum of £20m. for purposes of bribery in the area.[98]

But British freedom of action was drastically curtailed when in September 1940 General Ion Antonescu came to power in Rumania in partnership, at least at first, with the fascist-style Iron Guard – some of whom were under German control. The Germans then used Iron Guards in what the British Minister described as a 'terrorist campaign' against the British, particularly anyone capable of organising sabotage in the oilfields.[99] Almost all Britons were ordered to leave the Ploeşti area and six British subjects working there – some connected with S.O.E. – were arrested by Iron Guards and badly beaten up under interrogation. However, Antonescu himself did not want to quarrel with Britain and following pressure from the British Minister, the six were either released or expelled; all left the country in October. By the end of the month most British subjects and all British engineers had been expelled or 'squeezed' out of Rumania.[100] In late September Hankey wrote: 'for the future our hopes of stopping oil seem to rest almost entirely on air operations, supplemented by anything that can be done of a less regular character'.[101]

For 'irregular' work, S.O.E. had to rely from then on almost entirely on Iuliu Maniu, the National Peasant Party leader and a veteran politician of great prestige and influence. He was willing to accept money from S.O.E. 'as a loan'.[102] A S.O.E. report of December 1940 reported that Maniu had revealed an unexpected 'conspiratorial strain'; if, as was then expected, he left Rumania, 'the men in whose hands he intends to leave his organisation are excellent practical people from whom at least competent work may be expected'.[103] In reality, Maniu was much more interested in politics than sabotage. When Hoare saw him early in 1941 and spoke of the need for 'definite evidence of opposition in Rumania to German penetration', Maniu said he had an

organisation capable of sabotage, but did not show 'any signs of con-
viction that successful sabotage would in fact be carried out'.[104]

In mid-January 1941 Antonescu came into open collision with his
Iron Guard partners and fighting broke out. The Foreign Office and
S.O.E. agreed on 23 January that 'seeing that a [Iron Guard] revolt
had started, even though perhaps at half-cock, it would be better to
take advantage of the situation. There might be valuable opportunities
of interfering with German troop movements, as well as generally
creating trouble . . . the result of which would not only interfere with
Rumanian oil supplies to Germany, but also make it difficult for them
to launch an attack through Bulgaria.'[105] Cadogan referred the proposal to Eden and Churchill, who agreed that S.O.E. activities,
originally planned for the following month, when the British Legation
was due to leave, should now be advanced. S.O.E. sent a telegram to
Bucharest: 'in view general chaotic condition Rumania urgently
instruct all channels open to you in Rumania to carry out all possible
plans for causing disruption and increasing chaos. Spare no costs. Above
has been approved by H.M.G.'[106] Cadogan noted in his diary on 23
January that he had had a meeting with Sir Frank Nelson of S.O.E.
about Rumania: 'seeing that turmoil has begun there, decided to jump
in at once, even though our arrangements not complete.'[107]

After all this, anti-climax. Antonescu, with German backing, quickly
got the Iron Guard under control. Hoare reported on 25 January:
'forces of disorder have now been dispersed or driven underground . . .
Moment is therefore not propitious for direct subversive action but
indirect measures are being taken.'[108] The Foreign Office replied that
S.O.E. representatives in Bucharest were being instructed to concentrate on indirect measures such as bribery 'and to go slow for the time
being as regards direct methods, e.g. acts of major sabotage'.[109] British
efforts to exploit the Antonescu–Iron Guard clash had flopped.
Berthoud reported that refineries had worked normally all through the
'civil disturbances', though oil exports were held up for about four
days; there was no indication of acts of sabotage to the oil industry
apart from 'small damage to stocks and transport material'.[110]

In fact Maniu made it plain that he would only order sabotage if
it could have the cover of Allied air attack, even if only token attack.[111]
When the British Legation finally left in February, Hoare gave warning that this was the position. Eden, then in Cairo, thereupon urged
strongly that a minimum of one additional heavy bomber squadron
should be sent out for the Rumanian operation, to be based on Greece:
'time factor is all important'.[112] Dalton, as Minister of Economic Warfare, urged bombing if only on a light scale as a prelude to subversive
activities in Rumania.[113] From Istanbul, Hoare telegraphed that he had
the impression that excessive hopes were entertained in London about
the results which sabotage organised by S.O.E. and the National

Peasant Party could achieve; 'unsupported sabotage would alienate public opinion . . . sabotage without air action is worthless'.[114] Berthoud reported that 'the Rumanian population expected the withdrawal of the Legation to be followed by bombing attack . . . the bombing would give encouragement to the dissatisfied elements'.[115]

There was no bombing and no sabotage. For the reasons, it is necessary to go back to the Italian attack on Greece in October 1940. This had raised hopes that Britain would be able to use air-bases in Greece for bombing the Rumanian oilfields; and on 27 November Churchill told the War Cabinet that preliminary arrangements should be made.[116] On the same day he sent an ACTION THIS DAY minute to the Chief of Air Staff: 'we should at once begin to establish in Greece ground staff and nuclear stores to enable at least two squadrons of Wellingtons to bomb the Rumanian oilfields. We are late enough already.'[117]

At first it seemed as though the Greeks would agree. King George II sent a letter to King George VI, of which a copy reached the Foreign Office on 2 December, apparently pressing the British to establish air forces in Northern Greece: 'as I see it . . . you may not only deal the Italians crippling blows, but you may even deter the Germans from moving against Greece for fear of losing Rumanian oil . . .'[118] But it soon became clear that – probably because of skilfully conveyed German threats – the Greek government were anxious not to provoke German suspicions that the British were being given facilities to bomb the oilfields.[119] Churchill, in spite of his earlier toughness about the scruples of neutrals, replied gently that the Greeks should be promised that there would be no attacks from Greek bases on Rumanian oilfields without their permission; but reconnaissance work should be carried out by British officers in plain clothes.[120] Meanwhile all operational British air bases remained south of the Mount Olympus–Arta line.

The British believed, however, that the German attack on Greece, which they were sure would come, would still allow time for the use of Greek air bases against Rumanian oil. A report by the Chiefs of Staff to the War Cabinet on 24 February 1941 on the pros and cons of sending a British force to Greece said that one advantage would be that 'it would enable us to establish a platform for the bombing of Italy and the Rumanian oilfields'.[121] The next day Eden, from Cairo, sent a personal telegram to Churchill: 'if there is anything in the view so often reiterated to us that oil is Germany's weakness, we have in Rumania the means . . . of striking Germany a blow many times more severe than we can hope to land her by many months bombing of oil targets in Germany.'[122]

The answer from London was that it would take well over two months before a new squadron from Britain could be in action in the Middle East. Churchill also again stressed that 'the Greeks must have the last word'.[123] On 2 March the Greek Commander, General Alexander Papagos, was still reluctant to agree to the use of Greek airfields for bombing Rumania.[124] King George II said that once the Germans had attacked Greece, the British would be free to bomb, but not before.[125]

The combination of Greek fears and British lack of aircraft meant that nothing could be done. When in April the Germans attacked Greece, they moved so fast that there was small chance for the British to bomb Rumania from the Salonika area. On 9 April the Chiefs of Staff agreed that the bombing of Rumanian oilfields was a most desirable objective, but that 'given the very large number of even more urgent calls on our exiguous bomber force, there could be no question of pressing the Commander-in-Chief to go for them at the present time'.[126] The Air Officer Commanding, Air-Vice-Marshal Longmore,[127] feared very heavy losses from air attack on Rumania, which the R.A.F. could not afford.[128] Berthoud, who visited Athens during April to advise on bombing of oil targets, hoped that Wellingtons would carry out a raid as a 'swan-song' before they left Greece, but at the last moment Longmore withdrew his approval.[129] When the British withdrew from Greece, the last hope went.

The accusation was later made, both in the United States and in the House of Commons, that the British deliberately refrained from destroying the Rumanian oilfields because of the influence of British financial interests or of the Foreign Office.[130] The charge was clearly untrue. British failure was due to lack of resources and bases and to lack of Rumanian support, perhaps also to inefficiency – but not to lack of the will to destroy the oilfields.

SABOTAGE AND SUBVERSION IN YUGOSLAVIA, HUNGARY AND BULGARIA

In Yugoslavia, both Section D and M.I.(R) were concerned with other things as well as blocking the Danube. Under M.I.(R)'s auspices an 'unofficial' mission under General Sir John Shea, G.C.B., K.C.M.G., D.S.O., visited Yugoslavia in November 1939 to contact the Yugoslav General Staff, and recommended that British officers should be attached to existing Yugoslav 'guerilla cadres' (a proposal that remained without effect), and that the press should be subsidised.[131] At the same time Julius Hanau was very active in organising sabotage and subversion, on Section D's behalf. Apart from his Iron Gates projects he arranged for sabotage against German rail communications in Austria, carried out by a small group of Slovene Liberals with strong irridentist claims against Italy or Germany.[132] Tampering with the axle-boxes was a favourite method. On the Dalmatian coast there was some sabotage of shipping in which D. T. (Bill) Hudson, later to go as first British Liaison Officer to occupied Yugoslavia, was involved. As a result of these activities, not only Hanau had to leave Yugoslavia; in the summer of 1940 the Yugoslav government expelled Captain Malcolm Burr, against whom 'the German authorities' had brought the charge of being implicated in sabotage on German railways. The British Minister said this was untrue and protested, but the Yugoslavs replied that if Burr was not guilty, 'some British subjects certainly were', and as a result of German pressure, they had no alternative but to expel him.[133]

In the propaganda field, subsidies were given to certain Yugoslav newspapers. A news agency, Britanova, owned by the British government and supplied it information through British official channels, but ostensibly independent, was started in December 1939, with its headquarters in Belgrade and branches in Budapest, Bucharest, Sofia, Athens and Istanbul.[134] In Belgrade its editor was Gradimir Kozomarić, a Yugoslav economic journalist (who later died in a German concentration camp). Julian Amery was actively involved, with one foot in the Press Attaché's office and another in Section D. When British diplomatic representatives met in London in April 1940 they were told that 'considerable success' had attended 'the special propaganda effort' launched in Yugoslavia, largely due to the cooperation built up between the Press Attaché and Section D.[135]

In Hungary, Britanova was run by the journalist and writer, Basil Davidson: it was practically the only activity which the Minister, O'Malley, would permit. In Bulgaria, Rendel was also very reluctant to approve subversion, but he eventually allowed Section D to contact the left wing Agrarians led by G. M. Dimitrov, the group of dissident army officers led by Colonel Damian Velchev, and the left wing Macedonian revolutionary organisation known as the Protoguerovists. All were strongly anti-Boris. Small subsidies were granted and some propaganda material disseminated, but the difficulties were enormous and no sabotage had been undertaken by the time the German troops entered Bulgaria in March 1941. Before then – in January 1941 – Section D, now S.O.E., had persuaded Rendel to overcome his scruples about unorthodox behaviour in a neutral country and to allow them to smuggle out Dimitrov nailed up in a packing-case in a lorry taking Legation material to Istanbul.[136] This was an act of diplomatic courage on Rendel's part and physical endurance on the part of Dimitrov, who emerged from many hours doubled up in his packing-case ready and eager for more hours of lively political discussion with S.O.E.'s Istanbul representative, W. S. (Bill) Bailey.[137] He then went briefly to Yugoslavia in the hope of launching a small 'expedition' into Bulgaria but the German invasion killed the project.[138] Another Bulgarian Agrarian politician, Dimitri Matsankiev, also left Bulgaria with S.O.E.'s help.

Towards the end of 1940 Foreign Office and S.O.E. representatives met to review anti-Axis activities in South-East Europe. Among points discussed was 'the employment of large-scale bribery in Jugoslavia and

Bulgaria'. This presumably covered the subsidy of £5,000 a month to the Serbian Peasant Party started in July 1940 and smaller subsidies to the small Independent Democrat Party and the Narodna Odbrana, a long-established Serbian patriotic organisation,[139] and also the subsidies to the Bulgarian groups.[140]

At the same meeting the Foreign Office asked about sabotage at the Allatini chrome mines and other mines in Yugoslavia; 'it was generally agreed that it would be useful to have plans in readiness, but that these must depend on the cooperation of the Yugoslav General Staff, and that in turn depended largely on whether we embarked on a large-scale scheme of bribery'.[141] S.O.E. later reported that plans were already in existence in Belgrade for the destruction of the Trepča and Allatini mines, though it was not certain whether the Yugoslav government were aware of them.[142] Whatever plans there may have been and however large the bribes to the Yugoslav General Staff, no sabotage was carried out at the mines, either before or during the German invasion.

GREEK SHIPPING FOR BRITAIN

Perhaps Britain's greatest success in economic warfare during this period was over Greek shipping. Very early in the war Britain approached the Greek government in the hope of acquiring control of a large sector of the Greek merchant shipping fleet. The Greek government could not act officially but gave informal advice to Greek ship-owners to put their vessels at the disposal of the British by one means or another. The ship-owners responded (on favourable terms). So too did Greek seamen. From December 1939 on, the Germans protested repeatedly but without effect. When the Germans attacked Greece in April 1941 and published a White Book, they displayed the shipping question as perhaps their main complaint against Greece.[143]

The record of British economic warfare, sabotage and subversion in neutral South-East Europe up till April 1941 was patchy, with a great deal of promise but a good deal less achievement; there were some notable failures, but these probably mattered less than it seemed at the time, since the economic warriors considerably over-estimated Germany's dependence on Rumanian oil and foodstuffs and raw materials from the area. They also under-estimated the practical difficulties of destroying the oil-fields. And they over-estimated the willingness of General Staffs or politicians of the area to run big risks for the sake of British bribes or support.

But the British had at least come to take a serious interest in South-East Europe and to realise its economic, military and political potential. S.O.E. had established certain political contacts which influenced British policy in the years following Hitler's conquest of the Balkan peninsula. Startlingly, its failures did not shake the deep-seated belief in the omniscience and all-powerfulness of the British Intelligence Service.

What was striking was the lack of any top-level decision on priorities – between diplomatic, strategic and economic requirements. But given human fallibility this was perhaps no great loss.

5 Albania, 1939-41: the Revolt That Never Happened

Britain's first experiment in encouraging guerilla warfare in South-East Europe was made in Albania. This was natural: the tiny, remote, mountainous country, bordering on the southern Adriatic, seemed just the right place. But there were problems – the antagonism between the tribal chieftains in the mountains of the north and the more urbanised Albanians of the south and the coastal towns, together with inter-tribal feuds in the north itself. An even bigger problem was the hostility towards Albania of Britain's ally, Greece, which became still sharper when the Italians launched their attack on Greece from Albania in 1940. Yugoslavia's attitude was less of a problem; already possessing a large unruly Albanian minority, it was much less eager to acquire Albanian territory than the Greeks were.

When the Italians first occupied Albania in April 1939, they did not have much trouble. After they had chased out Zog – a tribal chieftain from the north, a self-made king and a forceful personality – they set about creating an Albanian Fascist Party, and the Albanian national flag was preserved, though adorned with the Crown of Savoy. The British gave *de facto* recognition of Albania's 'new status' as Italian-occupied territory by appointing Laurence Grafftey Smith as Consul-General in Durazzo on 31 October 1939. His main job was to report on the state of feeling in Albania. Early in 1940 he gave information on student demonstrations in Korca and Scutari. He also reported that the Italians were sponsoring claims by Albanian politicians to Yugoslav territory, especially Kosovo: 'the Italians seem anxious to keep alive the idea of a Greater Albania'.[1] (Shortly before the Italians invaded Albania, they had offered to partition it with Yugoslavia, but this had been turned down by Prince Paul, who, when he was staying at Buckingham Palace in July 1939, told Halifax that he felt he had been right to do so.)[2] In May 1940 a delegation of the Albanian High Fascist Council went to Rome and presented King Victor Emmanuel with a declaration of the 'absolute loyalty of all the Albanians', saying that they were grateful for the good done to their country.[3]

At the outbreak of war the British, anxious to keep Italy neutral, did not think seriously about stimulating Albanian resistance. When early in October the War Cabinet were discussing policy in South-East

Europe and the Lord Privy Seal, Sir Samuel Hoare, asked whether there were any plans for stirring up disaffection in Albania, 'in the event of a hostile Italy', the Deputy Chief of the Imperial General Staff said that it would be left to the Turks to stir up trouble through the Moslem population in Albania.[4]

But by April 1940 M.I.(R) had hatched a scheme for raising a revolt in Albania, and Section D in Yugoslavia was asked on 29 April to do 'the preliminary work involved'. Section D accordingly got in touch with three organisations already working from Yugoslavia into Albania. One was run by Jovan Djonović, former Yugoslav Minister in Tirana, with headquarters at Podgorica; it was supposed to cover the frontier area from the coast to the Yugoslav town of Peć. Section D gave this organisation money and claimed to have acquired considerable influence over its leaders. The second organisation was run by Albanian exiles in Yugoslavia led by Gani Bey Kryeziu and his brother, who had been enemies of Zog, though related to him, until just after the Italian invasion, when they became reconciled with him. They were working from the area lying between the Yugoslav towns of Peć and Prizren, where they had their headquarters. The third organisation was led by a Colonel Kokosi, based on Debar, near Lake Ohrid, in the south. The two latter organisations ran couriers into Albania to get information on Italian troop movements and other things. Section D reported that prospects were good for 'incidents' and a fairly general rising in the east of Albania, especially the Mirdites' tribal territory.[5]

In the early summer of 1940 the French were thinking on different lines. When the fall of France was near, the French Minister in Belgrade told Prince Paul that if Italy attacked the allies, Yugoslavia should in its turn attack Italy in Albania; it was a chance which might not recur; 'it was moreover for Jugoslavia not only a question of interest but of honour'. But Prince Paul pointed to the Allies' failure to supply arms to Yugoslavia; he did not reject the idea but did not accept it.[6]

Italy entered the war, France fell, Yugoslavia did not move. King Zog came from France to England in a British ship, and the British had to decide what to do with him. Grafftey Smith, home from Durazzo, said there was no pro-Zog party in Albania, the King was discredited and his entourage unpopular, though he still carried some weight with his own tribe, the Mirdites, in the north-east.[7] On 3 July Zog was politely told to go to the United States, but he replied that he had hoped to place himself at the head of the Albanians outside Albania and take part in any allied military operations – perhaps from Salonika. He also made contact with influential people in London. On 17 July Halifax said it was not worth while insisting on Zog leaving Britain if he was going to 'mobilize his friends' to be allowed to stay. Zog was then told that he could stay for the present, provided he did not take part in any political activities without British authority.[8] From then on British experts on Albania argued hotly whether Zog was or was not an asset in stimulating Albanian resistance.

At the end of June 1940 Section D was so hopeful of promoting revolt from Yugoslavia[9] that they asked for money to buy 5,000 old rifles. But at this point the C.-in-C. Middle East said that 'he definitely did not want a rising in Albania at that moment'. On 5 July Section D in Belgrade received instructions that they should not precipitate trouble but should remain in touch with their Albanian 'friends' and go on subsidising them, and should gather information without doing anything to provoke incidents. By this time Section D was also making some preparations in Greece, establishing contact with Albanian exiles (including Mustafa Ghinishi in south-east Yugoslavia), and establishing dumps of demolition materials near the Albanian frontier, at Janina and elsewhere. Section D also recruited agents in Greece who made two 'exploratory journeys' into Albania, though under strict orders not to stir up trouble or give the Italians an excuse for invading Greece. Towards the end of August the C.-in-C. Middle East approved Section D's programme for Albania, which was to be under the control of its Istanbul representative, Colonel Wilfred Stirling.[10]

In the autumn of 1940 the Foreign Office was still opposing any role for Zog in resistance plans. On 7 September they telegraphed Cairo that owing to Zog's many enemies and the fact that his followers were largely discredited, it was unlikely that he could play any prominent role.[11] The Foreign Office also turned down a suggestion by Section D that Zog should send a letter giving his blessing to an Albanian committee to be formed in Istanbul.[12]

One reason why the Foreign Office was so negative about Zog was that they did not want to commit themselves to restoring an independent Albania. When Italy entered the war, it was stated in the House of Commons that the British government 'hold themselves entitled to reserve full liberty of action in respect of any undertakings given by them in the past to the Italian government concerning the Mediterranean, North or East African and Middle East areas'. This tortuous phrase withdrew their earlier *de facto* recognition of Italian occupation of Albania, but a Foreign Office minute said that it did not imply recognition of an independent Albania, 'though it enables us to proceed to that step at a further date'.[13] When in September 1940 the Foreign Office drew up a directive for the B.B.C. broadcasts to Albania which were about to begin, it banned 'all specific promises of restoring Albanian independence'.[14]

The Italian invasion of Greece, from Albania, in October created a new situation and unleashed a fresh burst of activity both by Zog and by S.O.E. (as Section D was now called) in Yugoslavia. Churchill was persuaded to authorise the despatch of a message to the Albanian

Committee – now successfully launched by S.O.E. – in Istanbul, that 'H.M.G. have the cause of Albania very much at heart'.[15] In London Zog suggested to the British on 8 November that he should go to Istanbul, where there were '14,000 Albanians', organise a force to be landed at Salonika with the consent of the Greek government, and form a small fighting front.[16]

At this point the Foreign Office – presumably impressed by the need to help the Greeks at all costs – softened their attitude to Zog. After Foreign Office–S.O.E. discussions in London, S.O.E. put to its Istanbul representative the question whether Zog should 'fly to Greece urgently'.[17] The Foreign Office put to Athens, Ankara and the C.-in-C. Middle East the suggestion that Zog might broadcast a 'rallying speech' from Radio Athens on Albanian Independence Day: would the Greek government agree, provided that this did not imply restoration of Zog or the reconstitution of an independent Albania? The British Minister in Athens, Michael Palairet,[18] replied promptly that the Greek Prime Minister, Ioannis Metaxas, had the 'greatest doubts' about using Zog; 'he would not welcome his presence in Greece'.[19] Three days later the Foreign Office told Athens that in view of Metaxas' attitude, the plan to send Zog to Greece had been abandoned; as an alternative, what would the Greek government think of landing Zog in northern Albania 'with the object of leading the operation he suggests?'[20] To this Palairet replied: 'I do not think it politic to raise the question again', since Metaxas had been 'emphatic' in his objection to Zog.[21]

Metaxas clearly wished to keep his hands quite free over Albania. In a broadcast on 27 November he said that the Greeks were fighting not only for their own existence but for the other Balkan people and for the 'liberation' of Albania. In the Foreign Office Dixon[22] minuted that 'liberation' in Greek did not mean 'independence'. He also wrote: 'the Greeks have always coveted Albania. They may well hope to recompense themselves in their present struggle by demanding to be given Albania. I am certain the Greeks will require a rectification of the southern boundary.' This, he thought, was the reason for the Greek opposition to Zog.[23]

So there was little hope for the proposal put by George Taylor of S.O.E. to the Foreign Office on 2 December, that the British government should declare that the future status of Albania would be a matter for the peace settlement. Against this Dixon argued that 'Albania was never likely to be able to stand alone', that such a declaration would upset the Greeks, and that after the war it might be 'convenient' to let the Greeks keep any parts of Albania they might hold. The Foreign Office and S.O.E. then agreed that the proposed declaration should make no mention of an independent Albania, and that the approval of both Greeks and Yugoslavs should be obtained. Also, the plan for landing Zog in northern Albania was to be abandoned, for the time being at least.[24] Instead, the Foreign Office and S.O.E. agreed on a policy of bribing the Albanian chieftains to resist the Italians.[25]

However, the Foreign Office persisted with the idea of a watered-down British declaration, suggesting to Athens and Belgrade that this should be: 'H.M.G. wish to see Albania freed from the Italian yoke and will give the Albanians all support in their power . . . At the issue of the victorious struggle it will be for the Albanians themselves to decide their own future. At the same time safeguards will have to be devised to prevent the recurrence of such events as those which have of recent years reduced Albania to foreign vassalage.'[26] But from Athens, Palairet replied that the proposed declaration would be 'unwise' and 'undesirable'.[27]

The Yugoslavs felt differently. A senior Foreign Ministry official told the British a little later that the Greeks were being very short-sighted in contemplating the partition of Albania; this would be against the 'real wishes' of the Yugoslav government who wanted the independence and integrity of Albania, on the principle of 'the Balkans for the Balkan peoples'.[28] But neither the Yugoslavs nor the British were prepared to argue with the Greeks, who were fighting for their lives. On 23 January Eden told Lord Cecil, a strong champion of Albanian independence, that while H.M.G. was 'no doubt in principle in favour of an independent Albania', they were bound at the moment to conform their policy to the wishes of the Greeks.[29]

Even if the Yugoslavs disagreed with the Greeks over Albanian independence, they wholly agreed with them over Zog. Their War Minister told the British early in December that the Yugoslav commander on the Albanian frontier, who was secretly in constant touch with the Albanians, said the one thing they were united on was their unwillingness to have Zog back.[30]

It became clear at this point that Prince Paul was worried about British activities in Albania. At the end of November S.O.E. reported from Belgrade that it was essential to get Prince Paul's co-operation over arms supplies to Albanian 'irregular levies'. The Foreign Office asked Campbell to mention the matter to Prince Paul in the hope that 'he would at least be ready to give instructions for a blind eye to be turned to our activities'. But Prince Paul's answer was that the Italians left plenty of rifles lying about in Albania which the Albanians could get hold of. Campbell thought this meant that the Yugoslavs themselves were already helping the Albanians; while Prince Paul could rely on the discretion of his own people he could have no guarantee of secrecy if the matter were left to the British, whose Albanian contacts he could not control. To press him any further would be merely to receive a rebuff. A few days later Campbell again talked to Prince Paul, but again got the impression that 'for obvious reasons . . . there

will be a tendency to keep out British intervention . . . They have . . .
shown doubt that it is possible for us to judge with certainty the reli-
ability of Albanian contacts.'[31] One reason for Prince Paul's anxiety
may have been that the Italians had already complained to the
Yugoslav government about the operations of a number of Yugoslav
officers in northern Albania.[32]

Nevertheless S.O.E. remained eager to raise a revolt in northern
Albania through their contacts in Yugoslavia. S.O.E. Belgrade reported
on 18 December that Gani Bey was ready to enter north-east Albania
immediately and was convinced the entire North would rally to him.
He would occupy Kukes and proclaim an Albanian national government, referring to the allied Greeks in 'very friendly terms'. But it
would be essential for the British immediately to promise full moral
and material support, publicly. £60,000 would be needed to maintain
the Albanian army for at least a month, and British air support would
be needed to provide arms, clothing and food.[33]

Surprisingly, the Foreign Office seem to have accepted this plan with
little reservation. But at this point London and Athens got oddly out of
step, perhaps because of delays in transmission of telegrams. On 18
December the Athens Legation telegraphed that Alexander Glen, of
S.O.E. Belgrade, was in Athens, and together with the head of the
British Military Mission, Major General T. G. Heywood, had discussed
the plan with Metaxas. The outcome was agreement that in present
circumstances 'Anglo-Greek interest will be best served by co-ordinated
activities of several small bands'. Athens also reported that a consign-
ment of captured rifles from the Middle East had been promised for
this purpose.[34] The next day S.O.E. Athens (presumably Glen) telegraphed to S.O.E. Belgrade that the arms would not be available for
at least three weeks and the R.A.F. would not be able to give any help
for the time being; so action would depend on what arms S.O.E. could
get locally.[35]

Yet on 20 December the Foreign Office still thought that the plan
for a revolt was on the table; they sent a telegram to Athens about it,
adding that the proposed British declaration of support for an Albanian
'government' would contain a promise of British aid in the 'liberation'
of Albania, and concluding, 'please obtain consent of General Metaxas
at once'.[36] The next day they told Athens that it might be desirable
to get Zog to send a message of support to Gani Bey.[37] On 20 December the War Office said that it approved in principle the attempt to
start a rising, and the Air Ministry said that the proposal for a revolt
had been approved in principle by the Chiefs of Staff, and urged that
an effort should be made in the Middle East to supply food and
materials to the rebels by air.[38]

But this house of cards built in London was swiftly knocked down
by Athens. On 21 December Palairet said he had 'every reason to think

that the Greek government are most averse to the establishment of any provisional government', adding that the R.A.F. in Greece said they had not the technical equipment for dropping rifles, which was an essential part of the scheme. He had no hope of persuading Metaxas unless the scheme was practicable in all details.[39] He also reported that the Greek General Staff and British 'military experts' agreed that the only practical scheme at present was action by 'small bands of irregulars'; the Greeks agreed that this should be done from Yugoslavia. Palairet went on caustically: 'I hope that the zeal of the experts on Albania will not be allowed to outrun their discretion and that we shall not thrust any such ambitious but ill-considered schemes on the Greek government who are after all chiefly responsible for the conduct of the campaign in Albania.'[40]

On 26 December Dixon minuted that the proposal had been abandoned for the moment while enquiries were made whether a special flight of British aircraft could be sent out for dropping military supplies. The next day S.O.E. told the Foreign Office that there was no chance of aircraft being sent from England.[41] S.O.E. London then sent a stiff message to its Belgrade office: 'you must clearly understand decision for or against Albanian rising . . . must be made by military authorities in Cairo and Athens and your role is simply to put all the possibilities of the situation before them in greatest detail and then take your instructions from them.'[42] Eden minuted on 28 December: 'S.O.2 seem to have rushed ahead without much thought.'[43]

S.O.E. Belgrade hardly deserved this snub, seeing that the Foreign Office and Chiefs of Staff had at first blessed the plan for a revolt. Nor was it unreasonable to assume that Metaxas would welcome any diversion of Italian forces in Albania from the Greek front, however short-lived the diversion might be. But the Greeks were still having surprising successes against the Italians, so he can have been in no mood to tie his hands in any way over Albania; and approval of a large-scale Albanian revolt might have laid him – and still worse, the British – under a political obligation.

S.O.E. Istanbul did not give up hope. In late February it sent to London a proposal by the Albanian Committee in Istanbul for setting up an Albanian national government with British help and with a British promise to restore the Albanian State as it was before the Italian invasion: the result would be an Albanian army of 100,000 men. S.O.E. suggested that the proposed government should include Gani Bey Kryeziu and a former Albanian Minister in London, Mehmet Bey Konitsa.[44] The Foreign Office did not even reply to this.[45]

After the Belgrade coup d'état of March 1941 the British – as the French had done in June 1940 – urged the Yugoslavs to attack the Italians in Albania, collecting large quantities of Italian arms in the process – the arms which the British themselves could not supply. But the Belgrade government was far too disorganised and nervous to commit what would technically have been an act of aggression. It was left to Captain Dagvall Oakley Hill of S.O.E. (like Stirling, a former officer in the pre-1939 Albanian gendarmerie) to set out from Yugoslavia with a band of anti-Zog Albanians, without arms or radio communications or air support. The band was dispersed and Oakley Hill captured by the Italians.[46]

*   *   *

Such were the political minefields in the way of S.O.E.'s perhaps rather unrealistic effort to help an ally and harm the enemy. If this was an object lesson for the future, so also was the frustration produced by S.O.E.'s complete dependence on the R.A.F. – over which it had no control – for essential support in its operations.

6 Bulgaria, 1939-41: No Key for Britain

When Halifax told the War Cabinet in September 1939 that Bulgaria was 'the key to the Balkans', he should have added that it was a peculiarly difficult key for Britain to turn. Apart from Albania, it was the poorest and least developed country of the area, with the smallest middle class. It was ruled by King Boris, an obstinate but nervous man. He had good reason to be nervous. He had come to the throne as a result of his country's defeat in the 1914–18 war. The landmarks of his rule had been a brief period of dictatorial government by a forceful revolutionary peasant leader, Alexander Stamboliski, an abortive Communist rising, the plots and intrigues of Macedonian revolutionaries, an army conspiracy against the throne. The Peasant Party – the natural representative of the majority of the people – had split into factions, and because of a strong under-tow of pro-Russian feeling, the peasants were liable to turn to Communism if they had no satisfactory representation of their own. There was also, as the British Minister, Rendel, reported, a 'small but very active industrial population' which was 'Communist in the modern sense' and 'working directly for union with Russia'. It included the factory workers and nearly all the port workers at Burgas and Varna.[1]

King Boris knew the strength of Soviet influence and though he might make some concessions he was determined not to fall a victim to it. He does not seem to have liked Hitler, but certainly saw Germany as the lesser evil, especially if it restored lost territory to Bulgaria. There was no reason why he – or other Bulgarians – should like the British, who were the friends of Bulgaria's enemies, and had given guarantees to two countries against which Bulgaria had territorial claims.

Britain's only hope of influencing Bulgaria was to instil belief in the certainty of Germany's defeat and to give warning that Britain would ultimately reward its friends and treat its enemies according to their deserts. (This hardly fitted in with the declared British aim of a just post-war settlement, but any such discrepancy could be glossed over.)

One early difficulty was that though Britain encouraged Bulgaria to declare its neutrality on the outbreak of war, it gave no answering public promise to respect Bulgarian neutrality – the French wished to keep their hands free. (King George VI did however give King Boris an assurance in a private letter in the autumn of 1939.)[2]

The British set out, as part of their policy of building a Balkan bloc, to try to improve Bulgaria's relations with its neighbours. During the winter of 1939–40, Rendel worked hard at bringing Bulgaria and Turkey together, with some success. A visit to Sofia by the head of the Turkish Foreign Ministry, Numan Menemenjoglu, was followed by a visit by the Foreign Minister, Sarajoglu, himself, which in Rendel's view produced 'an immense improvement in the atmosphere'.[3]

Rendel was less lucky in his efforts to promote better Bulgarian–Yugoslav relations: in Belgrade, Campbell knew all too well Prince Paul's distrust of King Boris.[4] In April 1940 Rendel suggested that King George VI should write to Prince Paul urging him to overcome his suspicion of Boris; but Campbell wrote in May that when he last saw Prince Paul, he had 'never known him so hot on the subject of Bulgaria and King Boris', so the idea of the letter was dropped.[5] Seven months later the Southern Department minuted: 'the chief obstacle to any Bulgarian–Yugoslav rapprochement is still the Prince Regent's dislike and distrust of King Boris'.[6] Boris on his side had perhaps still more reason to mistrust the Yugoslavs, since there were very close links between the Serb Peasant Party headed by Milan Gavrilović and the left wing of the Bulgarian Agrarians led by G. M. Dimitrov: both wanted a South Slav state uniting Bulgaria and Yugoslavia, which meant abolishing the Bulgarian monarchy, and both were working with S.O.E. In November 1940 the Bulgarian War Minister complained of the anti-Bulgarian activities of the Yugoslav Legation in Sofia, said to be working against the Bulgarian dynasty.[7]

Rendel's main task, as he saw it, was to warn Bulgaria of the dangers of falling into Hitler's clutches. With the government of Georgi Kioseivanov, in the early war months, he had some success. But this was replaced early in 1940 by a government headed by Boris Filov, who was much more friendly to the Germans. Rendel could seldom get any change out of Filov, so he had to rely on his sporadic interviews with King Boris to get results. The King listened politely; but he was above all preoccupied with his dilemma – the need to choose between Russia and Germany. In January 1940 he remarked to an English friend that his father had shown himself Russophobe in a Russophil country and that 'his son would not repeat the mistake'.[8] So in the winter of 1939–40 he concluded a civil air agreement and a commercial agreement with Russia.[9] But he told Rendel in April that he was haunted by the fear of a rapid spread of Communism in Europe if Germany was crushingly defeated; he therefore hoped for a negotiated peace.[10]

When in July 1940 Rumania repudiated the British guarantee,

Britain could for once use a territorial bribe. Rendel was instructed to tell Boris that since Rumania had 'thrown in her lot with Germany' and could no longer be regarded as fully independent, the British government 'would fully understand and sympathize with any desire which Bulgaria might now have to effect an early settlement' of the question of southern Dobruja.[11] Rendel gave the good news to Boris on 19 July; the King said it caused him utmost satisfaction to see that Bulgaria's claim had been at last recognised on all sides. However, Rendel reported, he appeared 'nervous and frightened'.[12]

Unfortunately, the British move over the Dobruja came too late to steal Hitler's thunder; it was obvious that it was Hitler's bullying of the Rumanians which compelled them to give up southern Dobruja peacefully by the Craiova agreement of 8 September. Halifax felt it necessary to expound British philosophy on frontier revision, telling the House of Lords on 5 September:

> H.M.G. have never supported a policy based on a rigid adherence to the *status quo*. On the contrary the principle to which H.M.G. have lent their support is that they would be favourable to a modification of the *status quo* provided always that such a modification is just and equitable in itself and is reached by means of free and peaceful negotiation and agreement between the interested parties and without aggression or compulsion . . . It is for that reason that H.M.G. can regard with satisfaction the conversations . . . in regard to . . . the southern Dobruja.

This Chamberlainesque statement can have cut little ice with Bulgarians; more to the point was Churchill's statement in the Commons: 'personally I have always thought that the south part of the Dobruja ought to be restored to Bulgaria'.[13] (This was true: in September 1939 Churchill had told the War Cabinet that Britain 'should put considerable pressure on Rumania to offer to Bulgaria the southern portion of the Dobruja, which was entirely inhabited by Bulgars and which Rumania had seized after the last Balkan war'.)[14]

In October 1940 the British became worried by reports of heavy German pressure on Bulgaria coupled with offers of an outlet to the Aegean. The Foreign Office asked Rendel to deliver a message from King George VI to Boris, welcoming the Dobruja settlement and urging that Bulgaria should maintain its neutrality and refuse 'to be lured by specious promises into a state of belligerency in the course of which she might well become the battlefield between the contending parties'.[15] Rendel delivered the message on 15 October. Boris seemed pleased by the first part of the message but 'looked somewhat disturbed' by the last part. Once again Rendel noted that the King seemed 'depressed and frightened': 'I think he is probably being bullied by the Germans. He has also obviously been impressed by the character of German assistance to Bulgaria over the Dobruja'. A day later Rendel commented 'I do not think [King Boris] has sold himself to the Germans . . . But I think he feels he is in a cleft stick and we shall not be able to help him.' A week later Boris sent an answer to George VI: 'placed as it is, in a particularly delicate position, my country cannot at the present moment do more than play the smallest part and its attitude is dictated by its anxiety to safeguard as far as may be possible its vital interests'.[16]

The Italian attack on Greece on 28 October inevitably heightened tension and added to King Boris's fears. Rendel was instructed to warn the Bulgarian government to refrain from any action 'which would render more difficult the task of the Greek government', and to make it plain that 'at the end of a victorious war [Britain] would know how to deal both with friends and enemies'. Rendel slightly softened this message in conveying it to Filov, who 'repeated over and over again that [Bulgaria's] situation was dangerous and delicate'.[17]

It was at this point that the Soviet Union stepped on to the stage, though hardly into the public limelight. Since May it had been encouraging the Yugoslav government, at least in words, to stand up to Axis pressure; on 7 November Andrei Vyshinski told the Yugoslav minister in Moscow that the Soviet government were interested in the Balkans 'and interested in a practical way'.[18] But Soviet interest in Bulgaria was far greater than in Yugoslavia. Since the Filov government was outspokenly pro-German, the Soviet Union was making use of the Bulgarian Communist party, which was active and well-established, and guided at long distance by Georgi Dimitrov, secretary of the Comintern, in Moscow.

Rendel kept a close eye on Communist leaflets. In April the Central Committee had violently attacked 'Anglo-French war-mongers' for trying to convert the Balkans into a theatre of war, for attacking Germany and then Russia. Bulgarians, it said, did not want to become 'the executioners of Soviet and German workers . . . Down with the capitalist plunderers!'[19] But in August a Communist Party manifesto attacked 'the advocates of active intervention by Bulgaria in the war on the side of the Berlin–Rome Axis'.[20] The arrival of a Soviet football team at Sofia airport gave the Communist Party a chance to organise a welcoming demonstration by 70,000 to 100,000 people, resulting in about 500 arrests.[21] In mid-October Rendel reported that Communist pamphlets, 'obviously issued with the approval of Moscow' were taking 'a definitely anti-German tone'.[22]

The Soviet Union was therefore steadily increasing its pressure on Bulgaria. In mid-November Molotov arrived in Berlin, hoping, in Stalin's words, for 'a long-range delimitation of mutual interests'. He asked Hitler what Germany would say if Russia gave Bulgaria a guarantee exactly like the guarantee Germany had given Rumania.

Russia was also ready to give Bulgaria an outlet to the Aegean. Hitler stalled, saying he did not know of any request by Bulgaria for a guarantee; and he set out to divert Soviet ambitions elsewhere. Molotov persisted, saying that Russia was interested not only in Bulgaria but also Rumania, Hungary, Yugoslavia and Greece.[23] After the meeting the two sides exchanged draft documents providing for Soviet adherence to the Tripartite Pact. The German draft mentioned no South-East European country except Turkey; the Soviet draft contained a secret protocol 'recognizing that Bulgaria is geographically located inside the security zone of the Black Sea boundaries of the Soviet Union and that it is therefore a political necessity that a mutual assistance pact be concluded between the Soviet Union and Bulgaria, which in no way shall affect the internal regime of Bulgaria, her sovereignty or independence'.[24]

The Germans never replied. On 17 November – just after Molotov left Berlin – Hitler summoned King Boris to Berchtesgaden. The visit was supposed to be secret; on 21 November Rendel learned unofficially that Bulgaria had been asked to join the Tripartite Pact but that Boris had said 'he could not join unless the Soviet Union was also a party to it' – in the circumstances, a clever answer; Hitler had dangled an Aegean outlet, but Boris side-stepped saying that Bulgaria would not use force.[25]

Four days after Boris got back from Berchtesgaden, the Soviet Assistant Commissar for Foreign Affairs, A. Sobolev, arrived in Sofia, and proposed a Soviet–Bulgarian mutual assistance pact; Rendel heard that he also asked for Soviet bases at Varna and Burgas and an airfield at Plovdiv.[26] It was only later that the British heard that the Russians presented the proposed pact as a defence against Turkey rather than Germany, coupling it with an offer of Turkish territory in Thrace up to the Enos–Midia line.[27] This devious approach must have been an ostrich-like attempt to avoid direct confrontation with Hitler.

To back up Sobolev's approach, the Bulgarian Communists – in the words of the Party history – 'unleashed a broad campaign for acceptance of the Soviet proposal'; petitions were sent from factories and workshops to the Filov government.[28] *The Times* described this campaign as 'the greatest subversive activity organised from abroad in the country's recent history; thousands of telegrams poured into Sofia, many deputies requested an audience with the King; many Communists were arrested'. *The Times* concluded: 'no government could now declare Bulgaria to be on the side of the Axis without risking severe internal difficulties'.[29]

The Filov government politely declined the Soviet offer, but from then on Boris was in a stronger position to resist pressure from Hitler. The Foreign Office wanted to add a British warning and on 1 December instructed Rendel to say that H.M.G. would view 'with grave concern'

Bulgaria's adherence to the Tripartite Pact, and – for the first time – to
give a formal assurance that Britain would respect Bulgaria's neutrality
'so long as it is respected by others and provided that Bulgaria
genuinely maintains her neutrality and does not, by infiltration of
German technicians and tourists, by the conclusion of a military agreement with Germany, or in any other manner such as adherence to the
Tripartite Pact, allow that neutrality to be eaten away or rendered
nugatory'.[30] Rendel replied that no warning was needed at the moment
since, as a result of Soviet pressure, the danger of Bulgaria's joining the
Tripartite Pact was very much less. As for a British declaration about
Bulgaria's neutrality, it would have been valuable a year ago, but now
it 'would come too late'.[31] Perhaps the Foreign Office were relieved at
this negative answer: the Rumanian oilfields could not be bombed
without violating Bulgarian air space and Bulgarian neutrality. However, Sargent minuted that he was 'not very worried' about this, since
if the British ever had enough bombers to be able to attack the oilfields,
they would be in a strong enough position 'to commit technical violations of Bulgarian territory with impunity, in just the same way as we
commit technical violations of Swiss territory when bombing towns in
Northern Italy'.[32]

The Sobolev visit brought into the open the clash between Germany
and Russia over Bulgaria, which could only be welcomed by Britain.
At this point British interests coincided with Soviet interests and the
British and Russians had been exerting pressure in the same direction
for the same end. But there had been no co-operation between them.
When Rendel asked the Soviet Minister about Sobolev's visit, he was
told it was 'purely one of courtesy'.[33]

The Foreign Office continued to believe that the Soviet Union would
not, when it came to the crunch, stand up to Hitler. When in January
1941 the War Cabinet discussed the Soviet government's statement
that they had not been consulted about German troops going through
Bulgaria, the comment of Cripps was that Russian policy would continue to be dominated by fear.[34] Later in January Cripps reported
from Moscow that the Soviet Ambassador in Berlin has made it clear
that Russia would not resist a Soviet invasion of Bulgaria, any more
than it had resisted the German take-over in Rumania.[35] At the end
of January Eden tried to get from the Soviet Ambassador, Ivan Maisky,
some statement of the Soviet view on a probable German forward move
in the Balkans; he failed.[36] In late February Cripps reported that
Vyshinski was saying that the situation was 'grave and very complicated'; German troops were on the Bulgarian frontier; but 'the Soviet
government will know how to secure . . . their interests when the
moment comes'. Cripps thought that the Russians had 'accepted their
inability to prevent the Germans entering the Balkans but wished
resistance by others to be as strong as possible so that they may be

subsequently in a position to profit from the resulting weakness of both combatants'.[87]

This seems the only possible explanation of Soviet policy not only towards Bulgaria but also towards Yugoslavia. The Soviet Union failed to follow up the Sobolev visit in any practical way. Rendel reported that pro-Russian Bulgarians 'complained bitterly, when the Germans eventually arrived, that Russia had abandoned them to their fate'.[38] From the British, the Bulgarians knew they had nothing to expect but rather unconvincing warnings. In February, when German troops in plain clothes were streaming in, Rendel was instructed to tell the Filov government that if they gave way to German demands, the British would 'take such measures as they may consider necessary to meet the situation; nor would they at any eventual peace settlement be able to forget Bulgaria's action'.[39] Undeterred, Filov signed the Tripartite Pact in Vienna on 1 March and on the same day German troops in uniform entered Sofia.

Rendel, whose Bulgarian staff had been harassed by the police while an official in the Passport Control Office had disappeared without trace, now said he thought the time had come to break off relations. On 3 March he had his farewell interview with King Boris. He said that Bulgaria's accession to the Tripartite Pact 'would mean that the war would now spread to Bulgarian soil', at which the King 'looked perturbed'. Boris said that Bulgaria had not had fair treatment, had always been blamed for everything that went wrong, and had been a victim of world events. Rendel reported that 'the King was personally most friendly . . . but the interview was extremely painful'.[40] Later he wrote, 'I said good-bye to His Majesty with real regret . . . he was not of a character and calibre to take command of events.'[41]

Rendel's last interview with Filov had less pathos. Rendel expressed 'deep regret' that the British policy of trying to preserve Bulgarian independence had failed; Filov replied that this was a question with which the Bulgarian government was competent to deal without British help.[42] Rendel and his staff – except for the unfortunate Passport Control official – were safely out of Bulgaria by 12 March; but two girl typists were killed by a bomb planted in the party's luggage which exploded in their Istanbul hotel. Eden suggested that Sofia should be bombed in retaliation (also for other better reasons) but was overruled by the Air Officer Commanding Middle East.[43]

The Soviet Legation remained in Sofia throughout the war, as a useful centre for collecting information on South-East Europe (which was not passed to the British) and to prepare the way for the Red Army's arrival in September 1944.

7 Hungary, 1939-41: a Corridor, Not a Base?

Relations between Britain and Hungary in the first nineteen months of war had a certain atmosphere of drawing-room comedy, with black overtones. This came partly from the character of the Hungarian political élite, drawn from the aristocracy or gentry and possessing sophisticated skills, learned under the Habsburgs, in obstructing superior might or playing off opponents against one another. (Perhaps Hitler, of Austrian origin if of a very different social class, took the measure of the Hungarians better than the British did.) The élite held all power in its hands. The peasants, many of them landless, had no real political representation; there were opposition parties, but where national interests were at stake they tended to line up with the élite. There was no mass party, like Maniu's National Peasant Party in Rumania, with which the British could intrigue against the government.

The British therefore dealt with the political establishment, and with it alone. This suited the inclinations of the British Minister, O'Malley, a man of strong and sometimes eccentric personal views and an intense individualist. Because of his prickly personality, his relations with the Foreign Office were not always easy. One Foreign Office minute read: 'Mr. O'Malley scarcely conceals his contempt for his instructions' [that is, from the Foreign Office].[1] Before the war started he had led the Foreign Office into embarrassment by urging an approach to Rumania over the highly sensitive question of frontier revision in Transylvania. (see p. 8 above.) Of this he later wrote in an official report: 'Mr. O'Malley expressed to the Foreign Office his unrepentance.'[2] Sargent minuted in February 1940: 'the Hungarians are always very persuasive and plausible, and . . . they have an eloquent advocate in the person of H.M. Minister at Budapest.'[3] O'Malley's own formula for handling the Hungarians was 'sympathy, encouragement and gentle and rather infrequent advice'.[4]

Halifax's definition of Hungary, in April 1940, as a 'weakly-held outpost' of a British-supported Balkan front was somewhat misleading. The Hungarians saw the idea of a neutral bloc as a Rumanian ploy; O'Malley made it clear that he thought the Hungarians would never accept it until Rumania was willing to 'talk frontier revision'; without that 'Rumania alone stood to gain by the proposed pact'.[5] In February

1940 Sargent defined the position differently from Halifax: 'from the beginning of the war we have all along recognised that it would be impossible to establish any "front" in South-East Europe which would include Hungary. For this reason there was never any question of guaranteeing her against Germany as we did Rumania. In other words, we have recognized Hungary to be in the German sphere, and nothing we can *say* will change this.'[6] If this was something of an over-state-ment, it helps to explain the curiously fatalistic and resigned attitude which the British took towards Hungary.

In the winter of 1939–40, the Hungarians themselves had not finally accepted submission to Hitler. They were still putting some faith in Mussolini whom they had seen since 1934 as a rival to Hitler and a supporter of their own attempts to maintain their independence. At the beginning of the war, Mussolini backed them in their refusal of Germany's demand that its troops should pass across the north-east corner of Hungarian territory to Poland,[7] which they had linked with a threat to 'blow up the tunnels' – or so O'Malley reported.[8] But a meeting between the Hungarian and Italian Foreign Ministers, Count István Csáky and Ciano, in January 1940 led to misunderstandings and a cooling-off; Italian support waned.[9] In April the Foreign Office wrote that 'the latest indications are that Hungary could not rely upon Italian assistance in the case of German aggression'.[10]

However, the Hungarian government did not give up its policy of resisting German demands within the limits they judged safe. But they wanted a reward from Britain for good behaviour, in the form of a softer British attitude over Transylvania. On 9 February the Hungarian Minister in London, G. de Barcza, left a note on Hungarian territorial claims, linked with a statement that Hungary was ready to defend its independence and honour against any foreign aggression. Sargent's response was 'since Hungary can render us no service in the war, it is not worth our while to make any sacrifices on her behalf'.[11]

O'Malley however followed his own path. He suggested that on 1st March, the anniversary of Admiral Miklós Horthy's accession as Regent of Hungary, the British radio and press should pay tribute to him as a champion of Christian and gentlemanly principles who was continuing the Hungarians' traditional task of acting as a bulwark against oriental barbarism; nothing however should be said which could embarrass Horthy in relation to Germany.[12] He himself visited the Regent on 1st March and gave him a signed photograph of George VI together with a 'verbal message of goodwill' from the King. Horthy, O'Malley reported, 'dwelt on the sombre nature of the decision he would have to take if Germany, determined to make a dash for the oilfields of Rumania, offered Hungary a choice between the re-acquisition of Transylvania on the one hand and armed oppression on the other'. But Horthy refused to tell O'Malley what the decision would be.[13]

A few days later the Prime Minister, Count Pál Teleki – a distinguished geographer who had just sent the Foreign Office a long and learned study of his own on the Transylvanian problem – also told O'Malley that he could give him no assurance how he would act if he got 'a telephone message in the evening and the Germans . . . arrived in Budapest the next morning'.[14]

The moment of truth came on 23 April. Csáky revealed almost casually to O'Malley that he expected that the Germans might ask for the use of the lines running through the north-east corner of Hungary, and this time, 'Hungary would not in any way resist' the German request. When O'Malley pointed out that this was a serious decision, Csáky asked what else the Hungarians could possibly do. If Hungary resisted, it would be all over in a few days, there would be a German occupation of the whole country and a puppet Nazi government would be installed; moreover, the Hungarians would in fact only be sacrificing themselves to defend Rumania. O'Malley commented, 'it is impossible not to sympathise with the Hungarian government' and drew a parallel with the position of the Austrian Chancellor, Kurt von Schuschnigg, when threatened by Hitler in 1938.[15]

In the Foreign Office Sargent, presumably feeling it was useless to bully Hungary, showed a good deal of understanding for O'Malley's attitude and agreed that he should react very mildly: he should write to Csáky a 'personal letter' telling him that H.M.G. could not remain indifferent to a Hungarian decision to permit the passage of German troops, since this would be entirely inconsistent with Hungarian neutrality; he was to warn Csáky of 'the consequences as regards Anglo-Hungarian relations', but it was not spelt out what this meant.[16]

The Soviet ultimatum to Rumania, demanding Bessarabia and Bukovina, on 26 June sparked off the inevitable Hungarian demand for Transylvania. Hitler did not want fighting between Hungary and Rumania, especially since the oilfields might have suffered; so negotiations started, with the Hungarians confident of success.[17] O'Malley, basing himself on the Foreign Office's recent directive about 'embroiling Germany and Russia' seized the chance to urge that the moment was ripe for 'the complete reversal' of the British attitude over Transylvania,[18] in a pro-Hungarian direction. The Foreign Office again said no. To incite the Hungarians against the Rumanians, they argued, might not necessarily embroil Russia and Germany; for one thing Russia was not yet ready to stand up to Germany and for another, Hitler would not let Hungary fight Rumania.[19] Instead, the Foreign Office decided to incite the Rumanians, through B.B.C. broadcasts and by local propaganda, to resist Hungarian claims on Transylvania.[20] This inevitably provoked protests from the Hungarians, who were also incensed by the British decision to recognise the Czechoslovak government of Eduard Beneš at the end of July.

O'Malley's summing up of the position in August was that 'Hungarian opinion inclines to the view that Germany cannot possibly be beaten and that the United Kingdom . . . cannot . . . exercise any appreciable influence on the settlement of purely continental questions . . . Since the German destruction of the Versailles settlement has greatly assisted Hungarian attacks on the Trianon settlement, the Hungarian government are congratulating themselves on the results so far achieved by playing up to Germany.' But, he added, the Hungarians still wanted to preserve their independence and hoped that once their own territorial claims had been settled, Germany would be weakened.[21]

Hungarian resentment against Britain over frontier revision was in no way soothed by statements made in Parliament on 5 September by Churchill and Halifax, giving their blessing to Bulgaria's recovery of southern Dobruja but not to Hungary's recovery of northern Transylvania. They were slightly assuaged by Churchill's phrase, 'personally I have never been happy about the way in which Hungary was treated after the last war', but this was cancelled out by Halifax's statement – endorsed in vaguer terms by Churchill – that the Vienna Award, giving northern Transylvania to Hungary, was 'the result of a dictation by the Axis Powers, imposed on Rumania under duress', and that Britain would not therefore recognise it.[22]

One outcome of the Vienna Award was that the Germans acquired the right to enter Rumania. This meant that the Hungarians had to implement the decision they had taken in April – to allow German troops to pass through. On 9 October a high-level Hungarian source, referred to by O'Malley discreetly as 'my friend', admitted to him that German soldiers were passing through in civilian clothes, adding that Greece was among possible targets for Hitler's invasion plans.[23] A few days later the Hungarian Director of Military Intelligence told the British Assistant Military Attaché that Hungary had granted transit visas to Rumania for 7,000 German 'civilians' in the last three weeks, adding that German strategy was to force a decision against Britain in the Mediterranean.[24]

On this, Strang[25] minuted: 'it is a curious position when we maintain relations at all with a government which permits the passage of enemy troops whose object – as the Hungarian military authorities admit – is to establish a base of operations against us in the Middle East.' 'But,' he added, 'there is this to be said for the Hungarians, that they have behaved much better to us than have the Rumanians.' The Foreign Office sent very mild instructions to O'Malley: 'if you see Regent . . . you might point out that although we understand the difficulty of resisting German pressure we cannot condone the action of the Hungarian government in permitting German troop movements . . . designed to establish a base of operations against us in the Middle East'.[26]

But before these instructions arrived, O'Malley had already seen the

Regent. He reported later: 'having let the Regent know I should like to see him, but did not want to embarrass him by asking in the ordinary way for an audience, he invited me on October 19 to come, but arranged for me to enter the palace on foot by a side door. His welcome was as warm as always. He said he had wanted to see me for some time, but had hesitated to propose it without knowing how I would take such a furtive entrance . . . Germans had agents even in his own palace . . .' Horthy told O'Malley that Hungary still hoped to get the rest of Transylvania from Rumania and then 'hinted' that Hungary would shortly be pressed to join the Tripartite Pact and would be unable to refuse. O'Malley asked plaintively whether Hungary, when it came to a post-war settlement, would not find 'cause to regret having so thoroughly alienated British–American sympathy'. But 'the Regent was deaf, as is all his government, to all arguments of this kind'. O'Malley commented sadly: 'this Legation can hope to achieve little more than to keep alive friendship with Britain and admiration for the British way of life'.[27]

On 20 November – just after the Molotov visit to Berlin and King Boris's visit to Berchtesgaden – Hungary signed the Tripartite Pact, bowing to the German pressure which Bulgaria had resisted. Hungary, of course, had not the advantage of counter-pressure from the Soviet Union, such as had temporarily helped Boris. In July the Russians had invited Hungary 'in very friendly terms' to send a delegation to Moscow to negotiate a trade agreement,[28] but this initiative was not followed up. In August O'Malley reported that 'numerous remarks made to me in the Ministry of Foreign Affairs show that the Hungarian government regret that Russia is so little help as a counterweight to Germany'.[29] The Vienna Award led Molotov to display resentment at German failure to consult the Soviet Union, which he regarded as a violation of the Soviet-German Pact of 1939; German conduct, he said, had not been entirely in good faith, since the Germans could have been in no doubt that the Soviet government was interested in Rumania and Hungary. Molotov reiterated Soviet interest in Hungary, along with other South-East European countries, during his Berlin visit.[30] In late November, using the usual roundabout Soviet technique, the Soviet News Agency 'denied a German press report' that 'the accession of Hungary to the Tripartite Pact was achieved with the cooperation and full approval of the Soviet Union'.[31]

Even if Moscow had wanted to exert pressure on Hungary, there would have been no active, well-organised Communist Party, such as existed in Bulgaria, which could be mobilised to agitate in support of Soviet diplomacy. After Béla Kun's short period of Communist rule after the First World War, the Communists had been too brutally suppressed in Hungary to survive as a live force, and their surviving leaders, notably Mátyás Rákosi, were in the Soviet Union.

O'Malley's reaction to Hungary's signature of the Tripartite Pact was very relaxed. When Hungarians asked him whether Britain was likely to break off relations, he said it was not clear what rights and obligations Hungary had assumed, and he did not suppose the British government were 'particularly interested' if Hungary's adherence had really altered nothing; British–Hungarian relations depended not so much on 'this sort of window dressing' as on the actual conduct of the Hungarians. O'Malley reported that the Hungarians seemed to be very anxious to avoid any action which would make it difficult for the British Legation to remain. He himself thought it should stay. The Foreign Office agreed.[32]

Horthy still wanted to keep open his lines to the British. On 7 December he summoned the Naval Attaché and kept him for 'one and a half hours of very friendly and intimate talk'. He said that in return for signing the Tripartite Pact Germany had promised that Hungary should be 'independently represented at the peace conference' and meanwhile would not have to take on any fresh responsibilities.[33] In London, de Barcza told Cadogan that he was personally distressed by Hungary's signature of the pact, but that geographical facts made it inevitable.[34] During December, Csáky found himself in political trouble at home, not for signing the pact, but for showing enthusiasm about it: for this he was heavily criticised by the elder statesman Count István Bethlen, the Smallholders' Party leader, Tibor Eckhardt, and other 'leading Hungarians'. Horthy told O'Malley during a shoot that the effect of this enthusiasm had been very bad in the United States.[35]

In late December 1940, Hungary agreed to a German request to station railway transport officers at Hungarian stations, notably on the Austrian frontier, the Rumanian frontier and in Budapest itself. This was admitted to O'Malley on 23 December; he recommended to the Foreign Office that no action should be taken about it, since 'anti-German feeling is increasing in Hungary and the presence of German soldiery will strengthen it'.[36]

The German R.T.O.s were in fact preparing the way for the vast flood of German troops which poured into Rumania in the following weeks, to be used either for Hitler's drive south into the Balkans or for invading Russia. For Hitler's purposes, it was essential to neutralise or immobilise Yugoslavia. The Germans therefore approved Hungarian plans for a friendship treaty with Yugoslavia. The British Assistant Military Attaché in Budapest, visiting the Szeged area in December and observing German military dispositions, deduced that the Germans were initiating measures 'which would serve as a form of blackmail on Jugoslavs in negotiations', adding that a Hungarian–Yugoslav treaty might later 'act as a brake on Yugoslav anti-Axis policy', and that 'should diplomacy fail', there might be a German attack on Yugoslavia through Hungary.[37] Horthy told the British Naval Attaché that he was 'in personal and almost daily correspondence of very friendly character with Prince Paul'.[38] From Belgrade, Campbell reported that while Horthy had been impressing the Yugoslavs with his strong pro-British feelings, the obvious danger of the proposed pact was 'the risk it involved of Yugoslavia being drawn into the German-Italian orbit'. He thought the British attitude should be to show interest in the development, provided Prince Paul realised the risks.[39]

The Hungarian–Yugoslav pact was signed in December, and broken by Hungary the following April.

In January 1941, the inner circle of the Hungarian political establishment devised a plan by which Hungary, while complying with German demands, could keep the good will of Britain and the United States. (O'Malley later claimed to be himself one of the originators of the plan.[40]) At the time he reported that Horthy had received Bethlen (probably the most influential politician in Hungary), Eckhardt (whose mildly reformist views on the peasant problem would be acceptable in the West) and other notabilities for a very secret discussion. The plan was that when Germany demanded 'something definitely inconsistent with Hungarian sovereignty', Horthy would appoint a government of politicians who would by that time be abroad and out of danger of capture by the Germans. Horthy himself would stay in Hungary but resign and refuse all co-operation with any quisling régime set up by the Germans.[41] On 26 January Horthy received O'Malley and confirmed to him that this was indeed the plan. From other sources O'Malley learned that Bethlen was to head the exiled government, residing in London, while Eckhardt would go to Washington. (He in fact left Hungary in January.) O'Malley told the Foreign Office that he had let it be known that the British would facilitate Bethlen's journey to London, adding 'I should presumably consider myself as more or less accredited to Count Bethlen and collaborate with him wherever he went'. He thought that Horthy might, when it came to the crunch, give more to the Germans than 'we should wish to see him do', but he was 'very stubborn and personally quite fearless'.[42]

It is not clear what Halifax thought of this scheme, but after learning of it he saw the Hungarian Minister and told him that British forbearance had limits, and the Hungarian government should realise that Britain's post-war attitude would be influenced by the degree and manner in which the Hungarians had tried to withstand Axis pressure. De Barcza replied that the Regent was personally pro-British, but Germany had offered much as regards frontier revision, and in any case German troops were not allowed to detrain in Hungary.[43]

Halifax also told O'Malley that he agreed to Bethlen's coming to London.[44] But the plan for a government in exile somehow evaporated. On 20 March the Hungarian Foreign Minister went to see Ribbentrop in Munich; on his return he refused to tell O'Malley what had passed.

On 24 March the British Military Attaché received information of
German motorised artillery formations in the neighbourhood of the
Yugoslav frontier.[45] On the same day Yugoslavia signed the Tripartite
Pact, with extremely important reservations. On 27 March the coup
d'état took place in Belgrade. Hitler decided to invade Yugoslavia. On
2 April the Hungarian Prime Minister, Count Teleki, shot himself.

The next day, O'Malley went to see Horthy, and condoled with
him on Teleki's death. Horthy said he would tell 'the whole story':
Hitler had offered Hungary, as reward for co-operation, Croatia and
Fiume (former historic lands of the Hungarian Crown, but not territory usually claimed by post-Trianon Hungary). On 1st April the
Hungarian Crown Council had decided to accept the offer, if Croatia
should split off from Serbia, or if the Yugoslav army should retire into
the mountains leaving a vacuum to the south of the Hungarian–Yugoslav frontier. Teleki, Horthy said, favoured this decision; but the next
day he received a telegram from de Barcza in London reporting that
'someone in authority' had said that if Hungary now became Germany's accomplice against Yugoslavia, its name would be completely
dishonoured. Teleki then shot himself, leaving one letter to his wife,
who was herself dying, and another to the Regent saying that the
course to which the Hungarian government was about to commit itself
was not consistent with his honour or his conscience.[46]

To O'Malley, Horthy justified Hungary's decision by its historical
association with Germany, the sacred duty of restoring ancient frontiers,
and the hopelessness of looking to Britain for any help for this purpose.
O'Malley, who must have been suffering a bitter personal disappointment, replied with an emotional outburst 'in language which I . . . had
hardly expected ever to use to the head of a State': if the Regent
entered into such a corrupt bargain with Germany or acted as a Hungarian jackal to the German lion against a State with which he had
just signed a treaty of eternal friendship, Hungary could expect no
sympathy and no mercy from a victorious Britain and United States,
and Horthy himself 'would be covered with well-deserved contempt
and dishonour'. There followed what O'Malley described as a 'passionate and lengthy but intimately friendly conversation' during which
Horthy 'was almost moved to tears'; but there was no sign that he
intended to change course.[47]

By 6 April O'Malley had simmered down and reported that he had
learnt that Germany had uttered threats to obtain Hungary's com-
pliance, adding (rather unfairly, since Teleki could not give his side
of the story) that he also learnt that it was Teleki himself who 'first
induced the Regent to start upon the ignoble path upon which his feet
are now set, and his suicide was in part due to remorse'. (Teleki's
painfully sincere letter ended: 'we shall become robbers of corpses, the
basest of nations . . . I am guilty'.)[48] Bethlen, O'Malley said, was going

to stay in Hungary to 'restrain the Hungarian government' from committing itself further to Germany.[49]

On the same day the Foreign Office instructed O'Malley to leave Budapest, but Britain did not declare war on Hungary.[50] By marching into Hungary in the wake of the Germans, Hungary acquired a considerable slice of Yugoslav territory – but not Croatia or Fiume.

In the Foreign Office, Frank Roberts[51] summed up British policy: 'it was . . . because Hungary seemed to be making some effort to pursue an independent policy and so long as she remained a corridor, but not a base, for German troops that we made allowances for her difficulties and maintained relations with her. Our attitude only changed when Hungary became a base for a German attack upon Yugoslavia, shortly to be followed by a Hungarian attack.'[52]

British policy at that time was open to the criticism that British diplomats had allowed themselves to be duped by Hungarian charm and wiles, while the Hungarian governing classes were allowing themselves to be duped by Hitler's bribes; or that the British had failed to contact and work through the more democratic elements in Hungary. On the other hand, if the Russians could not produce a social revolution in Hungary, still less could the British; and outside the governing élite there were no real centres of power, such as the opposition parties in Serbia or Rumania, with which the British could work. (Prince Paul once remarked enviously on the complete solidarity of all political elements in Hungary around the Regent.)[53] O'Malley's policy of keeping on friendly social terms with the Regent and the political establishment was therefore probably wiser than it sometimes looked, even if it reeked of what Hugh Dalton called 'the Servants' Hall mentality'.[54] Again, if British attempts to organise sabotage in Hungary were minimal, this was partly because O'Malley opposed them, but also because it was hard to find people to take the necessary risks. As for the Hungarian governing class, if they wanted to have their cake and eat it – to accept Hitler's bribes and stay on good terms with the Western democracies – that was only to be expected, and righteous indignation on Britain's part could be little more than an empty gesture.

8 Rumania, 1939-41: Maniu or Nothing?

If in Hungary there was on the surface an atmosphere of drawing-room comedy, in Rumania there was one of crude melodrama. This was mainly because of the fierce vendetta between King Carol and the Iron Guard, the extreme radical movement which, on one side, campaigned for the peasants' rights, a clean-up of political corruption and some kind of social revolution, and on the other, used the trappings and violent methods of a Nazi-type party, and was at least in part manipulated by the Germans. Its members ranged from idealistic young men, including former Communists, to thugs and sadists. Carol had tried hard but vainly to suppress it, earning its undying hatred through the killing of its idolised leader, Corneliu Codreanu. Codreanu's father and a group around him were set on vengeance.

The King had also made a personal enemy of Maniu, the most respected politician in the country and leader of the party which commanded the loyalty of most peasants and most Transylvanians: Maniu was himself from Transylvania and had done much to unite it with Rumania after the First World War. He strongly disapproved of the political influence of Carol's mistress, Magda Lupescu.

So Carol's position on the outbreak of war was shaky. But he and his government – in particular Gafencu – were well-disposed to the Western Allies, and Britain had no interest in working against him. The Minister, Hoare, was a shrewd observer; he was also remarkably outspoken in telling Rumanians what he thought of them, in a way that sometimes alarmed the Foreign Office; but his charm of manner perhaps softened his words. Early in 1940 he watched with scepticism King Carol's efforts to create a 'National Renaissance Front' of his own, complete with uniforms and compulsory membership for State officials, while formally suppressing all other organisations. This was mainly directed against the Iron Guard, but provoked Maniu to long and closely-argued protest.[1]

Hoare regarded with almost equal scepticism his own government's policy of guaranteeing Rumania without providing the arms for its defence, let alone possessing the capacity to give military aid. He urged the supply of anti-tank and anti-aircraft guns and aircraft. He urged – in vain – that the British guarantee should be extended to cover attack by Russia. He knew that this was what Carol feared most, and that if Britain did not help him to meet the Soviet threat he would inevitably turn to Germany. When Hoare saw him in May 1940, he reported that Carol 'made it fairly plain that he would dislike the utter defeat of Germany . . . almost, if not quite as much as a great German triumph, and he said almost in so many words that wisdom lay in an early peace and the conclusion of a Holy Alliance against Russia'.[2]

By this time the King had already taken note of German victories in the west; in late April he had released all Iron Guards from the concentration camps. At the beginning of June he got rid of the pro-western Gafencu and replaced him as Foreign Minister by a pro-German nonentity. After the fall of France he tried to consolidate his own position by taking over personal leadership of the National Renaissance Front and re-christening it the 'National Party'.

But when the blow fell and Russia demanded Bessarabia and Bukovina, and Ribbentrop, on 27 June, advised Rumania to yield, there was a sort of total moral breakdown of the Rumanian governing class. Hoare wrote later: 'it is impossible to over-estimate the effect of the Bessarabian crisis on Rumania . . . Having a thoroughly bad conscience about the gross mismanagement of what should be a tolerably rich country, the bourgeoisie is today terrified of communism and social unrest. They hope profoundly that in the course of this war the present régime in Russia will be shattered. If Germany does it she will have their warm support.'[3] Not only the bourgeoisie, but also the Rumanian army were demoralised by the abandonment of costly and elaborate defences and a hopelessly disorderly flight from Bessarabia. Some Rumanians – mostly Jews – fled in the opposite direction, into Bessarabia.[4]

The British reaction to the Soviet annexation of Bessarabia and northern Bukovina was resigned and passive. In the Foreign Office Philip Broad[5] minuted: 'it was almost inevitable that this should happen sooner or later. From our own purely selfish point of view this . . . does not greatly change the position. Rumania has gone too far towards the Axis Powers for there to be any question of her thinking of appealing to our guarantee.'[6] Rumania in fact denounced the guarantee a few days later, to please Germany. When R. A. Butler,[7] then Parliamentary Under-Secretary at the Foreign Office, saw the Rumanian Minister after the Soviet annexation, all he offered was a statement that 'no occupation of territory of a friendly government could be a matter of indifference to H.M.G.' and that he could 'express the sympathy of the British government at the severe fate which had befallen the provinces so dear to Rumania'.[8] Britain did not recognise Soviet occupation of Bessarabia and northern Bukovina _de jure_.[9]

Butler's nebulous statement was unlikely to breathe courage into

Carol, who in desperation appointed a fully pro-German government and – in Hoare's words – set about 'trying desperately hard to earn one of Hitler's rare embraces'. Hoare added – over-optimistically – that Rumanian opinion 'strongly objects to the King's present mood which is to place his country and himself at Hitler's disposal'.[10]

The wretched King was rapidly thrown into a far worse crisis, over Transylvania, which finally lost him his throne. The British saw their opportunity. They hoped, by encouraging Rumanian resistance to the cession of Transylvania to Hungary, to topple Carol's pro-German government and bring in a more pro-western government under Maniu; at worst, they could at least cause trouble to the Germans in an economically important and sensitive area. Hugh Seton-Watson,[11] then attached to the British Legation, was in touch with Maniu, and reported in July that Maniu had been proposing a Government of National Concentration, representing all the political forces of the nation, but the King had so far rejected the idea. Robin Hankey,[12] then First Secretary at the Legation, wrote on 22 July: 'there is one conceivable if desperate alternative to the present régime . . . It is the return of a National Peasant government under M. Maniu . . .' A few days later Hankey telegraphed that the Iron Guards as well as Maniu were opposing any frontier revision and were said to have the support of many army officers; 'if a diversion in the south-east of Europe would be convenient to H.M.G. . . . it would pay us to encourage resistance to Hungary in Rumanian broadcasts'.[13] Seton-Watson also reported that Maniu wanted 'an understanding' between England and Russia and Hankey telegraphed that Maniu was in 'indirect touch' with the Soviet Legation.[14]

In London, the Foreign Office was considering the idea of bringing Manin to power by encouraging resistance to Hungarian demands. On 6 August, the Foreign Office told Bucharest that it was inclined to favour it: 'the restoration of Rumania to a position of real neutral independence is obviously most desirable, and even if this were prevented by forcible intervention by Germany, such intervention would in itself serve our purpose, since it would bring about a situation which might well be conducive to a clash between Germany and Russia.'[15]

In this crisis, Russia's attitude was obviously of key importance. Since its annexation of Bessarabia and northern Bukovina, there had been a number of reports that Russia was not satisfied and might take more Rumanian territory. What the Rumanians, above all Maniu, wanted was an assurance that if they were involved in conflict with Hungary, Russia would not attack them in the rear. But there was no British–Soviet discussion of this question, and the outcome of Maniu's contacts with the Russians was obviously negative.

In early August a manifesto was circulating signed by Maniu, the Liberal, George Bratianu, and other politicians, though not the Iron

Guard. On 9 August the British Legation reported:' we are encouraging resistance movement by direct clandestine propaganda, some of which has already met with remarkable success'. The resistance movement was however largely confined to civilians, while a considerable part of the army seemed 'profoundly demoralized'.[16] Seton-Watson, on a visit to Transylvania, reported that Maniu was travelling about talking to local personalities; clandestine circulars were being sent round urging people to resist. The 'intellectual youth' composed a declaration completely rejecting any negotiations with Hungary.[17] The British Consul

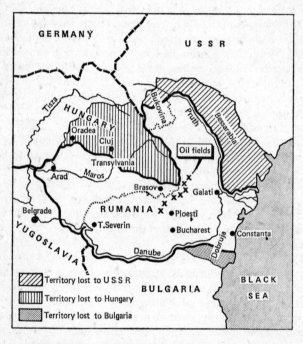

MAP 2. Rumania's Territorial Losses, 1940

in the Transylvanian town of Cluj reported that there were many Transylvanian regiments stationed in the area which might support Maniu.[18]

In spite of this resistance, Carol agreed to negotiations with Hungary which started on 16 August, but the Rumanians remained unwilling to yield anything of substance to the Hungarians. Hungary then forced Hitler to intervene by threatening military action against Rumania, so Hitler imposed the Vienna Award on Rumania, threatening – according to the Rumanian account – that if the German terms were not accepted by 3 a.m. on 1st September Rumania would be invaded by Hungary and the Soviet Union simultaneously.[19] At the time, there was a good deal of speculation in the Foreign Office, whether or not there had really been a Soviet threat, or Soviet–German collusion.[20] In the light of the German documents there was obviously no collusion; the Russians were indignant at German failure to consult or inform them in advance.[21]

The Vienna Award did not at first put an end to British hopes of stimulating a resistance movement. Demonstrations against it were reported in many parts of Transylvania, and attacks on the German consulates at Cluj and Braşov.[22] But it soon appeared that the demonstrations were small-scale.[23] However, Maniu continued his political activity, publishing his declaration at the Crown Council on 30 August: 'I protest against the fact that we should repeat in Transylvania what has happened in Bessarabia and Bukovina . . . Better defeat in battle than shameful retreat . . .' An organisation was launched to keep alive a spirit of resistance, intended to unite outstanding men of various parties, but under the guidance of Maniu, and backed by the British; it was known as Pro-Transylvania or Ardealul.

But Maniu was too obsessed with constitutional and legal questions and the type of political bargaining practised in the Austro-Hungarian empire to be able to grasp power with the ruthlessness required in 1940. Hoare wrote that Maniu had 'preserved a rugged and obstinate adherence to principle in this land where expediency rules supreme'.[24] Adherence to principle was not a very useful virtue, however admirable, in the turmoil and near-anarchy in Bucharest in early September, created by the psychological shock of the Vienna Award and the rampaging of the Iron Guard. Carol lost grip of the situation. But it was not Maniu who stepped into the void. It was General Ion Antonescu, a distinguished soldier who had offended Carol; he now emerged from retirement to try to form a government. He soon found it impossible since neither the Iron Guard nor Maniu nor other reputable politicians would serve under the King. The Iron Guard agitated for his abdication. The British Military Attaché believed that if Carol abdicated both the Iron Guard and the National Peasant Party would agree to serve in a national all-party government.[25] But then Hoare reported that the process of government building was hanging fire: 'delay is widely attributed to M. Maniu's refusal to cooperate . . .'[26]

Maniu had obviously set his terms for entering an Antonescu government too high. Hoare reported on 11 September: 'Maniu's . . . conduct during the present crisis suggests that he remains as negative as ever. Antonescu's position is however still extremely weak and Maniu therefore has a considerable nuisance value.'[27] The Foreign Office concluded that in view of the 'rather feeble' part Maniu had played throughout the Transylvanian crisis, there was not much point in supporting him publicly; 'whether we support him through less obvious channels is of course another question'.[28]

The solution of the crisis was that Antonescu, pressed by the Iron Guard, forced Carol to abdicate and the Iron Guard then entered the government. A section of the Iron Guard then harassed the British so badly that the Foreign Office, early in October, considered breaking off diplomatic relations straight away, but took no definite decision.[29] In Bucharest the Legation and S.O.E. took measures to prepare for sabotage and political resistance after relations were broken. On 24 October, at a meeting in the Foreign Office, the head of S.O.E. reported that Maniu 'had now agreed to leave the country when the right moment came'. The meeting agreed that it would be more useful for Maniu to establish himself in Istanbul or Cairo than in London. It was decided *not* to form a Rumanian committee in London under the former Minister, Tilea.[30]

By then German troops were already moving into Rumania, and the decision to bring Maniu out of the country meant that the British had decided to pin their hopes on him as leader – or at least figure-head – of a resistance organisation to the Germans in the months and years ahead. His great prestige could be expected to outweigh his 'negativeness'. He had a wide-spread and fairly efficient party organisation – in theory a great asset for underground work.

On 20 November R. A. Butler told the House of Commons that the Rumanian government had invited German troops to enter the country and that they had been arriving in 'ever-increasing numbers'. This obliged H.M.G. to regard the Rumanian government as being 'no longer in full control of their own country or its foreign policy'. But he refused to say whether the Legation was going to leave. On 23 November Rumania signed the Tripartite Pact, three days after Hungary. This provoked no strong British reaction; the Legation stayed on.

In January 1941 came Antonescu's show-down with the Iron Guard. After he had triumphed, with the help of the German military, he reconstituted his government on a non-party basis and strengthened his position. In the Foreign Office Dixon minuted bitterly on 11 February: 'the National Peasant and Liberal leaders, continuing their spineless attitude, appear to have accepted the inevitable and to have determined to support the new government such as it is.'[31]

Maniu turned his energy to winning the support of disillusioned members of the Iron Guard. He told Hoare, just before the Legation left in mid-February, that the dead Iron Guard leader, Codreanu, had left a sort of will designating Maniu as leader; a large section of the Iron Guard might now be ready to follow him, and if they were gangsters, possibly for present purposes they were more useful than 'the respectabilities'. Hoare's final impression was that 'though Maniu's intentions are the very best, he is sadly lacking in inspiration . . . However, there is nobody else who could head a patriotic movement, and so at present it is Maniu or nothing.'[32]

S.O.E. also felt it was Maniu or nothing. At a meeting at the Foreign Office on 20 February S.O.E. representatives said their programme in Rumania was 'entirely dependent' on the co-operation of Maniu's supporters, on whom they would also have to rely for their communications with Rumania once the British Legation had left.[33]

In late February Hoare and the Legation staff left Rumania. Maniu did not. All through March S.O.E. were waiting for him to come, and sending messages to him. They had left a W/T transmitter with him, but no explanation came of Maniu's reasons for not leaving, in spite of his promises to Hoare and to the S.O.E. representative, Gardyne de Chastelain. On 29 April a short message came that public opinion in Rumania was anti-German and that Rumanians were not demoralised by the German advance in the Balkans.[34] A message also arrived saying that the Germans intended to attack Russia on 15 June.[35]

Perhaps one reason why Maniu did not leave was his expectation of a German–Soviet clash – rumoured for months past in Bucharest – which would raise the question, for Rumania, of recovering Bessarabia and Bukovina. Over this, Maniu would have a political role to play which would hardly be approved by the British. He may also have wished to be with his own people at a time of great danger and stress. But most probably the main reason was his temperamental inability to make up his mind to positive action.

9   Yugoslavia: Prince Paul or a Coup?

British policy towards Yugoslavia between 1939 and 1941 was plagued by three problems: geography, or the impossibility of giving military help to Yugoslavia without controlling either the Adriatic or Salonika; the Serb-Croat division; and uncertainty over Prince Paul. All had grave consequences.

BRITISH DEMANDS: NO BRITISH AID

In the early months of the war, the inability of the Western allies to help Yugoslavia had been solved, in French eyes, by the Salonika front plan; but the British had not believed in it, nor, once he realised allied weakness in the Eastern Mediterranean, had Prince Paul.

When in April 1940 there were signs of an imminent Italian threat to Yugoslavia, in Dalmatia, the War Cabinet had an inconclusive discussion on what, if anything, could be done. The only practical suggestion that emerged was that a discreet and 'unofficial' warning should be given to the Italian Military Attaché in London that Italy 'could not attack Yugoslavia with impunity'.[1] When in mid-May Halifax saw Princess Paul of Yugoslavia in London, she asked what Britain would do if Italy attacked Yugoslavia. Halifax told her that 'we should naturally wish to do anything in our power to help but . . . we must recognize that if the Italians, as . . . was likely, mined the entrance of the Adriatic, the navy would presumably not be able to do much'. She then asked about the order for aircraft placed some time ago by Yugoslavia. The reply was that the British were throwing everything they could into the Western battle and it was quite impossible to predict its issue; it was very difficult to spare military aircraft which the British needed themselves.[2]

At the beginning of June, the Joint Planning Committee, in a preliminary draft paper, recommended that Britain should inform Yugoslavia that it would declare war on Italy if it attacked Yugoslavia. But in the Foreign Office Sargent thought that Britain ought not to take the initiative, though 'once Italy is fighting against us we should welcome intervention by the Balkans on our side. Meanwhile we should be careful not to give them the impression that we are trying to push them into the war purely for our own ends.'³ Italy rapidly settled the argument by entering the war against Britain and France, and giving Yugoslavia an official assurance of peaceful intentions. The Yugoslav Foreign Minister told the British Minister, Campbell, that Yugoslavia would remain neutral: 'Yugoslavia was not like Greece, accessible to help from the Allies, and would be overrun.'⁴

The French collapse, Campbell reported, produced bewilderment and incomprehension in the Serbs. 'As a martial race . . . they one and all draw a comparison with those years of the last war when their country was overrun and they . . . retreated to Salonika enduring terrible hardships . . . They assert that France should have continued the struggle . . . It is likely that many hopes will be turned to the Soviet Union.'⁵

The idea of withdrawal to Salonika continued to dominate Serb thinking; so too did the hope of Russian protection. The first step towards the Soviet Union – with which Yugoslavia had never had official relations – had already been taken in March; Prince Paul, though known for his 'notorious hatred of Bolshevism', had prompted the move.⁶ A Yugoslav delegation went to Moscow and negotiated the establishment of commercial relations, announced on 15 May. The delegates were received by Molotov in an 'exceptionally cordial way';⁷ one of the delegates, the Croat economist, Budolf Bičanić, reported that Molotov said that Yugoslavia should aim at increasing its military and political power and that Russia wished to be 'useful'.⁸ In June, full diplomatic relations were established and Milan Gavrilović, leader of the Serb Peasant Party and closely associated with the British Legation and Section D/S.O.E., went to Moscow as Minister. The arrival in Belgrade in early July of the first Soviet Minister was the occasion of enthusiastic demonstrations by the extremely active if small Yugoslav Communist Party. This caused the government some embarrassment since by then it was taking up an outwardly pro-Axis attitude.

One thing the Yugoslavs particularly hoped to get from Russia was arms – the arms which the British could not supply. The new Soviet Minister advised the Yugoslavs to resist all German pressure: if they asked for help, the Soviet government would give it.⁹ In August the Yugoslav Director of Military Intelligence was sent to Moscow as military attaché, and told the British that he meant to ask 'immediately and brutally' whether the U.S.S.R. wanted a strong and independent Yugoslavia: if so, it must supply arms, aircraft and tanks. He said he had high hopes.¹⁰ But Prince Paul told Campbell he was 'more than doubtful',¹¹ and it turned out that he was right. There was complete silence on the Soviet side for three months.

Probably to counteract the shock of the fall of France, the Foreign Office suggested in June that King George VI should send a letter of encouragement to Prince Paul. The letter, when sent, was warm and friendly: '. . . my thoughts have often been with you and with the extremely difficult position in which you have found yourself . . . Here in England we have all admired the skill and foresight you have shewn in guiding the policy of your country, and we are confident that you will succeed in maintaining this policy on the firm and independent lines you have chosen . . .'[12] This was supplemented by a personal message that the Duchess of Kent (the Prince's sister-in-law) had seen his two children, who were being educated in England, and that they were well and happy.[13]

But Prince Paul remained fearful of the future. He told Campbell in mid-August that he always told everyone, especially the Germans, that Yugoslavia would fight. But he added that Yugoslavia could lose two million men and last perhaps a fortnight before being overrun.[14]

When Mussolini attacked Greece in October 1940, Yugoslavia declared its neutrality and offered mediation. The British military attache, Col. C. S. Clarke, saw the Yugoslav Chief of Staff, General Petar Kosić, who was 'in a depressed and nervous state', repeating several times: 'what can we do? We are completely surrounded.' Clarke concluded that it was unlikely that Yugoslavia would help Greece.[15] When Campbell said the British hoped the Yugoslavs would 'go as far as they could to assist Greece', Prince Paul replied that Yugoslavia would reject demands for the passage of Italian troops, or for Yugoslav territory; it was less certain that it would refuse passage to German troops. In the Foreign Office, Dixon minuted on this: 'it is no doubt to our interest that Yugoslavia should not enter the war against the Italians . . . Such action would certainly lead to an immediate German attack'. Dixon added that the two essentials were that Yugoslavia should maintain a 'benevolent neutrality' in the Italian-Greek conflict, and should reject all German, as well as Italian, demands 'incompatible with Jugoslav sovereignty'.[16]

The Foreign Office proposed a fresh letter from King George VI to Prince Paul; it was almost friendlier than the July letter: ' . . . Italy's attack on Greece has brought the war nearer to you than ever before. I know and realise how difficult your position is, and that you may have to make concessions to the Axis on non-essential matters. At the same time I am sure you will never give way where the sovereignty of your country is concerned, and I do admire the skill and patience with which you are conducting a very difficult policy'. The letter expressed regret that Britain could not at present supply badly needed armaments, but it was 'only a matter of time' till it would be able to do so.[17]

One move in Belgrade in November encouraged the British: the War Minister, General Milan Nedić, was replaced by General Petar Pešić, reputedly more anti-German.[18] The British military attaché found Pešić 'most friendly and greatly impressed by the British war effort'.[19]

On 23 November – the day on which Rumania, following Hungary, had signed the Tripartite Pact – Campbell telegraphed that Yugoslavia was exposed to 'the immediate possibility of most severe Axis pressure' and urged a formal British communication to 'strengthen the hands of the Prince Regent and other staunch elements'; 'in particular Prince Regent would then have justification before history for the decision to expose his small and in materials weakly armed country to the armed might of the Axis. This is especially important in view of his position as trustee for young King.'[20] On this Churchill minuted: 'the moment is appropriate and the action needful ... Is there any aid and assistance we can give them, except by carrying on the war by ourselves as we are doing .. ? If we cannot promise any effective material aid, we can at any rate assure them that, just as we did last time, we will see their wrongs are righted in the eventual victory.'[21] The Chiefs of Staff said the Navy might be able to keep open the supply line through Salonika, though that was dependent on a number of conditions; sustained operations in the Adriatic were not possible, though submarine operations might be undertaken. Any air assistance could at best only be effective over southern Yugoslavia; 'it is not possible for us to assist Jugoslavia with land forces'.[22]

In these circumstances, the British assurance was inevitably nebulous: '... if the Yugoslav government and people should be called upon to defend again their freedom and independence, they may rest assured that H.M.G. will make a common cause with them ... Yugoslavia will be fighting side by side with us and our allies, and we could look forward once again to achieving a victory by our joint effort that would secure to Yugoslavia all her rights and interests'.[23] In giving this assurance, the British were in fact demanding a supreme act of faith in British victory; they could promise nothing before then.

At this moment of crisis, the Soviet Union made what seemed to be a far more concrete promise than the British – an offer of arms. The Soviet military authorities suddenly told the Yugoslav military attaché in Moscow that they would supply at once 'all the war material they wanted at whatever price they cared to fix', requesting a reply by noon the same day. The Russians said that the aircraft they could supply would, until the following August, be neither very modern nor very fast; they suggested that Yugoslavia should send barges down the Danube to collect the arms which could be hidden under cargoes of wheat to escape German notice. The whole thing should be kept secret.[24]

It was against the background of these British and Yugoslav moves that the Yugoslav Foreign Minister, Alexander Cincar-Marković, was invited on 26 November to visit Ribbentrop. Prince Paul at once told Campbell and said he had given very strict instructions that the Foreign Minister was not to commit Yugoslavia to anything.[25] The Foreign

Office immediately told Campbell that they sympathised with Prince Paul in the difficult position in which the German invitation placed him, but the Yugoslavs should make it clear that they would 'stand four-square against any Axis demands designed either to assist Italy in her difficulties or to advance German military aims in the Balkans'. Above all, the British government counted on the Yugoslav government refusing to join the Tripartite Pact.[26]

This was the first time that this precise British demand, which became so insistent in the following months, was made to Yugoslavia. On this occasion, however, Prince Paul told Campbell that the Germans did not directly ask Yugoslavia to join the pact, though 'one or two hints were thrown out'; 'you can take it we are still being good', he said. In the Foreign Office Nichols minuted: 'I don't myself believe the Prince Regent is guilty of suppressing the truth.'[27] This comment suggested that doubts about the Prince were already creeping into some British minds.

While the British kept up pressure – so far polite – on Yugoslavia, the Soviet Union took no steps whatever to fulfil its lavish arms offer. The Soviet Minister in Belgrade, at a convivial lunch with several Yugoslav Ministers in early December, joked about the number of aircraft – anything from 150 to 500 – that Russia might send Yugoslavia. Questioned whether the Soviet government was interested in peace or war in the Balkans, he answered 'both'.[28] In the Foreign Office Dixon commented: 'the Soviet government appear to blow hot and cold according as (1) they feel confident or frightened about Germany's intentions towards them, and (2) they judge that Yugoslavia is or is not menaced ... '[29] The main reason why they did nothing was presumably that they were hoping for a deal with Hitler over South-East Europe, and gave this higher priority than stiffening the Yugoslavs.[30]

Yugoslavia therefore had to face the Balkan crisis of early 1941 without arms supplies from any quarter. The new War Minister, Pešić, told Campbell in December that German deliveries had suddenly stopped about the time he had taken up his post. But, he said, Yugoslavia would fight whether fully equipped or not; it asked for nothing, and would yield nothing.[31] These were brave words but were perhaps not intended to be taken quite literally.

THE CROATS AND THE DEFENCE OF YUGOSLAVIA

At the root of the problem of Yugoslavia's defence strategy lay the Serb-Croat problem. The voluntary union of independent Serbia with the Croats, Serbs and Slovenes of the Austro-Hungarian empire in 1918 had saddled the new State with great difficulties which only supreme political patience and flexibility could have solved. These were not qualities for which the Serbs of Serbia were noted: their struggle for liberation from the Turks had required quite different virtues. On the eve of the Second World War, Prince Paul had managed to bring about an agreement with the Croat Peasant Party leader, Vladko Maček, which gave a considerable degree of autonomy to an enlarged Croatia. This caused great resentment in Serbia and gave Serb opposition politicians a fresh grievance against Prince Paul. But he was determined to maintain his political partnership with Maček, so as to keep Yugoslavia intact until young King Peter came of age, at eighteen, in 1941.

There were many dangers. Even though resistance to Italian threats to Dalmatia was a relatively popular idea with Croats, a threat from Germany, especially accompanied by promises and bribes, was quite another matter; cautious neutrality seemed the only sensible course. Maček told Roosevelt's special envoy, Colonel William Donovan, in January 1941 that he had no doubt Great Britain would defeat Hitler in the end but 'we had to preserve our own skins until that British victory seemed assured'.[32]

The British were well aware of the Croat problem, through the reports of their Consul-General in Zagreb, Terence Rapp,[33] and through meetings between Maček and Campbell in Belgrade.[34] But they did not seem to see its full impact on the defence of Yugoslavia. They still tended to think in terms of alliance with the gallant little Serbia of the 1914–18 war. The British military attaché, Col. Clarke, in a report at the end of 1940, forecast that the Yugoslav army would 'prove itself in every way worthy of the great Serbian fighting traditions'.[35]

This left open two questions: whether the Croats were prepared to fight; and whether the Serbs were willing – or able – to fight for Croatia. In mid-November 1940 Col. Clarke had already come to the conclusion that it would be wrong to defend Croatia. He reported that the Yugoslav General Staff had two main plans. One, drawn up by General Dušan Simović when Commander-in-Chief, was to defend Yugoslavia's frontiers; Clarke thought this rash and said 'there would now appear no military justification whatever for retaining it'. The second was that the Yugoslavs should concentrate their forces 'for active defence of Serbia': this, Clarke thought, should be adopted, even though it meant the sacrifice of much territory and abandonment of the defences on the northern frontier – though now that the Germans were in Rumania, these would in any case be useless. The Yugoslav Chief of Staff, Kosić, himself told Clarke that for strategic reasons there was no doubt that the second plan was right, but the government might veto the movement of forces away from Croatia and the army might be forced to adopt the strategically unsound first plan.[36]

Prince Paul told Campbell at the end of November that although the Yugoslav armed forces should already be being withdrawn to a defence line further south, this was for obvious reasons politically impossible, since it would mean leaving Croatia defenceless. Campbell, rather suprisingly, asked whether the 'Croats could not be brought to see that in the interest of facilitating resistance of the whole country ... it might be preferable to forgo defence of Croatia in the confidence of recovering it after victory'. Prince Paul, with more realism, said this was too much to expect. But he said about a third of the army was mobilised in the extreme south and more and more Serbs were being sent there.[37] In the Foreign Office Dixon minuted: 'this conversation confirms our supposition that political considerations will militate against the adoption of the right strategic plan ... i.e. abandonment of Croatia and withdrawal to old Serbia.'[38] The British seemed to pay no heed to Prince Paul's determination to keep Yugoslavia intact for King Peter, or the probability that if Croatia was once deliberately 'abandoned' it would never willingly return to a Yugoslav State.

What worried them more was the danger that even if the Serbs forgot about Croatia, it was not certain that they would try seriously to defend Serbia, preferring retreat and withdrawal and 'continuing the fight on foreign soil' as in the 1914–1918 war. The British Naval Attaché, Captain Despard, reported on 22 November that a 'secret government committee' was studying this problem and had instructed Miloš Tupanjanin, acting leader of the Serb Peasant Party, to approach him unofficially to find out whether Britain would be able to supply 'at least part of shipping required and organize supply of local shipping' for the evacuation of a force of 300,000 men, probably through Salonika or Kavalla.[39] The Foreign Office minuted that Campbell should urge 'a spirit of resistance without too much thought of withdrawal'.[40] But this idea of a mass withdrawal continued to dominate the thinking of both the Yugoslav military leaders and the Serb politicians.

PRINCE PAUL AND THE BRITISH

The British attitude towards Prince Paul was to treat him as a kind of honorary Englishman, but one who could not altogether be trusted to put British interests first. Prince Paul's personal inclination seems to have been to enjoy the role of honorary Englishman; but he put what he believed to be Yugoslav interests ahead of British interests. However, he had frequent and intimate conversations with the British Minister (first Sir Ronald Campbell, then Mr Ronald Ian Campbell) and regularly handed over confidential information received from Yugoslav diplomats in various countries, or other sources. When he asked tentatively whether the Minister could give him some confidential information in return, the Foreign Office said he could be shown certain papers, but not those marked 'secret' without special permission from London.[41] So it was a rather one-way relationship.

In any case the British thought it as well to have in the cupboard an alternative policy to all-out support of Prince Paul. During 1940 Section D (later S.O.E.) was particularly active in Belgrade, cultivating politicians and leaders of patriotic organisations and handing out subsidies to the Serb Peasant Party, the Independent Democrat Party and the Narodna Odbrana (see p. 45 above). They were also in contact with the exiled Bulgarian left-wing Agrarians.[42] In July 1940 Campbell told the Foreign Office that he had learnt (presumably from Section D) that there were elements, particularly in Serbia, 'who are thinking of utilizing the discontent which is felt at the pro-Axis policy of the present government to attempt a coup d'état and simultaneously to declare common cause with Great Britain'. Behind the plan were patriotic organisations such as the Narodna Odbrana, the Orthodox Church, important sections of the army, and, particularly, 'the peasants'. There would be a simultaneous coup in Bulgaria by the Bulgarian Agrarians. The Yugoslav Regent would be removed 'if necessary by violence' but the dynasty would be maintained under the young King; the Bulgarian king would be removed 'by violence' as a step on the way to Yugoslav–Bulgarian federation. The Yugoslavs would attack Albania to promote revolution and provoke Italy. The coup organisers would declare common cause with Britain and try to get Soviet support. If the Germans invaded, the Yugoslavs would offer 'maximum military resistance' and carry out 'maximum sabotage'. Britain would be expected to recognise the new government immediately and offer an alliance.

Such was the plan reported by Campbell, who added that his own view, apart from objections to violence, was that until the Axis had been militarily weakened, the British aim of bringing about conflict between Germany and Russia in the Balkans would not be helped by premature action; so he had given instructions that 'the scheme should not be encouraged by any members of the Legation'. He added that no member of the Legation had taken the initiative in 'seeking out contacts with the originators of the plan who are solely responsible for it'.[43]

To judge by Julian Amery's account of Section D's activities, a key figure in the plan must have been Jovan Djonović, a Serbian politician and former Minister in Tirana.[44] Others must have been Milan Gavrilović and Miloš Tupanjanin of the Serb Peasant Party, and Ilya Trifunović Birčanin, a noted Serb guerilla leader of the 1914–18 war.[45] The Narodna Odbrana, of which he was head, was described by the Foreign Office as 'a patriotic youth organization lately engaged in anti-fifth column activities'.[46] But it was much more than that. It was created in the years before the 1914–18 war to work both openly and conspiratorially for the union of the Serbs of the Austro-Hungarian empire with independent Serbia, and on 23 July 1914 it was formally

charged by the Austro-Hungarian government with responsibility for
the murder of the Archduke Franz Ferdinand, which led to the outbreak of the war. According to the official Austrian dossier it was by
this time 'completely dependent on the Serbian Foreign Ministry'. In
1917 the Serbian government themselves accused the Black Hand, a
conspiratorial group of Serbian officers, of responsibility, instead of the
Narodna Odbrana. But in any case there were close links between the
two, and Trifunović Birčanin recalled to Amery his friendship with
Apis-Dimitriejević of the Black Hand.[47]

In July 1940 the first reactions of the Foreign Office to the plan, as
reported by Campbell, were relatively favourable. Nicholls minuted
that while Halifax thought it would be premature to encourage the
movement at present, later on it 'might be of first class importance to
H.M.G.'[48] Dalton, as Minister responsible for S.O.E., minuted: 'we
cannot afford to neglect any chance, however slight, of improving our
prospect of victory within a tolerable time'. He suggested a slightly
more encouraging reply to Belgrade than the Foreign Office were contemplating; the Chiefs of Staff agreed. So on 3 August a telegram
went to Belgrade: 'you should indicate orally that this plan does not,
at present, enjoy the support of H.M.G. . . . You should also indicate
that the main reason why H.M.G. adopt this attitude is that they
regard the questions . . . as of such importance that the eventual success
of some such scheme must not be endangered by premature action,
more especially at a moment when they are unable to give a guarantee
of any support'. H.M.G. would in any case not support violence to the
Regent.[49]

So the matter rested for the moment. In October, the German move
into Rumania stirred things up again. Campbell reported that there
were persistent rumours of 'an imminent substitution for the present
government of a strong military one which would cease the policy of
concessions to the Axis'; there might be a 'spontaneous movement' on
the part of the army 'and/or Serb elements' dissatisfied with the
government's attitude towards Germany. He asked whether a change
of government would be in Britain's interest.[50] This time the Foreign
Office was more cautious than in July, saying they shared Campbell's
own view that in a crisis Prince Paul 'would be in a position to enforce
a stand', though they regretted that no hope could be held out of any
material aid except 'naval pressure'. The Yugoslav government's
attitude, the Foreign Office said, remained of great importance to
Britain over three matters: resistance by force to Axis attack, refusal
to make any territorial concessions, and, in particular, refusal to permit
passage of Axis troops.[51]

If the British had stuck consistently to these three demands, there
would have been no quarrel between them and Prince Paul. But the
events of early 1941 moved the British to make further demands – in

effect, that Yugoslavia should abandon neutrality and enter the war. It was this that opened their breach with the Prince.

At the end of 1940 Churchill became convinced – through intercepts of German communications[52] and from other sources – that Hitler was going to drive south into the Balkans, and told Dalton to make preparations for action in Yugoslavia by S.O.E. Dalton sent out George Taylor to Belgrade, on what was described as a 'mission ordered from the All Highest'.[53] Churchill also decided that a mechanised force including tanks and artillery should be sent to Greece in addition to the R.A.F. squadrons already there, and on 11 January the Foreign Office instructed Campbell to tell Prince Paul. The Regent's reaction was emotional; he expressed 'dismay at the British decision which he firmly believed would cause the Germans immediately to overrun the Balkans'. Britain, he said, 'theatened to destroy the few remaining free countries in Europe'; he did not think it fair on the Balkan countries still at peace. His own responsibility was to keep his country from war and destruction if possible. Paul did however give Campbell a definite assurance that he would refuse any German demand for the passage of troops across Yugoslavia – yet partly withdrew it the next day by sending his Minister of Court to say that if the British were determined to constitute a 'Salonika front', Yugoslavia might be forced to modify its attitude.[54]

The British neither liked nor expected the Prince's reaction. On 14 January Churchill minuted that Paul's views left him 'unchanged'; it was for the Greeks to say what they wanted. He added that 'the evidence in our possession of the German movements seems overwhelming. In the face of it Prince Paul's attitude looks like that of an unfortunate man in the cage with a tiger, hoping not to provoke him while steadily dinner-time approaches.'[55] The Prince's views were also made known to the Greeks, and, according to the Greek Minister in London, influenced them in their decision to decline the offer of British land forces when first made by Wavell in mid-January.[56]

However, until mid-February the Foreign Office remained confident that Yugoslavia would resist any Italian or German demand for passage of troops through the country, and seemed content with this.[57] But then Eden and the Chief of Imperial General Staff, Dill, set out for Cairo with sealed orders from Churchill, first to 'send speedy succour to Greece', and second 'to make Jugoslavia and Turkey fight or do the best they could'.[58]

So the problem was now, how to make the Yugoslavs fight, whether attacked or not. One constructive idea came from Moscow, where Gavrilović suggested to Cripps that the Croats might be won over if the British government would recognise the Yugoslav claim to the Istrian isthmus and the Italian islands off the Yugoslav coast. Campbell agreed; the Foreign Office examined the problem and eventually told

the War Cabinet that there seemed to be a strong case on an ethno-
graphical basis for revising the existing Italian–Yugoslav frontier; a
map was produced showing Trieste as Italian, but Gorizia as lying
within the Yugoslav-inhabited area. The Foreign Office concluded that
although H.M.G. had so far adopted the general rule that they could
not discuss any territorial changes during the war, 'the decision of the
Jugoslav government at the present juncture is of such importance that
it would be worth while to disregard this rule ... if by so doing we
could induce Jugoslavia to intervene forcibly on behalf of Greece'.[59]
With the approval of the War Cabinet, Eden was authorised to offer
British support for revision of the Italian–Yugoslav frontier.[60]

Another move was a further message from King George VI to
Prince Paul in late February, aimed at bringing him into the open:
'there is today great uncertainty over the attitude which Yugoslavia
intends to take with regard to coming events in the Balkans ... My
government are faced with decisions of vital importance ... which
depend to a large extent on the attitude of Yugoslavia as the central
factor of South-East Europe.' The King made a 'personal appeal'
that Prince Paul should as soon as possible make a 'full statement' of
his government's position.[61]

A parallel enquiry in this sense was sent to Prince Paul by Eden
after the first Anglo-Greek talks in Athens on 22 February.[62] The
Prince's reply, which reached Eden five days later, was regarded as
unsatisfactory; he confirmed that he would not let Axis troops pass
through Yugoslavia, but refused to say precisely what Yugoslavia
would do in the event of a German move through Bulgaria against
Greece.[63] But this was what the British wanted: that the Yugoslavs
should go to war, even if their country was by-passed. Eden then summoned Campbell to Athens to discuss Prince Paul's position and sent
him back to Belgrade with a personal letter urging the Prince to resist
German demands and 'join with ourselves and the Greeks'.[64]

By the time Campbell got back to Belgrade, Prince Paul had – with
his government's approval but without telling the British – secretly met
Hitler, who had demanded that Yugoslavia should sign the Tripartite
Pact. Since German troops were pouring into Bulgaria, so that Yugoslavia was militarily hemmed in by the Axis on three sides, it must have
required some courage for Prince Paul to refuse an answer. Playing for
time, he agreed to Eden's suggestion that he should send a staff officer
to Athens for talks with the British and Greeks.[65] But he side-stepped
a series of pressing proposals, from 29 February onwards, that he or his
Ministers should meet Eden, openly or secretly.[66] This obviously
offended Eden.

The visit to Athens of the Yugoslav staff officer, Major Miloslav
Perišić – who travelled on a British passport under the name of L. R.
(Last Ray) Hope[67] – brought little satisfaction to either side. The

British and Greeks decided that as the Yugoslav attitude was so uncertain, they should only give general replies to his questions and so
did not tell him that the proposed British defence line lay south of
Salonika or that there were plans for demolitions in the Salonika area.
The Major was mainly interested in finding out what help the Yugoslav armed forces could get in withdrawing either through Greece
to the Aegean (that is, Salonika or Kavalla) or westwards to the
Adriatic so that they could if necessary be evacuated from Adriatic
ports.

On this second point the British answered that 'the naval problem
involved' was difficult; the running of naval convoys up and down
the Adriatic would be 'onerous' though they would of course do their
best if 'our Allies were cut off in that sea'.[68] Behind this extremely
vague statement lay the fact that, as Admiral Cunningham, the Naval
Commander in the Mediterranean, wrote to Eden, so long as British
forces were being moved to Greece, he had absolutely no ships to
spare 'except possibly an occasional submarine', though in two or three
months' time, it would be possible to reconsider the situation.[69]

Neither the nebulousness of British assurances, nor the fact that Mr
Hope's highly secret visit was immediately known to the Germans[70]
can have given much cheer to Prince Paul. The question of British
naval support in the Adriatic was particularly singled out by Paul
and his Ministers when they got 'Mr Hope's' report on the Athens
talks. Campbell therefore suggested that 'some fairly strong reassur-
ance on prospects of support and supply by the Royal Navy in the
Adriatic is of great importance ... to satisfy military authorities and
Croats'.[71]

Prince Paul, on his side, was playing for time by negotiating with
the Germans about stiff conditions for Yugoslavia's accession to the
Tripartite Pact, while at the same time holding his government together and, in particular, keeping Maček and the Croats in line. It was
just possible to get the Croats to agree to defend Yugoslavia's
neutrality and frontiers against attack, but not to start military action
outside the frontiers. Yet, during March, the British showed more and
more clearly that this was just what they wanted. In the short term,
while the British expeditionary force was moving into position in
Greece, it suited them well enough that Prince Paul should keep the
Germans in play,[72] since they wanted to delay a German attack. But
at the same time the British wanted the Yugoslavs to attack northern
Albania, to help out the Greeks, and above all to promise that if the
Germans attacked in the direction of Salonika, they would treat this
as an attack on Yugoslavia itself and act accordingly.[73] But the Croats
saw Salonika as a Serbian interest, not a Yugoslav or Croat interest.
For this reason, Prince Paul told Campbell, the Croats would see a war
for Salonika as an unnecessary war, and having unified the country

he could not wittingly split it. Nor could he retire: he could not leave 'the Boy' [the young King] since that would be complete treachery.[74]

Paul obviously tried, without telling everything, to hint to the British what he was thinking. On 10 March he told Campbell that the decision facing him was a terrible one; the military authorities told him Yugoslavia could not hold out for more than a week nor in their opinion could the Greeks, even with British help. He made it clear that joining the Tripartite Pact was a possibility.[75] Prime Minister Cvetković seemed honestly to hope that by dragging out the negotiations or making unacceptable demands the Germans could be provoked into making a break. He said that in any case three things were certain: Yugoslavia would resist attack, refuse passage of troops or use of its railways, and would not 'sign Tripartite Pact with its military clauses'.[76]

Eden apparently did not notice the qualification attached to this last undertaking by Cvetković, and noted 'with satisfaction' his statement that Yugoslavia 'will not sign the Tripartite Pact'.[77] This misunderstanding may have added to Eden's anger when the Yugoslavs eventually *did* sign, *without* the military clauses, and his refusal to take any account of the other important conditions which the Yugoslavs had got Hitler to accept. These were strongly hinted at by Cvetković on 17 March when he told Campbell that the Germans were 'daily' pressing Yugoslavia to sign, adding that it would never agree to sign clauses requiring participation in hostilities, passage of troops or use of Yugoslav territory: 'without these, the pact would merely be an empty shell'.[78]

But Eden wanted much more than this. On 17 March he wrote a personal letter to Prince Paul, delivered by Terence Shone,[79] a friend of the Prince, urging him to 'maintain his position against Germany', attack the Italians in Albania, and have fresh contacts with British military representatives.[80] But on 19 March a Crown Council was held to discuss whether to sign the pact, on the conditions which Cvetković – probably also the Prince – had hoped the Germans would reject – no passage of troops or use of Yugoslav railways, no military clauses, a guarantee of Yugoslavia's integrity. It was agreed to go back to the Germans and demand that the 'secret clauses' should be published. The Germans agreed that the Yugoslavs should publish two of them and that they themselves would not repudiate them. On 21 March the crucial meeting of the Crown Council was held. Three members of the government resigned rather than agree to signing the pact – Branko Čubrilović, of the Serb Peasant Party, Srdjan Budisavljević, of the Independent Democrat Party (both parties were subsidised by S.O.E., who were in close touch with both men) and Mihajlo Konstantinović, an independent nominee of Prince Paul's, over whom Budisavljević and Tupanjanin (of the Serb Peasant Party, also in constant touch with S.O.E.) had acquired considerable influence.[81] The rest voted for signature or abstained. Hitler agreed to a slight delay while the gaps in the government were remedied. On 25 March Cvetković and Cincar-Marković signed the pact with Vienna.

To Eden, this act obviously came as a personal blow, perhaps even an affront, in no way softened by the 'secret clauses'. The Yugoslavs had gone their own way, in spite of all his pressures and promises. Although Prince Paul and Cvetković had dropped very heavy hints about what they were doing, they had not officially informed or consulted the British. They had in fact no formal obligation to do so, but that did not make their failure any less wounding.

THE BRITISH AND THE COUP OF 27 MARCH

One reason why Prince Paul did not tell the British must surely have been that he knew the British were in touch with his opponents both among the politicians and in the armed services and were plotting against his policy. Since Dalton, spurred on by Churchill, had sent George Taylor to Belgrade early in 1941, S.O.E. had stepped up their activities, aiming, first, by means of political agitation and propaganda to deter Prince Paul from signing the pact, and second, if that failed, to stage a coup against him.[82] Agitation against the pact became vociferous from early March on. Campbell reported on 7 March that petitions had been addressed to Prince Paul by the Narodna Odbrana and other leading patriotic societies urging action 'in the sense desired' – that is, by S.O.E., with whom the Minister was by now working closely.[83] But a statement issued a day or two later by the Serb opposition parties did not please Campbell; he had asked S.O.E. to urge them to put in the form of a promise to support Prince Paul in resistance to the German demands, but in fact the statement distributed was 'pure defeatism in that (for reasons of internal politics) it threw doubt on Croat loyalty'. Nor did it please Prince Paul, when he learnt that two members of the parties in question had gone to the German Legation to say that the statement was not directed against Germany but was purely for internal political consumption.[84] It is clear therefore that up to a certain point Paul found S.O.E.'s agitation useful, even if it sometimes misfired. Tupanjanin was playing an extremely active if somewhat ambiguous role, in constant touch both with S.O.E. and Campbell and with Prince Paul and Cvetković.

On 16 March Campbell warned Cincar-Marković that 'popular opinion was highly excited' and was looking to the dynasty to refuse to put the country in a position where Germany could act as in Rumania; there might be a 'strong reaction', if this was not done.[85] Up to this point the British were still hoping to prevent signature of the pact; but by 18 March S.O.E. had come to the conclusion that it would almost certainly be necessary to bring down the Cvetković government; and at a meeting held at the British Legation on 19 March this was agreed.[86] On the day on which the Yugoslav government decided to sign, Eden, from Cairo, asked Campbell about the 'practical possibility' of a coup; the next day, Campbell replied that feeling in Serbia 'may be ready, if led' to burst out, and asked for H.M.G.'s view. On the same day Churchill sent a message to Eden: 'you must settle this in Cairo . . . play the hand as you think best', while from Cairo Eden authorised Campbell to give assurances of British support if Yugoslavia were involved in war.[87] On 21 March Dalton noted in his diary: 'bad news from Juggery . . . Wire sent to use all means to raise revolution. G. [Gladwyn Jebb[88]] screws this through the F.O.'[89] On 24 March Eden told Campbell he had full authority for any measure he might think it right to take to further a change of government or régime, 'even by coup d'état'. On the same day Campbell reported that the best chance lay with a 'military movement' and that it would be important to make a firm offer of military supplies, perhaps also to promise to bomb Durazzo. On this telegram Churchill wrote: 'I am very doubtful about all this'.[90]

What Campbell's reference to a 'military movement' meant was that while S.O.E.'s contacts with Serb political parties and patriotic organisations were very useful for purposes of agitation and propaganda, they were not enough in themselves to produce a coup against Prince Paul. The Serb Peasant Party was small and lacked the necessary political base; the leaders of the opposition parties were elderly politicians, not revolutionaries. The Narodna Odbrana seemed to have lost its original conspiratorial fire. The best hope lay with the Air Force, and with the younger army officers: the General Staff, whatever bribes S.O.E. may have lavished, were too cautious and fearful to take action.[91] So when it came to the point it was not S.O.E.'s contacts, but the contacts of the Air Attaché, Group Captain Macdonald, with Air Force officers such as General Simović and General Bora Mirković, which kept the British informed of what was being planned. On 26 March Macdonald reported that Simović was head of an organisation intending to carry out a coup d'état, and had said that 'we should not have to wait more than a few days'.[92] In reality, Simović was the figure-head and Mirković the moving spirit, who brought forward the date of the coup to 27 March.

In the following year, when Mirković was in the Middle East, he was reported to have said that he had been an 'agent of the British' before the coup. On this Campbell (by this time Minister in Washington) commented that 'if he was indeed an "agent" I did not know of it. I knew he was in confidential contact with the Air Attaché and told him that a coup d'état was being planned, but he never furnished any details or dates, and I should doubt that he received pay from any of our intelligence or other services.'[93]

It is clear that in fact Mirković was the director of the operation, keeping in touch with the British, but in no way their agent; his most important collaborators were the Knežević brothers – the politician, Radoje, and the young Guards officer, Živan. But the British equally clearly gave every encouragement. The fact that the coup was blood-less and completely successful shows the efficiency of Mirković and his associates, not of the British. Yet S.O.E. could fairly claim that they had done a great deal to prepare Serb political and popular opinion, so that the coup was accepted in Serbia with enormous enthusiasm. It is perhaps worth recording that in Belgrade the Communists had played a prominent part in the anti-pact demonstrations, though they had no foreknowledge of the coup.[94]

The British – anyhow in London and Cairo – at first totally mis-calculated the implications of the coup. When the War Cabinet met on 27 March they were told that 'the repudiation of the government which had signed the three-power pact was a clear rebuff to our enemies'. Churchill said he had authorised Campbell to tell the new government that, 'on the basis that they were determined to denounce the pact with Germany, and to help in the defence of Greece', Britain recognised them as the government of Yugoslavia. He had also sent a telegram to Roosevelt urging him to encourage resistance in the Balkans.[95]

But the new Simović government which emerged from the coup neither denounced the pact nor offered to help Greece. It carried on Prince Paul's policy with virtually no change; the new Foreign Minis-ter, Momčilo Ninčić, immediately informed the German Minister of this,[96] and hoped to go to Hungary for fresh talks with Hitler.[97]

The British were left in painful uncertainty. A few days before the coup, they had been toying with an alternative scheme. The Greek commander, Papagos, who was anxious to win over the commander of the Yugoslav Third Army in the extreme south, had sent an emissary to Skoplje to get in touch with him and encourage him to resist the Belgrade government's policy and combine operations with the Greek Army on the Albanian front. The British commander in Greece, General Maitland Wilson, warned Papagos against the danger of dis-integrating the Yugoslav army and so playing the German game, but referred the matter to Cairo.[98] Eden, after discussion with the Middle East Command, suggested that Wilson, to 'secure maximum Jugoslav forces . . . to defend Vardar and Monastir gaps', should arrange for British officers to get in touch with military commanders in southern Serbia 'and if possible coordinate plans'.[99] Wilson, Papagos and Cairo then became involved in a discussion of what 'financial assistance' or 'personal inducement' should be offered to Yugoslav officers or men.[100] In the Foreign Office, Sargent surmised that this undertaking might lead to the secession of the Yugoslav army in the south and the setting up of a 'separatist government' such as Venizelos set up in Greece in 1915.[101] But the coup seems to have put a stop to this alternative scheme. So the British had nothing for it but to hope against hope that Simović could be induced to stand up to the Germans. (See pp. 104–7 below.)

THE OSTRACISM OF PRINCE PAUL

Prince Paul, deposed from his office as Regent by the coup, went by train to Athens after urging the Croats to co-operate with the Simović government.[102] In Athens the British Legation was instructed by Eden to refuse to see him. But King George of Greece – who had probably suffered a more bitter disappointment over the pact than Eden – met Paul at the station and was quite willing that he should stay in Athens.[103] But the Simović government raised objections, suspecting the Prince of intriguing against them, so he had to move on.[104]

When Eden visited Athens in early April, he refused to see Paul. The Prince's uncle, a former Tsarist Russian Minister in Athens (and an old Etonian), Prince Demidoff, told Palairet that Paul had been hurt by Eden's not seeing him. Reading this in a telegram from Palairet, Churchill underlined the sentence and wrote 'Good' in red ink in the margin. Palairet, clearly following Eden's line, told Demidoff that he could not believe that 'a friend of England would have concluded a pact with her enemies and the enemies of freedom'. As for Paul's belief that Hitler would keep his word to Yugoslavia about the passage of troops, Palairet said that nobody but a fool could believe that. To this Demidoff replied that Prince Paul might be a fool, but he was not guilty of treachery. At the bottom of Palairet's telegram Churchill wrote: 'Foreign Secretary. The sooner Palsy is interned and out of the way the better. WSC.'[105] Prince Paul was sent to Kenya.

Some members of the Simović government or their hangers-on circulated discreditable stories about the Prince, for instance, that he had aimed to become king and had been promised the Crown by Hitler, or had plotted against King Peter's life;[106] this in spite of the fact that Ninčić had told Campbell on 4 April that he did not believe the story of Hitler's offer of the Crown; on which Campbell had commented: 'presumably he would still less believe the poisoning story'. Yet Eden minuted on 11 July: 'if half the reports . . . are true Prince Paul played a sinister role in Jugoslavia. He deserves no tenderness from us.'[107]

On 18 August 1914 Prince Paul wrote to the Duke of Kent, whose wife was his sister-in-law. The letter was a plea in defence of his political record: '. . . I worked and walked hand in hand with your country till the last minute when I was unable to act differently owing to internal complications, when my effort tended to prevent the splitting up of my country ... As to what concerns Anthony [Eden] it's again linked with our ... fright of Germany ... We carried on negotiations with Germany, and asked for terms which were very difficult for them to accept, and which we were sure they couldn't accept but it gave us time to mobilise ... I was longing to see him personally ...' but '... we were surrounded with spies.' As for the coup, Prince Paul wrote that 'one of the chief objects ... was the wish of a few ambitious (v. few) military people to get hold of Peter and through him rule the country ... I must at all costs be kept away from the child so that he shouldn't fall "under my influence".'[108] On this, Dixon minuted in the Foreign Office: 'Prince Paul's explanations are entirely unconvincing,' and Sargent echoed: 'unconvincing'.[109] Prince Paul had lost his reputation.

Dalton was as remorseless as Eden and Churchill in his attitude to Prince Paul.[110] It is hard not to see in this remorselessness, bordering on vindictiveness, a side-effect of British disappointment over the way in which the coup of 27 March – from the British standpoint – mis-fired, and over the subsequent British defeat in Greece.

10   The Balkan Campaign, 1941

The reasons why the British insisted so strongly that Prince Paul should abandon his benevolent neutrality and that Yugoslavia should go to war, whatever the cost, why they in fact forced Hitler to undertake an operation against Yugoslavia which he had not intended, at any rate at that time, can be understood only in the light of their doubts and fears about the outcome of the Balkan campaign of 1941. This campaign – so strongly criticised after the event – was seen from the start as a military gamble, justifiable only in so far as it enabled Britain to keep or win allies on the continent of Europe.

The first problem was how to keep Greece as an ally, under a régime about which the British had many misgivings. General Ioannis Metaxas, who had been in power since 1936, was not much loved in Greece, nor in Britain either. Palairet, in a despatch of February 1940, put the rhetorical question: 'can a régime admittedly so unpopular (as a result of its despotic and arbitrary treatment of its opponents and critics) be trusted to lead the nation into war? May not the outbreak of hostilities open the flood-gates of discontent which will sweep away General Metaxas and even the King . . .?' There was also, Palairet said, the 'undesirable effect on British opinion of the activities of M. [Constantine] Maniadakis, the "Himmler" of Greece'. As for the Greek army, the British military attaché reported that though he had no evidence that it was not loyal, the régime was unpopular with everyone; and the King had always set his face against the return to military service of the Venizelist officers dismissed in 1935. On the other hand the military attaché thought the present commander, General Papagos, 'exceptional among Balkan military personalities' and if he were removed it was uncertain whether the Venizelists could replace him adequately; nevertheless, 'a dangerous situation might be produced should we have to sustain the present régime against the will of the Greek people'. Palairet himself, while forwarding the military attaché's views, reached the conclusion: 'it will be wiser for us not to interfere in any way in Greek internal affairs. We had better shut our eyes to the disagreeable elements of the régime.'[1]

In the Foreign Office, Sargent agreed with Palairet: 'Metaxas still continues to govern Greece efficiently, however unpopular he may be among the dispossessed politicians, and what is more his policy conforms to our interests and meets our requirements.'[2]

Nevertheless when the King and Metaxas defied the Italians and went to war in October 1940, there were worries – at least in S.O.E. – first, whether Metaxas could keep the country together, next, whether he might not come to terms with the Axis, or at least with Germany. S.O.E. therefore set about contacting Venizelists both in Greece and abroad (General Nikolaos Plastiras was in the south of France and Sophocles Venizelos was in the United States). The removal, in the 1914–18 war, of a Greek king suspected of pro-German policies and the instalment of a pro-allied Venizelist government was an obvious precedent. But at a meeting with the Foreign Office on 9 December S.O.E. only said that 'Mr Bailey [Col. W. S. Bailey, later attached to General Mihajlović in Yugoslavia] had been at work in Athens with the object of promoting a united front'; his aims were '(a) to ensure that exiled politicians were allowed to return; (b) to ensure that the Greek government were aware of the undesirability of having two anti-Italian but pro-German ministers in the government; (c) to bring people of Venizelist sympathies in line with the present régime'. Even this mild version of S.O.E.'s activities rather alarmed the Foreign Office who 'expressed doubts' as to their 'utility' and suggested that no steps should be taken without Palairet's express approval.[3]

But fears that Metaxas might came to terms with the enemy haunted the Foreign Office as well as S.O.E., all the more since during the winter the Germans put out various rumours of peace feelers directed at the Greeks. Even before the Italian attack the Foreign Office had written to the Chiefs of Staff: 'hitherto Greece has shown a remarkably stiff front to Italian demands but whether she would continue to do so in the event of a German threat through Bulgaria is more than doubtful.'[4] Soon after the Italian attack, Dill wrote to Churchill that it was likely that Hitler would offer to mediate between Italy and Greece 'with a pen in one hand and a sword in the other'.[5] In December the German Foreign Ministry was reported as suggesting that it would much appreciate a Greek declaration that the war 'was not aimed at Germany' and that Greece would not allow British forces to land.[6] However on 7 December Metaxas said he would never agree to any attempt to drive a wedge between Britain and Greece, and soon after he authorised a senior Greek official to tell Palairet that he would treat any German threat exactly as he had treated the Italian ultimatum.[7] On 24 December Palairet, in reply to a Foreign Office enquiry, said he thought there was no danger of Metaxas, of his own accord, concluding a separate peace with Italy 'whatever threats or blandishment Germany may employ'.[8] Yet three days later Philip Nichols, in the Foreign Office, minuted that it might be difficult to persuade Greece where its true interests lay.[9]

In mid-January, the British military attaché in Ankara reported that the Germans were said to be waiting for Greek ammunition supplies to

run out at the end of February and that they would then offer to
arrange peace, with Greece receiving part of southern Albania, at the
same time threatening invasion if Greece refused.[10] On 19 February
King George II told the British that the German military attaché was
saying that Germany would shortly ask Greece to terminate the war
with Italy and return to its old frontier; it might also be 'necessary for
Germany to occupy Salonika'.[11] Also in mid-February Palairet sent a
memorandum on the probable impact of a German attack, concluding:
'we should not build any exaggerated hopes on the . . . resistance to
Germany by Greece as a united country unless both Yugoslavia and
Turkey . . . are prepared to go to war as Greece's ally.'[12] However,
the British were heartened and reassured by the firm attitude of the
Greeks when the Anglo-Greek conversations opened in Athens on 22
February,[13] and on 28 February the Foreign Office, in a circular
telegram. affirmed that the Greek government remained 'in uncompromising mood alike towards Italy and Germany'.[14]

But privately the British were still worried. On 8 March the Foreign
Office sent to Eden in Athens a message from a reliable but unquotable
source that Prince Paul had been asked by Hitler to 'induce Greece
through medium of dynastic ties to join New Order', and to 'inform
Greece that if she refused her future sacrifices would be immense'. The
Greek Royal House were expected to receive the message 'direct
through Hohenzollerns'.[15] On 11 March the Foreign Office was told
by the Greek Legation that Franz von Papen, the German ambassador
in Ankara, had told the Turkish President that 'Greece would be
granted an honourable peace' and it would be a good thing to bring
pressure to bear on the Greeks to accept it; he 'hoped the British would
not formulate objections'.[16]

This intensive German peace campaign was presumably intended as
psychological warfare, to drive a wedge between Greece and Britain
and soften up the Greeks so that they would crumble before a German
threat of attack. The other alternative, that Hitler genuinely wished
to avoid war with Greece, and only moved because he 'discovered'
that British troops had arrived on the Greek mainland, as he often
maintained, seemed highly unlikely in the light of German military
planning in the autumn of 1940. Talking to the Bulgarian Prime Minister, Filov, on 7 January 1941 Hitler said that if any power were to
land on the Continent, he would 'immediately repel the invader';
Germany had 230 divisions 'unemployed' and could carry through the
operations in Greece without the slightest risk. Hitler concluded by
offering Bulgaria an outlet to the Aegean.[17] On 26 January the German
military attaché in Ankara said flatly that the Germans proposed to
move into Salonika as soon after 2 March as weather conditions per-
mitted: 'there was no question of this move being conditional or any
attempt by the British to occupy that area, Germany's aim being to

have permanent bases on the Mediterranean' – at Salonika and elsewhere.[18] Hitler, writing to the Turkish President on 28 February, said
equally flatly that his aim was to 'eliminate British influence on the
European continent'; he was therefore taking certain 'preventive
measures'.[19]

These statements were made *before* the move of British land forces
to Greece. The German threat against Greece was therefore no inven-
tion of the British. It is also clear that the Greeks never responded to
German overtures. The German White Book of 6 April 1941, recount-
ing supposed German efforts to induce the Greeks to return to 'genuine
neutrality', said, 'the Greek government set at nought all these warnings. They also never – this must be expressly stated – approached the
German government with the object of discussing with them even the
possibility of a return to neutrality.'[20]

Nevertheless, one powerful effect of the German peace campaign
was to make the British determined to acquire fighting allies for Greece,
to stiffen the Greek will to resist – first and foremost Yugoslavia, if
possible also Turkey. Moreover the British doubted whether the unpopular Greek régime, which had managed to keep the nation surprisingly united through the first, victorious, phase of the war against Italy,
would be able to maintain this unity and keep up army morale without
the psychological and material support which Yugoslavia could bring
as a fighting ally. The Greeks themselves, both Metaxas and Papagos,
always insisted on the need to bring in Yugoslavia. Shortly before his
death in January 1941 Metaxas told the British military attaché that
Yugoslavia's attitude was of 'utmost importance'; if the Yugoslavs
resisted an Axis attack and sent very small forces into Albania, they
would rapidly complete the defeat of the Italians and release Greek
forces to help the Yugoslavs; but if Yugoslavia allowed the passage of
German troops, this would be 'tantamount to a declaration of war
against the allies'.[21]

THE BRITISH SEARCH FOR ALLIES

The British themselves, in the autumn of 1940, were beginning to feel
a certain psychological and strategic need for allies in South-East
Europe. Since June 1940 they had been shut out of the European continent after a series of more or less humiliating defeats; their chances
of returning to the continent, or even engaging the German army on
land, seemed very far off. So long as they were engaged in the Battle
of Britain and coping with Hitler's invasion threat, they had plenty to
think about. By October 1940 the invasion threat was receding; the
British were fighting Italians in north Africa, but they were not fighting
the German army. A chance to return to the continent and to fight
Germans was therefore something to be grasped if possible. As R. A.

Butler – normally a peaceable man – minuted in late 1940: 'surely it is important for us to aim at involving part of the huge German army somewhere.'[22]

The Greek appeal to Britain for help in resisting, first the Italians, then the Germans, gave an opening which the British were themselves beginning to seek. Already at the beginning of October 1940 Metaxas told Palairet that he expected an Italian attack and begged for all possible British aid, pointing to the 'deplorable consequences' for the British, both moral and strategic, if in spite of their guarantee Greece were to be over-run.[23] But at that time the British were expecting a German drive through Bulgaria against Turkey and the Middle East,[24] so their inclination was to continue to give priority to Turkey, particularly in arms supplies. Ten days before the Italian attack, Palairet telegraphed: 'if we continue to send quantities of equipment to Turkey only, without providing for any of Greece's vital needs, we shall provide the Axis with a very dangerous weapon.'[25] From Turkey, Knatchbull-Hugessen had just reported that 'the Turks are very far from being able to use either tactically or technically the large amount of British equipment already supplied to them, and would certainly be unable to deal with more by the spring' – though he added that the political effect of cutting down supplies would be very serious.[26] Yet on 21 October the Chiefs of Staff continued to recommend sending 'all the material aid we could possibly spare' to the Turks; the most they would offer was 'a small token gift of anti-aircraft or anti-tank guns' to help encourage the Greeks.[27]

Nevertheless when the Italians attacked on 28 October, a message from King George VI to the Greek king and people was broadcast from London saying 'we are with you in this struggle; your cause is our cause'; and on the same day Churchill sent Metaxas a message: 'we will give you all the help in our power.'[28] Palairet was informed: 'we are doing our utmost by sea, land and air . . . Land and air action on a scale which involved considerable risk elsewhere have been set on foot . . .'[29] But luckily for the British, the Greeks did not then want 'land action'. The king and Metaxas said what they wanted first and foremost was air action, and the despatch of the 'maximum possible number of squadrons'.[30]

On 4 November Churchill told the War Cabinet that it was of the utmost importance to help Greece resist the Italian attack, and that British public opinion was 'most anxious for British intervention in Greece'. Halifax welcomed Churchill's decision: 'to have sent no help to Greece would have undermined the will to resist of the other Balkan countries'. He added, revealingly, that 'the difficulty was to find a way of heartening the Greeks without disclosing our weakness in the Middle East'. The Greek king and Metaxas were therefore to be told 'in strict confidence' how many squadrons were to be sent.[31]

Perhaps it should rather have been 'how few'. During the first half of November two Blenheim squadrons arrived in Greece,[32] while a British Military Mission was established in Athens. But the British had a toe-hold on the continent. What was more, they were giving practical help to a country which they had guaranteed, instead of standing helpless, as they had done with Poland and Rumania. But until they had secured the defence of Egypt they could not think much further ahead.

For some, however, wider vistas were opening up. On 1st December Leo Amery, Secretary of State for India, a close friend of Churchill and father of Julian, just home from his S.O.E. work in the Balkans, made a speech at Newmarket. He said:

If we can enable Greece to hold her own until we have disposed of the Italians in Egypt, we shall have secured for our armies a foothold from which we might threaten the flank of any German attack upon Turkey. Last but not least, from that foothold we might eventually, with our own armies and with the new allies whom our growing strength will gather, deal a mortal thrust at the German dragon, not against the scaly armour of the Siegfried line, but against his soft under-side.

This caused alarm in Athens and Belgrade; Amery was unrepentant.[33]

This 'soft under-belly' concept was typically Churchillian, just as the Salonika front idea had aroused him in 1939. The concept won a new and potentially influential supporter in January 1941 in Col. William Donovan, who was touring South-East Europe on a special mission on President Roosevelt's behalf. One of his conclusions was: 'it is a truism to say that the will of [the German people] must be broken and her armies must be at some point thrown on the defensive and beaten in the field. The Balkans offer perhaps the only place for such a defeat. The British must then retain a foothold there, and this can only be done by inducing Jugoslavia, Greece, Turkey and if possible Bulgaria to stand together with England.'[34]

At the beginning of 1941 the British became certain that the Germans were going to drive south from Rumania. (Among other sources, the Rumanian oil industry had provided the British with valuable information about the location of the lines of petrol and oil cans they had been ordered to lay out, in preparation for the German move.[35]) On 6 January Eden sent Churchill a minute: 'a mass of information has come to us over the last few days . . . all of which tends to show that Germany is pressing forward her preparations in the Balkans with a view to an ultimate descent upon Greece'.[36] It was in these circumstances that Wavell visited Athens in mid-January to offer a small British land force, only to be told by Metaxas that nine British divisions would be needed to meet a German attack, and he did not want anything less than that.[37] The British took Metaxas's refusal with good grace; Eden told the Greek minister in London that they had always recognised that it was for the Greek government to decide whether further British help was timely or not.[38]

The situation then changed rapidly. Metaxas died. The Greeks got into difficulties in Albania and became convinced that the Germans were about to move into Bulgaria. On 8 February Metaxas's successor, Koryzis – a much less forceful man, certainly acting on the order of the king, who was now the real power in Greece – asked what help Britain could give.

The Greek request coincided with a surprisingly quick British military success in Africa, which seemed to create a rather unreal atmosphere of optimism, even euphoria, in London and Cairo. Churchill told the War Cabinet on 10 February that the position in the Eastern Mediterranean was altered by the capture of Benghazi at a much earlier date than had been expected, and put the question, in what way British forces in the Middle East should now be employed. The Defence Committee was asked to discuss this.[39] The outcome was the despatch of Eden and Dill to the Middle East with Churchill's sealed instructions, which set as the ultimate aim 'perhaps to use the Balkan theatre as the stage on which to inflict a military defeat on the Germans when the will to resist of the German people was on the point of breaking down'.[40] Churchill also sent instructions to Wavell that if the Greeks had a 'good plan', 'it would be worth while to back it with all our strength and fight the Germans in Greece, hoping thereby to draw in both Turks and Yugoslavs'.[41]

No firm decision to send a force to Greece had yet been taken. On 16 February the Director of Military Operations, General J. M. Kennedy, gave Churchill a very gloomy appreciation of the outlook for a campaign in Greece.[42] Churchill sent Eden a message: 'do not consider yourselves obligated to a Greek enterprise if in your hearts you feel it will only be another Norwegian fiasco . . . But of course you know how valuable success would be.' It was fairly clear where Churchill's own heart lay. On the same day Eden replied, 'it is of course a gamble to send forces to the mainland of Europe to fight Germans at this time . . . We are not without hope that it might succeed to the extent of halting the Germans before they overrun all Greece . . . The stakes are big. If we fail to help the Greeks there is no hope of action by Yugoslavia and the future of Turkey may easily be compromised . . .'[43]

The wider political and long-term strategic factors influenced not only Churchill and Eden but also the Chiefs of Staff. When from Athens Eden reported 'agreement with the Greek government on all points', the Chiefs of Staff considered whether to endorse the agreed policy. The first advantage they listed was that by going to Greece 'we take the only remaining chance of forming a Balkan front, and of getting Turkey, and possible Yugoslavs, to enter the war on our side'. Their last conclusion was: 'if we are to undertake this commitment, every possible effort should be made to get the Turks and Yugoslavs to join in the struggle on our side. Without the support of one or the other our help to Greece is unlikely in the long run to have a favourable effect on the war situation as a whole. If both came in, however, the Germans would be seriously embarrassed, at least temporarily, and we should have a good chance of successfully building up a Balkan front.'[44]

The Anglo-Greek talks which started in Athens on 22 February also high-lighted the military and political importance to the Greeks of getting Yugoslavia to enter the war, and the Yugoslav question-mark played a big part in the argument between Papagos and the British military representatives over whether or not to try to hold Salonika. Arguing against the British pressure for the Aliakmon line, further south, Papagos, reluctant to abandon Salonika and a large slice of Greek territory, declared: 'if Yugoslavia said tonight that she was going to fight, the Greeks would hold the Nestos line and ask the British to land at Salonika and Kavalla.' The outcome of the argument – or so the British believed – was a compromise: Greek advanced troops would begin to withdraw southwards, while Eden would try to find out Prince Paul's attitude, though without letting him know too much about British-Greek plans.[45]

But when the Anglo-Greek talks resumed ten days later, Eden had failed to budge the Turks an inch from their refusal to stir outside their frontiers,[46] and had obtained no clear answer from Prince Paul; as he put it to the Greeks, 'we need not despair of Prince Paul but could not count on him'. The Greeks on their side had not started troop withdrawals southwards, on the grounds that no final decision was to be taken until Prince Paul's attitude was known, since, as Papagos said, if Yugoslavia did enter the war, the Aliakmon line was not the best.[47]

In the end, Papagos was over-ruled by the Greek king who himself intervened in favour of the Aliakmon line and a Greek withdrawal southwards, saying that 'General Papagos, now that he had decided to face the Germans, would do it with the same determination whatever troops were available and whatever plan was adopted'.[48] (From this personal act, perhaps, stemmed much of the British government's later sense of gratitude and obligation to George II.)

Eden made further unsuccessful moves to pull in the Turks and Yugoslavs. On 9 March Churchill appealed to Roosevelt: 'at this juncture the action of Yugoslavia is cardinal. If they will fall on the Italian rear in Albania there is no knowing what might happen in a few weeks. The whole situation might be transformed.' He asked for American diplomatic support.[49]

THE BELGRADE COUP AND AFTER

The Belgrade coup of 27 March naturally roused fresh hope of a 'Balkan front' in both Greeks and British. At an Anglo-Greek meeting on 28 March, Papagos said that an effort should be made to constitute 'a solid continuous defensive front from the Adriatic to the Black Sea', cleaning up Albania with Yugoslavia's help and moving all available Anglo-Greek forces northwards since 'we were practically obliged to defend Salonika if the Yugoslavs came in'. Eden suggested four-power talks between Britain, Greece, Yugoslavia and Turkey 'to form a common front to aggression'.[50] Churchill telegraphed to Eden that the Yugoslavs, Greeks and Turks should send a 'triple note' to Germany saying that if it attacked any one of them, it would be at war with all three.[51]

On 31 March Churchill, in the War Cabinet, was still taking a very hopeful view of the Belgrade coup. He also used it to counter serious doubts about the Greek campaign felt by Australia and New Zealand, which were supplying a major part of the force in Greece. He sent a personal and most secret message to the Acting Prime Minister of Australia: 'when a month ago we decided upon LUSTRE [the movement of troops to Greece] it looked a rather bleak military adventure dictated by noblesse oblige . . . Events in Belgrade show far-reaching effects of this and other measures we have taken on whole Balkan situation . . . We may cherish renewed hope of forming a Balkan front with Turkey comprising about 70 allied divisions from the four powers concerned.' (This phrase surely carried echoes of Weygand, and of Gamelin who in December 1939 had foreseen 'a Balkan front of 111 divisions'.)[52] Churchill added more cautiously: 'this is of course by no means certain yet. But even now it puts LUSTRE in its true setting not as an isolated military act, but as a prime mover in large design . . . Result unknowable but prize has increased and risks have somewhat lessened.'[53]

Developments in Belgrade quickly destroyed such hopes. Apart from the Simović government's decision not to renounce the Tripartite Pact, there were other disquieting signs. It later became known that after one of the first cabinet meetings Simović wrote a note saying that there must be no marked friendship for Great Britain on the part of the Yugoslav government.[54] Instead, the government put its energies into conciliating Russia and Italy. Carrying on an initiative taken under the aegis of Prince Paul, who had sent a 'special confidential emissary' to Moscow in the hope of negotiating a military alliance,[55] the new Foreign Minister, Ninčić, sent a delegation to Moscow in the expectation of signing such a pact. But in spite of the toughness of Gavrilović, all that the Yugoslavs could obtain from Stalin was a non-aggression pact, signed on 5 April. This irritated Hitler without providing Yugoslavia with any security. As for the Italians, the British air attaché in

Belgrade reported on 3 April that he learned that 'negotiations were proceeding', and while these were going on, the Yugoslavs did not intend to attack Albania.[56] From this it was clear that Papagos's long-standing hope of a Yugoslav move was most unlikely to be realised.

This point was made quite plain at the highly clandestine Anglo-Yugoslav talks when Dill visited Belgrade secretly on 31 March and 1 April. Dill urged the Yugoslavs to take the initiative before Germany was ready and to attack in Albania, 'where they would have an easy victory and secure quantities of much needed equipment'. But Simović said this would provoke an immediate German attack from south-west Bulgaria and Yugoslavia was not yet ready. As Prince Paul had done, Simović 'regretted his inability to receive Mr Eden', since this would provoke the Germans. And as Prince Paul had done he stressed the Croat problem: if the government took any 'provocative action' the Croats would defect. But if the government could show that they had not provoked a German attack, then the Croats and Slovenes would fight. Agreement to hold British-Yugoslav-Greek staff talks at Florina was the only outcome of the Dill visit.[57]

These in turn were a fiasco. The Yugoslav representative, General Miloje Janković, read out a note declaring that if the 'freedom of Salonika' were to be threatened by the Axis, the Yugoslav army would intervene to ensure its security, which was vital to itself. This looked, at last, like the declaration which Eden had asked for so often. But Janković destroyed its value by adding that 'the necessary decision will be taken by the Yugoslav government at the appropriate moment'. There was only a vague general discussion of Yugoslav military plans. One point which caused trouble was that while in Belgrade Dill had said that Britain would ultimately have 150,000 men on the Aliakmon line and was already 'somewhere near the half way mark', General Maitland Wilson now said that Britain would have one armoured brigade and three infantry divisions 'in about six weeks' time'. Janković declared that Yugoslav plans had been based on Dill's considerably higher figure of the forces already in place, and that 'news of the lesser British forces would be an acute disappointment'. The meeting ended without any clear agreement and – to judge by the British record – left a feeling of mutual mistrust.[58]

So when Hitler launched his Balkan campaign on 6 April, against Yugoslavia and Greece, there were no joint plans agreed with the Simović government; and uncertainty over Yugoslavia had left the differences between the British and Greeks over defence policy basically unsolved. As Field-Marshal Wilson later wrote: 'the Greeks were angling for Yugoslavia to come in with them and this consideration had priority over anything we might offer or undertake ... This wooing of Yugoslavia obtruded itself in all discussions on strategy like a motif running through an opera.'[59]

The speed of the Yugoslav collapse produced some unfairly caustic comment in London. When on 11 April, after the flight of the Simović government from Belgrade, Campbell reported that Simović was asking for the 'immediate despatch of two armoured divisions', Sargent commented that the Yugoslavs were responsible for their own troubles by refusing staff talks before the German attack. The two armoured

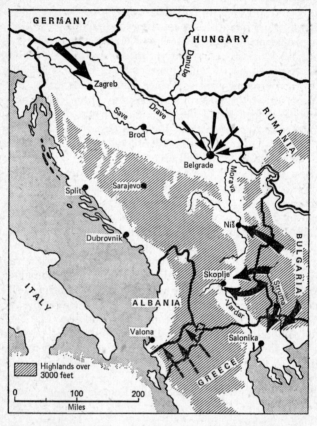

MAP 3. The German Attack on Yugoslavia, April 1941

divisions were of course out of the question.[60] Two days later Churchill sent a message to Campbell: 'we do not see why the King or government should leave the country, which is vast, mountainous and full of armed men. German tanks can no doubt move along the roads and tracks but to conquer the Serbian armies they must bring up infantry. Then will be the chance to kill them. Surely the young king and the ministers should play their part in this.'[61] But immediately after this the king and government left Nikšić without consulting Campbell, though Mirković demanded the help of the British assistant air attaché in facilitating their flight to Greece. Campbell then managed to get some of his staff and certain 'compromised' Yugoslavs away in two British seaplanes; he himself and others of his staff, together with several members of S.O.E., were taken prisoner; a British submarine sent into the Gulf of Kotor to take them off arrived too late.[62]

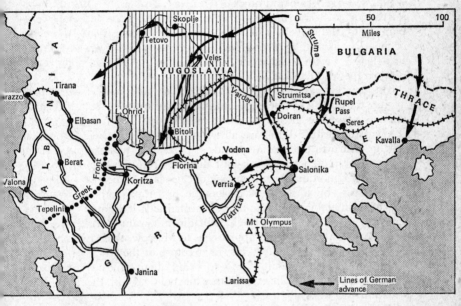

MAP 4. The First Phase of the German Attack on Greece, 6–9 April 1941

The British bore no ill-will towards the Simović government for these events. They were unfailingly tolerant towards the Turks, who had stubbornly resisted all Eden's pressures – even more stubbornly than Prince Paul. Eden's conclusion towards the end of April was that 'the most we can hope for is that Turkey will remain benevolently neutral and resist if attacked ... We now have no alternative to riding the Turks on an easy rein ...'[63]

As for the campaign on the Greek mainland, the British saw this at the time as a defeat but not a disaster. On 1st May the Chiefs of Staff reported to the War Cabinet that about 60 of the 130 aircraft based on Greek aerodromes had got away safely, and all but about 100 of the 1700 R.A.F. personnel had been evacuated. The total number of army personnel in Greece had been between 55,000 and 56,000; 43,000 had been got away.[64] It was the subsequent fighting in Crete which caused much graver losses.

Politically, the outcome of the Balkan campaign was more difficult to assess. Against the British, it could with reason be said that they had egged on small countries to oppose overwhelming force, knowing that this was a gamble and without giving anything like adequate support. It could also be said that they had – perhaps carelessly rather than deliberately – led these small countries to believe that British aid would be larger-scale and quicker than was possible. The British themselves ran risks and made sacrifices, but on no scale remotely comparable to the Greeks and Yugoslavs, now facing years of enemy occupation. Of the '300,000' Yugoslav troops who – it was once hoped in Belgrade – were to have been evacuated by the British, about 1,000 reached the Middle East.

Yet few Greeks or Yugoslavs seemed actually to feel resentment against the British on these grounds; most continued to regard them as allies who would come back one day victoriously.

What the British did above all was to demonstrate their determination to return to the continent and, in particular, to stake out a claim to an active presence in South-East Europe. From the summer of 1940, the Soviet Union had begun staking out its claim to post-war influence in the area, by a series of diplomatic or propaganda manoeuvres, backed neither by arms supplies nor armed aid; it wanted the South-East European countries to fight, but did not want to risk war itself. In spite of tentative British approaches to Moscow, these two processes were totally unco-ordinated. The later course of the war showed painfully clearly how difficult it was to bring about any convergence of British and Soviet policies – military or political – in the area, even when the two were allies.

To Hitler, the British declaration of active involvement in South-East Europe caused continuing worry, even after his victory of April 1941. He always expected the British to try to come back. This fear could later be exploited to divert his energies from greater concerns.

PART TWO

UNWILLING ALLIES AND RELUCTANT ENEMIES

South-East Europe in
British War Strategy, 1941-5

The Balkan campaign of 1941, though strongly condemned after the event by most military experts, left the British convinced that they would return to South-East Europe one day. This belief persisted even after the Quebec conference of 1943 had demonstrated the determination of Britain's closest and most powerful ally, the United States, to prevent any serious Anglo-American commitment in the area, and the Teheran conference had shown the even stronger determination of Russia to exclude the British so far as possible. At the very least, it lived on in the mind of Churchill who, whatever the scepticism of his own military advisers, and even though he had formally accepted strategic decisions which seemed to rule out any such return, still believed that the unexpected might happen, the opportunity might offer itself, to be seized and exploited eagerly.

As for Churchill's motives, until the spring of 1944 these were clearly strategic: he believed that through the entry of Turkey into the war, the action of the Greek, Yugoslav and Albanian resistance movements, or the defection of the Axis satellites, Rumania, Hungary and Bulgaria, Germany's collapse might be speeded and the war shortened. On the other hand, from the end of 1941 Eden and the Foreign Office saw a military return to South-East Europe as probably the only means of holding back post-war Soviet expansion into the area. In the spring of 1944, when the Russians were already poised on the Rumanian frontier, Churchill came to share this view. From then on he had a double interest – strategic and political – in a return to South-East Europe. But for Hitler's fanatical obstinacy and the extraordinary staying-power of the German forces in Italy and the Balkans, the unexpected opportunity for which Churchill hoped against hope might have offered itself. As things turned out, it never did. All that the British could do was to return to Greece and hold it, by a hair's breadth, at the end of 1944.

A SECOND FRONT – WHERE?

In the first months after the German attack on Russia, Stalin was willing and eager to take help from any quarter. He was quick to

demand the immediate opening of a second front. In September 1941
he urged Churchill that Britain should send a considerable number of
divisions either to Archangel or through Persia to 'the southern regions
of the USSR'.[1] Churchill replied encouragingly but non-committally:
' . . . the two flanks, north and south, certainly present the most favourable opportunities . . . In the south the great prize is Turkey; if Turkey
can be gained another powerful army will be available . . .'[2]

The matter was left open for discussion when Eden first visited
Moscow in December 1941. The British then said that a second front
had been opened by their operations in North Africa; Stalin countered
by asking whether the British would be able to open a second front in
Europe by a landing in the Balkans. The British replied that a landing
on the continent in the immediate future was not probable but that one
objective of the Libyan campaign was to secure a base for an attack
on Italy. Stalin then switched the discussion by suggesting British aid
for a Soviet attack on Petsamo in the extreme north.[3] It is unclear
whether Stalin seriously wanted a Balkan front, or was merely probing
British intentions, probably with the aim of diverting British energies
elsewhere.

At this time, a Balkan front was certainly one of the options considered by the British military planners; and it had not yet been ruled
out by the Americans. A memorandum by the U.S. and British Chiefs
of Staff at the Washington war conference in December 1941 forecast
that though no large-scale land offensives against Germany were likely
in 1942, 'in 1943 the way may be clear for a return to the continent,
across the Mediterranean, from Turkey into the Balkans or by landings
in Western Europe'. Meanwhile the main methods of wearing down
Germany would be air bombardment, aid to Russia, the Blockade and
'the maintenance of the spirit of revolt in the occupied countries, and
the organisation of subversive movements'.[4] (At this time almost the
only resistance movement to have emerged was in Yugoslavia.)

During the early part of 1942 Soviet pressure for a second front
continued to mount and took on unpleasant overtones. There was
some speculation in London about the possibility of Stalin's making a
separate peace with Hitler.[5] These were among the reasons why Britain
pressed ahead with negotiation of an Anglo-Soviet treaty and why
Roosevelt and Churchill agreed on the need to open a front in North
Africa in 1942. In their directive to the Commander-in-Chief North
Africa in August 1942, they set the aim – among others – of insuring
communications through the Mediterranean and facilitating operations
against the Axis on the European continent.[6]

The North African operation had immediate repercussions on South-
East Europe. It caused the undertaking in late November of the highly
successful British-led destruction of the Gorgospotamos bridge on the
main north–south railway by which the Germans could carry reinforce-

ments through Greece. It also gave fresh impetus to the re-examination of the Yugoslav resistance and the rival merits of Mihajlović and Tito, which was being undertaken by the British in the autumn of 1942.

But on the further strategic outlook for South-East Europe, the British and American military planners began to diverge. Churchill, in a paper for the Casablanca conference, pounced with delight on a suggestion by Roosevelt that a survey should be made of future possi- bilities 'including forward movement directed against Sardinia, Sicily, Italy, Greece and other Balkan areas and including the possibility of obtaining Turkish support to an attack through the Black Sea against Germany's flank'. This chimed with Churchill's own desire 'to strike at the under-belly of the Axis in effective strength and in the shortest time' – in the first place, to attack Sicily or Sardinia; Churchill also pressed for 'a supreme and prolonged effort' to bring Turkey into the war in the spring by means of guarantees of territorial integrity and increased military aid.[7]

The British Chiefs of Staff, in their own final paper for the Casa- blanca Conference of 31.12.42, argued in greater detail the need for further operations in the Mediterranean before attempting an assault on North-West Europe. They said that 'by amphibious operations in the Mediterranean, aimed at bringing about the collapse of Italy, we can give the maximum relief to Russia, wear out the German Air Force and ultimately threaten Axis economic resources in the Balkans'. Moreover if Italy were knocked out, Turkey would be more likely to come into the war: 'with Turkey on our side, we should be well placed for offensive action against the Balkans'. Pointing out that the Balkans were mainly garrisoned by Italian troops the British argued – over- optimistically – that Germany would be unable to undertake the two new commitments of garrisoning both the Balkans and Italy without devastating effects on the Russian front. They therefore thought that in the Balkans the aim should be, first, intensification of subversive activity and supply of arms and equipment for 'the patriot forces in Greece, Jugoslavia and Albania', and next, 'when the time is ripe, the despatch of Allied land and air forces to act as a rallying point for offensive action of insurgent forces in this area'.[8]

All this was far from the minds of the American Joint Chiefs of Staff who countered British plans with a reminder of American strategic doctrine: offensive action in North-West Europe and the Pacific and Burma, and 'the strategic defensive in other theatres'. This meant exploiting success in North Africa only by intensive bombing of Ger- many and Italy from North African bases, possibly also, if Turkey should later enter the war, by air operations from Turkish bases. Land operations against Italy, let alone the Balkans, were totally absent from the American plans.[9]

The outcome of the Casablanca Conference of January 1943 was a compromise; the Americans agreed to attack Sicily so as to secure the Mediterranean lines of communication and intensify pressure on Italy; also to create a situation 'in which Turkey could be enlisted as an active ally'. But they did not promise to attack Italy itself.[10] The British and American planners also agreed to draw up a comprehensive cover plan for the Mediteranean: 'the possibility of carrying out feints or minor operations in the Eastern Mediterranean will be examined'. The British were to be left to handle all matters connected with Turkey.[11]

To the British planners, this compromise still left open the possibility of following up a successful attack on Sicily by an assault on the Italian mainland with all the possible implications for South-East Europe. The requirements of strategic deception also focused fresh interest on this area. So for the first time, in the spring of 1943, the British military leaders began to give serious thought to building up the resistance movements there and making the necessary aircraft and supplies available – and in particular of getting aircraft of sufficiently long range out of the Americans. It seems likely that just as S.O.E. often had to exaggerate the scale of their achievements or hopes in order to get support and facilities from the British Chiefs of Staff and commanders, so the British Chiefs of Staff – or Churchill himself – tended to exaggerate British achievements and hopes in the Balkans to get aircraft out of the Americans, as for instance when it was a question of getting Liberators for use in Yugoslavia out of General Eisenhower, in Algiers, early in 1943.[12]

There was an enormous amount to be done in the field of resistance. The first British officers had only been dropped in Greece in November 1942; in Yugoslavia until the end of 1942 there was only one British officer, with Mihajlović, who was moody and at times hostile, excusing his inactivity by British failure to send any supplies worth mentioning. There were no British officers yet in Albania. As for the Axis satellites, S.O.E. maintained sporadic contact with Maniu in Rumania but to little effect; there was virtually no contact with Bulgaria; and the first tentative approaches from the Hungarians, early in 1943, had been quickly 'blown' by the Germans. If therefore the British were to fulfil the minimum aim of holding down and weakening the Germans in South-East Europe – let alone diverting German troops there or bringing about a German withdrawal – things had to be changed fast.

It was in these circumstances that the British took the decision in March 1943 to contact Tito's Partisans in Yugoslavia, and soon after to contact Albanian groups, which were in fact also Communist. Directives were sent to British Liaison Officers (BLOs) in Greece to develop large guerilla forces, and up to May these directives assumed that there would be allied landings in Greece in 1943.[13] These directives pushed the BLOs to rely increasingly on the Communist-led EAM/ELAS to carry out the necessary actions, especially for purposes of strategic deception, as cover for the operations in the central Mediterranean. At this stage the long-term political consequences of backing Communist forces in South-East Europe were not considered by the military planners; nor were they pressed by the Foreign Office. The demand of the Chiefs of Staff for a 'tuning up' of guerilla operations in the Balkans was taken as imperative.[14]

When it came to persuading the American planners to agree to an invasion of Italy, the British tried to dangle alluring prospects in South-East Europe as a carrot. The Joint Planning Staff argued in May 1943 that although the final blow against Germany must be delivered in North-West Europe, not the Mediterranean, a great deal could be done to exhaust the Germans first by attacking the Italian mainland. One consequence could then be that the Germans would have to replace the 32 Italian divisions in the Balkans and the Aegean. The Joint Planners forecast with great optimism:

> Sustained at comparatively little cost to the Allies ... up to 300,000 guerillas could harass the enemy's vulnerable communications, denying him important economic resources in Yugoslavia and Greece, facing him with seriously increasing recalcitrance and throttling his garrisons in Greece to such an extent that it is difficult to see how they could be maintained . . . Ploeşti itself would for the first time be brought within range of offensive air attack, from Italy . . . The Rumanians . . . are unlikely to show much firmness under air bombardment . . . In the Aegean, the Dodecanese would be weakened and might well be taken, and the way opened for Turkey to enter the lists ...

A bridgehead should be seized at Durazzo with four assault brigades and two infantry divisions: 'this force alone would activate the guerilas and we could support it with up to 500 bombers and 300 transport aircraft from the mainland.'[15]

These happy British dreams found no favour with the American planners, who riposted with a paper assuming that 'no amphibious operations will be undertaken in the Mediterranean' after the invasion of Sicily, and that all available forces and landing craft should be moved to the United Kingdom for the invasion of North-West Europe in April 1944.

Once again the outcome was an Anglo-American compromise, reached at the Trident conference in May 1943. Action was to be taken to 'eliminate Italy from the war and to contain the maximum number of German forces', but after the invasion of Sicily four American and three British divisions were to be withdrawn to the United Kingdom. No mention was made in the final report of operations in the Balkans or a bridgehead at Durazzo. The Americans were to try to bomb the Rumanian oil fields from North Africa.[16]

In spite of American coldness to British plans for the Balkans, from early May 1943 onwards Churchill's personal interest in the area was very keen, and in Yugoslavia in particular, he sought his own sources of information, by-passing S.O.E. and the Foreign Office.[17] At the beginning of July, just before the landings in Sicily, he sent a message to General Alexander: 'I presume you have read about the recent heavy fighting in Yugoslavia and the widespread sabotage and guerilla beginning in Greece. Albania should be a fertile field . . . If we can get hold of the mouth of the Adriatic so as to be able to run even a few ships into Dalmatian or Greek ports the whole of the western Balkans might flare up with far-reaching results.'[18]

When Mussolini fell he sent a memorandum to Roosevelt, who agreed to it with slight changes:

It will become urgent in the highest degree to get agents, Commandos and supplies by sea across the Adriatic into Greece, Albania and Yugoslavia. It must be remembered that there are 15 German divisions in the Balkans . . . Nevertheless once we have control of the Italian peninsula and of the Adriatic, and the Italian armies in the Balkans withdraw or lay down their arms, it is by no means unlikely that the Hun will be forced to withdraw northwards to the line of the Save and the Danube, thus liberating Greece and other tortured countries.

Churchill added that the effects of Mussolini's fall on Bulgaria, Rumania and Hungary might be profound; and the collapse of Italy should be the moment of putting the strongest pressure on Turkey. Roosevelt asked for the words to be inserted: 'we believe that in any important negotiations affecting the Balkans the concurrence of Russia should be obtained if practicable'.[19]

NO BALKAN FRONT

For a few weeks, Churchill's euphoric forecast seemed to have some validity. But the Quadrant conference at Quebec, starting in late August, showed that whatever Roosevelt might say, the American planners remained determined to concentrate on North-West Europe and to stop the British drawing off forces – as they saw it – for a prolonged campaign in Italy or hare-brained schemes in South-East Europe. The British had to agree to an operation in southern France in support of Overlord in North-West Europe, and to accept that, in the matter of scarce resources, Overlord must have absolute priority. Operations in the Balkan area were to be 'limited to supply of Balkan guerillas by air and sea transport, to minor Commando forces, and to the bombing of strategic objectives'. It was stated that, militarily, the time was not ripe for Turkey to enter the war, though the Turks should be asked to keep German shipping out of the Black Sea and stop supplying chrome to Germany.

Even though the Trident verdict seemed to rule out any sizeable British military operation in South-East Europe, it is doubtful whether Churchill took it as final and irreversible, still less that he took it as implying the exclusion of Britain from the area. For the time being, it left it open to the British and Americans to exploit the effects of the Italian collapse in South-East Europe to a modest extent. Tito could be supplied much more plentifully by sea and air, though no permanent bases could be established on the Adriatic coast, and the Germans could not be prevented from regaining control of the coastline and most of the islands from Tito's Partisans. A Hungarian peace feeler, prompted by the Italian collapse, was discussed by Churchill and Roosevelt during the Trident conference and given an encouraging response (see p. 252 below); and from then on Churchill took a lively, if sporadic, interest in the possibility of detaching one or other of the Axis satellites from Germany, whether by bombing or political coup d'état.

The British Chiefs of Staff also remained keenly interested in the strategic possibilities of the area, giving the opinion, in early October, that 'we should not relax our efforts to contain as many German divisions as possible in Greece and Jugoslavia'. They thought it possible that things could be made so hot for the Germans that they might voluntarily evacuate the Balkan peninsula, or at least its southern part.[20] This view was initialled by Churchill without comment. On 12 October the Chiefs of Staff asked S.O.E. to report 'what further efforts could be made to nourish the activities of the guerillas', since they were very anxious to back them up as soon and as much as possible.[21] Four days later the Chiefs of Staff, after receiving S.O.E.'s report, told Churchill that there were 'some 230,000 guerillas operating in organised parties and 80 British missions all of whom are in W/T contact with Cairo'. These were said to be containing 'some 17 German and 8 Bulgarian divisions' (a controversial figure). The Chiefs of Staff felt strongly that 'great opportunities now exist in the Balkans for assisting the campaign in Italy and these should be seized immediately'.[22] They advocated a reorganisation of the command structure in the Mediterranean which would enable aircraft and shipping to be obtained more easily (from the Americans) for support of the Balkan guerillas.

At a meeting of the Chiefs of Staff a few days later, Churchill made it clear that if the British alone could decide strategy he would favour reinforcing the Italian theatre and 'entering the Balkans', but added that they could not take a unilateral decision and a further meeting with the Americans would be necessary for this.[23] However, Churchill's remarks did not result in any action; and in November a suggestion of his for establishment of bridgeheads on the Dalmatian coast, together with the use of the First British Airborne Division and all available

Commandos, showed his preoccupation with the problem, but was turned down by the Chiefs of Staff and by General Alexander himself.[24] By this time the growing difficulties of the Italian campaign were casting a long shadow over prospects for easy gains in South-East Europe.

While Churchill was grappling with the strategic problems of the Mediterranean and his relations with the Americans, now becoming increasingly the dominant partner, Eden was taken up with the political problems of relations with Russia. At the Moscow conference of Foreign Ministers in October 1943 he made a series of proposals on the South-East European countries, designed to get information about Soviet intentions and if possible establish a working partnership in the area. Virtually all were evaded or rejected.[25] (See p. 137 below.) In retrospect – though this was not how Eden saw it at the time – it seems clear that Stalin was mainly interested in finding out what the British were up to in South-East Europe and what likelihood there was of British military operations there, so that he could react accordingly.

U.S. STATE DEPARTMENT ALOOFNESS, O.S.S. ACTIVISM IN SOUTH-EAST EUROPE

One thing which the Russians must have seen clearly at the Moscow conference was the difference of approach between the British and Americans over South-East Europe – between Eden's policy of active intervention, and the extreme reserve of Cordell Hull, the American Secretary of State. Yet at the same time they must have found the Americans puzzling. Hull opted out of all discussions on South-East Europe whenever he decently could, as though the whole subject were distasteful, leaving matters to be settled separately by Eden and Molotov. Yet on 23 October he suddenly asked General Deane of the U.S. delegation to speak to the conference. Deane said that the American Chiefs of Staff felt that there were great opportunities in the Balkans, 'particularly in the winter months', to intensify subversive activities. They wanted to do this by utilising the Office of Strategic Services, who would penetrate the area by air and other means to create cells of unrest and sabotage. He hoped this would receive the support of the Soviet government on the understanding that its purposes were purely military. Molotov, obviously somewhat taken aback, asked for 'a clearer picture'. Deane said that was 'not entirely possible as such operations were largely opportunistic'.[26]

If Molotov was surprised, so probably was Eden. It was only on the day before Deane's statement in Moscow that Roosevelt sent Churchill a telegram which, considering Churchill's passionate interest in Balkan resistance and his pride in British achievement, must have been wounding. Roosevelt said he was worried about the chaotic condition in the

Balkans: 'in both Yugoslavia and Greece the guerilla forces appear to be engaged largely in fighting each other and not the Germans . . . the only hope I see for immediate favourable action is the presence of an aggressive and qualified officer'. He then proposed General Donovan – now head of O.S.S. – as the man: 'being a fearless and aggressive character he might do much good'. 'If we decide to send him', Roosevelt added, 'all agencies of ours now working in the Balkans should be placed under his direction and the resources we put into this effort should be at his disposal'.[27]

In 1941 Churchill had paid high tribute to Donovan's 'magnificent work' in the Balkans, telling Roosevelt that he had carried everywhere an 'animating and heart-warming flame'.[28] But following the formation of O.S.S., under Donovan, in June 1942, a 'treaty' had been made between S.O.E. and O.S.S. in September 1942 by which S.O.E. was to have the directing role in the Balkans.[29] In 1943, Churchill did not take kindly to the idea of putting the whole network of BLOs, which had been built up so painfully, under the control of an American. He answered politely but smartly: '. . . We British have about eighty separate missions under General Wilson's control working with partisans and patriot bands scattered over these immense mountainous regions 900 miles by about 300 miles in extent. Some of our officers there of Brigadier's rank are very capable and have in numerous cases been there for two years. I have great admiration for Donovan, but I do not see any centre in the Balkans from which he could grip the situation. If however you would like him to go to Cairo and meet General Wilson, he will be given the fullest information . . .' Churchill added that the enemy now had 'not less than 25 German and 8 Bulgarian divisions' in the Balkan theatre (thereby adding eight to the number of German divisions given by the British Chiefs of Staff a week earlier) (see p. 117 above). He concluded: 'we hope soon to compose the Greek quarrels but the differences between Tito's partisans and Mihajlović's Serbs are very deep-seated'.[30]

One of Donovan's reactions to Churchill's brush-off – which was followed by a S.O.E.–O.S.S. clash in Cairo – was to detach O.S.S. activities in Bulgaria and Rumania from Cairo – and so from British supervision – and move them to Istanbul, where they were placed directly under Washington: in late November Donovan told the U.S. Chiefs of Staff that he was sending a mission to Turkey under Colonel Jadwin.[31] This quickly led to Anglo-American friction over Bulgaria. (See p. 217 below.)

O.S.S. work in South-East Europe in the following year and a half was for the most part conducted independently of the British – sometimes in collaboration, sometimes in rivalry, and in one case in flat contradiction to British policy (Col. Robert McDowell's mission to Mihajlović in 1944). O.S.S. was independent of the State Department;

S.O.E. was not similarly independent of the Foreign Office. Problems of co-ordination were therefore especially awkward.

TEHERAN: STALIN DEFLECTS THE BRITISH FROM SOUTH-EAST EUROPE

At the Teheran conference in December 1943 Stalin, forearmed by the Moscow conference, had ample chance of exploiting and widening Anglo-American differences over South-East Europe, taunting the British with disloyalty to the agreed strategy of a second front in North-West Europe and casting Roosevelt in the role of chief opponent of Churchill's supposed Balkan ambitions. Churchill himself later wrote that all he wanted was the postponement of Overlord for a few weeks, and the consideration of 'a right-handed movement from the North of Italy, using the Istrian peninsula and the Ljubljana Gap, towards Vienna' – a suggestion first rashly put forward by Roosevelt, not Churchill – as alternative to the planned landing in the south of France. He also wanted – in defiance of the views of the American and British Chiefs of Staff – a fresh effort to get Turkey into the war.

These three points, Churchill wrote, 'I pressed upon the President and Stalin on every occasion, not hesitating to repeat the argument remorselessly. I could have gained Stalin, but the President was oppressed by the prejudices of his military advisers . . . Our American friends were comforted in their obstinacy by the reflection that "at any rate we have stopped Churchill entangling us in the Balkans".'[32]

It seems very doubtful whether Churchill could really have 'gained Stalin'. It was true that Stalin agreed that 'it was most desirable' that Turkey should come into the war before the end of the year; he may however have been gambling on the near-certainty that the Turks would, as usual, refuse, thereby putting themselves in the wrong, or that if they did come in, they would remain passive and would not advance into the Balkans – a prospect for which he could have had no enthusiasm. Certainly the forcefulness with which Stalin backed the southern France operation against the Ljubljana Gap plan cannot have been prompted only by Soviet devotion to orthodox conceptions of strategy. In the light of the entirely negative Soviet stand against British initiatives over South-East Europe at the Moscow conference, he must have been moved, at least in part, by the long-term aim of keeping the British out of the area.

Yet even after Teheran, in Churchill's mind the option of some form of operation in South-East Europe remained open. Wilson, as Supreme Commander in the Mediterranean, continued to regard Rumania and Bulgaria as 'within his sphere of responsibility', even though, so long as the Germans controlled the Aegean, there was 'no method by which he could introduce any ground forces'.[33] Wilson also raised the question of reaching an understanding with the Russians on military policy in the area[34]; the Anglo-Americans were already bombing the Axis satellites. But the Chiefs of Staff thought it most unlikely that the Russians would give any information on their plans,[35] and even in October 1944 Stalin was evading British suggestions for 'direct coordination of Wilson's operations with those of the Soviet forces in Hungary and Yugoslavia'.[36]

In the Foreign Office, a belief that there might be a British occupation of South-East Europe persisted. The British had been planning for some time, under the aegis of the Middle East Command, for a period of military administration in Greece, Albania and Yugoslavia, and had been training civil affairs officers for the purpose in Egypt.[37] In May 1944 a Southern Department official wrote: 'in the case of Yugoslavia there will probably be no occupying troops and as regards Bulgaria we are at present trying to decide whether we shall have troops to send in.'[38] Sargent wrote to Knatchbull-Hugessen: 'while it is true that it is part of our policy to endeavour to work hand in hand with the Russians in the Balkans, this in no way means that we are intending to divide the area up into spheres of influence . . . We do not yet know how many troops we shall have available for occupation purposes when the moment of collapse comes'; in Rumania, however, Russian occupation was geographically inevitable.[39] As late as August 1944 the Balkan Air Force's Policy Committee suggested that it might be a mistake to bomb Hungary, on the grounds that it might be against British interests to produce chaos there 'before we were ourselves in a position to enter and take control of the country'.[40]

STRATEGIC DECEPTION IN SOUTH-EAST EUROPE

For the outside world, both allied and enemy, the possibility of Anglo-American operations in South-East Europe remained a live issue well into the autumn of 1944. This was partly due to wishful thinking, for instance, among non-Communist politicians in Hungary, Rumania and Bulgaria, or anti-Communist leaders such as Mihajlović, or to deep-rooted fears on the part of Hitler or the rather different fears of militant Communists in Yugoslavia, Greece and Albania. But it was also due to the plans for strategic deception, related to Overlord, set on foot at Teheran. Churchill wrote later: 'I asked if there would be any difficulty in the three Staffs concerting cover plans. Stalin explained that the Russians had made considerable use of deception by means of dummy tanks, aircraft and airfields . . . He was entirely agreeable to the Staffs collaborating with the object of devising joint cover and deception schemes.' The three leaders formally agreed that 'a cover plan to mystify and mislead the enemy . . . should be concerted'.[41]

The Western allies were thinking of something much more elaborate

than dummy tanks. Already before the invasion of Sicily, the BLOs in
Greece had been instructed to conduct operations to create the impression that the invasion would be in the southern Balkans: the result was
the extremely successful Operation Animals lasting from 21 June till
14 July.[42] BLOs in Albania seem to have been told to spread the idea
that the Balkans were to be invaded: when Brigadier 'Trotsky' Davies
was dropped into Albania in September 1943, he was pressed by Enver
Hoxha, the resistance leader, to give information on this point.[43]

After Teheran the Controlling Officers, as they were known, set to
work in London, Moscow and elsewhere not only to devise a cover
plan, but also to vet a whole range of proposals in the light of this plan.
In 1944, therefore, surrender negotiations with leaders in the South-
East Europe satellites became unnecessarily tortuous because they could
not be told flatly to abandon hope of the arrival of Anglo-American
troops[44] to save them from the Russians; they had to be kept guessing
so that the Germans should be kept guessing. The deviousness of the
reasoning involved is shown in a note from the 'Controlling Officer' to
the Chiefs of Staff on whether or not a Rumanian offer to surrender to
the Allies, early in 1944, should be rebuffed:

Negotiations with Rumania:
1. In our cover plans for the Mediterranean theatre we wish the
Germans to believe that the following are our intentions in regard
to the Balkans:
    (a) during April Anglo-American and Polish forces will be estab-
    lished in Greece and Albania
    (b) during May Russian forces will be established in Bulgaria.
2. If the above were our *real* plans the following points would
emerge:
    (a) no allied forces could reach Rumania before June
    (b) Russian forces are the only ones which could get there by that
    date; any others would arrive much later
    (c) Anglo-American forces could not reach Rumania until after
    Salonika had fallen, which could not be much before August.
3. Were our operations in Greece real they would be greatly assisted
if the Germans had simultaneously a hostile Rumania on their hands.
It is therefore suggested that we would try to secure Rumanian agreement to the following arrangements, if our real intentions were as
described in para 1 above:
    (a) Rumanians to be ready from end of March onwards to declare
    for the Allies immediately a landing in Greece was announced
    (b) Rumanians to oppose the Germans with Allied air assistance
    alone until early June
    (c) Russian forces from Bulgaria to go to Rumanian assistance
    early in June.

4. In order to assist the Mediterranean cover plans it is therefore suggested the following points should be borne in mind: *No suggestion should be made that we shall not be ready to take advantage of the Rumanian offer this spring.* If it is necessary to elaborate this:

(i) no surrender is required before the end of March in any case
(ii) after that date surrender should be made when requested by the Allies
(iii) the first Allied force to support the Rumanians must be Russian since they are much nearer and alone have direct access to Rumania.[45]

When in Albania, in the summer of 1944, the question was raised whether it was worth supporting nationalist guerillas as well as the Communists, the British Chiefs of Staff pointed out that not only was it part of allied Balkan strategy to contain as many enemy forces as possible in Albania, but also 'our deception plan includes a notional assault on the Albanian coast'.[46] But they doubted whether any operations likely to be undertaken by the Albanians would do much to support Allied deception plans.[47]

Given the complexity of the cover plans, it seems possible that at times the British may have deceived not only the Germans – which they did – but also themselves; or at least it seems uncertain down to what level British officers or officials knew what was fact and what was fiction.

CHURCHILL'S ATTEMPT TO HOLD BACK RUSSIA

During the early part of 1944 Churchill was stung by Soviet rebuffs over Poland and the dropping of two British officers in Rumania, by difficulties with Tito and by a prolonged Greek crisis, to turn his mind to the long-term political aspect of strategy in South-East Europe. In early May he minuted to Eden about 'the brute issues between us and the Soviet government which are developing in Italy, in Rumania, in Bulgaria, in Yugoslavia and above all in Greece. Are we going to acquiesce in the Communization of the Balkans and perhaps of Italy? ... If our conclusion is that we resist Communist infusion and invasion, we should put it to them pretty plainly ... evidently we are approaching a show-down with the Russians ...'[48]

Eden momentarily diverted Churchill's energies into an effort to reach a political understanding with Russia on South-East Europe. But his perception of the Soviet threat coloured his impassioned strategic arguments during June and July 1944, when he – and, perhaps half-heartedly, the Chiefs of Staff – tried to persuade the Americans to drop the landing in the south of France. Until mid-June the American Chiefs of Staff were still ready at least to consider an operation at the head of the Adriatic as an alternative; General Wilson, Supreme Commander in the Mediterranean, and General Alexander, the commander in Italy, both favoured this course. But General Marshall, backed by Roosevelt partly for domestic political reasons, over-ruled them.[49] Roosevelt wrote that since the landing in the south of France had been agreed with Stalin, strategy could not be changed without consulting him.[50] Churchill replied that though for short-term military reasons Stalin might welcome the Trieste–Ljubljana gap operation, 'on a long-term political point of view he might prefer that the British and Americans should do their share in France . . . and that East, Middle and Southern Europe shall fall naturally into his control'.[51] Stalin was not consulted. Churchill gave way; the landing in the south of France took place.

But in late August Churchill again wrote to Roosevelt: 'I have never forgotten your talks to me at Teheran about Istria, and I am sure that the arrival of a powerful army in Trieste and Istria in four or five weeks would have an effect far outside purely military values. Tito's people will be awaiting us in Istria. What the condition of Hungary will be then I cannot imagine, but we shall at any rate be in a position to take full advantage of any great new situation.'[52] (The Rumanian change of front on 23 August had caused a political upheaval in Hungary in a direction favourable to the allies.) Roosevelt replied that Trieste and Istria could be discussed at the coming Quebec conference.

At Quebec in mid-September, Churchill formally raised the idea of giving 'a stab in the Adriatic armpit' and welcomed the American decision to leave certain landing-craft in the Mediterranean for the purpose, if wanted. He added that one reason for the plan was 'the rapid encroachment of the Russians into the Balkan peninsula and the dangerous spread of Soviet influence there'. Roosevelt replied with a highly optimistic forecast of early German withdrawal from the Balkans and in Italy. On 13 September Churchill was able to tell the War Cabinet that there was 'almost complete agreement'. 'There is to be no weakening of Alexander's army till Kesselring has bolted beyond the Alps or been destroyed. We are to have all the landing-craft in the Mediterranean to work up in the Northern Adriatic in any amphibious plan which can be made for Istria, Trieste etc. The idea of our going to Vienna, if the war is long enough and if other people do not get there first, is fully accepted here.'[53]

In the view of the British military historian, Michael Howard, however, no 'serious calculations' were produced to show that such an operation was feasible, and 'it may be doubted whether any were ever made'. The difficulties would have been considerable.[54]

In any case, it was already too late to achieve Churchill's aim of stopping Soviet 'encroachment' into the Balkan peninsula. By the end of August Soviet forces controlled Rumania; on 9 September they had been welcomed in Bulgaria by a new pro-Soviet government. On 18

September Tito flew secretly to Moscow. The Red Army was to enter Hungary on 26 September and Yugoslavia on 1 October and was to liberate Belgrade later that month. But the Germans held on stubbornly in Italy throughout the winter. At Yalta in February 1945 Stalin suggested to Churchill that he could leave 'a few British divisions' in Italy and transfer the rest to Yugoslavia and Hungary and direct them against Vienna. Churchill wrote later: 'it cost him nothing to say this now, but I made no reproaches. "The Red Army," I answered, "may not give us time to complete the operation".'[55] The only military operations – apart from Commando raids – which the British conducted in South-East Europe were to prevent a Communist take-over in Greece, and to prevent Tito's forces from establishing themselves in Trieste.

It has been powerfully argued by the official British war historians[56] that in the dispute of 1943 over Mediterranean strategy Churchill and the British Chiefs of Staff were concerned only with shortening the war, ensuring the success of Overlord and helping Russia, not with keeping the Russians out of South-East Europe. Their evidence is very strong. The fact remains that it was these strategic decisions, and the tenacity with which the Americans stuck to them in 1944, which determined the fate of South-East Europe after the war. It is also clear that in accepting the 1943 decisions, Churchill had no intention – still less the Foreign Office – of handing over South-East Europe to the Russians. He was simply putting first things first. From the spring of 1944 onwards he was constantly haunted by fear of Soviet domination of all South-East Europe, which he wanted to prevent, not purely to serve British interests, but also, it seems fair to say, to save small independent states from extinction. Whether his plans for military intervention in South-East Europe could have succeeded in practice is another matter.

All that can be said is that the activities which the British actually carried out in the area, through support of resistance forces and contacts with opposition groups in the satellite countries, helped to a limited extent to defeat Germany. But they left Britain virtually powerless – except in Greece – to exercise any influence on the post-war settlement.

12 Britain, Russia and South-East Europe, 1941–5

Throughout the years when Britain and the Soviet Union were allies, South-East Europe was a sensitive spot. Each suspected the other's long-term aims in the area. Until late 1943, both subordinated their suspicions to the needs of joint war strategy. From then on, their conflicting long-term aims played an increasingly open part, influencing their political relations and military policies. But although there were minor local clashes, a major open clash over South-East Europe was avoided until the war against Hitler was won.

THE TURKISH PROBLEM

On the edge of South-East Europe, Turkey was a peculiarly sensitive point in Anglo-Soviet relations. This was true even before Hitler invaded Russia. By the time the British were driven from Greece in April 1941, they had become convinced that this was to be Hitler's next move, though Stalin persisted in ignoring British and other warnings. The British, who after the fall of France had set themselves the aim of 'embroiling' Germany and Russia, could only welcome the prospect. But they had also to try to fulfil their other aim of making sure that Turkey should *not* become embroiled with Russia nor side with Germany.

This was not altogether easy. Hitler was well placed to make trouble. On 28 February, just before German troops entered Bulgaria, he had sent a very smooth letter to the Turkish President Ismet Inönü, promising that German troops would keep away from Turkey's frontier.[1] The Germans could, and did, inflame Turkish suspicions of Russia by making known the Soviet offer to Bulgaria, in November 1940, of Turkish territory up to the Enos–Midia line, and Molotov's demand for Soviet bases on the Straits. These suspicions had been only slightly soothed by the Soviet declaration of 9 March 1941 – prompted, and publicly welcomed, by Britain – that Russia would remain neutral if Turkey were attacked. (See p. 27 above.) The British defeat in Greece made the Turks all the more inclined to listen to German warnings and wooing.

On 23 April a Foreign Office memorandum noted that 'as a preliminary to any attack on the Soviet Union, it is essential from the German point of view that Turkey should be unable to open the Straits to us. An attack on the Ukraine and the Caucasus would be hazardous if there remained the possibility of the British fleet entering the Black Sea.'[2] On 18 May the British ambassador, Knatchbull-Hugessen, reported that Germany had 'decided to frighten Turkey with the spectre of a joint German-Russian threat unless Turkey comes to terms with Hitler'.[3] Two days later he telegraphed that the Turkish Foreign Ministry thought it in Turkey's interest for a war between Germany and Russia to take place.[4] Thereafter in spite of strenuous efforts by Knatchbull-Hugessen and a personal plea from Eden, Turkish-German negotiations moved smoothly and on 18 June a treaty of friendship was signed. Four days later Hitler attacked the Soviet Union.

The Turks seemed to feel that they could claim some of the credit for this; in any case the Turkish government hailed the German attack 'with unconcealed delight'.[5] The British, even if they had failed to stop the Turks from signing a treaty with Hitler, had at least preserved the Anglo-Turkish treaty in existence. Turkey remained as neutral as before – even if for a time this neutrality had a more pro-German bias than before, especially over chrome deliveries. Britain was unable to bring aid to Russia through the Straits into the Black Sea.

Britain's swift welcome to Russia as an ally cast a blight on British-Turkish relations, and this was not dispelled by the identical assurances given to Turkey by Britain and the Soviet Union, on British prompting, on 10 August 1941, promising fidelity to the Montreux Convention and scrupulous respect for Turkey's territorial integrity. Knatchbull-Hugessen commented: 'the Turkish government . . . placed the fullest confidence in British sincerity, but they did not relish our joint action with the Soviets and they were far from ready to place the same confidence in the Russian word'.[6]

This same distrust of the Russians continued to rule Turkish policy and to block British efforts, in the following years, to bring Turkey into the war. The more successful the Russians were militarily, the nearer they came to South-East Europe, the greater was Turkish suspicion and fear. As early as January 1942 President Inönü, looking ahead to a German defeat, remarked: 'then Russia will be master of Europe, what are you going to do to control her?' On this Eden minuted: '. . . there's the rub . . .' but he did not suggest an answer.[7]

STALIN'S OPENING BID

At the time of Hitler's attack, it is unlikely that Stalin had much thought of controlling Europe. His military problems were too vast. Nevertheless within five days Molotov was proposing to the British

ambassador, Cripps, the conclusion of 'a political agreement to define
the basis of cooperation'. Cripps, perhaps recalling the unhappy outcome of his effort, a year before, to discuss with Molotov the restoration of a European balance, replied that 'it was better to wait till we
had learnt to trust each other'.[8]

But by October Molotov was pressing Britain to display political
solidarity with Russia by declaring war on Finland, Rumania and Hungary. (Bulgaria was not at war with the Soviet Union, so was not
mentioned.) In March 1941 Britain had considered declaring war on
Bulgaria and Rumania but had decided against it, since it was not in
the British interest 'to increase the numbers of our enemies', and there
was strong pro-British feeling in Rumania and anti-German feeling in
Bulgaria.[9] On 26 October Eden told the War Cabinet that the Soviet
government clearly attached very great importance to British acceptance of its request, and 'we naturally are anxious not to rebuff or
discourage them . . . A refusal might arouse their latent suspicions as to
our motives.' On the other hand, Eden set out various practical objections to the step.[10] Churchill put some of these objections to Stalin on
4 November; 'Rumania and Hungary: these countries are full of our
friends: they have been overpowered by Hitler and used as a cat's paw.
But if fortune turns against that ruffian they might easily come back to
our side. A British declaration of war would only freeze them all and
make it look as if Hitler were the head of a grand European alliance . . .
Do not pray suppose it is any want of zeal or comradeship that makes
us doubt the advisability of this step . . .'[11]

In spite of Churchill's friendly tone, an angry, aggrieved answer
came from Stalin, saying that 'an intolerable situation' had been
created: the problem was being discussed in the press and 'after all that
the British government informs us of its negative attitude to our proposal. Why is all this being done? To demonstrate the lack of unity
between the U.S.S.R. and Great Britain?'[12] Eden told the Soviet
ambassador, Maisky, that this message had surprised and pained
Churchill and the Cabinet.[13] But finally Churchill turned the other
cheek and proposed that Eden should visit Moscow; he would be ready
to discuss post-war problems. 'We expect,' he wrote, 'that Soviet
Russia, Great Britain and the U.S. will meet at the Council table of
the victors as the three principal partners . . . The fact that Russia is
a Communist state and Britain and the U.S. are not and do not intend
to be, is not any obstacle to our making a good plan for our mutual
safety and rightful interests.'[14]

To create a good atmosphere for Eden's visit, the British government
decided after due deliberation and advance warnings to declare war on
Finland, Rumania and Hungary.

When Eden got to Moscow he was faced by political demands which
Stalin probably thought extremely reasonable; they were a good deal

more moderate than those put to Hitler a year before, all the more if set against Cripps's supposed offer of Soviet leadership in the Balkans in June 1940. Stalin's main demand was simply that Britain should make a political agreement recognising the Soviet claim to the Baltic States and to the 1941 frontiers in Finland and Rumania; Poland, as a particularly sensitive issue for Britain, could be left for later settlement. He did however make two further demands, for Soviet bases in Rumania and Finland; to balance these, Britain could acquire bases in North-West Europe – at one point he suggested Boulogne and Dunkirk – perhaps also in Norway and Denmark. He must have thought this a very fair offer.

As for Turkey, Stalin was very careful; he made no mention of the Straits, but suggested that Turkey – as part of a far-ranging 'secret protocol' on the post-war European settlement – should acquire Bulgarian territory south of Burgas, together with the Dodecanese islands. When Eden objected that these were strongly claimed by Greece, he said there could be an 'exchange of islands' between Greece and Turkey. Other points in Stalin's 'secret protocol' were the restoration of Yugoslavia and its territorial extension at Italy's expense, guaranteed independence for Albania, the restoration of Greece to its old frontiers, and an extension westwards of Rumania, at Hungary's expense – it was not clear whether this meant only the return of Northern Transylvania or something more – and a Soviet guarantee of Rumania against Hungary.[15]

Stalin may well have thought that since he was safeguarding Britain's special friends, Turkey, Greece and Yugoslavia, there was nothing Eden could not easily swallow. He perhaps genuinely failed to understand Eden's repeated statement that he could not sign on the dotted line without consulting the Cabinet, and that Britain had promised the United States not to make secret agreements about post-war frontiers. One weakness in Eden's position on this last point was that Britain had already made one exception, in offering to back Yugoslav claims against Italy in Istria. (See pp. 87–8 above.) As Eden told Stalin: 'Mr. Roosevelt was worried because he had heard somewhere that I had offered the Yugoslav government some territorial extension and he was nervous about this . . . Even before Russia was attacked Mr. Roosevelt sent a message to us asking us not to enter into any secret arrangement as to the post-war reorganisation of Europe without first consulting him.'[16] The degree of British deference to American wishes was obviously a surprise to Stalin, who did not seem to take it at its face value. The War Cabinet however confirmed Eden's stand on the principle of no post-war commitments, and so deadlock developed over what Stalin regarded as the key issue.

THE BRITISH COUNTER-BID: CONFEDERATION

The deadlock over frontiers created a bad atmosphere for discussion of the proposal which Eden had taken to Moscow – that encouragement should be given to confederations in post-war Europe. The British case was that there would be a need in any eventual settlement to strengthen the smaller European countries 'so as to put them, both economically and strategically, in a position to resist successfully pressure by Germany'; Britain therefore welcomed the negotiations going on between the exiled Czechoslovak and Polish governments, and hoped that 'the various Balkan States may combine to form a similar system'.[17]

At his first meeting with Eden, before British opposition to secret agreements had emerged, Stalin said that 'if certain of the countries of Europe wish to federate, then the Soviet Union will have no objection'. This however was in the context of a proposal military alliance of 'democratic countries' with an international military force. Thereafter confederations were lost in the arguments over post-war frontiers; and very soon after the Moscow talks they became an object of intense Soviet suspicion. It can only be guesswork whether, if Eden had been able to do a deal over post-war frontiers, Stalin would have been less mistrustful of British plans for confederations.

Clearly Eden himself did not think Stalin's frontier demands unreasonable. When he got back to London he sent a message to Churchill – then on his way to talks with Roosevelt – that he thought that for Stalin this question was an 'acid test of our sincerity'; he asked Churchill to take the matter up with Roosevelt.[18] Churchill's reply was crushing: '. . . We have never recognized the 1941 frontiers of Russia except de facto. They were acquired by acts of aggression in shameful collusion with Hitler . . . This also applies to Bessarabia and Bukovina.' As for Eden's 'acid test', Churchill countered: 'I, on the contrary, regard our sincerity involved in the maintenance of the principles of the Atlantic Charter to which Stalin has subscribed.'[19]

But in the end Eden got his way, although Roosevelt declared that 'under no conditions would be subscribe to any secret treaty'.[20] Eden argued that after the defeat of Germany there would be no counterweight to Russia in Europe; Britain would therefore have to co-operate with Russia. Refusal to meet Stalin's demand might end any prospect of fruitful co-operation. Eden added that 'Stalin might have asked for much more, e.g. control of the Dardanelles, spheres of influence in the Balkans . . .'[21]

So Anglo-Soviet negotiations for a treaty started, while the Americans remained rather huffily aloof. The British aim was to persuade the Russians to leave aside Stalin's proposal for a 'secret protocol' on the future map of Europe and limit the territorial side of the treaty to the Baltic States, Finland and Rumania. In return the British would expect to get 'formal Soviet approval of the principle of confederation as applied to the weaker countries of Europe, especially in the Balkans and as regards Poland and Czechoslovakia'.[22] Dixon of the Southern Department minuted: 'it would probably be sufficient to require . . . merely a general assurance . . . An alternative would be to seek specific assurances that they agree to the constitution of a south-east European federation in which the enemy states, Bulgaria and Rumania, would be included as units. The object of this would be to ensure the emergence after the war of an independent Rumania in regard to which country Soviet designs are dubious . . .'[23]

Dixon also thought it would be in Britain's interest, but impracticable, to get a 'hands off' assurance that the Soviet government had no ambitions in the Adriatic and recognised that Yugoslavia would lie in the British sphere of influence after the war. The Russians should however be asked to recognise the existence of Greek claims to the Dodecanese and southern Albania.[24] (At a meeting held by Sargent it was agreed that 'nothing need be said to Stalin about the Greek desire to obtain Cyprus'.)[25]

Out of all these desirable things, confederation loomed largest for the British. Unfortunately, for Stalin this had become an 'acid test' of British sincerity. By the end of 1941 the Greek and Yugoslav exiled governments had negotiated a formal agreement creating a 'Balkan Union', and the Foreign Office had been debating whether or not they dared say openly that they hoped that Bulgaria and Rumania would eventually join in, or whether this would provoke too much Soviet suspicion.[26] They decided to play safe, but when faced with a direct question in the House of Commons on 4 February, Eden replied: 'what I can say for sure is that this Greece–Yugoslav treaty is definitely to form the basis of a Balkan confederation.'[27]

The Yugoslav politicians in London made it very clear that their interest (though not the Greek interest) in a Balkan Union was as a barrier against Communism and Sovietisation. Their ambassador in Moscow, Gavrilović, had come to London and was warning all and sundry not to trust any Soviet undertakings to refrain from pressing towards the Aegean and Mediterranean and establishing a sphere of influence in the Balkans.[28] The Croat and Slovene politicians echoed these warnings. Simović and others urged the Foreign Office to see that a British expeditionary force would have to be sent to the Balkans to prevent a Soviet take-over.[29] The Foreign Office was fairly sympathetic; Sargent minuted on 11 January that there was a genuine danger: one instrument at Britain's disposal for countering Russian penetration was 'the policy of a Balkan confederation', while the other was an expeditionary force.[30]

All this Yugoslav talk must have reached Soviet ears. In any case King Peter of Yugoslavia, at a lunch to celebrate the signing of the

Yugoslav–Greek agreement, spoke of it as 'an important beginning for the realisation of a great political and economic union in South-East Europe', and suggested it might be linked with a Central European Union based on the Czechoslovak–Polish agreement, to form 'a great organisation with a single common Supreme Organ'.[31] Given the suspicions which the Russians already had about the Polish General Sikorski, this was certain to alarm them still more; the Soviet ambassador to the exiled governments, Alexander Bogomolov, adopted a 'very chilling' attitude to the Greek–Yugoslav pact, while in Kuibyshev Vyshinski was said to have shown clearly the Soviet government's 'suspicion and distaste' for it.[32] The Greek Prime Minister, Emanuel Tsouderos, was worried at Soviet coldness and the indiscretion of King Peter and General Sikorski.[33]

Nevertheless, the Foreign Office remained devoted to confederation; and in their draft for an Anglo-Soviet treaty, given to Maisky in April, there was an article 5(a) on the encouragement of confederations in Central, Eastern and South-East Europe. Maisky asked Eden: why these in particular and why not Western Europe too? His government, he thought, would like some more general geographical description.[34] Cadogan minuted: 'our dotting of the i's and crossing the t's has evidently aroused Russian suspicions,' adding that the reference to Central, Eastern and South-East Europe would probably have to be dropped. Eden agreed.[35]

When Molotov arrived in London for the final negotiations, he said flatly that 'the Soviet government had certain information to show that some federations might be directed against the Soviet Union'; the question was one for the future. Eden assured him that Britain would never, 'of course', be party to any scheme directed against the Soviet Union; federations were intended only as a defence against Germany.[36] It is unlikely that Molotov believed him; any way he continued to press for something very much vaguer than the British draft.

This however was not the key point in the talks, which hinged mainly on Molotov's demand for mutual assistance treaties with Rumania and Finland, in addition to restoration of the 1941 frontiers. Eden pressed Molotov to say whether these were intended as 'punishment' and meant the stationing of Soviet troops. Molotov slid away from an answer and suggested, as an alternative, a much vaguer formula about Soviet security interests in the Gulf of Finland and the north-west part of the Black Sea. Eden liked this still less, since he felt it contained 'implications which would arouse all sorts of suspicions'.[37]

The negotiations became so difficult, and American unhappiness so intense, that Eden put forward an alternative draft treaty making no reference to frontiers but offering Russia a post-war alliance against German aggression: Molotov, after reference to Moscow, accepted this, thereby pleasing the Americans, and departed to Washington.

The alternative treaty omitted not only frontiers but also confederations. Sargent hoped that it might still be possible to persuade Molotov, on his way home to Moscow through London, to agree to a joint Anglo-Soviet statement advocating 'the establishment in suitable cases of regional understandings and confederations between states on the basis of friendly relations towards the U.S.S.R. and Great Britain'.[38] On this Cadogan minuted sceptically: 'even if the Russians *say* this, will they not – if that is their desire – work just as hard against such a policy?'[39] Undaunted, Sargent prepared a detailed paper on confederation in South-East Europe, likely to produce some confusion in the reader. A South-East European federation, he wrote, may be said to offer resistance to Russian influence; the Russians think that it would be directed against their legitimate interests; the confederation would have to rely on Russian good will. But just how this could be done, did not emerge.[40]

Eden did not in fact tackle Molotov, on his way back to Moscow, about confederation. Instead he raised an issue which had just cropped up: the Soviet offer to sign a new treaty with the exiled Yugoslav government, providing for post-war political co-operation. Eden might perhaps have been expected to welcome this. Since November 1941 he had been trying to persuade the Soviet government to help Britain stop the feud between the Yugoslav Communist Partisans and the leader backed by the exiled government and by Britain, Dragoljub Mihajlović. He had totally failed. Better relations between the exiled government and Russia might be expected to help matters.

But Eden did not like the idea of Moscow concluding a series of post-war treaties with the South-East European countries; perhaps he correctly sensed that this was the Soviet riposte to the British plan for confederations, just as in the early post-war period it was Stalin's answer to Tito's dreams of a South-East European federation. So Eden proposed to Molotov on 9 June that both Britain and the Soviet Union should refrain from concluding treaties covering the post-war period with 'the lesser allies'; he did not want 'a treaty-making race', but a 'self-denying ordinance'. Molotov seemed rather puzzled and put out; but he eventually agreed to report to Moscow that Eden wanted an understanding that Britain and the Soviet Union would agree between themselves before they concluded a treaty with any of the lesser allies.[41] On 14 July – according to the British record – Maisky said his government agreed with Eden's proposal.[42]

So no new Soviet–Yugoslav treaty was signed. But also in July Communist propaganda organs started publicising the supposed treasonable activities of Mihajlović and soon after the Russians gave the exiled Yugoslav government – and also the British – a sort of charge sheet against him. Relations between Russia and the exiled government were maintained but became increasingly bitter.

In September 1942 the Foreign Office took a fresh look at confederation. One official described the policy as irritating Russia to no useful
purpose.[43] The general conclusion seemed to be that Britain was
publicly committed to support confederations and so could not well
discard the policy, but the Americans should be restrained from showing undue enthusiasm for it. The Soviet ambassador to the exiled
governments went on working against it. Sargent minuted in January
1943: 'so long as we make no move the Soviet government, or at any
rate M. Bogomolov, will continue without interruption to undo all the
work which has been done in the last two years in the matter of preparing the ground for future confederations in Eastern Europe'.[44]

At the beginning of 1943 there was a fresh discussion inside the
Foreign Office about relations with Russia over South-East Europe,
sparked off mainly by the growing crisis over Mihajlović and his feud
with the Communist Partisans, and the Soviet refusal to intervene.
Douglas Howard[45] minuted: '... the obvious and easiest solution would
of course be that we and the Americans by an invasion of the Balkans
should be on the spot and in a position to police that part of the world
and thus prevent ... Communist risings'. But Christopher Warner,[46] in
the Northern Department, dealing with the Soviet Union, minuted:
'... our only chance of preventing the Balkans from falling completely
under Russian control will be by securing Russian agreement to Anglo-
Russo-American collaboration there.' Sargent wrote: 'I assume that
H.M.G. are definitely opposed to the policy advocated by Professor
[E.H.] Carr in *The Times* that we should tacitly disinterest ourselves
from Central and South-East Europe, and that now and at the peace
settlement we should recognise all this part of Europe as falling within
the exclusive Russian sphere of influence.' Against this, Eden wrote in the
margin the word 'Yes'. 'We must always remember,' Sargent added,
'that even though the Soviet government are as regards the Balkans
in a strong position to dictate their terms ... we also may have a card
or two to play ... (1) the possibility that at the end of the war there will
be British and American armies in the Balkans (2) that Turkey may be
a belligerent ... (3) the fact that we and the Americans will control the
relief organisation which will have to feed the starving population
throughout the Balkans ... '[46]

The outcome was that the new British ambassador in Moscow,
Archibald Clark-Kerr[48] was asked to raise the whole question of 'the
post-war reconstruction of Europe' in Moscow. The results were small.
Molotov did not oppose confederations as such but was 'rather reserved'
about existing schemes. In London, Maisky told Eden on 10 March
that Moscow was 'not enthusiastic' about federations and preferred
a 'bloc of the United Nations' headed by the Soviet Union and
Britain.[49]

Soviet dislike of the whole idea was sharpened by an unfortunate approach which the British made in February 1943 to Turkey about confederation in South-East Europe. They hoped, by discussing the idea with Turkey, to 'bring her out of her shell of neutrality'.[50] This initiative misfired; it made the Turks more rather than less neutral. Taking the bit between their teeth they assumed that the aim was a neutral bloc with an anti-Russian slant, and that they themselves would be founder members; and they approached the three Axis satellites, Rumania, Hungary and Bulgaria about the idea. In the Foreign Office, the Southern Department minuted: 'it is . . . most deceitful of the Turks to go and discuss these matters without telling us . . . If the Russians get to know . . . their suspicions may be justifiably aroused.'[51] It was obvious to diplomats in Ankara that what the Turks wanted was a scheme for building up security against Russia in the future.[52] The British tried belatedly to restrain the Turks, but inevitably the Russians came to know of the affair.[53]

Not surprisingly, on 7 June, Molotov told Clark-Kerr that the Soviet government were 'unwilling to pledge themselves' to federation in Eastern and Central Europe.[54] There could be no doubt that the Russians particularly disliked federation in South-East Europe and that there was little hope of winning them over by diplomatic persuasion. On 1st July Eden put to the Cabinet a memorandum on post-war Europe in which he wrote: 'so far as the Balkans are concerned, we are doing our best to encourage the Greek–Jugoslav confederation, but it is difficult to make much progress . . . while the governments of these countries are exiled and we cannot say what the position will be when the Axis collapses. Much will depend on whether we ourselves are in occupation of that area.'[55]

At that time, the impending Italian collapse made Anglo-American occupation of South-East Europe seem a practical possibility. It was one that roused sharp Soviet interest. Maisky, back in London from Moscow at the end of August, saw Eden and probed him on the prospects of knocking Italy out of the war in 1943; he asked whether the British had given any thought to the possibility of operations in the Balkans. It seemed to him that there would be 'great opportunities' there. Eden replied that it should be possible to organise operations in the Balkans with comparatively small contributions in man-power; a few Commandos might suffice. He urged the Russians to work with the British in the political sphere and agree policies about the Balkan countries.[56] Maisky replied encouragingly, and went on to say that there were two ways of organising Europe after the war – a division into Soviet and Western spheres of influence, each excluding the other, or, 'as his government would greatly prefer', each should admit the right of the others to an interest in all parts of Europe. If the second were accepted, the West would have to understand Russian concern in France and the Mediterranean.[57]

Illogically, Maisky simultaneously complained bitterly about Britain's supposed veto on a Soviet–Czechoslovak treaty much desired by President Eduard Beneš. It was true that Eden had been upset by the projected treaty since he believed that in June 1942 Molotov had agreed to a 'self-denying ordinance' on treaties with lesser allies. This Molotov now denied, saying that there was no such thing, and no provision for it in the Anglo-Soviet treaty.[58] So it looked as though Stalin wanted to have it both ways: Russia was to be free to conduct relations with Central and East European countries as it wished, but there must be the principle of three-power interest in all parts of Europe, giving Russia a right to concern itself with France and the Mediterranean. But this contradiction did not worry the Foreign Office. Oliver Harvey[59] minuted on 15 September that three-power co-operation in all areas of Europe was far preferable to the policy of 'dividing Europe into a Russian East and an Anglo-American West'. If Stalin could be got to agree to the self-denying ordinance, this would be best, but the Soviet–Czechoslovak treaty was not a matter for breaking with Russia. Eden agreed.[60]

Maisky himself may perhaps have believed in three-power co-operation. Dalton, now President of the Board of Trade, saw him in mid-September and asked straight out 'whether the Russians had any objection to British and American troops invading the Balkans; did they regard any part of this as being within the Russian sphere of influence?'. Maisky replied that 'they would be very glad if we invaded the Balkans'; they took the whole of Europe as their sphere of influence and 'hoped we did the same'.[61] When Maisky was passing through Cairo soon after, he told the Minister of State that Russia wanted to see broad-based governments, not excluding Communists, in countries such as Greece, Yugoslavia and Italy: they should be progressive not reactionary.[62]

So far as South-East Europe was concerned, Maisky's words were in line with Soviet propaganda, as observed by the British; it worked consistently for the formation of 'patriotic fronts' or 'liberation fronts' based on an alliance of 'peasants, workers and intellectuals', together with 'patriotic elements' in the bourgeois parties or armed forces. There were Soviet-based and Soviet-controlled freedom stations – Free Yugoslavia, Hristo Botev (Bulgarian), Romania Libera, Kossuth (Hungarian) – all following this line. So it was fairly easy for British propaganda to align itself, roughly speaking, with Soviet propaganda to South-East Europe in encouraging broadly-based anti-German fronts, though the British laid more emphasis on the peasants and the agrarian parties than the Russians did. It seemed reasonable to hope that these war-time 'fronts' might lead at the end of the war to coalition governments, stretching from Communists on the left to anti-German 'bourgeois' politicians, formed with the joint blessing of

Britain and Russia. In retrospect this belief seems naive; at the time it did not.

By the autumn of 1943, it was in any case the only hope. The strategic decisions taken at the Quebec conference had made British or Anglo-American occupation of South-East Europe very unlikely. Eden therefore had a further motive to try to reach agreement with Russia on political co-operation in the area. It was in this spirit that he went to the Moscow conference in October, with a string of proposals designed to achieve this aim in respect of Yugoslavia, Greece, Bulgaria, Hungary and Rumania. But Molotov blocked British proposals on the Axis satellites, apart from a harmless formula calling for mutual consultation on peace feelers.[63] (See p. 208 below.) He fended off Eden's pleas for joint efforts to stop the Mihajlović–Tito feud, but suggested sending a Soviet mission 'to be with the British Mission' with Tito – a suggestion which Eden immediately welcomed; when Eden suggested that Russian officers might also go to Mihajlović, Molotov said he might prefer to have no mission at all than one with each side.[64]

On more general questions, Molotov repudiated the self-denying ordinance, while Eden gave his belated blessing to the Soviet-Czechoslovak treaty. And Molotov finally killed off British plans for confederation with a long statement condemning 'premature and possibly artificial attachment of these countries to theoretically planned groups' by the decision of émigré governments who might be imposing decisions not in conformity with the people's wishes. Moreover, Molotov said, 'some of the plans for federations remind the Soviet people of the policy of the "cordon sanitaire" directed, as is known, against the Soviet Union'.[65]

The Russians also revealed what sort of meaning they gave to the principle of three-power co-operation in all parts of Europe, as advocated by Maisky: they asked for deletion from a British draft of a Four-Power declaration of an undertaking that there would be joint action in all matters relating to 'any occupation of any enemy territory and the liberation of other states held by the enemy'.[66] This seemed to show that Stalin was determined to keep his own hands free to act as he wanted in territory occupied by the Red Army, and that this was more important than trying to shackle the Anglo-Americans in territories they occupied.

THE TURKS REFUSE TO BUDGE ONCE AGAIN

The Turks, at any rate, were perfectly clear about the outcome of the Moscow conference. At Moscow, Eden's pleas for joint efforts to bring Turkey into the war must have faced Stalin with the same kind of dilemma between short-term military interests and long-term political

interests as the British faced in backing Communist-led resistance movements in Greece and Yugoslavia. If Turkey came into the war, Hitler
might be defeated more quickly – but the way might be opened up for
British forces to appear in Bulgaria, even Rumania; and this, in the
long view, Stalin could not want. Stalin's response to Eden was therefore rather wavering, but tactically clever: by insisting on a time-limit
for Turkey's entry into the war – the end of 1943 – he made it virtually
certain that the Turks would refuse. On the other hand Stalin volun-
teered that if Turkey, as a result of coming into the war, were attacked
by Bulgaria, Russia would declare war on Bulgaria.[67]

This pleased Eden; but when, after Moscow, he saw the Turkish
Foreign Minister, Numan Menemenjoglu, in Cairo, and urged Turkey
to come in, Numan showed the utmost suspicion that an 'Anglo-Soviet
deal' had taken place, hinting that 'the Russians had refrained from
insisting on a second front in exchange for a free hand from H.M.G.
with regard to the Balkans'. The Turks, he said, were fearful of a territorial fait accompli in Rumania and Bulgaria, because they did not
wish to see the Russians in the Balkans. Turkey was unable to enter
the war 'without a clarification of the intentions of Russia in the
Balkans'. Eden denied strongly that there had been an Anglo-Soviet
deal, but probably heightened Turkish suspicions by refusing to tell
the Russians that Turkey would not come in without a guarantee from
the Russians about their intentions.[68]

There was complete deadlock, and neither then nor after the Teheran
conference could the Turkish leaders be persuaded to budge. Thereby
Turkey – unintentionally – obstructed British efforts to bring about the
surrender of Bulgaria, Rumania and Hungary before the Red Army
arrived, and so helped to make it quite certain that the Russians would
dominate South-East Europe. On the other hand, Turkey itself survived with its strength intact, capable of enlisting Anglo-American
support in resisting Soviet demands on the Straits in 1945.

THE SOVIET ATTEMPT TO STOP BRITISH PENETRATION
OF SOUTH-EAST EUROPE

At Teheran, Stalin consolidated Molotov's negative position at the
Moscow conference by throwing his weight against British pleas for a
Trieste-Ljubljana Gap-Vienna operation. From then on there were
clear signs of a Soviet policy of checking and curtailing British (and
American) activities in South-East Europe. These may well have seemed
to Stalin more formidable than they really were: 80 British missions in
Greece, Yugoslavia and Albania, all in wireless contact with Cairo;[69]
plans to contact Bulgarian partisans through Serbia; wireless contacts
with important groups in Rumania and Hungary. All this – to Russian
eyes – could look like a British attempt to rob the Soviet Union of the

rightful fruits of victory in South-East Europe. The Russians themselves had their contacts in Bulgaria through their Legation in Sofia,
but did not seem to be making active use of them; whatever contacts
they had with Communists in Rumania and Hungary were for the
moment of little value. Eden was undoubtedly sincere in offering full
information and co-operation to the Russians, with the aim of shortening the war; but he also still hoped that Britain would keep some
post-war influence in South-East Europe, and even a foot-hold in
Rumania. Stalin presumably discounted British offers as Machiavellian
cunning.

The despatch of a Soviet mission to Tito at the beginning of 1944
was probably seen by Stalin as a means of countering British influence
in Yugoslavia. In this matter, Anglo-Soviet relations were outwardly
most friendly, although the Minister responsible for S.O.E., Lord
Selborne, objected strongly to the Soviet mission's out-trumping a British
brigadier with a full Red Army major-general. But the Russians cannot
have been pleased when they heard – after the event – that a British
mission had been dropped into Rumania in late December 1943 (see p.
230 below). Nervous about Soviet displeasure, Eden vetoed the sending
of a British party to Hungary (see pp. 255–6 below). However, the
Russians agreed to use British services in initiating surrender negotiations in Cairo, in March 1944, with Rumanian representatives speaking
for Maniu (see pp. 228–31 below).

It was in April that a crisis blew up in Anglo-Soviet relations. During
the early part of 1944, relations between the British and the Communist-led E.A.M./E.L.A.S. in Greece seemed to be at breaking point.
E.A.M./E.L.A.S. were clearly determined to destroy all possible Greek
rivals and set up a sort of government of their own, the Political Committee of National Liberation (P.E.E.A.), in the mountains. There were
then serious mutinies in the Greek armed forces in the Middle East.
Churchill appealed to Molotov for co-operation. Molotov, in a message
delivered to Churchill at the end of April, complained that the British,
in their efforts to form a broadly-based government, had not taken into
consideration 'the legitimate desires of those Greeks who are the representatives of the Greek national movement'. Molotov added: 'it is
apparent that the British government controls Greek affairs and the
Greek government in the most direct manner. On the other hand you,
of course, understand that the Soviet government cannot accept any
responsibility for Greek affairs or for the measures taken by the British
government.'[70]

Simultaneously Molotov sent Churchill an offensive message about
the British mission dropped into Rumania in December, who had been
captured and held by the Rumanian government and were now being
used by it to transmit messages to the British in Cairo (all of which
were shown to the Russians). This, Molotov said, must mean that there

was 'a definite agreement' between the British and Rumanian governments behind Russia's back.[71] (See p. 234 below.)

This accusation of bad faith stung Churchill to the quick. Eden, to
avoid further trouble with Moscow, put a ban on the dropping of all
missions to Rumania, whether by S.O.E. or other organisations.[72]
Churchill was furious with S.O.E. (in this case, quite unfairly): 'it does
seem to me that S.O.E. barges in in an ignorant manner into all sorts
of delicate situations. They were originally responsible for building up
the nest of cockatrices for E.A.M. in Greece ... It is a very dangerous
thing that the relations of two mighty forces like the British Empire
and the U.S.S.R. should be disturbed by these little pinpricks inter-
changed by obscure persons playing the fool far below the surface.'[73]
Eden, though he did not follow up Churchill's first angry suggestion
that S.O.E. should be 'divided up between the Military and the
Foreign Office' – which was far from novel – was also inclined to try to
lay the blame on S.O.E. His irritation boiled over when Selborne – who
had not been consulted – wrote to Eden about his ban on the dropping
of S.O.E. parties into Rumania. 'It seems to me,' Selborne wrote, 'that
we have been taking too weak a standpoint. S.O.E., at the request of
the F.O., has undertaken the transport of Russian agents into Germany,
Austria, France and Italy[74] and none of these countries can be considered as Russian spheres of influence. We have not questioned whether
the agents we dropped were Communists or what was the purpose of
their missions . . . Why then should we cancel our operational parties
[to Rumania]? . . . I am sure appeasement does not pay, even with
one's best friends.'[75]

Selborne's letter was described by Eden in a Foreign Office minute
as 'gross impertinence'.[76] The accusation of 'appeasement' was
obviously intended to wound; and it was particularly embarrassing to
Eden at a moment when he was trying to reach an understanding with
Russia on spheres of responsibility in South-East Europe.

THE ANGLO-SOVIET PERCENTAGE AGREEMENT

Stung by Soviet hostility over Greece and Rumania, Churchill minuted
to Eden on 4 May: 'evidently we are approaching a show-down with
the Russians.'[77] The next day Eden saw the Soviet ambassador, Feodor
Gusev, and 'casually' mentioned the possibility of some sort of understanding on the problems of Greece and Rumania[78] – as Eden put it
later 'agreeing between ourselves as a practical matter that Rumanian
affairs would be in the main the concern of the Soviet government
while Greek affairs would be in the main our concern, each government
giving the other help in the respective countries'. After a fortnight's
delay Gusev told Eden that Soviet agreement would be dependent on
the prior consent of the United States.[79]

In the light of later events, it seems clear that Stalin knew enough of American thinking to be sure that the Americans would be very unhappy about the idea – as indeed Cordell Hull and to a lesser extent Roosevelt were, to say nothing of other Americans who thought they smelt traces of British imperialist interest-seeking. Eden knew that he might also have difficulties at home, from politicians who thought as Selborne did about 'appeasing' Russia. Probably for this reason, he got the Foreign Office to prepare a paper on Soviet policy in the Balkans which he put to the War Cabinet on 7 June. This set modest aims for Britain: 'to focus our influence in the Balkans by consolidating our position in Greece and Turkey . . . and, while avoiding any direct challenge to Russian influence in Yugoslavia, Albania, Rumania and Bulgaria, to avail ourselves of every opportunity in order to spread British influence in those countries'. This would need 'careful handling . . . to avoid an open contest with the Russians . . . but in the long run it might be effective inasmuch as there are elements in those countries which will be frightened of Russian domination and anxious to reinsure with Great Britain. This, indeed, probably applies to General Tito himself . . .'[80]

Hoping that this cautious policy statement would disarm critics, Eden pressed ahead. In mid-June Roosevelt told Churchill that he agreed to the proposal on a three months' trial basis; the War Cabinet noted this 'with satisfaction' and invited Eden to tell the Soviet government.[81] But at this point Stalin decided to approach the Americans directly,[82] thereby eliciting such an unhappy and ambiguous memorandum from the State Department, deploring any suggestion of 'spheres of influence',[83] that neither Churchill nor Eden could interpret it clearly, and Stalin had an excellent excuse for further delay.

The Russians used this delay to good effect. During the summer, the Red Army remained static on Rumania's 1941 frontier, exercising a heavy threat while the internal situation evolved: the 'bourgeois' opposition parties and the King were induced to accept the Communists as allies in a group prepared to take over power at the right moment. In Bulgaria, from March onwards, Russia exerted increasingly heavy diplomatic pressure so as to bring about a steady shift of power away from pro-German elements, first to pro-Western politicians and ultimately to the pro-Soviet Fatherland Front. Hungary had been occupied by German troops in March, and since then contacts with the Anglo-Americans had been interrupted, so Russia had little to fear. In Yugoslavia the Russians had not brought Tito under full control, but they were working to create suspicions of the British – as for instance when Stalin warned Milovan Djilas in Moscow that the British might try to assassinate Tito as (he alleged) they had killed the Polish General Sikorski; this, Djilas wrote later, was probably the reason why Tito did not tell the British before flying secretly to Russia in September 1944.[84]

Greece remained a question-mark for the Russians. They did not know the value of E.A.M./E.L.A.S. Presumably to settle this question a Soviet mission of eight officers, after misleading the British, arrived at a S.O.E. landing ground in E.A.M./E.L.A.S. territory on the night of 25–26 July. This was alarming in itself for the British, and the timing was particularly awkward because on 27 July Eden, answering a parliamentary question on Greece, made it clear that the British government might feel bound at some later date, in view of the 'continued intransigeant attitude' of E.A.M., to cut off supplies to E.L.A.S. and to withdraw British missions. Cadogan minuted that 'the presence of a Soviet mission at E.L.A.S. H.Q. can only encourage the latter to remain intransigeant'. Eden himself minuted: 'on the face of it this may be a Russian attempt to complete Communist domination of the Balkans and I think we should make it pretty plain that we are not standing for it in Greece'.[85] To Gusev, Eden expressed pained surprise. The Chiefs of Staff said on 3 August that this 'attempt by the Russians to build up E.A.M. means that probably 80,000 rather than 10,000 British troops would have to be sent to Greece'.[86]

A few days later, the Russians infiltrated a small mission to the Communist Partisans in Albania; once again Eden expressed pained surprise to the Russians.[87] To Churchill, he commented: 'unheralded despatch of this mission following on despatch of Soviet mission to E.L.A.S. smells of a Russian attempt to communize the Balkans under our noses.'[88] But when Molotov saw Clark-Kerr on 21 August, he played down the whole affair: there had been no Soviet-British agreement on prior consultation and no agreement about Greece; the journey of the officers was 'so trifling a matter' that it hardly called for a decision by his government.[89]

Information from Greece suggested that the arrival of the Soviet mission had not increased the militancy of E.L.A.S. The head of the British mission, Col. C. M. Woodhouse, thought its leader, Col. Gregory Popov, was unimpressed by E.L.A.S.'s fighting qualities,[90] and a few days after Popov visited E.A.M./E.L.A.S.'s political organ, the P.E.E.A.,[91] this body, which had been holding out stubbornly for seven seats in a British-sponsored Government of National Unity, suddenly agreed to make do with five. The government, under George Papandreou, was then successfully formed on 2 September. So it was arguable that the Russians were acting in the spirit of the understanding proposed by Eden in May.

The Russians, at this moment, had plenty on their own plate. On 20 August the Red Army advanced into Rumania; on 23 August King Michael carried out his coup taking his country over to the side of Russia and the western allies. (See pp. 239–41 below.) He thereby cut short the delays of the Rumanian politicians who had been hoping against hope for some form of Anglo-American military presence at the moment of changing sides as a counterweight to the Russians. This hope quickly vanished. The Cairo surrender negotiations were closed down by Russian wish and transferred to Moscow with the Soviet government playing the leading role.

Meanwhile King Michael's coup had opened the way for the Red Army to move not only against Hungary but also into Bulgaria, where, after a last-minute Soviet declaration of war, the pro-Soviet Fatherland Front took power.

To the British this brought immediate fears of a Red Army or Bulgarian move into Greek Thrace, in line with the territorial promises which Sobolev had made in Sofia in November 1940. Churchill, by now obsessed with the need to safeguard Greece, was willing to make concessions over Bulgaria. During the Quebec conference, Eden telegraphed to the Foreign Office, speaking for Churchill and himself, criticising Soviet 'pretensions and manoeuvres' in Bulgaria, but adding (inaccurately): 'we have always recognised that it is for the Soviet Union to take the lead in Bulgaria provided that they recognise that H.M.G. should take the lead in Greece'. This should be reflected in the Bulgarian armistice terms: there could be a Soviet Chairman of the Control Commission, though the British should be 'full members'. As for the other side of the bargain, Eden wrote, 'we would have to be assured that the Soviet Union recognises the predominant position of H.M.G. in all arrangements for Greece now and after the actual state of war has ended'. (So much for the British assurance to the Americans that any such arrangement over Greece and Rumania would be a temporary war-time affair; Eden admitted that the State Department would probably object.) As for Yugoslavia, Eden telegraphed, 'we should require the Soviet government to agree that . . . there should be close consultation between us and that it is our common interest that Jugoslavia should be a strong, united, independent and democratic state'.[92]

In this telegram Eden, under Churchill's influence, was willing to throw Bulgaria as well as Rumania to the Russian wolves in order to save Greece. But when he came back to London, he changed under pressure from his own senior officials. He telegraphed to Churchill on 19 September:

> I find that there is considerable objection to the proposal . . . that the Soviet Union should take the lead in Bulgaria . . . On reflection, I should be reluctant to offer such a bargain over Bulgaria. We can afford to allow Russians to play a predominant part in Rumania . . . but if we were to abandon . . . Bulgaria, which borders on Greece, Yugoslavia and Turkey and is a threat to all of them, our credit would suffer throughout the Balkans . . . We must of course stake our claim to a predominant position in Greece, but we can do this without selling out over Bulgaria.[93]

Eden followed this up with tough bargaining with Russia over the Bulgarian armistice terms and the Control Commission. But on 6 October he had to report to Churchill that there was deadlock: 'for the purposes of prestige alone . . . we have insisted on equal part in the control of Bulgaria. If we give way it will be represented as abdication on our part.' The British might, Eden said, sign a separate armistice with Bulgaria; but then 'we should be in the impossible position of being unable to enforce any terms, as we should have no troops on the spot'. So the only thing was for Eden and Churchill to raise the matter on their coming Moscow visit.[94]

Meanwhile Clark-Kerr had been instructed on 21 September to tell the Russians that a British force was about to be sent to Greece; he was also to recall Britain's special interest in Greece and say it was hoped that 'the Soviet government would not find it necessary to send Russian troops into any part of Greece except in agreement with H.M.G.' Two days later, rather surprisingly, Vyshinski said that the Soviet government 'confirmed' the agreement of May 1944 about theatres of operations, and had no intention of sending forces to Greece.[95]

So when Churchill and Eden reached Moscow in October 1944, they still hoped faintly for an understanding with Stalin on South-East Europe. Yet by this time, the Red Army advances had created a situation which in military terms Britain could do nothing to contest: quite apart from Rumania and Bulgaria, the Russians were in eastern Yugoslavia and had reached an agreement with Tito in Moscow (of which the British were not informed until 10 October);[96] they were fighting in eastern Hungary and a Hungarian delegation was about to sign an armistice in Moscow. In southern Greece, a very small British force was trying to establish a secure base for the Papendreou government.

Militarily, therefore, the position in South-East Europe was hopelessly unequal. In the Anglo-Soviet talks, Churchill tried to restore some sort of balance, with his half-sheet of paper setting out percentages for 'predominance' for the Russians and 'the others': 90–10 in Rumania, 10–90 in Greece, 50–50 in Yugoslavia, 50–50 in Hungary, 75–25 in Bulgaria. Stalin, after a glance, ticked the half-sheet with blue pencil. From Churchill's own account, he clearly realised the long-term significance of the deal, asking Stalin whether it might not be thought rather cynical 'if it seemed we disposed of these issues, so fateful to millions of people, in such an off-hand manner'? Stalin was not worried.[97]

Explaining his motives, Churchill wrote two days later to Stalin of these percentages:

They might . . . be a good guide for the conduct of our affairs . . .
We shall perhaps prevent several civil wars and much bloodshed and
strife in the small countries concerned . . . We certainly do not wish

to force on any Balkan state monarchic or republican institutions. We have however established certain relations of faithfulness with the kings of Greece and Jugoslavia . . . We are very glad that you have declared yourselves against trying to change by force or by Communist propaganda the established systems in the various Balkan countries. Let them work out their own fortune in the years ahead.[98]

To the War Cabinet at home, he played down the importance of the matter: 'the system of percentages . . . is not intended to be more than a guide, and of course in no way commits the United States, nor does it attempt to set up a rigid system of spheres of interest . . .'[99]

How hopeful Churchill really was about the long-term effects of the percentage agreement cannot be known. Molotov quickly tried to beat down Eden, in haggling over the Bulgarian and Hungarian armistices, to get him to alter the figures to Russia's advantage, proposing 75 to 25 for Hungary, 90 to 10 for Bulgaria and 60 to 40 for Yugoslavia. Eden stood firm on Yugoslavia and Bulgaria, saying the British 'must insist on having a greater position' in Bulgaria than Rumania. Molotov said he would refer to Stalin and the argument tailed off inconclusively.[100] The Foreign Office were worried that, on the basis of the percentages, Eden was yielding too much over the armistices.[101] Eden replied: 'as it now appears that the Soviet government intend to maintain forces in Bulgaria so long as the Control Commission operates, and as neither we nor the Americans are in a position to send troops to the country, I fear we must simply accept the realities of the situation, however disagreeable'.[102]

In practice, the British and American elements of the Control Commissions in Bulgaria and Rumania – and later Hungary – soon found themselves with small influence and no power. In April 1945 Churchill wrote to Stalin: 'we have given repeated instructions that your interest in Rumania and Bulgaria is to be recognized as predominant. We cannot however be excluded altogether . . .'[103] But there was no force behind such complaints.

As for Yugoslavia, in December 1944 Churchill appealed to the percentage agreement when some of Tito's commanders raised unexpected difficulties about British activities on the Adriatic coast intended to help Tito's military effort. In a personal message to Tito, sent also to Stalin, he recalled the Anglo-Soviet arrangement 'to pursue as far as possible a joint policy towards Yugoslavia', with their influence 'held on equal balance'. Tito's reply was conciliatory but he made no reference to this Anglo-Soviet 'arrangement'.[104] The British hoped that 'fifty-fifty' might be applied in practical terms by leaving the Russians to supply the Yugoslav army while the British would be responsible for the navy and air force.[105] But Yugoslav–British relations deteriorated rapidly in 1945, especially over Trieste. In June 1945 Churchill wrote to Stalin: 'our joint idea at the Kremlin in October was that the Yugo-slav business should work out around 50–50 Russian and British influ-ence. In fact it is at present more like 90–10 and even in that poor 10 we have been subjected to violent pressure by Marshal Tito.'[106]

The one country where the percentage agreement seemed effective – for a time – was Greece. Churchill wrote to Eden on 7 November: 'having paid the price we have to Russia for freedom of action in Greece, we should not hesitate to use British troops to support the Royal Hellenic government.'[107] When fighting broke out in Athens in Decem-ber 1944 between the British and E.A.M./E.L.A.S., the Russians – so the British believed – refrained from interference. The Foreign Office tele-graphed to Washington on 6 December complaining of an official U.S. statement criticising British policy in Greece: 'we find the American attitude all the more wounding in that Soviet government have so far scrupulously abstained from any similar conduct or comment.'[108] According to Harold Macmillan, then in Athens, the American ambas-sador, Lincoln MacVeagh, refused to allow British soldiers to use his well, although he drew British rations, for fear of compromising his neutrality.[109] The O.S.S., which had earlier taken an anti-E.A.M. stand, had now become very critical of British policy.[110]

Popov, the head of the Soviet mission, now in Athens, was seen to go round photographing in areas where fighting was going on, 'to the embarrassment of the British forces'; but this was not regarded as proving interference.[111] Earlier, Papandreou had told the British that the Greek Communist leaders were disappointed by the Soviet govern-ment's lack of interest in them.[112] The non-Communist though pro-E.A.M. Greek Col. Euripides Bakirdzis said in December that there was definite proof that the Soviet Union had supplied no financial aid.[113] On 16 December Eden telegraphed to Moscow that he had the impres-sion that the Soviet press was showing considerable restraint, though with some bias towards E.A.M., and was genuinely trying to give the views of both sides: Clark-Kerr, if he agreed, was to convey to Molotov Eden's appreciation of the Soviet government's action in this respect.[114] Four months later, when relations with Stalin were badly strained, Churchill wrote to him: 'I recognize the consideration which you gave me when we had to intervene with heavy armed forces to quell the E.A.M./E.L.A.S. attack upon the centre of government in Athens.'[115]

It is hard to tell how far Soviet restraint was due to respect for the percentage agreement, or to disillusionment with E.A.M./E.L.A.S. – or even to fears of trouble in Rumania and Bulgaria, over which British restraint would be useful.

One thing is clear. It is wrong to think that by concluding the per-centage agreement Churchill 'abandoned' or 'handed over' South-East Europe, except Greece, to Russia. The Red Army was already in military control of Bulgaria and Rumania and parts of Yugoslavia and Hungary before he concluded it on 9 October 1944. The agreement merely formalised an already existing situation, except that the original percentages, in so far as they had a meaning, under-stated actual Soviet predominance.

Britain and the Resistance
Movements of Yugoslavia
and Greece, 1941-5

The story of British policy – or policies – towards the various resistance
movements or groups in Yugoslavia, Greece and Albania seemed a
matter of muddle and inconsistency and conflict. Yet, in the light of
overall war strategy and the development of Anglo-Soviet relations, it
had its own logic and even inevitability.

From the strategic standpoint, British requirements of the resistance
movements changed during the course of the war. After the fall of
France, the planners attached very great importance to building up
resistance organisations in occupied Europe, less for short-term operational purposes than for the preparation of ultimate grand national
uprisings, planned and timed to coincide with the arrival of Allied
liberating forces; the British would give the order when the moment
was ripe, and would be in overall command.[1] This policy had the
advantage that for the time being it required the British to give only
minimum arms and equipment to the resistance movements; and until
the late summer of 1943 they were physically incapable of sending more
than very small quantities to South-East Europe. That was why in
March 1943 Churchill, though calling Mihajlović's anti-British attitude
'intolerable', added: 'it is not much use preaching to the "toad beneath
the harrow". We must not forget the very little help we can give.'[2] As
late as June 1943 Selborne told Churchill that there were only four old
Liberators 'on their last legs' available to S.O.E. for work in the
Balkans; the Halifaxes could not carry a useful load for more than 1,000
miles.[3]

But there were also serious disadvantages to any such policy towards
the resistance movements, especially in Yugoslavia. If the resistance
forces were expected to do nothing but prepare and wait patiently for
the great day of liberation, how were they to keep up their fighting
spirit and avoid a lapse into inactivity and demoralisation? And if the
British could not supply arms, how could they keep any hold over the
resistance forces? These were problems of which S.O.E. were more
aware than the military planners; and their answer to the first ques-

tion was to try to carry on the work which had been attempted before the Germans overran South-East Europe – sabotage of economic resources and lines of communication. At the end of 1941 Gladwyn Jebb, on behalf of S.O.E., disagreed flatly with the exiled Yugoslav government's condemnation of the Communist Partisans' sabotage activities in Serbia, 'more especially as such sabotage is directed against the Belgrade–Nish railway and the industrial area of the Kragujevac-Kraljevo-Kruševac triangle'.[4] Yet although in Greece, which was far more geographically accessible, S.O.E. were able to get the resistance forces to co-operate in sabotage, in Yugoslavia they failed with Mihajlović. Because they could not send him arms, they had very little influence over him; by the time they were able to send arms, their relationship with him was already wrecked beyond hope of repair.

During 1943 the British military planners came to have a new use for the resistance forces – that they should give immediate help by drawing off and holding down enemy forces which might otherwise be used in more important theatres: this they could do either by local military operations or by playing a role, whether consciously or unconsciously, in carefully planned exercises in strategic deception. This new conception of the role of the resistance organisations grew partly out of the overall development of war strategy, but partly too out of the unexpected potentialities which certain of the resistance organisations had shown themselves to possess. The new role required a new sort of relationship – a more equal partnership – between the British and the resistance leaders. Since the most powerful of these leaders were Communists, the relationship was bound to be particularly delicate.

Inevitably, the political problems of the relationship became acute. The Foreign Office had been aware of these problems from the end of 1941 but would have thought it inappropriate to press them strongly at a time when victory over Hitler still seemed remote. But from mid-1943 on, they began to urge on the military planners, and on S.O.E., the importance of taking account of Britain's post-war interests; and during 1944 they thought it right to stress, in the War Cabinet and elsewhere, what they saw as the Soviet threat to South-East Europe.

What might have been expected in such circumstances would have been a clash between the Foreign Office and the military – the Chiefs of Staff or the Commanders in the Mediterranean. Such clashes did in fact happen, but in an atmosphere of outward mutual respect and courtesy. When the two sides felt bitterness or anger, they turned them against a third party, S.O.E., which sometimes found itself violently attacked by both sumultaneously – mainly, though not solely, because, in its operations in the field, it had failed to solve the quite insoluble contradictions between Foreign Office policy and military policy.

S.O.E. was not however an entirely innocent scapegoat. As a temporary wartime organisation, it had to fight for survival and defend its interests against the well-established organisations, and to do this it was ready to use unorthodox weapons. These inevitably included the exaggeration of its achievements and the suppression of information. S.O.E. was also weakened in its relations with other organisations by its own internal upheavals, purges and periodic reorganisations, particularly at the Cairo end. Then too individual S.O.E. officers inside occupied South-East Europe inevitably tended to identify themselves with the particular resistance movement to which they were attached, so that there were conflicts of evidence between them. When S.O.E., in Cairo or London, tried to iron out these conflicts in their own 'appreciations' or 'situation reports', the results were sometimes bewildering and aroused suspicion. At a higher level, Lord Selborne, as Minister of Economic Warfare from 1942 on, was often visibly at loggerheads with his own senior officials, both in London and Cairo: he was a staunch anti-Communist and fervent champion of the Greek and Yugoslav kings at a time when S.O.E. in the field was strongly backing Communist-led resistance forces. In June 1943 when S.O.E. Cairo had lost patience with Mihajlović and were urging active support to Tito's Partisans, Selborne wrote to Churchill: 'my sympathy is definitely with Mihajlović, who kept the flag flying since 1941.'[5] The result was that, especially over the Greek king, some S.O.E. executives used highly unorthodox methods (to say the least) to counter their own Minister's views.[6]

These things made it easy for periodic onslaughters to be launched on S.O.E. – with the Foreign Office in the lead – with the aim of abolishing it and carving up the remains between the Foreign Office and the military. Even after S.O.E. had survived, with some loss of power, the most dangerous of these onslaughts in the autumn of 1943, the Foreign Office did not give up hope. When in February 1944, Sargent wanted to exclude S.O.E. totally from the Rumanian surrender talks, Cadogan minuted: 'I sympathize . . . but until we come to the point where Sir O. Sargent is prepared to put up a case for root and branch abolition of S.O.E. – and win it – I am not sure that the national interest will be served by slamming the door on them.'[7] And in May 1944 Churchill himself, infuriated by Molotov's gad-fly stings, returned to the idea of carving up S.O.E. Eden did not think the time ripe for this, but referred to Selborne and S.O.E. in a Foreign Office minute as 'this chip of the old blockhead and his disorderly crew'.[8]

Some of the bitterness between the Foreign Office and S.O.E. could be traced back to the first eighteen months of the war, when there was the inevitable clash between diplomats trying to cultivate good relations with 'friendly' neutral governments and the organisers of sabotage. (See p. 28 above.) As a hang-over from this period, it became instinctive for the Foreign Office to accuse S.O.E. of political bungling and deceit, and for S.O.E. to lay the blame for their failures on Foreign

Office obstruction. In June 1940 Dalton wrote to Hankey that as regards Rumanian oil 'we must pin our hopes on wreckage, deeply regretting that the gentlemen have already missed dozens of catches while the gangsters have been piling up the score; it is surely high time to cease being gentlemen, to become professionals, and to do a little body-line bowling at the Hun' – a view which Hankey shared.[9] It was perhaps partly because of this robust spirit of Dalton's that Churchill decided to give to him, rather than to the Director of Military Intelligence, responsibility for S.O.E. in July 1940 – in which capacity Dalton continued to campaign against the 'gentlemen' of the F.O. (Another possible factor in Churchill's choice was the belief that British efforts at subversion would rely heavily on left-wing elements in the German-dominated countries, and that a Labour politician would therefore fit the job.)[10]

So long as the mild Halifax was Foreign Secretary, Dalton's relations with the Foreign Office were passable. When Eden succeeded Halifax, the relationship became tense. There was obvious personal rivalry over the Belgrade coup of March 1941: both men had sent messages to Belgrade urging action; Eden, then in the Middle East, had less chance of claiming credit for the coup, when it happened, than Dalton did in London. As Dalton recorded in his diary, 'it is clear that our chaps have done their part well . . . The money we have spent on the Serb Peasant Party and other opposition parties has given wonderful value . . .'[11] Churchill instructed Ismay[12] to write to Dalton that 'it was a source of great satisfaction that the careful patient work of your people had reaped such a rich reward' and to convey cordial congratulations to all concerned.[13] Yet, as was clearly shown by a letter of 28 March from W. S. Bailey of S.O.E., formerly in Belgrade, then in Istanbul, S.O.E. had at least to share the credit with others: 'I feel very strongly,' Bailey wrote, 'that although the action immediately preceding the coup d'état may have been directed by others, the necessary preliminary conditions were established largely through the work of the S.O.2 [S.O.E.] staff in Belgrade during the past six months.'[14]

In these circumstances, Dalton's claims about the coup may well have seemed exaggerated to his rivals, or to those who suspected S.O.E. Matters were made worse when Churchill and Eden refused to accept Dalton's original estimate that the Danube had been blocked for three months by S.O.E.-instigated sabotage (see p. 39 above), and so – to Dalton's indignation – made no mention of it in a House of Commons debate early in May 1941.[15]

All this made for growing friction between Eden and Dalton. In early July 1941 Dalton heard that Eden had made 'a great harangue' to Cadogan complaining that Dalton 'interfered too much in foreign policy': 'am I Foreign Secretary or am I not?' Dalton then recorded in his diary: 'my relations with A.E. being for the moment suspended, I am not sending in various papers I otherwise would'.[16] Dalton tried to melt the ice of his relations with Eden with 'a little artificial sunlight' and then sent him the papers he had been holding up – notably an important report on the Belgrade coup and sabotage on the Danube.[17] But soon fresh trouble blew up over efforts in which Eden played a big part to detach propaganda to enemy and enemy-occupied countries from Dalton and S.O.E. and to place it under a newly-created Political Warfare Executive responsible to no less than three Ministers – of whom Eden was in practice the most powerful. This move led to further upheavals inside S.O.E., and the personal ill-feeling between Eden and Dalton must have influenced Churchill's decision to replace Dalton as Minister of Economic Warfare, in the spring of 1942, by Selborne, who thereby took over responsibility for S.O.E.

At first this change pleased Eden. But Selborne quickly developed a stubborn loyalty to S.O.E., and sent Churchill a report on its virtues 'to refute unjust and untrue rumours that were militating against S.O.E. receiving the confidence of other departments with whom it had to work'.[18] Thereafter, even though Selborne shared – in uncomfortably militant form – Foreign Office views on the need to back the Greek and Yugoslav kings and to keep the Communists and Russians in check, there was constant friction between him and Eden over S.O.E., with Eden accusing Selborne and S.O.E. of withholding information and Selborne pressing the charge he made against Eden in May 1944 (see p. 40 above) of 'appeasing' the Russians.

Yet another source of inter-departmental friction was the mistrust felt by the permanent Secret Intelligence Service about S.O.E.'s discretion, security and judgment. This meant that S.O.E. was at times starved of information which might have influenced its policies. There was obvious ill-feeling between the two organisations at higher levels, even if there were often (not always) good personal relations between indivduals in the field. S.O.E. also seems either to have been starved of information derived from intercepts of enemy communications, or else to have failed to channel this information to the right quarters at all times. As early as the autumn of 1941 complaints reached Dalton on this point.[19] Intercepts disclosing the activities of the Yugoslav Partisans seem to have been available to the War Office from 1941 onwards,[20] but not to S.O.E. Cairo until the autumn of 1942, and not to responsible officers in S.O.E. London as late as the spring of 1943.[21]

Personal antagonisms at the top and inter-departmental ill-feeling lower down made it still more difficult to reconcile the conflicting British requirements of obtaining the most efficient possible resistance effort in South-East Europe – which meant backing Communist-led resistance organisations – and securing British post-war interests – which, it was thought, meant backing exiled kings and anti-Communist resistance groups.

GREECE AND YUGOSLAVIA: THE FIRST CONTACTS

Towards both Greece and Yugoslavia, when they fell under Axis occupation in April 1941, the British government had certain moral obligations; in both, S.O.E. had certain contacts. In Yugoslavia, King Peter's

MAP 5. The Dismemberment of Yugoslavia, 1941

part in the Belgrade coup had been entirely passive, yet he had been made its figure-head, and both Churchill and Eden felt a sort of protective obligation to the 18-year-old boy, which persisted even when it became clear that he was changeable, unstable, and easily swayed by every outside influence. They felt little obligation of Simović who, though nominal leader of the coup, obviously lacked political grasp and authority. The government formed after the coup, which later came to London, was composed mainly of politicians from the traditional political parties, Serb, Croat Peasant and Slovene Clerical, who were so engrossed in their traditional quarrels and feuds that they soon lost the respect and interest of the British, who from the end of 1942 showed little sense of obligation towards them. At times the Foreign Office despaired of bringing Serbs and Croats together in a re-created Yugoslavia, and thought that one of the advantages of a Balkan confederation might be to provide a structure which Serbia, Croatia and Slovenia could join as independent units.[22]

As for S.O.E.'s contacts, the Serb Peasant Party played a relatively small part, though Tupanjanin established himself in the Middle East as a strongly anti-Communist, pro-Mihajlović element, while Gavrilović became absorbed in émigré politics in London. The Narodna Odbrana faded out; some of the Četnik groups, and Ilja Trifunović himself, quickly drifted into co-operation with the Italians, some too with the Germans, while others regarded themselves as loyal pro-Western royalists, rallying to Mihajlović. Trifunović's friend, Djonović, became an important figure as official representative of the exiled government in Cairo, holding in his hands responsibility for contacts with Serbia, in so far as these were not taken over and handled by S.O.E.[23]

Before the Axis invasion, some S.O.E. representatives in Belgrade – Julian Amery, Alexander Glen and George Taylor – had had personal contacts with Col. Dragoljub Mihajlović, already known as an expert on guerilla warfare, at one stage concerned with planning post-occupational activities;[24] but no joint plans had been made with him.

British relations with the Greeks were from the start rather different. Towards King George II, the British had good reason to feel real obligation for his personal role in the campaigns of 1940–41. As Palairet commented after the death of Metaxas in January 1941: 'this puts a very heavy responsibility upon the King, for H.M. is now obliged himself to take all important decisions in home, foreign and military affairs... There is no doubt that he himself is thoroughly pro-British.'[25] The king on his side was very conscious of the British debt to him. As late as December 1944 he reminded Churchill: 'I did not stop to consider that Greek soldiers would die at the side of your own men in Macedonia and Crete in a military enterprise doomed in advance, nor that Greece would have to suffer the tragedy of occupation. And when, after the German attack, the political leaders faltered and none came forward to assume responsibility, I took that responsibility, acting as my own Prime Minister for some time.'[26]

But from the start the king's character caused some misgivings; so too did his lack of political support. Palairet commented in January

1941: '. . . the King's difficulties are increased by his being by nature reserved and diffident and without great energy of character or power of initiative'; he added that probably slightly more than half the country remained Venizelist.[27] Since the king had banned the Venizelists from political life and even at that moment of national crisis was reluctant to include any in the government, he could hardly hope for broadly based political backing.

The Foreign Office saw this weakness, as did S.O.E., and during 1942 both wanted to get the king to make pronouncements of a democratic and conciliatory kind, in the first place, to promise that Greece would return to constitutional government after the war. This only aroused the King's deepest suspicions. In January the Minister of State in Cairo wrote of the King's 'intense blindness which one might suppose to have been an inheritance from the Stuart family.[28] In March the King told the Director of Naval Intelligence, Admiral Godfrey, that the Foreign Office was 'pro-Republican and anti-himself'; he made similar accusations to personal friends in London.[29] The Southern Department commented that such charges were 'quite absurd': 'this is all the thanks we get for our constant endeavour to "sell the King and Government to the Greeks".'[30]

But if the Foreign Office felt full of injured innocence, they were unwilling to defend S.O.E. against similar allegations. In March the Greek Prime Minister, Tsouderos, sent Eden a report from Cairo, said to show that 'certain British officials are continuing to indulge in political opposition to H.M. the King and ourselves, in a manner that conflicts with the policy laid down by you in this question'.[31] Eden replied discounting the charge, but certain British officials in Cairo were removed from their posts.

The fact was that S.O.E.'s chief contacts in Greece before the occupation had been with Venizelists (see p. 97 above) including Col. Euripides Bakirdzis, who had been purged from the army in 1935 and never reinstated; the Venizelists had their own underground organisation.[32] After the occupation S.O.E. remained in wireless contact with two men known as Prometheus II and Odysseus, and through them and by other means with Venizelists, in particular, Panayiotis Canellopoulos. Although some of these contacts were known to the Greek government, others were not, since they would have been 'not exactly persona grata', seeing that officially S.O.E.'s aim was whole-hearted support of the exiled Greek government.[33]

By the end of 1941, S.O.E. was in contact not only with Venizelists but also with Communists, hoping to induce them to undertake strikes and demonstrations; and by January 1942 'Odysseus' was trying to encourage the formation of 'a Popular Front' of Communists and other leftish groups.[34] At this time S.O.E. became convinced – and convinced the British Command in Cairo – that, to get a united front in Greece, the King must be induced to promise that after the war the Greeks would be free to choose their own form of government. S.O.E. put this to the Foreign Office who, however, were unwilling to push the King too hard, and who also rejected the idea that S.O.E. should 'unofficially' assure the leaders in Greece that Britain would not impose the King by force. At this point Selborne succeeded Dalton, and reversed previous S.O.E. policy on this question – at least for the time being.[35] However, Selborne's ruling seemed to have little effect on S.O.E. Cairo, who thought it a mistake when Canellopoulos, after leaving Greece in early April, entered the exiled government without first getting an assurance on the question of the King's return: they feared this would weaken Canellopoulos's position inside the country.

In fact, the Venizelists inside Greece, not wishing to go against British wishes over the King, drifted into inactivity, so leaving the field open for the Communists, who by the summer of 1942 had created E.A.M., the National Liberation Front. They were also instigating strikes and had been promised and received British financial help from S.O.E. E.A.M. guerillas under Ares Veloukhiotis took the field and were receiving British supplies. The Venizelist Col. Napoleon Zervas had been induced by Prometheus II – and British money – to promise to take the field with a guerilla organisation, E.D.E.S. (the National Republican Greek Association), but did not actually do so until July. In August S.O.E. received a report that E.A.M. was 40,000 strong. By then the E.A.M. Central Committee had been supplied with a British W/T transmitter through Evmaios (also known as Andreas Tsimas), who was to be the closest Communist contact of the British for some time to come. This W/T set was quickly captured by the Germans but the British resumed contact with E.A.M. in October.[36]

Canellopoulos, as the Greek government's Cairo representative, was told a good deal about these S.O.E. contacts, but it is not clear how much the King and Tsouderos knew about them. The King remained suspicious and in August 1942 Tsouderos complained again to the Foreign Office about S.O.E. activities. The Southern Department commented: 'while there is a good deal of heresy-hunting involved, fundamentally Tsouderos has reason to complain (though we are not prepared to admit as much to him).' The Department added that the aim should be to 'ensure harmony between S.O.E., Canellopoulos and Tsouderos, the ideal being complete identity of view on all major questions on the basis of the agreed official policy'.[37] But since official policy was that it was the British government's 'hope' that the King would be 'welcomed back' at the end of the war, such an ideal was plainly unrealistic. However, Selborne called home the reputedly anti-monarchist Ian Pirie of the S.O.E. Greek section in Cairo.[38]

At this point, war developments lessened the weight of Foreign Office views and put S.O.E. in a stronger position. With an eye on the coming North African operation, the Middle East Command asked S.O.E. Cairo for 'the most vigorous immediate action' against enemy lines of communication in Greece. S.O.E. had a chance to prove their worth, and were brilliantly successful. The first British officers, led by Col. Eddie Myers,[39] with Major Christopher Woodhouse[40] as adviser, were dropped in Greece on the night of 30 September; on 24 November, with the help both of Zervas, of E.D.E.S., and of Ares Voloukhiotis, of E.A.M., the Gorgopotamos bridge was blown, so cutting the Salonika–Athens railway and preventing the despatch of Axis reinforcements to North Africa.

S.O.E. Cairo could well feel that their left-wing anti-monarchist contacts had proved their value. Instead of withdrawing the British party, as originally planned, they decided to leave them in Greece. This was a major decision, with obvious political implications. On this, S.O.E. failed to consult the Foreign Office. However, Brigadier Keble of S.O.E. Cairo informed the Middle East Command in early December, writing that 'requests had been received from Greece' that Myers should stay on. 'Myers,' Keble added, 'is already now about to become a Mihajlović of Greece – at any rate a person to be built up.'[41]

YUGOSLAVIA: ORIGINS OF THE MIHAJLOVIĆ LEGEND

Keble's reference to Mihajlović was intended to be flattering to Myers; it was in fact inappropriate. By the end of 1942 the Foreign Office was already disillusioned with Mihajlović and moving towards an attempt to contact the Communist Partisans. While younger S.O.E. officers in Cairo strongly favoured this change of policy, S.O.E. London were strongly opposed.

The disillusionment had come in less than a year from the first British contact with Mihajlović in the autumn of 1941. The British had known much earlier that the exiled Yugoslavs were anxious to contact potential resistance forces. King Peter told a British diplomat early in May 1941 that he was interested in contacting 'troops fighting in the Yugoslav mountains'.[42] From July on there were reports from the neutral press and Moscow about guerilla fighting in western Serbia, Bosnia and Montenegro, sometimes attributed to Communists.[43] By 22 August Simović, as Prime Minister, was getting worried about German reprisals and asked that the British press and radio should be careful not to incite the Yugoslav population to resistance in any way. He wanted a message to be broadcast to Yugoslavia: 'wait till the nightingale sings on the pyramids'.[44] But he also asked Churchill to send a submarine to contact a 'working committee for action' in Split, which had sent out a courier.[45] This committee may perhaps have been linked with Ilya Trifunović, the Narodna Odbrana leader, who might have been expected to play a big part in resistance: Split was later his headquarters.[46] But there is no firm evidence and nothing came of this request.

However, Churchill's interest in Yugoslav resistance was kindled. On 28 August he asked Dalton what contacts S.O.E. had with the guerillas and what he could do to help.[47] Early in September Churchill suggested to the War Cabinet that 'encouraging references about Yugoslavia should be made in the Press ... and we should do everything possible to re-equip Yugoslav forces who were fighting on our side'.[48]

Just at this time, Mihajlović had managed to get through his first wireless message, picked up by the British in Malta. But he had clearly been in earlier contact with the Yugoslav authorities in exile, in particular Djonović, then in Istanbul.[49] British relations with Mihajlović were in fact plagued from start to finish by the fact that the exiled Yugoslavs, through their own channels, were sending different instructions to him from those sent by the British; and in 1942 there was a prolonged wrangle between the Foreign Office, backing the exiled government's demand for their own secret cyphers for communication with Mihajlović, and S.O.E., backed by the S.I.S. and all the intelligence departments, strongly resisting this demand.[50] The demand was finally rejected but the exiled government continued to get their own messages to Mihajlović by various routes. In consequence, Mihajlović never took British requests – even when avowedly supported by his government – at their face value, or paid much heed to them. The British particularly suspected the activities of Major Živan Knežević, who had played an active part in the Belgrade coup of 1941 and who, in London in 1942, dominated the aged Prime Minister Slobodan Jovanović, Simović's successor;[51] they believed that he had sent 'secret communications' to Mihajlović which caused Mihajlović to treat Bill Hudson, the first British officer to reach his headquarters, 'with great reserve, if not suspicion'.[52]

Hudson's mission seemed ill-fated from the start. He was landed by submarine in late September in Montenegro, the home territory of Djonović, along with two Yugoslav officers who had received instructions not known to the British, and who went straight to Mihajlović's headquarters; according to the war diary of Vladimir Dedijer, the Partisan, their arrival 'speeded up the general offensive of Draža Mihajlović's četniks against our forces'.[53] But Hudson, who had at first no specific instructions to join Mihajlović, spent some time with the Partisans in Montenegro before he was ordered to join him. The first messages sent after he arrived were such a confusion of Mihajlović's views and Hudson's that the British disregarded the mention of the Montenegrin Partisans. Eden, Churchill and Dalton – at this time at one with Eden – were only interested in news of Mihajlović and his resistance in Serbia. Yet the real situation in Serbia at this time – as stated six months later by the Serb Fascist leader Dimitrije Ljotić –

was that four-fifths of the country was in the hands of the Communists who held full power in 80 per cent of the communes.[54]

In ignorance of this, the British Chiefs of Staff telegraphed to Cairo on 15 October: 'from our point of view the revolt is premature, but patriots have thrown their caps over the fence and must be supported by all possible means'.[55] By the end of October, Eden was telling the War Cabinet that 'the rebellion in Jugoslavia appeared to be on a considerable scale'. It might however be necessary to do something about the coordinating of communications with the patriot forces, since this was not satisfactory.[56] This was because Simović had just told Eden that he had instructed the insurgents to go slow. In the Foreign Office, the Southern Department minuted that this was disturbing: 'we cannot be sure that the General has the right ideas about the Revolt'.[57]

But this problem did not decrease British enthusiasm. Dalton noted in his diary on 4 November: 'Juggery is on the bill. I am summoned to a nocturnal meeting . . . P.M. in a good mood . . . All possible to be done to help the guerillas'.[58] Mihajlović had already been sent five million dinars by courier 'to finance his operation until such time as further and larger sums can reach him by aircraft'.[59] S.O.E. Cairo estimated that 50,000 gold sovereigns a month would be required.[60]

At this point there was concord between the British and Russians over Yugoslav resistance. S.O.E. apparently told the N.K.V.D. both in Istanbul and in Moscow what the British knew and wanted to do;[61] Eden also discussed matters with the Soviet ambassador, Maisky, who was eager that the British should send maximum aid.

By mid-November, the British were beginning to worry about the Partisans. The first news had arrived of fighting between Mihajlović's četniks and the Partisans. The rather jumbled wireless message disclosing this, purporting to come from Mihajlović, included a passage which must actually have been inserted by Hudson: 'the impressions of an English officer are that the Communists at the head of the Partisans are also opposed to the Axis . . . The četnik leaders say openly that they prefer to collaborate with Nedić rather than the Communists'.[62] General Milan Nedić, sacked by Prince Paul because of his willingness to make concessions to Germany as War Minister,[63] was now head of the German-appointed government of Serbia. This was the first hint reaching London of collaboration between Mihajlović's men and the enemy; no serious notice seems to have been taken.

Another part of the jumbled message, also obviously inserted by Hudson, was: 'Partisans would compromise but Mihajlović believes he holds all the trumps'.[64] Hudson himself seems to have encouraged this belief, reporting a few days later: 'I told him that if both sides turned against the Germans I believed that immediate British aid would be at his disposal, and we could help to establish him as unconditional commander-in-chief.'[65]

This was what the British – both the Foreign Office and S.O.E. – wanted to happen; but first they told Mihajlović that he must settle the dispute with the Partisans and abandon his declared intention of liquidating them;[66] they also asked the Soviet government to urge the Communists to 'put themselves unreservedly at the disposal of Col. Mihajlović as the national leader'.[67] Not surprisingly, the Russians did not respond to this rather sweeping demand. But within a few days there was a message from Mihajlović saying rather vaguely that he had 'ended the internal fighting'.[68] On the strength of this alone, the Foreign Office asked the Soviet government to send a message to the Partisans 'expressing approval of understanding reached with Col. Mihajlović and urging them to maintain united front under his leadership';[69] and Eden told the Cabinet on 27 November that 'the dispute between the two parties taking part in the revolt had now been settled', and that it was of the utmost importance to send supplies.[70] On 1 December the Chief of Air Staff told the Cabinet that 'steps were being taken to send out aircraft to the Mediterranean in order to furnish supplies to the patriots in revolt'.[71]

On this extraordinarily flimsy basis, British relations with the resistance in Yugoslavia were founded. The Mihajlović–Partisan dispute had *not* in fact been settled; the breach between the two sides was complete. Mihajlović himself was in fact no longer fighting Germans, but was in flight, and from then on saw the Partisans, not the Germans, as his chief enemy, or anyhow, the enemy deserving top priority. The promised flow of British supplies did not arrive; contact with Mihajlović through Hudson was lost for several months;[72] and the aircraft were not available. The British therefore found themselves in the rather ridiculous position of publicly backing the physically and morally weaker party in an internal Yugoslav struggle, without the power of supplying the arms which were essential if the weaker party were to succeed.

Nevertheless, when Simović was forced by his colleagues to resign in January 1942, Mihajlović became War Minister in the new government headed by Slobodan Jovanović – an arrangement in which the British acquiesced, though with some slight hesitations.[73] Within a few months, Mihajlović had become a legendary hero of European resistance. This was the work of the Yugoslav government and its officials rather than of British propaganda. The Political Warfare Executive (P.W.E.) directive to the B.B.C. of 14 November 1941 was that Mihajlović should be mentioned as leader of the Yugoslav patriot forces as the occasion arose, 'but do not yet try to star him constantly as the big personality'.[74] On 19 December the P.W.E. directive gave a warning that there was little reliable information about operations in Yugoslavia: 'Mihajlović is probably on the defensive in the hills.'[75] In April 1942 P.W.E. said 'use reports of Mihajlović's operations with extreme care only to show world interest'; in May, 'reports of large scale action by Mihajlović are almost certainly untrue and must be avoided'; and later in the same month, 'Mihajlović's present relations with Communists appear bad'.[76] But at the same time P.W.E. directives consistently called for appeals to Yugoslavs to unite around Mihajlović.

The Mihajlović legend, once launched, grew largely of itself. At a time when there was little good war news, the emergence of the first great resistance leader – as it seemed – was exciting and stimulating, not only to the British but to others too. There was an inevitable tendency for newspaper correspondents and news agencies to attribute any item about Yugoslav resistance to Mihajlović, and this was inevitably reflected by the B.B.C.

But the Foreign Office and S.O.E. knew at least something of the truth. Early in 1942 reports reached London through exiled Slovene and Croat politicians showing clearly that the fighting was in fact being done by the Communists; through the same channels the Foreign Office had received the official Communist account of the abortive negotiations between the Partisans and Mihajlović in the autumn of 1941, and their eventual collapse.[77] But the Foreign Office – and S.O.E. – were almost entirely ignorant about the Yugoslav Communist Party. In April 1942 Douglas Howard[78] of the Southern Department wrote to Professor Arnold Toynbee, then head of the research department: 'we have recently been hearing a great deal about Communist activities in Yugoslavia, and as far as we can make out they are rapidly gaining strength . . . and are taking a leading part in sabotage and resistance to the German and Italian forces. Unfortunately we have very little idea who or what these Communists are . . .'[79] Toynbee was apparently unable to help.

Then in the summer of 1942 the Russians – after side-stepping all British requests for co-operation over Yugoslavia – started publicly attacking Mihajlović for collaborating with Nedić and the Italians, first through the Soviet-based freedom station, *Free Jugoslavia*, then through the Swedish Communist newspaper *Ny Dag*, and finally in a direct communication to the Yugoslav government, of which Maisky gave Eden a copy early in August. (See p. 133 above.) This seems to have arrived simultaneously with secret reports on similar lines. The Foreign Office began a serious review of the policy of all-out support for Mihajlović; Hudson was asked for his views; and his answers, though cryptic, showed that he believed Milhajlović had agreed to collaboration with the Italians and was 'capable of coming to an understanding' with the Germans.[80]

In September General Alexander sent a message asking Mihajlović to attack Axis lines of communication so as to help the Allied offensive in North Africa. Mihajlović replied effusively saying that he was already carrying out 'all possible kinds of sabotage' and would continue to do so; but he did not want anything said about it over the radio.[81] But an S.O.E. 'appreciation on Jugoslavia' of mid-November said: 'the General has reported from time to time sabotage on the railways and in one case the firing of a mine, but these reports, except that of firing the mine, have not been confirmed from any other source, nor is there any evidence to show that even if they were true, they were effected by the forces of General Mihajlović . . . So far no telegrams have been received from either of our liaison officers reporting any sabotage undertaken by General Mihajlović, nor have we received any reports of fighting against the Axis troops.'[82]

In Yugoslavia, therefore, S.O.E. could claim no equivalent to the Gorgopotamos operation in Greece.

From all this it might seem that since the autumn of 1941 the British had – wittingly or unwittingly – been co-operating in a gigantic hoax. But neither the Foreign Office nor S.O.E. saw things in this light. Both still hoped that Mihajlović might be coerced or coaxed into stopping his crusade against the Partisans and attacking the Axis instead, so becoming a respectable resistance leader, truly worthy of both short-term and long-term support. The Foreign Office hoped this, because they did not want to see a Communist régime come to power; S.O.E. hoped it, because they had invested so much of their own energies and prestige in Mihajlović. Both agreed in the autumn of 1942 that a senior liaison officer, Col. W. S. Bailey, should be sent to Mihajlović to carry out the job, by means of stern warnings combined with promises of material and propaganda support if he behaved. They also agreed to start exerting pressure on him straight away by allowing the B.B.C. to begin reporting favourably the activities of the Communist Partisans – though the name 'patriots' was to be used in preference to 'Partisans' (a compromise which satisfied no one). This immediately stung Mihajlović into violent protest – but not into action against the Axis.

In this awkward situation, there was a certain difference between Selborne and Eden. Selborne seemed quite content to stick to the policy of all-out support for Mihajlović, even when some of his own officers in Cairo, on the basis of enemy intercepts, had concluded late in 1942 that the Partisans were the main resistance force; at first their Chief, Brigadier Keble, did not see eye to eye with them, but when Churchill visited Cairo in January 1943 and displayed great concern with Yugoslavia, this completed Keble's conversion to the Partisan cause.[83] In London, however, Selborne went on fighting a long rearguard action against a change of policy and continued to back Mihajlović through thick and thin.

Eden, however, was far more sensitive than Selborne to the danger of appearing in the eyes of the Russians, the British Chiefs of Staff and British public opinion as the champion and defender of a man strongly suspected of collaborating with the enemy – of a man who 'is not fighting our enemies and is being publicly denounced by our Soviet ally', as Eden himself put it at the beginning of 1943, adding: 'I see no sense in such a policy and every likelihood that we and the Russians will come to an open clash.'[84]

But even if Eden did not want to clash openly with the Russians, he was determined not to give them a free hand in Yugoslavia, or to let them take control of the Partisans. It seems that early in 1943, through the N.K.V.D.-S.O.E. network, the Russians asked to send a Soviet party to Tito with British help, but were refused – thereafter complaining when the British themselves sent parties without first telling the Russians.[85] When in February the British Embassy in Moscow suggested that a joint Anglo-Soviet mission should be sent, Eden vetoed the idea, on the grounds that it would 'commit the British' too far.[86] So the British merely 'went through the motions'[87] of asking for Soviet help in contacting Tito, and were not surprised when they were turned down. The N.K.V.D. in Moscow, however, continued to taunt their S.O.E. colleagues about British 'determination to support a man known to be in touch with the Yugoslav Quisling and to be bent on building up his own position', when they might be helping the Partisans who were 'fighting the common enemy with great gallantry'.[88]

Behind all this jockeying for position with the Russians lay a British hope – shared by the Foreign Office and S.O.E. – that it would be possible to send a large enough number of British officers, both to the Partisans and to Mihajlović, to establish British control over all the various forces and eventually 'centralize' them under British direction.[89] Eden, approving this policy, minuted that it was 'clearly desirable' to build up the British position in Yugoslavia as far as possible, since 'a communist Jugoslavia would be a cause of unsettlement to all its neighbours'.[90]

This therefore was the political background to the British decision in the spring of 1943 to contact Tito's Partisans: S.O.E. hoped to acquire operational control of all resistance forces, and to achieve something like the position temporarily created by the National Bands Agreement in Greece, first mooted in April 1943. (See p. 164 below.) The Foreign Office apparently hoped to bring the Partisans under British rather than Russian influence, and to prevent the emergence of a communist Yugoslavia.

At this moment British policies towards Greece and Yugoslavia, starting from very different points, seemed to be converging. In Greece S.O.E. had from the start been in touch with anti-monarchist Venizelists and soon after with Communists, and was poised to use these contacts to develop large-scale guerilla forces; the Foreign Office however was trying hard to bring S.O.E. politically into line with the official British pro-monarchist policy. In Yugoslavia S.O.E. had backed a right-wing monarchist Serbian officer – which was in line with Foreign Office policy – but had been forced to admit him a failure as a resistance leader, and, under pressure from the Foreign Office, was about to extend its contacts to the Communist Partisans, clearly a far stronger resistance force.

1943: POLICIES TOWARDS GREECE AND YUGOSLAVIA DIVERGE

In the summer of 1943, military considerations prevailed without question over political considerations: Mediterranean strategy demanded a real and immediate contribution from the resistance forces of South-East Europe, and for the first time the British acquired the ability to supply these forces with modest quantities of arms. Churchill directed on 23 June that from the end of September deliveries to the Balkans should be stepped up to 500 tons a month. In the last quarter of 1943 the Yugoslav Partisans actually received 113.5 tons by air and 1,857 tons by sea;[91] figures for the other resistance forces are not available.

It was military considerations which tipped the balance in favour of sending military supplies to the Yugoslav Partisans from June onwards, in spite of Foreign Office scruples and reservations. It was Mihajlović's failure to respond to military requirements, and his obstruction of Partisan or British efforts at sabotaging German lines of communication in 'his' territory, that speeded the British decision to drop him, first seriously mooted in November 1943. It was for military reasons that by the end of 1943 British policy was to give all-out support to the Partisans, and, as a political afterthought, to try to bring about an understanding between the King and Tito. As Eden put it to the War Cabinet on 20 December: 'the King should ... go himself to Tito's headquarters and should fight for his people ... We ... should not worry very much ... about the position of Mihajlović or the present Jugoslav government'.[92]

In Greece, military considerations influenced developments, but not decisively. They saved the Communist-led E.A.M./E.L.A.S., in the first half of 1943, from British displeasure at its efforts to destroy all rival resistance groups, and gave it an important role in the highly successful 'Operation Animals' of June–July, designed to mislead the Germans about Allied intentions in the Mediterranean. As Keble of S.O.E. Cairo had informed Myers on 26 February, 'chief object will ... be to divert troops, aircraft (particularly German) and naval craft away from south Italy and Russia to the Balkans'.[93]

In July it seemed that perhaps military and political considerations had been reconciled through the National Bands Agreement, intended to preserve the smaller groups from destruction by E.L.A.S. and bring all formations under the command of G.H.Q. Cairo. But the acute crisis in Cairo in August over the visit of the six Greek resistance delegates (three of them Communist) seemed to destroy hopes for political conciliation. The resistance leaders, sent away from Cairo empty-handed, without any assurance that the King would not force himself on an unwilling people, were angry; the Communists had their chance and civil war followed, with E.A.M./E.L.A.S. trying to mop up all potential rivals in the expected struggle for post-war power. The crisis also led to a combined onslaught on S.O.E. by the Foreign Office and the Middle East Command, which S.O.E. only survived with some difficulty. (See p. 150 above.)

Tensions were heightened not only in Greece but also in Yugoslavia and Albania by the collapse of Italy and the resulting belief that British landings in South-East Europe would follow. There were fresh clashes between Tito's Partisans and Mihajlović's četniks, and a parallel sharpening of hostility between the Albanian Communist Partisans and the Nationalist Balli Kombetar.

Because of the increased military importance of South-East Europe, the British decided to raise the level of their military missions in the three countries, sending Brigadier Fitzroy Maclean to the Yugoslav Partisans, Brigadier C. D. Armstrong to Mihajlović, and Brigadier 'Trotsky' Davies to Albania. Brigadier Myers was expected to return to Greece, but because of the Greek King's hostility and a Foreign Office veto, this did not happen, and Woodhouse took command. At one point all four Brigadiers met in conference in Cairo and arranged to keep each other informed of their progress; but owing to practical difficulties this did not come about.[94]

The need for co-ordinating policies in the three countries was becoming obvious. On 3 October the Minister of State in Cairo, Richard Casey,[95] sent a telegram to Churchill asking for his 'personal views' on the situation in the Balkans. Casey said he realised that Allied troops were *not* going to be available, except on a very minor scale, for the Balkans, so that it would be necessary to rely on stimulating guerilla activities. This, he argued, would mean arming Left-wing guerilla forces to an extent that 'would enable them to dominate their respective countries militarily and so politically as soon as the Germans are thrown out'. There would then be little chance of the monarchy surviving in Greece or Yugoslavia and a considerable chance of Communist governments. This, Casey argued, meant that 'our military policy (to exert the maximum possible pressure on the enemy) and our political policy (to do nothing to jeopardise the return of the monarchies) are fundamentally opposed'. The solution, he suggested, would be to maintain existing pressure on the enemy without any 'formidable building up of the Left-Wing guerillas'; at the same time 'we should endeavour to build up Right-Wing elements by all means in our power'.[96]

Churchill's only immediate reaction was to ask Eden for his views.[97] Before Eden could give his, the Chiefs of Staff had given theirs, in clear-cut terms: on military grounds there should be no relaxation of the effort to contain as many German divisions as possible in Greece and Yugoslavia: 'if by this pressure we should succeed in making things so hot for them that they voluntarily evacuate the Balkan Peninsula, or even the southern portion of it, the military disadvantages which they will incur through the loss of raw materials and prestige will in the view of the Chiefs of Staff more than counterbalance any political troubles which may be imposed upon us'. Churchill initialled this without comment.[98]

Eden thought differently, drawing a firm distinction between Greece and Yugoslavia. He admitted that long-term political interests 'incline us to support the monarchies' while short-term military interests 'oblige us to support the most active elements of resistance, which happen to be Communist'. But, Eden wrote, 'the situation in Jugoslavia is different from that in Greece. In the former there is a Communist army fighting the Germans and Mihajlović husbanding his forces'; British policy was to prevent civil war between the two and unite them in resistance; Casey's remedy was not possible 'since the Communist-led army is of real operational importance to us'. In Greece, on the other hand, the Communist E.A.M. had established power in a large part of the country by terrorist methods and its main object was to set up a Communist dictatorship; 'but E.A.M. is not fighting the Germans as are the Yugoslav guerillas'. The S.O.E. policy of working through E.A.M., Eden added, was 'impossible to harmonize with the Foreign Office policy which is to support the King and Government until their return to Greece when free elections can be held'.

Eden then faced Churchill with the harsh dilemma which he had neatly side-stepped in the case of Yugoslavia: 'if the military value of the Greek guerillas makes it necessary to continue our support of E.A.M., we may have to abandon our policy of support for the King ...' By putting the question in this form, Eden must have known that Churchill's instinct, given his personal sense of obligation, would be to leap to the King's defence. However, Eden probably did not want a head-on collision with the military, so he added that he was going to discuss the matter in Cairo. Churchill then agreed to wait for the outcome.[99]

When Eden got to Cairo he sent Churchill a 'special message of greeting' from the Fourth Hussars, adding: 'am struggling with Greek and Yugoslav problems'.[100] This he did on a purely pragmatic basis.

What was important about Eden's reply to Casey's question was not that it offered any solution to the dilemma, but that it drew a sharp line between Greece and Yugoslavia. He was willing to admit the priority of military considerations in Yugoslavia, but not in the case of Greece.

Eden's differing attitudes to the two countries reflected, in part, the different degrees of British long-term political interest in them, partly, too, the very real differences in the strength of the Greek and Yugoslav resistance forces. In July 1943 the Joint Intelligence Sub-Committee had given a figure for Yugoslavia of 65,000 Partisans and perhaps 20,000 Mihajlović forces; for Greece of around 20,000 guerillas (without distinction between E.L.A.S. and Zervas).[101] In mid-October the Chiefs of Staff received a memorandum from S.O.E. giving a figure of 180,000 men for Tito's forces, organised in six Corps each of three divisions, in effective control of large areas of Yugoslavia and some 20 landing grounds; Mihajlović's forces were still estimated at 20,000. The Greek guerillas were said to number 25,000, and had 'proved their value in a number of successful operations'.[102]

From these figures it was obvious that Tito's forces in Yugoslavia were bound to be a much bigger military factor in Allied strategy than E.L.A.S. in Greece.

The S.O.E. memorandum also gave interesting evidence of the difference in the relationship between the British and the resistance forces in the two countries. In Greece, there were 53 British missions. In Yugoslavia, there were eight missions with Tito, and eleven with Mihajlović.[103] In Greece therefore the degree of British control, leadership and initiative was far bigger than with Tito's forces, which had grown up before the British had contacted them and which guarded their full independence fiercely. When Tito's representative, Svetozar Vukmanović-Tempo, first visited E.L.A.S. headquarters in the summer of 1943, he was deeply shocked by the degree of British influence on E.L.A.S. and the way in which E.L.A.S. allowed British officers to interfere in their internal affairs. He did not however stop the Greeks from signing the National Bands Agreement.[104]

The Yugoslav attitude to the British was also shown by the advice which Tempo gave to the Albanian Communists in 1943: they should receive the British officers, give them information about German and Italian troops, but not allow them access to their own Partisan staffs or allow them to meddle in Albanian internal affairs.[105] The Albanians followed this advice, as is proved by 'Trotsky' Davis's account of their refusal of his offer of British liaison officers to the staffs of three Albanian brigades.[106]

The eleven British missions with Mihajlović had been sent – nearly all during 1943 – in the hope of acquiring influence and control over his local commanders, if not over Mihajlović himself. They singularly failed, largely because Mihajlović was determined that they should, and gave orders accordingly.

In Greece, perhaps the greatest value of E.L.A.S. was to provide the

British with the bases and safe harbours from which they themselves could carry out operations and sabotage. The British missions on their side wielded a very considerable political influence as well as military control, for instance in the negotiation of the National Bands Agreement of July 1943 and the later Plaka agreement of 19 February 1944, ending fighting between E.L.A.S. and Zervas's E.D.E.S. by delimiting areas of operation.

In Greece, therefore, the British attitude was much more paternalistic than it could ever be in Yugoslavia. And at least until the end of 1943, the Foreign Office seemed to believe that the British could make or break E.L.A.S., if this were necessary to bring back the King; they did not believe they could break Tito and by the end of the year had even abandoned Eden's hope of uniting Tito and Mihajlović in a 'common front'. It had become a question of persuading Tito to allow the King to return, not of preventing Tito from coming to power.

1944: CIVIL WAR IN GREECE; THE TITO-ŠUBAŠIĆ AGREEMENT

The events of 1943 had caused British policies towards Greece and Yugoslavia to diverge. In 1944 this trend continued, as was shown by the top secret memorandum which Eden put to the Cabinet, in June, on Soviet policy in the Balkans. Tito, this said, would, 'by his own efforts and our own support', probably emerge as the 'governing force'; but in Greece, Britain would have to 'set about now building up a régime which after the war would definitely look to Great Britain for support against Russian influence'.[107] By the end of 1944 Tito had taken power in liberated Belgrade; in Athens the British had fought a civil war against E.A.M./E.L.A.S. to establish a pro-British government in power. The Greek King had finally been compelled, after very strong British pressure – and after Churchill's own great reluctance had been overcome – to accept the appointment of a Regent, instead of returning to Greece himself.

Before then the British had expended an enormous amount of time, thought, nervous energy and diplomatic activity in the effort to achieve their political aims without sacrificing their military needs. In Greece, solutions considered ranged from a total break with E.A.M./E.L.A.S. and the building up of Zervas as chief resistance leader to the more practical attempt to curb the power of E.A.M./E.L.A.S. on the ground and to bring the E.A.M. leaders into the Greek government. Before a decision had been taken, E.A.M. had set up a sort of government of its own in the mountains – the P.E.E.A. of Political Committee of National Liberation – in mid-March; and this had sparked off mutiny in the Greek forces in the Middle East. It was only then that the King was induced to announce, on 12 April, that Greece should decide by free vote, after liberation, what form of government it desired. Thereafter a former Venizelist, George Papandreou, came to Cairo from Athens and formed a new government which, at the British-sponsored conference in the Lebanon in May, negotiated with P.E.E.A. representatives and other politicians from Greece for formation of a wider government of national unity. The agreement finally reached with the P.E.E.A. representatives was repudiated by the Communists after their return to Greece, and the government could not actually be formed until 2 September. (See p. 142 above.)[108] A few days earlier, Papandreou had met Churchill, who had at last agreed that the King's return to Greece should be delayed until a plebiscite had been held.

Against this political background, relations between the British missions and E.L.A.S. had become increasingly strained during the summer of 1944; nevertheless, in September General Saraphis, the non-Communist commander of E.L.A.S., and Zervas concluded an agreement with the Supreme Commander, Mediterranean, General Maitland Wilson, by which all forces in Greece were placed under the new government of national unity, which in turn placed them under the British General Ronald Scobie, who was to command the small British force of two brigades which was about to land in Greece; and in practice E.L.A.S. did co-operate with the British in harassing the retreating Germans.

Even then, so long as E.L.A.S. and the E.A.M. police in Athens remained armed, and reluctant to give up their arms, the Papandreou government's hold was precarious. In November Churchill began to doubt Papandreou's will to stand up to the Communists, and in a fit of violent irritation wrote to Eden: 'when you think what we have done for them in troops, in operations, in food, in currency and in cash, one begins to ask one's self the question, "are we getting any good out of this old fool at all" and would it not better to let them adjust their political differences in their own way and without our being involved?' He enclosed a draft message from himself to Papandreou: 'as far as I can see from here you seem to be slipping more and more into the grip of E.A.M. and E.L.A.S. . . . Immense pains, trouble and expense have been used by us to get your Government installed in Athens. My agreement with Marshal Stalin has been faithfully maintained by the Soviets. I hope you will arouse yourself before we have to say good-bye and your country slithers into ruin for another decade.'[109]

Eden persuaded Churchill not to send the message, but Papandreou was duly stiffened; and in December the civil war broke out over the question of disarming the E.A.M. police in Athens. The moment this happened, all Churchill's inborn tenacity and obstinacy were aroused; he sternly goaded his representatives in Athens, sent military reinforcements – there were 75,000 British troops in Greece at the end of 1944[110] – and himself flew to Athens, accompanied by Eden, at

Christmas to supervise personally the opening of negotiations with
E.A.M./E.L.A.S. under the presidency of the newly-appointed Regent,
Archbishop Damaskinos (whom, incidentally, he himself had described
only a week before as 'a dictator who may very likely become a champion of the extreme Left').[111]

By the end of 1944 therefore the Papandreou government, and with
it British influence and a British presence, had been securely established
in Athens; the principle of monarchy had been preserved (though it
seems clear that Churchill had made the British task much more difficult than it need have been by his rigid loyalty to George II). Above all,
Greece remained outside the Soviet sphere in post-war Europe – an
outcome which could not have been guaranteed by the Stalin–Churchill
percentage agreement alone.

In Yugoslavia, the idea of a civil war against Tito was unthinkable;
and when early in 1944 the British sent liaison officers to the Partisan
units in Serbia – until then regarded as Mihajlović's private stronghold
– and could see the rapid strides Tito was making there, it became clear
beyond doubt that in practice he would control the whole country at
the end of the war.

How to persuade him to accept back the young King Peter, who had
been so closely linked with Mihajlović, regarded by the Partisans as a
traitor, was a very difficult question. Eden and Churchill agreed that
the attempt must be made – Churchill out of a sentimental fatherly
feeling for the rather helpless and bemused young man, Eden with an
eye on retaining some degree of British influence after the war; but
they disagreed on the method. Churchill wanted to clear the decks by
getting rid of Mihajlović promptly and then appealing personally to
Tito's better feelings; Eden wanted a process of hard political bargaining, retaining Mihajlović as an admittedly rather dubious bargaining
counter.

In February 1944 Eden gave way over Mihajlović and agreed that
a complete break should be made; but he also got Churchill to launch
out on complex political bargaining. This meant that King Peter had
to be bullied into dismissing his existing government – long-withheld
British approval for his marriage to a Greek princess was clearly
intended to sweeten the pill – and into appointing a mild Croat politician whom he did not like, Dr Ivan Šubašić, as Prime Minister, with
the sole task of coming to terms with Tito on the formation of a united
government.

This formula was similar to the Greek Government of National
Unity. But the reality was very different. Tito had a very solid power
base in Yugoslavia which the British could hardly hope to shake,
whereas Šubašić had none and the King – given the disintegration of
Mihajlović's forces after the British abandoned him – had very little.
Churchill's personal influence, exerted through letters and a personal

meeting with Tito in Italy in August, counted for something in the balance, but certainly a good deal less than Stalin's.

Early in 1944 a Soviet mission – as a result of the Eden–Molotov talk in Moscow in October 1943 – had arrived in Yugoslavia, but did not at first make any perceptible difference to Tito's attitude: Maclean wrote to Churchill in March:

> Marshal Tito has, in his reception of the newly arrived Soviet Mission, gone out of his way to emphasize that their status here is to be exactly the same as that of my Mission. Reconstruction and rehabilitation are urgent problems and the Partisans cannot but realise that their country is bound to depend on Great Britain and America not only for material support during the war, but for relief and the means of prosperity after the war . . . there can be no doubt that they have realised the advantages of maintaining good relations with other Great Powers beside the Soviet Union.[112]

Tito told Maclean that Yugoslavia would remain dependent on the Allies after the war: in return for relief he would gladly give Britain economic concessions.[113]

But during the summer of 1944 Soviet influences worked on Tito by one channel or another, and Stalin's tactic was clearly to warn him against coming under British influence or allowing British interference, while at the same time pressing him to compromise with the British over the king. Milovan Djilas's account of his meeting with Stalin in June 1944 makes this quite clear.[114]

Šubašić, the British nominee, was therefore at a serious disadvantage in his dealings with Tito, a subordinate who had to be content with the shadow instead of the substance of shared power. Two minor politicians nominated by Tito were included in the Šubašić government in London; then Tito vanished secretly on his unannounced visit to Moscow, to be followed soon after by Šubašić, after which they drafted an agreement on forming a united government. News of this draft agreement prompted General Maitland Wilson, early in November, to stress strongly the urgency, from an operational point of view, of the earliest possible British recognition of the proposed united government: 'it will be necessary for us to discuss with Tito at an early date future operations in Yugoslavia and it is of the utmost importance that the atmosphere . . . should be as favourable as possible.'[115] The Foreign Office reply was very chilly: the agreement was only a draft and Šubašić was in Moscow.[116]

The united government – in which Šubašić accepted a minor role – was not recognised by the Allies until the spring of 1945. Early in the year King Peter – to Churchill's great irritation, and possibly encouraged by the O.S.S.,[117] put up a last-ditch stand over the composition of the Regency council, a temporary face-saving device until the monarchy could be formally abolished, as it was in November 1945. Churchill beat down Peter's resistance somewhat brutally.

In the closing phase of the war the personally friendly relationship which Churchill had hoped to establish with Tito crumbled away as a head-on confrontation developed between Tito's forces and Field-Marshal Alexander's over Trieste. There was a moment of crisis when it seemed possible that Alexander might have to drive the Yugoslavs out of Trieste by force of arms. It was only after President Truman had taken a strong stand and agreed to a joint Anglo-American display of force that the Yugoslavs could be induced to withdraw and accept a demarcation line.

For this and other reasons, British influence in Yugoslavia at the end of the war could be reckoned a minus quantity – certainly very far from the hoped-for 50 per cent. It was not until after the Tito-Stalin break in 1948 that the seeds sown by British–Yugoslav war-time co-operation began to germinate.

14 Albania: Britain and the Resistance

In Albania, the British faced much less difficult problems than in Greece or Yugoslavia. For a start, they had no political obligations. The Foreign Office consistently rejected all King Zog's polite requests for recognition as an Allied leader, for acceptance of Albania as one of the United Nations, or for permission to rally his supporters in Albania to the Allied cause. But he was never awkwardly importunate, and the Foreign Office came to acquire a certain liking for him (in contrast to other exiled Balkan monarchs). Denis Laskey[1] of the Southern Department wrote in late 1944: 'I have much sympathy for King Zog. We have been able to give him no encouragement, yet he has shown great patience and has never tried to cause us embarrassment, as he could certainly have done if he had wished. There is no reason to doubt his pro-British convictions and our influence in Albania would be far stronger with him as King than with an F.N.C. [Communist] government. Unfortunately he now has little support in the country.'[2] In spite of this, as late as August 1944 the Foreign Office regarded Zog as 'a valuable pawn'.[3]

If this pawn was never used, it was less because of Zog's reputed unpopularity in Albania than because of Greek ambitions – and the Greeks did not hesitate to be importunate and cause embarrassment. These ambitions were long-standing, but since the Greek victories in southern Albania in 1940, they had acquired something of the nature of sacred rights in Greek eyes. The Greeks also felt very bitter against the Albanians as a whole, blaming their own military reverses partly on supposed Albanian treachery to the Allied cause; certainly some Albanians had supported the Italians. From 1941 on the Greeks did not only have a territorial claim to southern Albania, which they called Northern Epirus, but also called into question Albania's right to independent existence. They would have strongly resented the slightest encouragement given by Britain to Zog or any of the would-be Albanian freedom movements; and in 1944 they protested against British contacts with Albanian resistance forces.[4]

Largely because of this Greek attitude, the British were extremely hesitant even to say publicly that they favoured an independent

Albania. In July 1941 Dixon of the Southern Department wrote: 'we have never supported the cause of Albanian independence and are even less disposed to do so now that the prospects of stimulating Albanian resistance to the Italians are much less real than they were before the collapse of the Balkans.'[5]

In December 1941, however, Stalin told Eden that he favoured an independent Albania; in January 1942, Eden told Maisky that he shared Stalin's view, but added that in view of Greek and Yugoslav claims he was not anxious to commit himself on the subject at present. It was agreed that neither Britain nor Russia would commit themselves to Zog.[6]

The British decision early in 1942 to negotiate a treaty with the Soviet Union recognising its 1941 frontiers had repercussions on the Albanian question. At the end of March Dixon of the Southern Department wrote a minute on the assumption that such a treaty would make it necessary for the British government to make some statement on Albanian independence, partly to stimulate resistance, partly because 'after the establishment of peace it will undoubtedly be to our advantage to have a friendly population in Albania'; at the same time there would be some advantage in recognising Greek claims in southern Albania. Dixon's conclusion was that Britain should make a statement on Albania as soon as a treaty recognising Soviet 1941 frontiers was concluded; at the same time S.O.E. should be asked to look into the chances of stimulating Albanian resistance.[7] Eden agreed, but since the eventual Anglo-Soviet treaty made no mention of frontiers, the need for a statement on Albania did not arise.

S.O.E. were less cautious than the Foreign Office. In May and June 1942 Glenconner of S.O.E. wrote to the Foreign Office about S.O.E. plans for subversive activity in Albania, and asked for a British declaration on Albanian independence to help them. The answer from Dixon was that although H.M.G. favoured the reconstitution of an independent Albania after the war, the time for a declaration had not yet come; 'the S.O.E. angle is not in itself sufficiently weighty to justify us in making such a declaration now'. The right course, Dixon wrote, was to get on with subversive operations irrespective of whether a declaration was made or not.[8] It emerged that S.O.E. plans were still in a very early stage; its Istanbul representative, Colonel Wilfred Stirling, a former officer in the British-run Albanian Gendarmerie in Zog's time, was on the point of establishing communications to enable S.O.E. to finance activities inside Albania.[9]

On 11 July Sargent minuted: 'if we make a declaration of policy we are likely to stir up a small hornet's nest, for the Greeks and the Jugoslavs will, whatever reservations we may make, feel that they must not miss the opportunity for staking out their claims . . . The most it could do would be to enable S.O.E. to enlist a few more local agents . . . On the whole therefore I should be inclined to leave the declaration alone for the moment.' Eden agreed.[10]

Although S.O.E. did not know it at the time, the Albanian Communist Party, formed at a conference in Tirana in November 1941 under the urging and tutelage of two Yugoslav Partisan representatives, Miladin Popović and Dušan Mugoša, had elected a Central Committee with the young school-teacher Enver Hoxha as one of its members,[11] and was now becoming extremely active, mainly in the south, where the first Partisan units had been formed early in 1942.[12] In August 1942 it started publishing its clandestine newspaper *Zeri i Populit* (Voice of the People). Other groups of former officers, notably Major Abas Kupi, were also active, and news was reaching the large Albanian colony in Istanbul, which passed it on to the outside world.

S.O.E. therefore had good reason to try to build up its contacts. One idea at this time seems to have been to work through Col. Muharrem Bajraktar, a former gendarmerie officer who after quarrelling with Zog had gone to Yugoslavia in 1936. There were reports during the summer that he had joined Mihajlović;[13] and in September Djonović, the Yugoslav government representative in Cairo, sent him a message via S.O.E. and Mihajlović: 'it is up to you to lead the fight and I give you my personal opinion Zog will not return to Albania.'[14] This had little, if any, result. But news continued to reach London during the autumn of resistance in Albania, notably of a big youth demonstration in Elbasan, in which 70 students were arrested.

In September 1942 – though this was not known in London till later – the Albanian Communists, acting in accordance with the doctrine of the Yugoslav Partisans and the Comintern on the creation of a broadly-based liberation movement, brought about a conference at Peza attended by a number of nationalists and former officers including Abas Kupi, Muharrem Bajraktar and Myslim Peza. A National Liberation Movement – L.N.C. – was formed, under a General Council on which there were several Communists including Enver Hoxha;[15] Major Abas Kupi was also a member.

In November the Allied landings in North Africa led the Foreign Office to think again about a declaration on Albania's independence: Sargent minuted that 'we are now on the offensive in the Mediterranean and a declaration about the future of Albania would be interpreted in the Balkans as evidence of this offensive spirit . . . S.O.E. have told us that a declaration would help us in their work among the Albanian guerillas.'[16] (The fact that Sir Stafford Cripps had just publicly recommended the partition of Albania was a further stimulus.)

Early in December, the British told the Soviet and American governments their intention, and invited them to make parallel declarations. On 3 December the War Cabinet approved the proposed British statement.[17] This carefully avoided any commitment to restoring Albania to its pre-1939 frontiers; it did not mention frontiers at all. The Greek and Yugoslav exiled governments were informed. The Greek government, through its ambassador, replied that it could have no objection to the British decision on restoring the independence of 'purely Albanian territory' but trusted that the 'vital and legitimate rights of Greece' would be adequately safeguarded; it added that the British statement would make 'a very painful impression' in Greece.[18] The draft British statement was therefore expanded to include a specific pledge that the frontiers of the Albanian State 'would have to be considered at the peace settlement'. Nevertheless the Greek Vice-Premier, Canellopoulos, the government's Cairo representative, exploded and threatened to resign, and so provoked Eden that he wrote on a telegram: 'this young man needs spanking'.[19] Even if Eden did not take him altogether seriously, the crisis was unpleasant enough to threaten the British policy of broadening the base of the exiled Greek government, and it was with some difficulty that Canellopoulos was persuaded to remain in office.

There was another last-minute hitch because of a remark made by the Soviet ambassador, Maisky, and reported to Eden, that the British should have 'consulted' the Soviet government instead of simply 'informing' them about the proposed declaration, and that in consequence the British might have lost 'some hard-won ground'. This agitated Eden to such an extent that he put off making the declaration; however, it then emerged that Maisky had not even telegraphed to Moscow on the matter; so the declaration was duly made in Parliament one day late, on 17 December.[20] On the next day the Soviet Foreign Ministry also issued a statement speaking in glowing terms of the Albanian patriots' 'courageous struggle for freedom'; it made no reservations about Albania's frontiers.[21] The U.S. government also issued a statement – several days before the British – which sounded a good deal more enthusiastic than the British one.[22]

Such were the troubles besetting even the simplest political commitment to Albania. But they did at least impel the British to keep perfectly free hands in their dealings with Albanian resistance groups.

In February 1943, Brigadier Keble of S.O.E. Cairo instructed Myers, in Greece, to link up with Albanian and Yugoslav groups.[23] In April a party led by Lt.-Col. Neil McLean[24] was dropped into northern Greece, destined to get into Albania with E.A.M.'s help.[25] They were held up for some days on the Albanian frontier 'because they were thought to be Greeks'.[26] However they arrived safely and sent back favourable reports on the situation in southern Albania, reporting the existence of the National Liberation Movement or L.N.C., which was still operating successfully under its General Council; the guerillas were pro-Russian and had political commissars, used the clenched fist salute and wore the five-pointed red star (like the Yugoslav Partisans). The nationalist Bajraktar was however said to have lost prestige by contacting Mihajlović. In July S.O.E. told the Foreign Office that they were sending in more liaison officers; their appreciation was that 'Albanian unity is easier of achievement than is Greek or Jugoslav'.[27]

At the time of the L.N.C.'s conference at Labinot in July, attended by McLean, this certainly seemed true. But the estimate was premature. Allied operations against Sicily and Italy had almost bigger repercussions in Albania than in Greece or Yugoslavia, since Italians were the only occupying force. Outside Albania King Zog, apparently confident that he would soon return to a free Albania, told a representative of the Jewish Board of Deputies that Albania would be prepared to put 150,000 hectares at the disposal of the Jews, and about 200,000 Jews could settle there with full rights as citizens. The Board of Deputies consulted the Foreign Office, who replied that they could not say whether or not Zog would return to Albania.[28]

Inside Albania, the crumbling of Italian power produced tensions inside the L.N.C. General Council between the Communists and the others, such as Abas Kupi, and also brought into the open the cleavage between the L.N.C. and another group, the nationalist Balli Kombetar (B.K.), formed by certain rich and powerful Albanians soon after the creation of the L.N.C. in September 1942. At first the B.K. took a strongly patriotic anti-Italian line, though they were equally anti-Greek and anti-Yugoslav. But its enthusiasm for active struggle was lukewarm. Though the British did not know it at the time, the Yugoslav Partisan representative, Vukmanović-Tempo, whom Tito had instructed to contact the Albanian and Greek Communists, visited Albania in July 1943 and, at a time when Enver Hoxha was planning to hold talks with the B.K. leaders, urged that the correct line was to split the B.K., winning over the rank and file to the L.N.C. and denouncing those B.K. leaders who collaborated with the enemy. Hoxha was over-ruled, Vukmanović-Tempo's advice was taken, and the L.N.C.'s attitude to the B.K. sharpened. An agreement to set up a joint committee of National Salvation with the B.K., signed at the beginning of August by a L.N.C. representative, Imer Dishniça, was repudiated by the L.N.C. Central Committee, which decided instead to 'unmask' the B.K. leaders.[29]

Vukmanović-Tempo's intervention meant that British hopes of maintaining Albanian unity were undermined. However in mid-August S.O.E. wanted the B.B.C. to broadcast appeals to the B.K., the Communists and the L.N.C. to unite against the Axis – which meant, against the Germans, who were far less unpopular than the Italians. By this time, S.O.E. had nine officers and fifteen British other ranks and eight separate W/T links in Albania, still mostly in the south.[30]

The Italian collapse produced clashes in Albania similar to those in Yugoslavia and Greece. In mid-September a B.L.O. reported that in the coastal area the B.K. was being actively obstructive, informing the enemy of L.N.C. intentions, and frequent B.K.–L.N.C. clashes were taking place. At this time German troops were moving in, setting up a provisional government for an 'independent' Albania which was to be allowed to keep the formerly Yugoslav territory in Kosovo-Metohija which Italy had joined to it. This was attractive to many Albanians. The L.N.C. was breaking up and had in fact become almost purely Communist; Abas Kupi and Muharrem Bajraktar were forming a 'Zogist' party in central Albania, while the B.K. was anti-Zog. According to another report, while Kupi was willing to fight the Germans, Bajraktar refused to fight anybody.[31] But in the south the L.N.C. continued to co-operate with the British and to carry out operations against the Germans. In mid-October, the Foreign Office and S.O.E. held a meeting and agreed that 'the line of cleavage between Communists and anti-Communists, which was so familiar in Jugoslavia and Greece, was likely to manifest itself in Albania as well'.[32]

By this time the Chiefs of Staff were taking some interest in Albania. A S.O.E. memorandum submitted to them in October gave a figure of 4,000–5,000 active guerillas 'with an estimated potential reserve of 30,000'.[33]

This was the situation when Brigadier E. F., or 'Trotsky', Davies parachuted into Albania. As he wrote later, 'in Cairo I had been told to back any political party which would fight the Italians or Germans, and it had sounded very simple. In Albania I was to find the whole matter very complex and difficult.'[34]

Davies was first in contact with the L.N.C. and Enver Hoxha, who clearly expected to monopolise British support,[35] and who said he had given orders to his forces to attack the B.K., which could be done without weakening the L.N.C. effort against the Germans. Davies asked Hoxha whether he would drop his feud with the B.K. if the B.K. gave a promise to fight the Germans. Hoxha agreed, in the conviction that the B.K. would never give such a promise.[36] Davies met the B.K. leaders on 8 November and with considerable difficulty obtained their written promise to fight the Germans; Abas Kupi, now said to be representing 3,000 Zogists in the north, was also present and also promised. Davies did not take to Kupi, whom he thought 'foxy', but in view of his pledge he undertook that Kupi should receive three aircraft drops.[37] Hoxha was furious when he heard of the B.K. leaders' promise, accused Davies of interfering in Albanian affairs, and said he would destroy the B.K. just the same.[38]

Davies reported to Cairo that in view of the B.K. promise, he would not recommend exclusive support of the L.N.C., which nevertheless he regarded as the only group with which the British could co-operate, though in his view 'not effective'. He added that L.N.C. was Communist but under the influence of Tito, not the Russians. Davies concluded gloomily: 'I have personally done my utmost with all parties to avoid civil war, but without success.'[89] On 11 November he asked the L.N.C. to cancel orders to destroy the B.K., but they refused, accusing the B.K. of collaboration with the Germans.[40]

Gradually Davies's sympathies moved towards the L.N.C., who were under attack by the Germans. In December he promised them 15,000 gold sovereigns for purchase of food and clothing and most of the British arms dropped were going to the L.N.C.[41] On 17 December he sent a message: 'I now recommend a change . . . It is imperative now to denounce . . . the B.K. and the Zogists . . . In all recent actions fought by L.N.C. they have met mixed German–B.K. bodies'; Abas Kupi had not fought against the Germans in spite of his promise. Davies concluded: 'I therefore recommend an open declaration for the L.N.C.'[42] (Curiously, Davies makes no mention of this recommendation in the book he wrote a few years later.) Soon after, Davies was attacked by a B.K. band led by an Albanian named Biçaku, was wounded and captured on 8 January 1944, becoming a prisoner of the Germans. He later suspected that Hoxha had deliberately abandoned him, but could find no evidence for this.[43] Col. Arthur Nicholls, who was with Davies at the time of the attack, was given shelter by a friend of Abas Kupi, suffered frostbite and gangrene and died.[44]

The sudden disappearance of Davies saved the Foreign Office from the unpleasant task of taking a definite decision on his recommendation that the British should break with the B.K. and give all support to the L.N.C. This would have been altogether too much, coming on top of the simultaneous need to take a parallel decision over Mihajlović and Tito, or a decision in reverse over E.L.A.S. and Zervas. In Albania, both S.O.E. London and the Foreign Office felt early in 1944 that there was a third way: to build up Abas Kupi as a counterweight to the L.N.C.

Col. Neil McLean, who had been with the L.N.C. in southern Albania, came back to London to discuss the project, and received some friendly personal encouragement from Eden, who suggested that McLean should send him a direct message from Albania in case of need.[45] Since Abas Kupi was now known as the Zogist leader and at a conference in the hills on 21 November 1943 had christened his group the 'Legality' or 'Legitimacy' party,[46] McLean asked Zog to send a mesage to Kupi; but a text which would meet Foreign Office requirements could not be agreed. After some delay, McLean, Major David Smiley and Captain Julian Amery were dropped into northern Albania in April,[47] to start their task of persuading Kupi to fight the Germans instead of the L.N.C. (now re-christened National Liberation Front or F.N.C.) and if possible to join forces again with the F.N.C. To prepare the way, General Maitland Wilson issued a message to the Albanians: 'the quickest way to liberate your country is to avoid all collaboration with the Germans and to resist and harass them in every possible way.'

It was never quite clear whether the main motive behind the British effort to mobilise Kupi was political or military, but on balance it seems to have been political. One military argument was that the Partisans (or L.N.C. or F.N.C.) were non-existent in the north, where Kupi had his stronghold; Kupi, in March, claimed that he could put 25,000 men in the field.⁴⁸ But in June S.O.E. reported that he was only in control of a rather badly armed force of about 5,000.⁴⁹ At this time one B.L.O., Lt.-Col. T. N. S. Wheeler, said by S.O.E. to be 'very pro-Partisan', arived in Bari and inspired the view that it was 'not worth while supporting Kupi now . . . Partisans continue as in the past to be the only party fighting the Germans. Support given to Kupi now will cause L.N.C. to take action against him and thus detract from their effort against Germans.'⁵⁰

By June, the F.N.C. forces were estimated by S.O.E. to have grown to 25,000.⁵¹ On 16 June General Maitland Wilson, as Supreme Allied Commander Mediterranean, told the Chiefs of Staff that the Communist Partisans were growing rapidly in strength and organisation and were already 'an effective instrument for action against the enemy in the south where his main commitments (the defence of vital road communications from Greece) are placed'. Military aid should therefore not be given to the Zogists – that is, Kupi – until they had been reconciled with the Partisans.⁵² The Chiefs of Staff said that this confirmed their own provisional view that 'no encouragement should be given to the Zogist Party'.⁵³

The Foreign Office was sympathetic to the project of supporting Kupi on long-term political grounds, but sceptical about the outcome. In April the Southern Department commented on a report that Kupi was 'temporizing' with the Germans: 'more Mihailovism'.⁵⁴ In June there was a similar comment: 'the idea of bringing about an agreement between Kupi and the L.N.C. seems to me to be a beautiful dream which it will prove quite impossible to realise . . . It is the old story of Zervas and E.L.A.S. and of Mihajlović and Tito, and in neither of those cases have we yet found a solution.'⁵⁵ On the other hand, the idea of a L.N.C. (or F.N.C.) government was not liked by the Foreign Office: 'politically there would be disadvantage in this . . . for L.N.C., like the left-wing parties in Greece and Yugoslavia, is under a considerable measure of communist control and it is very doubtful whether a purely L.N.C. régime in Albania after the war would be the most satisfactory either for us or for the Albanians.'⁵⁶

In practice, the British had very little choice in the matter. Towards the end of May the L.N.C. (F.N.C.) held a Congress at Permet, clearly modelled on Tito's Congress at Jajce on 29 November 1943 when resolutions had been passed banning King Peter's return to Yugoslavia and proclaiming a provisional government. L.N.C. also formed a provisional government, banned Zog's return, denounced Abas Kupi and the B.K., sent telegrams to Tito and the Greek E.A.M., and asked the Allied Mediteranean Command to accept a L.N.C. military delegation, and the Soviet Union and the United States to send military missions to the L.N.C.[57] It was a large programme; but the L.N.C. seemed strong enough locally to attain some at least of their objectives. In any case they were supremely self-confident.

Kupi himself did little to help the British in their dilemma. When McLean arrived, Kupi, who had been concentrating on defensive measures against any L.N.C. incursion into his area in the north, said that he would and could only fight the Germans after the British had sent arms so that he could equip and expand his forces. The British answer was that he must attack Germans first and then he would get arms. But in spite of this deadlock, Kupi co-operated in June in an operation carried out by a B.L.O., Smiley, against a bridge on the Tirana–Scutari road.[58] Kupi professed himself ready to be re-conciled with the L.N.C.,[59] though there were doubts whether he was sincere.

In any case the L.N.C. made it perfectly clear that they were not going to be reconciled with Kupi. In July the British suspended sup-plies to the L.N.C., to stop them fighting Kupi,[60] but resumed them when the Germans started a drive which seemed a real threat to the L.N.C.[61] At this point Churchill sent Eden a minute: 'let me have a note on this showing which side we are on. W.S.C.'[62] Eden replied: 'I still have some hope that we may be able to reconcile the two factions.'[63]

The decisive factor was that the military, both at Supreme Allied Headquarters in Caserta and in Bari, wanted to keep on good terms with the L.N.C.[64] This produced what Julian Amery, after serving some months in Kupi's area, later described as 'the appeasing climate of Bari'.[65] The military were in fact beginning to plan for the expected German withdrawal from Greece through Albania. In any case the difficulties of the Allied campaign in Italy made it necessary to do everything possible to hold down Germans in the Balkans. From May to July 1944, supplies to Albania averaged 100 tons a month and were expected to rise to 160 tons in August.[66]

At the end of July, a L.N.C. delegation of three was escorted to Bari by Col. Alan Palmer for military talks with Air Vice-Marshal Robert Elliott of the Balkan Air Force. A military agreement was drawn up; the delegates demanded recognition of the L.N.C. provisional govern-ment and a permanent L.N.C. delegation in Bari. The British decided to reject the first and accept the second request. While the delegates were in Bari, the L.N.C. forces were moving north into Kupi's area, doing considerable damage to his frail organisation, but also killing 380 Germans, who were reported to be calling reinforcements from Greece.[67] At the same time a Soviet mission of two officers arrived in southern Albania.[68] In spite of these events, the negotiations in Bari continued and on 24 August, after long arguments over the question whether British supplies should be distributed by B.L.O.s or by the L.N.C., a British–L.N.C. military agreement was signed.

On the following day Hoxha told the B.L.O. at his headquarters that McLean, Smiley and Seymour were working against the Partisans; they must leave Albania or hand themselves over to the Partisans for evacuation; otherwise they would be captured and tried by a Partisan military court. This was an ultimatum which the British in Bari, however 'appeasing' the climate, could not take lying down. Palmer was sent back to Hoxha to get him to retract, under threat of cancellation of the military agreement.[69] In spite of the arrival of the Russians, Hoxha met Palmer in a friendly way[70] and withdrew his threat.[71] Later in September, when a L.N.C. commander arrested a B.L.O. with Gani Kryeziu, who had taken the field, while his wireless operator received 'disgraceful treatment', Hoxha apologised fully, saying the action had been taken against his orders.[72]

Meanwhile, the L.N.C. were continuing their drive northwards. In mid-September the British in Bari recommended that a last-minute offer by Kupi to attack the Germans should be disregarded and that no arms should be sent to him. By this time Kupi had only about 2,000 men of his own, and perhaps another 2,000 Nationalists were co-operating with him; meanwhile the L.N.C. had about 25,000 men and were doing very useful work by actively engaging the Germans, so in Bari's view it would be unfortunate to 'prejudice military relations' with them by sending arms to Kupi.[73] McLean's report that Kupi's men had been involved in three 'minor actions' against Germans did not alter this view.[74] (One of these was the action in which Julian Amery led a party of Turkestan deserters against the Germans.)[75]

Early in October, McLean and his colleagues were recalled to Bari. When they told Kupi, he said that he could only keep his forces in the field if he co-operated with the Germans against the L.N.C.: this he would not do, so he would disband his movement.[76] At McLean's personal request, Eden gave instructions that Kupi should be got out of Albania 'without it appearing that H.M.G. have been involved in the operation'.[77] The secrecy was thought necessary to avoid trouble with Hoxha. However, no clandestine operation was needed. Kupi and his two sons left Albania in their own craft and were picked up by a Royal Navy launch when their engines broke down.[78]

By this time the British were giving clear priority to good relations with Hoxha, now regarded as certain to take power when the Germans left, though there were still slight doubts whether he would stay in power. On 20 October Hoxha issued a declaration in Berat that the 'first Albanian democratic government' had been formed and that Britain, the Soviet Union and the United States would be asked to give it full recognition. The B.L.O. present reported: 'the town of Berat is in a state of fanatical excitement.'[79]

The British did not wish to commit themselves too quickly, and so informed the Soviet and American governments. On 17 November, the F.N.C. captured Tirana. On 3 December Col. Alan Palmer, who had been chosen to head a British Military Mission in liberated Albania, wrote to Eden (with whom he was on christian name terms): 'on the question of recognition of F.N.C., I can only express a hope that you will not withhold it for long. The Provisional Government now controls almost the whole country and there is no chance of any large-scale opposition from outside the F.N.C. in the near future . . . I hear that Billy [Neil] McLean and Julian Amery will be home shortly, so you will no doubt be getting a blast of more right-wing sentiments soon.'[80] Eden replied on 25 December: 'don't fear that I shall be corrupted by other visitors – unhappily I had to put them off . . .'[81]

During December relations between the British and the Hoxha government were shadowed by the civil war in Athens. There were E.A.M. representatives in Tirana. Palmer was instructed to 'make it plain to Hoxha that . . . it is clearly in Albania's best interests that they should not allow themselves to be drawn into internal Greek dispute'.[82]

It was not until November 1945 that the British, Soviet and American governments finally recognised the Hoxha government. In 1946 a British warship was badly damaged in the Corfu Channel close to the Albanian shore, and relations were broken – and never resumed.

In military terms, however, something had been achieved by the British support of the Albanian Communists. It was estimated that about 6,000–7,000 German troops were killed in Albania and 500 captured.[83] This had been achieved by Hoxha's L.N.C. with a little help from 40 men of the Long Range Desert Group dropped to the Peza area in September 1944. If, from the long-term political standpoint, the British failed to win any good will from the Albanian Communists, it can only be said that the Soviet Union was equally unsuccessful. Possibly the British, by feeding the youthful Hoxha's ego, helped to give him the supreme self-confidence to quarrel with all the big Powers except Communist China.

The British, the Balkan
Communists and Macedonia

In their dealings with the resistance movements of Greece, Yugoslavia
and Albania – also Bulgaria – the British were hampered by lack of
knowledge of the Communist parties involved and of their relations
with one another. Although in Greece they had contacts with Communists as early as 1941, in Yugoslavia and Albania until 1943 they
were almost totally ignorant of the leaders, and even after that of the
tensions inside the Communist parties or between the party leaders and
Moscow.

The British were not uniform in their attitudes to the Communists.
Churchill, though strongly anti-Communist on principle, was perfectly
prepared to try to make a personal friend of Tito. S.O.E., in their early
dealings with Greek Communists, seemed singularly free from the normal British prejudices and suspicions. In the case of Yugoslavia, S.O.E.
tried to play on Foreign Office fears of Communism to obtain support
for Mihajlović, so long as this suited them; thereafter they seemed to
have no ideological or political objections to close contacts with Communists, whether in Yugoslavia, Albania or Bulgaria. The same was
true of the British military commanders in the Middle East and the
Mediteranean. As for the individual British officers who lived and
worked in daily contact with Communists, they too seem for the most
part to have been quite open-minded and often remarkably tolerant of
Communist awkwardness, prickliness, or even outright hostility. Where
they found Communists whom they liked and respected, they seem to
have won similar liking and respect themselves, and sometimes to have
made lasting friendships, at least in Yugoslavia.

The Foreign Office attitude was inevitably different, since they
saw the Communists as a threat to their long-term aims in South-East
Europe.

THE BRITISH, SOUTH SLAV UNION AND MACEDONIA,
1939–42

In their fear of the spread of Russian influence and of Communism in
South-East Europe, the Foreign Office had two particular bugbears –
South Slav union and Macedonian independence. During the 1920s,

the Comintern had taken a very lively interest in the Balkans and its usual policy had been to call for a Balkan Communist Federation, which would solve the national quarrels between Bulgaria, Greece and Yugoslavia, perhaps Rumania too. In particular it would solve the bitter quarrels between Bulgaria, Greece and Yugoslavia over Macedonia, which would emerge as an independent or autonomous unit in the federation – its frontiers were never specified. None of the Communists liked the idea much except the Bulgarians who believed they would be able to control Macedonia.

The British, in the Second World War, seem to have ignored this Comintern policy, thinking instead in terms of Tsarist Russia and the threat of Pan-Slavism, which they expected to take the form of a South Slav union between Bulgaria and Yugoslavia or Serbia, and which would be an agent of Russian imperialism in South-East Europe. As for Macedonia, the word alone seemed to send a shudder down Foreign Office backs; at best, Macedonia would be a lynch-pin in a South Slav union which they did not want; at worst it would threaten their protégé, Greece, and so undermine British influence in the area.

The Foreign Office were particularly nervous of the Bulgarian Communist Party, which had won a world-wide reputation through its leader, Georgi Dimitrov, and his defiance of the Nazis at the Reichstag fire trial; they knew about him and his second-in-command, also in exile in Moscow, Vasil Kolarov. George Rendel, both while Minister in Sofia and later as ambassador to the exiled Yugoslav government, always believed that the Bulgarian Communists would play a leading role in Soviet schemes for dominating South-East Europe; he was supported in this view by the exiled Yugoslav politicians, especially Milan Gavrilović.

While still in Sofia Rendel reported regularly on Communist activities, for instance the big Communist-sponsored tobacco strikes of the summer of 1940,[1] and the Communist demonstrations and leaflets at the time of the Sobolev visit to Sofia in November 1940.[2] He also kept a close watch on Bulgarian attitudes towards Macedonia. In January 1940 he reported an approach from a sympathiser of the Internal Macedonian Revolutionary Organisation, which had been largely responsible for killing King Alexander of Yugoslavia in 1934, about possible British support for I.M.R.O. The Foreign Office response was that 'we should not have anything to do with the Macedonians . . . we would only burn our fingers'.[3]

The combination of Communists and Macedonia seemed even more dangerous than I.M.R.O. Rendel sent the Foreign Office the Bulgarian Communist Party's manifesto of August 1940 on Macedonia, which was remarkable for its far-reaching concessions to Yugoslavia, and was presumably a by-product of the Soviet decision to establish diplomatic relations with Yugoslavia. Until then, Bulgarian Communists had never accepted that Macedonian territory which they regarded as rightfully Bulgarian should be attached to Yugoslavia. Now they seemed to agree that Yugoslavia should keep this territory:

> Very justly the Macedonians of Jugoslavia are now directing their efforts to the attainment of autonomy for Macedonia. By striving together with all South Slav peoples for the preservation of peace . . . the Jugoslavs of Jugoslav Macedonia will unite their efforts with those of all progressive forces in Jugoslavia towards completion of the process . . . which will lead to democracy and federal reconstruction, giving autonomy to the other Jugoslav nations as well as to Macedonia. Having in this way attained its independence, Jugoslav Macedonia will seek to secure the adherence of the other parts of Macedonia, and to become a connecting link with the other Balkan countries . . . Macedonians in Bulgaria can have no other policy than that of the core of the Macedonian people living in Jugoslav Macedonia.'[4]

If the Bulgarian Communists had stuck to this policy over Macedonia – which was virtually identical with the one developed by Tito in the following years – they would never have quarrelled with the Yugoslav Communists over Macedonia; and there might have been a degree of unity between the two Communist parties which would have seriously threatened British efforts to keep Greece territorially intact and free of Communism – and also Stalin's post-war efforts to keep Tito in his place.

In 1940, not only the Bulgarian Communists but also the Protoguerovists – the break-away left-wing of I.M.R.O., with whom S.O.E. were in touch – were willing to accept Macedonian autonomy inside a federal Yugoslavia.[5] It also seemed to be accepted inside Yugoslav Macedonia: a report from the British Vice-Consul in Skoplje early in 1941 said that I.M.R.O. had lost ground there, and former I.M.R.O. members were now prepared to accept autonomy inside Yugoslavia.[6] The Vice-Consul added that although the Communist Party was proscribed in Yugoslavia, 'communism is strongest among the . . . youth . . . Its latent strength, in so far as the strength of an underground movement can be gauged, is probably very considerable'; and it had just received instructions from the Comintern to do its utmost to combat 'Fascism'.[7]

In fact, the situation in Yugoslav Macedonia was much more confused than the Bulgarian manifesto or the Vice-Consul's report suggested. When Vukmanović-Tempo visited Macedonia on behalf of the Yugoslav Communist Party in 1940, he came up against a veteran Communist and former Comintern official known as Sharlo-Shatorov, whom he regarded as pro-Bulgarian and wrong-headed, but whom he had to accept as secretary of the newly-formed (Yugoslav) Macedonian

Communist organisation largely because he was reputed to 'stand well' with Georgi Dimitrov in Moscow.[8] Tempo's own efforts to build up the party organisation, during his visit, clearly met with only limited success. The Sobolev visit to Sofia in November 1940 suggested a swing of Soviet interest and support away from Yugoslavia and back to Bulgaria; and the Bulgarian occupation of most of Yugoslav Macedonia in 1941 after the break-up of the Yugoslav State made it virtually impossible for Bulgarian Communists to stick to the line of their 1940 manifesto. Inside Yugoslav Macedonia, a number of Communists were arrested or shot, and the first partisan detachments suffered badly.[9] Meanwhile there was a bitter struggle between the Yugoslav and Bulgarian Communist parties over the right to control Yugoslav Macedonia, with Sharlo-Shatorov aligning himself with the Bulgarians, and the Comintern giving a slightly equivocal ruling in favour of the Yugoslavs in August 1941,[10] which did not end the dispute.

The Foreign Office, meanwhile, were worrying about the possibility of a South Slav union, which they disliked just as much when propounded by anti-Communists as by Communists. Before the German occupation of Yugoslavia, S.O.E.'s protégés, the Serb Peasant Party and the Bulgarian left-wing Agrarians, had wanted such a union. (See p. 85 above.) When Milan Gavrilović arrived in London from Moscow at the end of 1941, he continued to champion the idea strongly with his exiled colleagues and with the British, arguing that it would be the best way of stopping Bulgaria from going Communist and checking the spread of Soviet influence in the Balkans. But he came up against Ninčić, who saw himself as the creator of the Greek–Yugoslav pact and the champion of a Balkan Union to be formed on this base, and argued that a Yugoslav–Bulgarian union might serve as a vehicle for Soviet influence rather than a barrier.

The Foreign Office sided with Ninčić, taking it as a fixed article of faith that a Bulgarian–Yugoslav union, whether between anti-Communists or Communists, would be a threat to British aims. In March 1942 when the British were preparing for an Anglo-Soviet treaty, the Southern Department minuted: 'it would be useful, but no doubt impolitic, to seek an assurance that the Soviet government will take no steps to promote Pan-Slav movements in the Balkans or to constitute a South Slav bloc, since any such development would be incompatible with the principle of a Balkan Federation'.[11] No such assurance was sought. In the following June, Sargent set out in detail British opposition to 'Panslavism in the Balkans', by which he meant Bulgarian–Yugoslav union: 'Bulgaria, where opinion is overwhelmingly pro-Russian, would provide a spearhead for Soviet penetration of the Balkans, and the Russians would easily find support in Macedonia and in Serbia for the constitution of a compact block stretching across the Balkans from East to West and isolating Greece . . .'[12]

TEMPO, THE BALKAN COMMUNIST PARTIES AND RESISTANCE
STRATEGY

If the Foreign Office had known about the activities of Tito's representative, Vukmanović-Tempo, in relation to the Balkan Communist
Parties and Macedonia from the end of 1942 on, they would certainly
have been alarmed and suspicious, and might have had very grave
misgivings about supporting Tito's Partisans.

Tito sent Tempo to Yugoslav Macedonia towards the end of 1942
with special authorisation from the Yugoslav Communist Party Central
Committee to develop the armed struggle on the territory of Macedonia and Kosovo-Metohija, and to make contact with the Communist
Party Central Committees of Albania, Greece and Bulgaria so as to
organise co-operation in the struggle against the German-Italian
occupying powers.[13] By his energy, courage and devotion to Communism he was well fitted for the job – but not perhaps by his temper-
ament. A young Montenegrin – he was 30 in 1942 – he was, by his own
showing, headstrong in his convictions, headlong in his actions and
reactions, arrogant in demolishing the views of others, and outspoken
to a point where he was bound to cause offence. In the summer of 1943
the Yugoslav Central Committee told him that in his dealings with the
Balkan Communist Parties he should be 'tactical' and should take
account of the fact that they were independent parties, though where
political questions were concerned he should not be 'pliant'.[14] In so far
as 'tactical' meant 'tactful', this Tempo certainly was not; by vaunting
Yugoslav achievements and harshly criticising the achievements (if
any) and policies of his fellow Balkan Communists he must have put
many backs up, especially those of older and more experienced comrades. Towards the end of 1944 Tito, in a moment of irritation, told
Tempo that in his talks with the Balkan Parties he had behaved like
a bull in a china shop.[15] Given the national rivalries and quarrels
which persisted between Communist Parties almost as much as between
nationalists in the Balkans, this verdict had some truth.

From the start, Tempo made it clear to his fellow Balkan Communists that the Yugoslav resistance strategy was the only right one and
that all others were wrong. In Macedonia, early in 1943, he was involved in long argument with a delegate of the Bulgarian Communist
Party Central Committee, Bojan Balgaranov, who had been sent to
Macedonia to co-ordinate action with the Yugoslav party. Tempo set
out the basic Yugoslav doctrine, forged by the experiences of the
Partisans from the summer of 1941 on. This was that there must at all
times be armed struggle, involving the organisation of whole-time
fighting units in the countryside; these were the heart of the national
liberation movement; workers and others should be induced to come

out of the towns and cities and join the armed formations and create liberated areas. This, the Yugoslavs held, was the only way in which the Communists could be sure of taking power at the moment of victory, since they would have arms and an experienced fighting force in being. Tempo was perfectly frank in stating this aim.[16]

This was the doctrine which Tempo expounded not only to Balgaranov, but also to Enver Hoxha and other Albanian Communists,[17] and to the acting secretary of the Greek Communist Party, George Siantos[18] during the summer of 1943. Tempo accused the other parties of following an inactive policy, failing to fight the enemy, and making a grave error by relying on the organisation of subversion or sabotage in the towns as the main centre of resistance.

Balgaranov, a former Comintern official, argued back: Bulgarian policy was in accord with the wishes of Stalin who wanted strikes and 'diversion'; and conditions in Bulgaria – which was not occupied – were quite different from those in Yugoslavia. This stimulated the suspicion in Tempo that Moscow did not approve of the Yugoslav resistance strategy of all-out armed struggle.[19] Certainly Tempo does not seem to have had much effect on the Bulgarian Communists who, with a minor deviation in the Yugoslav direction early in 1944, carried on their 'Stalinist' resistance policy with little change. The first B.L.O. in contact with the Bulgarian Partisans, Major Mostyn Davies, reported in February 1944 that while there were said to be 12,000 Partisans, he had been told that a much larger number were enrolled in the 'militia' which had been formed within the army and the police. The Bulgarian Partisan leaders had set the following priorities: first, recruitment of 'militia' and sabotage in industrial areas, next, penetration and subversion of the army and police, and last, Partisan action in country districts and small towns. Mostyn Davies commented that this showed that the Bulgarian movement, unlike the Yugoslav movement, laid emphasis on disruptive work in the towns rather than guerilla activity in the hills; the 'ultimate revolt' would depend on large-scale support by the army co-ordinated with the rising of the 'militia' in the towns.[20] ('Militia' in the Bulgarian sense clearly meant an underground organisation.)

The Greek, Siantos, met Tempo with a rather similar argument. In Greece, he said, half the population lived in big towns, and 'who holds the towns, will hold power in the whole of Greece'; that was why the Communists made the towns the central point of their work, not the countryside. (The guerilla leader, Arcs Veloukhiotis, thought differently.) As for seizing power, Siantos said that the Communists would propose the formation of a united coalition government with all the bourgeois parties, if they were opposed to the return of the King, whether or not they had taken part in the struggle against the occupiers. When Tempo objected that these parties would then, with the help of the Allies, become the dominant force and eliminate the Communists, Siantos replied that the first thing to do was to eliminate the King, and that in any case the Communists would demand the ministries of the Interior and the Army; the Greek people could express their will in free elections held by the coalition government. To this Tempo replied forcefully that the Yugoslavs would never allow a government including the 'old' parties to carry out 'free' elections – they had not made so many sacrifices for that – nor would they allow Allied forces to come to their country. To this Siantos replied: 'you Yugoslavs decide everything by force, but we Greeks make use of politics. Our way is easier.' Tempo answered: 'our way is harder but more efficacious. We shall certainly succeed, but I am not sure about you.'[21]

At an earlier meeting another leading Greek Communist, Tsimas (Evmaios) had told Tempo that Greece was in a special position: the interests and influence of England were dominant and the Greeks therefore gave publicity to the English only among the big allies. To this Tempo replied: 'do you think you will succeed in deceiving the English?'[22]

Although Tempo did not convince either Balgaranov or Siantos of the rightness of Yugoslav strategy, his arguments had a certain limited influence. E.L.A.S. expanded its area of action and became increasingly anti-British, while the Bulgarians belatedly started to form permanent fighting partisan units on a larger scale – with Yugoslav help and advice – in the first part of 1944. In Albania Hoxha, in accordance with Tempo's advice, not only broke off relations with the Balli Kombetar but – aided by the Italian collapse – greatly expanded the L.N.C.'s military activity and carried out large-scale recruitment. In these developments, Britain's public support and praise for Tito – and the remarkably rapid growth and success of Tito's forces – must have played a part. In the internal arguments inside the Greek Communist Party over military and political strategy, it must have been doubly difficult to withstand Yugoslav arguments about all-out armed struggle when the British were backing Tito with such enthusiasm.

Tempo did not however succeed with his personal suggestion to the Greek and other Balkan Communists that there should be a 'Balkan Staff' to co-ordinate the war effort against the occupiers, and perhaps too efforts to prevent 'reaction', after liberation, from profiting from the fruits of war. As a first step, there should be radio links between the existing Partisan staffs.[23] When, in the summer of 1943, Tempo put this to Tsimas and Ares, no decision was taken: Tsimas was to go to Athens to see the Party leaders about it. A few weeks later, when Siantos saw Tempo, he expressed reserve about a 'Balkan Staff': 'our enemies would accuse us of founding some sort of Balkan International'. At this, Tempo taunted the Greeks with placing themselves under the British Middle East Command while rejecting a Balkan Staff, adding that such a staff would have political significance as the first step towards a Balkan federation. Siantos merely said the time was not ripe.[24]

But with the Albanians Tempo had better luck. According to the report which he sent to the Yugoslav Central Committee on 8 August 1943, Hoxha had accepted the proposed Balkan Staff.[25] So also, according to Tempo, had the Bulgarian Communist Party.[26] An official Bulgarian Party history, published after the Tito–Stalin break had let loose a flood of mutual accusations by Sofia and Belgrade, still admitted that there had been regular links between the Partisan Staffs of the two countries, and, 'as far as possible', joint action.[27]

Nevertheless, the Yugoslav Central Committee, after receiving Tempo's report of August 1943, sent him instructions that his initiative on a Balkan Staff was politically incorrect and harmful and that he should drop it entirely. He did so.[28] It would be interesting to know whether instructions from Stalin, or at least from Georgi Dimitrov, Tito's regular contact in the Soviet Union, lay behind this Yugoslav veto on Tempo's initiative.

THE BALKAN COMMUNISTS AND THE BRITISH

When Tempo told the Greeks – Tsimas, Sarafis and Ares Veloukhiotis – in the summer of 1943 that he was shocked by the way in which they allowed the British to interfere in their internal affairs, and when he told the Albanian Communists that they should not allow the B.L.O.s access to the staffs of their Partisan units (see p. 167 above), this was partly an expression of the Yugoslav Partisans' spirit of uncompromising and prickly independence, partly caused by the intense bitterness which Tito's forces felt at the fact that the British were sending arms to Mihajlović's četniks (they cannot have known how few these were) which were then used against the Partisans. Partly, too, it stemmed from the deep suspicion felt by Tempo, and other leading Yugoslav Partisans, though perhaps not by Tito himself, that the British would try to impose the King and exiled government upon them by force of arms.

Tempo later recounted, in a slightly self-critical vein, how when he first visited E.L.A.S. headquarters in the summer of 1943, he refused to speak to Myers, on the grounds that the British had supplied arms to the četniks – an action which he violently attacked in a speech to E.L.A.S. officers in front of Myers. By refusing to speak to him, he kept himself in ignorance of the fact that Tito had just welcomed a British mission.[29]

A particular point of Tempo's, and other Yugoslav Partisan leaders, was not to take money from the British. Tempo criticised the Greeks for taking money and clothing, thereby inspiring Ares Veloukhiotis to make a fiery speech declaring that the English should not think they could buy E.L.A.S. with under-pants or gold: 'we need arms, not under-pants'.[30]

When a few months later Tempo himself had to receive a British mission in Yugoslav Macedonia, he said he was willing to fight the Germans and destroy enemy installations; but if the British wished to stay on his territory, they must supply arms, explosives and ammunition – but not clothing, food or money. If the British sent these things and not arms, as they did in Greece, they should leave Macedonia – a warning which he followed up a few days later by an ultimatum, to show that 'this people cannot be corrupted'.[31]

At other times and places the Yugoslav Partisans did, in dire need, take food and clothing from the British – but not money. In Greece, E.L.A.S. were paid, as Zervas was, irregularly at first, but from July 1943 at the rate of one gold sovereign a month for each enrolled guerilla, plus one sovereign for his family. According to Woodhouse, then second-in-command to Myers, E.L.A.S. 'collared the lot and spent the proceeds at their own discretion'.[32] The Albanian L.N.C. did not hesitate to ask the British in 1943 for 15,000 sovereigns. (See p. 179 above.) 'Trotsky' Davies wrote later that this sum was needed to feed the growing Partisan forces and the Italian soldiers who had deserted after the Italian armistice; he added that in all about £80,000 was sent to Albania,[33] though not all of this can have gone to the Partisans. At a later stage, when relief was in question, the Foreign Office wrote that the Albanian Communist leaders 'look to us for supplies and for gold'.[34] As for Bulgaria, in 1944 the Treasury authorised the expenditure of £50,000 on the Partisans.[35]

In Yugoslavia things were different. Money of course had from the start been sent to Mihajlović; but when Fitzroy Maclean was about to be dropped into the country, and S.O.E. suggested that he should take in an 'enormous sum in gold sovereigns', he turned it down, saying that if he found he needed money, he would let them know. In fact Tito made it clear to him from the start that he would not accept money from the British and did not want them to try to spend sovereigns in Yugoslavia. Maclean sacked one British officer who did have some money dropped in, allegedly to buy mules.[36] John Henniker-Major,[37] from his experience with the Partisans in Serbia in 1944, also said that no money was given to them, though the British paid for their own board and lodging. The Partisans, when procuring food and supplies from the local population, paid in promissory notes to be cashed after liberation, which were apparently accepted willingly enough.[38]

THE BRITISH AND THE YUGOSLAV AND BULGARIAN PARTISANS

However suspicious Tempo was of the British, and however hotly he argued with Bulgarian Communists, he and other Yugoslav Partisan leaders were very helpful to the British in their efforts to make contact with the Bulgarian Partisans and to encourage resistance inside Bulgaria, as also to carry out demolitions in Yugoslav Macedonia. The British had known of the existence of the Fatherland Front in Bulgaria (see p. 213 below) since 1942, and had known that it included not only Communists but also elements with whom S.O.E. had been in touch before April 1941 – the Left-Wing Agrarians and the Military League led by Col. Damian Velchev. But S.O.E. had failed to make contact with it either through Istanbul or Mihajlović (see p. 212 below), and the only hope was to work through the Yugoslav Partisans. British contacts with the Bulgarian Partisans, operating under the Fatherland Front, were in fact a more or less integral part of British operations in Yugoslavia.[39]

It was in early October 1943 that the first B.L.O. reached H.Q. Yugoslav Partisans Macedonia and established W/T contact with Cairo. Another B.L.O. (Major Mostyn Davies) soon joined him, en route for Bulgaria. The two B.L.O.s had a long talk with Tempo, and also with a Bulgarian Communist presented to them as 'Sergei' who gave information about the Bulgarian Partisans. The B.L.O.s reported that Macedonia H.Q. were 'quite ready to cooperate with our missions in attacking enemy lines of communication and economic targets... Regarding the Allatini chrome mine... there are many Partisan supporters amongst the employees... it should be easy to initiate sabotage... Tempo offered to instal a British W/T set with a Macedonian operator at Skoplje. This would act as a centre for obtaining intelligence of enemy troop dispositions.'[40]

The B.L.O.s also reported that Macedonia H.Q. had offered to help the B.L.O.s to reach the Bulgarian H.Q. south of Trn [a town very close to the Yugoslav–Bulgarian frontier], which was in contact with the Fatherland Front in Sofia, said to include 'Agrarians, Socialists, Communists, Military League and Protoguerovists'. They had been told that there were 8,000 Bulgarian Partisans 'well organised but ill equipped'.[41]

This optimistic report was welcomed in Cairo. A party was quickly dropped to reinforce the mission at Macedonia H.Q. with orders to say that G.H.Q. Middle East was 'most interested' in the possibility of attacking the Skoplje–Djevdjelija line and the Allatini chrome mine and would supply the necessary materials.[42] However a 'large-scale expedition' against the Skoplje–Djevdjelija line, in November, failed, though the Partisans derailed a train on another line killing 200 Germans.[43]

Meanwhile Mostyn Davies was making his way slowly towards the
Bulgarian Partisans, observing the operations of the Yugoslav Macedonian Partisans as he went.[44] An 'appreciation of the military situation'
by Force 133 (S.O.E.'s new name in the Middle East) of 19 November
commented: 'it should be noted that when we wished to send a British
officer to Bulgaria, it was not possible to infiltrate him from the Mihajlović groups a few miles from the frontier, but it was necessary to
arrange the long journey from Partisan H.Q. Macedonia under
Partisan escort'.[45] In mid-December S.O.E. said that Mostyn Davies
hoped shortly to meet the Bulgarian Partisan leader in Trn.[46] This he
did – on the Yugoslav side of the frontier.[47]

According to Tempo, there were at this time two Bulgarian Partisan
battalions, both based inside Yugoslavia, the Hristo Botev, which was
under Yugoslav command, and the Vasil Levski, under Bulgarian
command, formed in the Crna Trava region from workers and peasants
who had come from Sofia and other parts of Bulgaria. Tempo had
agreed with Balgaranov that the Bulgarians could use 'free territory'
in Yugoslavia close to the Bulgarian frontier as a base for developing
their activity inside Bulgaria. The Yugoslavs promised to supply food
and weapons for new fighters, in so far as this was not done by the
newly-arrived British mission. The Hristo Botev battalion would be
handed over to Bulgarian command. Following this agreement, Balgaranov went to Sofia to organise the mobilisation of new recruits, and
came back with a proposal that bases should be prepared on Yugoslav
territory for the Bulgarian Partisan General Staff and the Communist
Party Central Committee, so that from there they could complete the
mobilisation and form new partisan battalions. Tempo agreed – but
the idea was not popular among the Serbian villagers who would have
to supply the food. However, the Bulgarian General Staff was formed
and started mobilising and equipping new Bulgarian units. Soon they
had not enough weapons available; Tempo, to help out, ordered a
Serbian unit to hand over its weapons to the Bulgarians.[48]

In February and March 1944, the British thought the outlook for
developing Bulgarian resistance was promising. Mostyn Davies and the
young Communist poet, Frank Thompson, who had joined him in
January, were preparing to move into Bulgaria hoping to establish
contact with Partisans in the Sofia, Plovdiv, Kazanlik and Rila areas,
and to arrange to receive British supplies there. More B.L.O.s were
ready to go in. There seemed to be special opportunities for co-
ordinating Partisan actions with Anglo-American air attacks on Sofia,
and the Chiefs of Staff and S.O.E. were in contact on this.[49] (See
p. 209 below.)

However, the whole plan for using Yugoslav 'free territory' as a
secure base for developing operations was stopped by a telegram from
Moscow from Georgi Dimitrov – according to Tempo – asking why the

Partisans had left Bulgaria and moved to Yugoslav territory: how did they think they were going to take power in Bulgaria? Behind this Tempo saw the old dispute over resistance strategy, and Bulgarian insistence that what mattered was not partisan warfare but an uprising in the towns. The two Bulgarian brigades duly moved into Bulgaria, and suffered very heavily.[50]

It was presumably because of the policy dictated by Dimitrov that Mostyn Davies and Frank Thompson also moved into Bulgaria. On 23 March Mostyn Davies was captured and shot by the Bulgarian police.[51] Thompson took charge, equipped about 500 Bulgarians, and set off with them on an expedition which seemed doomed from the start: it was ambushed; Thompson, with others, was captured, sentenced at a 'trial' in Sofia, shot and buried with the others in a common grave.[52] His name was engraved on a large head-stone among those of his Bulgarian comrades in 1946. It was left to Major John Harington, who arrived in Greek Thrace in April, to try to make a fresh contact with the Partisans. He was joined in July 1944 by Major Ian Macpherson, but they did not contact the Fatherland Front until July and did not enter Bulgaria until August, when some British supplies were sent.[53]

The British effort to arm and develop a Bulgarian Partisan force, with Yugoslav Partisan help, was therefore a failure. But the fault did not lie with the Yugoslav Partisans or the British – except in so far as they imagined, quite wrongly, that the Bulgarian Partisans would turn out to have the same qualities and fighting capacity as the Yugoslavs. The cause was to be found in the internal Bulgarian situation and the internal disputes inside the Bulgarian Communist Party.

THE BRITISH, THE YUGOSLAVS AND THE MACEDONIAN PROBLEM 1943–5

If there was satisfactory co-operation between Tempo and the British over the Bulgarian resistance, the same could not be said about their relations over the Macedonian question, on which both sides were extremely sensitive. When Tempo arrived in Macedonia in February 1943 as the delegate of the Yugoslav Central Committee, one of his first tasks was to help reorganise the Communist structure, which had suffered badly under the Bulgarian occupation. At the end of February an 'independent' Macedonian Communist Party was formed, with Lazar Koliševski as secretary of its first Central Committee: this was seen by Macedonians as a firm indication of Tito's policy towards Macedonia, as one of the nations of a future federal Yugoslavia, with equal rights with Serbs, Croats and others, publicly defined at the Jajce conference of the Yugoslav Anti-Fascist Council in November 1943. It meant that the Yugoslav Macedonians were from then on

much less liable to fall under Bulgarian influence. It also created a
good atmosphere for the formation of new and more effective Partisan
units and the development of a Macedonian national consciousness.
By the end of the year the first liberated territories had been formed.

Tempo had no intention of confining his activities to the old Yugoslav frontiers. When he met Tsimas, Sarafis and Ares Veloukhiotis in

MAP 6. The Macedonian Question, 1943–5

Greece in the summer of 1943, he urged the need to overcome divisions
between the Macedonians of Yugoslavia, Greece and Bulgaria. All
previous Balkan governments, including Greece, he said, had oppressed
the Macedonians. He was not suggesting that the question of frontier
changes should be raised, but rather that all the Balkan Communist
Parties should promise national freedom and equality of rights to all
nations, including the Macedonian nation; that all should form
Macedonian partisan units with their own flag and using their own
language, together with the five-pointed red star used in Yugoslavia;
and that Macedonians should be given the feeling that frontiers would
cease to have reality if the national liberation movements in all the
Balkan countries triumphed. This meant that there should be Slav

Macedonian partisan units in Greece, just as there were Albanian partisan units in Yugoslavia.[54]

A few weeks later at an extremely secret meeting near Larissa, Tempo saw Siantos, who agreed that the Yugoslav Partisans should cross into Greek territory and encourage the local Slav-speaking population to join E.A.M./E.L.A.S., under guarantee of national freedom and equal rights; Slav-Macedonian units could be formed, though they must be under E.L.A.S.; Macedonians should be told that they would win the right of self-determination only through the armed struggle.[55]

In line with this understanding Tempo and a Yugoslav Partisan formation crossed the Greek frontier in the Kajmakcalan area, planning to cut the Salonika–Djevdjelija railway. They met E.L.A.S. units who were most alarmed to hear of this plan, saying it would not be permited by the E.L.A.S. General Staff. Tempo took no notice and went on to the neighbourhood of Salonika where the Yugoslavs were welcomed and sheltered by villagers who – to their disappointment – turned out to be, not Slav-speaking Macedonians, but Greeks from Asia Minor.[56] When Tempo repeated the operation in larger force in February 1944, he reflected that perhaps the reason why they met with only one single traitor in all the Greek villages where they sheltered was that E.L.A.S. had been totally inactive in the area, so that the villagers had no experience or fear of reprisals by the occupiers.[57]

On the other hand, Yugoslav efforts to recruit Slav-speaking Macedonians in western Greek Macedonia were all too successful for the good of relations between the Yugoslav and Greek Communist Parties, and led to some very bitter exchanges in the second half of 1944.[58] E.L.A.S. decided that things had got out of hand and began to disband the Macedonian units, which were wearing the (Yugoslav) Macedonian flag, and send them to southern Greece, which led some Slav Macedonians to flee to Yugoslavia, where they were formed into Partisan units under Yugoslav command, while E.L.A.S. and Tempo mutually accused each other of interference in each other's internal affairs.[59] According to a later Yugoslav Macedonian account, E.L.A.S. also arrested and killed some leading Slav Macedonians.[60] The same account attributed this action to 'opportunist and short-sighted attitudes of the Greek Communist Party and E.A.M. towards the exiled government and the English'.[61] A generation later Yugoslav Macedonian secondary school-children were taught that the failure of Tempo's attempt to co-operate with the Greeks stemmed from the decision of the E.A.M./E.L.A.S. leaders to subordinate themselves to the British Middle East Command, thereby destroying their own independence and falling under the control of the Western Powers: this had done great harm to the liberation movement and to the Macedonians of Greek Macedonia in particular, including the death of some of their leaders.[62]

Much as the British disliked any Macedonian movement which

might, in their view, harm their Greek allies, it is very doubtful whether their influence over E.L.A.S. was as strong as this account suggests. E.L.A.S. did not need outside prompting when it came to oppressing the Slav-Macedonians.

A remarkably favourable report on Yugoslav activities in the Florina area from March to October 1944 came from a B.L.O., Captain P. H. Evans, who had observed the situation at first hand. He said that the region was predominantly Slav, not Greek. Metaxas had made the Slav language illegal and fed people on castor oil for speaking it. The Yugoslav Partisans had been much more successful in organising the Slav villages than E.L.A.S., since the Slavs mistrusted E.L.A.S's supposedly Slav formations, known as S.N.O.F., or the Slav national liberation front. Evans quoted Tempo as calling for a 'free Macedonia' including Florina and Salonika, and for a plebiscite on the issue, and concluded: 'if such a plebiscite were freely and fairly held it is more likely than not that a free Macedonia would result'.[63]

Until late in 1944, Tempo does not seem to have approached the Bulgarian Communists about organising the Macedonians of Bulgarian (Pirin) Macedonia. Perhaps he thought the Bulgarian resistance movement too weak to make the effort worth while. Moreover, the attitude of the Bulgarian Communist Party on the Macedonian question was still equivocal. When the B.L.O., Mostyn Davies, had his first talks with the Bulgarian Partisans in February 1944, he reported that while close Bulgarian–Yugoslav co-operation was part of their programme, they did not think the question of federation should be raised until after the war, and their attitude over Macedonia was not clear. Their illegal newspaper, *Rabotnichesko Delo*, called for an 'integrated, free, independent Macedonia', but said nothing about frontiers.[64] The mere mention of Macedonia was an alarm signal for the British, and it was suggested in Cairo that Mostyn Davies should be warned of 'the innumerable snags in Bulgaria's relations with our Greek and Jugoslav allies' and instructed to 'dissociate himself as pointedly as possible' from all but the military aspects of the Fatherland Front programme.[65]

The events of the late summer and early autumn of 1944 led to a minor crisis over Macedonia and South Slav union. On 2 August the Anti-Fascist Assembly of National Liberation of Macedonia, or A.S.N.O.M., met for the first time – an assertion that a Yugoslav Macedonian State was already in existence, in fulfilment of the policy laid down by Tito at the Jajce conference.

The British were already worried over this policy, as a possible threat to British and Greek interests. In April 1944 a statement by Tito on complete autonomy for Macedonia was welcomed in Moscow by the newspaper *Red Star*. This led Churchill to send a minute to the Foreign Office: 'let me have a note of not more than one page on the Macedonian issue, illustrated by a map. Comment please upon the question of "an autonomous Macedonia".[66] He sent a further minute to Cadogan: 'how should we feel towards a Bulgar–Yugoslav bloc? It certainly does not seem very pleasant at first sniff.'[67] Eden replied that ethnographically such a bloc had the advantage of providing a solution of the Macedonian problem, for Macedonia would be an autonomous unit in the federation; against this, the Greeks hated the idea. From the purely British point of view, Eden added, 'such a bloc is a doubtful proposition. It would overshadow Greece both politically and militarily. It would undoubtedly give the Russians a preponderating position in the Balkans. It might advance claims to Greek territory ... In present circumstances it would in practice mean having the Russians on the Aegean'.[68] (Eden did not explain just why it meant this.)

In August 1944, Eden told Churchill he was worried about Soviet softness towards Bulgaria, suspecting that this meant that the Russians were preparing for Bulgaria to enter a South Slav State, led by Tito, which might take in 'a bit of northern Greece'. Eden suggested Churchill might bear this in mind when he saw Tito in Italy.[69] On 12 August Churchill duly 'sounded a note of warning to Tito', but also minuted: 'it will be difficult to stop'.[70]

What the British did not know was whether Tito was content with an autonomous Macedonia inside the pre-1941 Yugoslav frontiers, or whether he wanted to add Greek and Bulgarian Macedonia to it. The coming to power of a Fatherland Front government in Bulgaria on 9 September aroused fresh fears. On 10 November the British mission in Sofia sent the Foreign Office a manifesto issued by A.S.N.O.M. in Yugoslav Macedonia proclaiming its 'justified and persistent demand for the unification of the whole Macedonian people on the basis of the right to self-determination', and inviting all Macedonians in Greece and Bulgaria to 'participate actively in the general struggle for the complete defeat of Fascism and its satellites'.[71] On 16 November the British Mission now established in Belgrade reported rumours of 'a secret agreement' between Tito and the Bulgarian government whereby Pirin Macedonia would be 'returned to Yugoslavia.'[72]

It was true that Tito had signed an agreement with a newly-appointed Bulgarian Partisan General, Dobri Terpeshev, whom no one in Bulgaria took very seriously, about co-operation in the war effort. Terpeshev himself also seemed quite ready to let the Yugoslavs have Pirin Macedonia: in December he told A.S.N.O.M. that Fatherland Front Bulgaria 'considers that that part of Macedonia which at present lies within the boundaries of Bulgaria should be united with Macedonia in Yugoslavia'.[73] But this was not the view of more serious Bulgarian Communists, and when Tempo visited Sofia, together with Lazar Koliševski and the Yugoslav Macedonian Partisan Commander, General Mihajlo Apostolski, they had rather stormy conversations with

Traicho Kostov, Tsola Dragoicheva and other leading Communists. The Yugoslavs urged the Bulgarians to grant autonomy to Pirin Macedonia, as Yugoslavia had done to Vardar (Yugoslav) Macedonia; to appease the Yugoslavs, the Bulgarians agreed on an intensification of contacts between Yugoslav Macedonia and Pirin Macedonia, which might perhaps prepare the ground for ultimate union. But any idea of a grant of autonomy to Pirin Macedonia was subsequently vetoed by Georgi Dimitrov, who telegraphed from Moscow that it would be premature to raise the question, and conditions must first ripen.[74]

The British were worried not only by Yugoslav–Bulgarian contacts – rather prematurely – but also by reports of the formation of a battalion of Greek Macedonians in Bitolj, on the Yugoslav side of the frontier. These were clearly S.N.O.F. refugees from E.L.A.S., but the British saw the event as a prelude to a Yugoslav move to annex Greek Macedonia. When, in November, Eden read the first telegram on it, he wrote: 'very bad. Should we not have a show down about all this with Russians, Tito etc.?'[75] Fitzroy Maclean, on taking up his position as head of the British Mission in Belgrade, was instructed to protest to Tito, who explained that the brigade had been formed from refugees from 'oppression' in Greece, and promised that the brigade would not cross the Yugoslav frontier.[76]

What made Eden really angry, however, were the reports of speeches made on 7 November at the National Theatre in Belgrade to the Serbian Anti-Fascist Assembly on the Macedonian question. Tempo declared that the whole of the Macedonian people wished to achieve complete unity; the Aegean province and the Pirin province should join the federal state of Macedonia (inside Yugoslavia). He added that he had travelled through Pirin and Aegean Macedonia and found that the people there wished to join their 'mother country'.[77] Milovan Djilas accused 'forces under the command of the Papandreou government' of 'violently terrorizing our Macedonians in Greece' without justifiable reasons; the Macedonians only wanted to use their own language in organising for the struggle against the Germans. Djilas added that no sufficiently strong force had yet been found to offer successful resistance to this 'chauvinistic policy'.

The telegram from Bari reporting this pointed out that Djilas, who had recently been in Moscow, was speaking in the name of the Central Committee of the Yugoslav Communist Party, so was presumably expressing the official party line. Eden wrote on the telegram: 'who is this animal? and should we not complain to Russia of his sauciness? or to Tito?'[78]

On the same occasion Dimitar Vlahov, a veteran Macedonian revolutionary, now Vice-President of the Yugoslav Anti-Fascist Assembly, A.V.N.O.J., spoke about the 'terrorization' of Slavs in Aegean Macedonia and claimed the right of self-determination for Macedonians in Greece, Bulgaria and Yugoslavia.[79]

All this was calculated to rouse the worst fears in the Foreign Office. After the first report of Djilas's speech, instructions were sent to Belgrade: 'Marshal Tito should be told of H.M.G.'s strong disapproval of such utterances.' The passages relating to Greece were 'peculiarly offensive' since they were an attack on 'the government of one of the United Nations with whom H.M.G. are in special relations'.[80] The Foreign Office asked the Moscow Embassy to inform the Soviet government of these representations and express the hope that the Russians would 'see fit to express their disapproval also to Tito'.[81]

The Foreign Office however took little notice of the statement made by the Bulgarian, Terpeshev, on the same occasion, admitting the right of Pirin Macedonia to join Yugoslav Macedonia as part of the Yugoslav federal state, and declaring that there was no obstacle to a 'friendly alliance' between Bulgaria and Yugoslavia.[82] At that moment they inclined to the view that the Bulgarian–Yugoslav negotiations were 'a typical Macedonian conspiratorial intrigue' – whatever that might mean.[83] In Sofia the British political representative was assured by Petko Stainov, the non-Communist Foreign Minister, who spoke rather scornfully of Tito and the Yugoslavs, that there was no agreement on the return of Pirin Macedonia to Yugoslavia.[84] It is certain that even if some of the Bulgarian Communists – though not Kostov – were willing to cede Pirin Macedonia, the non-Communist members of the government, then in a majority, were not.

On 30 November Sargent produced yet another paper on Macedonia and Yugoslav–Bulgarian union, reiterating that

'although we would welcome a federation between all the Balkan States . . . we cannot agree to an exclusive union or federation between Yugoslavia and Bulgaria because it would disturb the balance of power between the Balkan States, because it would isolate Greece and endanger her position as a Balkan State, and because it would enable Bulgaria . . . to escape . . . from the consequences of her acts . . . Although we are prepared to acquiesce in the creation of a Macedonian State in the future federal Jugoslavia, we must insist that this State shall not annex nor lay claim to any territories whatsoever belonging to either Bulgaria or Greece, on the ground that these territories are 'Macedonian'.[85]

On 5 December Eden presented this paper to the War Cabinet which discussed it six days later. Eden said it might be 'rather optimistic to hope that we should in fact be able to veto a Yugoslav–Bulgarian combination', but that was the more reason why we should talk without delay to the Russians and make it clear that if the object of the manoeuvres was to enable Bulgaria to acquire Greek territory or an Aegean outlet, 'we should be strongly opposed to this'. Churchill, probably with an eye on the Greek civil war and mindful of the percentage agreement, said it was important to avoid a clash with the Russians: there could be little question under present circumstances that Communist influence, under Russian patronage, was in due course, even without specific action by Russia, likely to establish itself throughout the Balkan peninsula, save possibly in Greece. Stability, Churchill said, should be restored in Athens before there were talks with the Russians.[86]

One serious difficulty was to know just what was happening in Macedonia. On 2 December Sir Reginald Leeper, the ambassador in Athens, reported that there was no form of frontier control between Greece and Yugoslavia and 'E.L.A.S. and Tito's bands are probably able to cross at will'; there was evidence that the Macedonian question was becoming a bone of contention between the Greek Communist 'extremists' (by whom he presumably meant the leaders in Athens) and 'the local E.L.A.S. who disapprove of Macedonian separatism'. But, he added, Tsimas, now E.L.A.S. representative with Tito, probably favoured it.[87] On 13 December the Foreign Office was told of reports that the Bulgarians were forming a brigade of Greek Macedonians.[88] On 16 December they heard from Maclean in Belgrade that a few days earlier the Yugoslav Macedonian Partisan commander, Apostolski, had told the British mission that they were not needed and must leave; however Maclean had at once written to Tito who replied that Apostolski had acted without authority and had been instructed to keep the mission.[89]

Tito took the same conciliatory line on the more important issues, giving Maclean a personal assurance that he had no aggressive intentions against Greek Macedonia, that he had instructed Tempo and his other commanders to make no more mention of Greece or the Macedonian question without first referring to him, that any Yugoslav claims would be held over till the peace conference, and that the activities of which the British complained had taken place without his knowledge or approval.[90] He does not seem to have been asked for, or given, assurances about Bulgarian–Yugoslav union.

The Foreign Office was a little soothed. But on 27 December telegrams were sent to Moscow and Washington, saying there had been signs that the idea of a Yugoslav–Bulgarian federation was entertained with favour in the Yugoslav national liberation movement and – unfairly putting the blame on the Bulgarians instead of the Yugoslavs – that 'the Bulgarians' were preparing to foster agitation for 'a greater Macedonia at the expense of Greece'. The Soviet and American governments were informed of British views as set out in Sargent's paper of 30 November; Tito and the Bulgarian government were to be similarly informed later.[91]

At the beginning of February 1945 the Soviet government replied that they knew that Yugoslavia and Bulgaria were negotiating a pact of alliance, and that they favoured this; but they considered 'the question of a Balkan Federation and in particular of a Yugoslav–Bulgarian Federation' was 'not at present actual . . . and of no practical importance'.[92] Tito had not informed the British that he was negotiating with Bulgaria, and the Foreign Office thought it clear that the pact was intended to be the first step towards a federation, and suggested that the matter should be discussed at Yalta.[93]

At Yalta Eden proposed to Molotov and Edward Stettinius that since Bulgaria was still under an armistice régime, the Bulgarian and Yugoslav governments should be told that an alliance between them could not be approved. Stettinius however suggested that the matter should be left for Molotov to discuss with the British and American ambassadors in Moscow. Molotov agreed.[94]

According to later Yugoslav accounts, negotiations about a Bulgarian–Yugoslav federation had started in December, on Yugoslav initiative, but had reached deadlock on the question whether Bulgaria should merely be one unit, along with six others, in the federal state, or whether Yugoslavia and Bulgaria should be two equal units in a much looser federation. Stalin came down first on the Bulgarian side, later on the Yugoslav side. But the negotiations came to nothing and even the draft treaty of alliance was shelved – so the Yugoslavs believed – because of Anglo-American intervention.[95]

The British had therefore done something to stop the dreaded Bulgarian–Yugoslav union and the unification of Macedonia. But it seems doubtful whether they would have succeeded if Stalin had not begun to think that he too had an interest in preventing it. Certainly by 1948 Stalin had decided firmly that he was not going to allow it: the Soviet interest was to keep Yugoslavia and Bulgaria at loggerheads over Macedonia. This later became a permanent tenet of Soviet policy. The Russians eventually reached a position rather similar to the war-time position of the British, each seeing a Bulgarian–Yugoslav union as a threat to their interests in the Balkans.

The weaknesses of Britain's war-time policy were lack of inside information about the inner workings of the Communist parties, a belief that the Communist world was monolithic, and a failure to understand that in the Balkans, Communists were swayed as much as anyone else by national passions and prejudices, or at least by the need to play on such feelings in their followers.

16 Britain and the Reluctant Satellites, 1941–5

On the western side of the Balkan peninsula, the British found themselves in contact with Communist resistance leaders who were allies, but
who suspected and feared British 'invasion' plans. When in 1944 Stalin
asked Tito what he would do 'if the British really forced a landing in
Jugoslavia', Tito answered: 'we should offer determined resistance'.[1]
The Albanian and Greek Communists would almost certainly have liked
to give the same answer but might have thought it impracticable.

In Hungary and Rumania the situation was reversed. Both hoped
against hope for the arrival of British or Anglo-American forces, or
even a token force. If Britain had been able to send one, these two Axis
satellites would probably have tried to break with Germany much
earlier than they did. But the British were prevented by geography and
war strategy from any such attempt. The third Axis satellite, Bulgaria,
was in a rather different position. Until late summer 1944, most Bulgarians did not share the Hungarian and Rumanian fears of Russian
domination. Instead they looked to the Russians to protect them against
the vengeance of the British, seen as the champions and protectors of
their Greek and Yugoslav neighbours. In the last weeks before the Red
Army arrived on their frontier, non-Communist Bulgarians began to
think differently and, like the Hungarians and Rumanians, to hope
against hope for the arrival of Anglo-Americans. Once again for geographical, strategic and political reasons, this was impossible.

The Turks, who might perhaps have opened the way into Bulgaria
and Rumania, were nearly as anxious to see the British there and to
keep out the Russians as the Rumanians and Hungarians themselves.
But they were so obsessed by their fear of Russia and Russian designs
on the Straits that their strongest instinct was to keep their heads down
and preserve their strength intact rather than risk entry into the war.
They also doubted Britain's capacity and will to keep the Russians out
of South-East Europe. So they did not even break off diplomatic relations with Germany until August 1944, by which time the Russians
were about to sweep into Rumania, Bulgaria and Hungary.

In their dealings with the Axis satellites, the British were faced with
strong temptation to act behind Russia's back and to encourage their

defection from Germany by promises of support against Russian demands and Russian vengeance. They could even have argued that they were thereby shortening the war against Germany. Except for one or two minor failures to follow the Soviet line or keep the Russians informed, the British government were painfully scrupulous in resisting all such temptations as though they came from the devil himself, and in telling the Russians every detail of their dealings with the satellites. The Russians did not reciprocate. They must have thought the British either extremely naive or diabolically but inexplicably cunning.

Apart from this rigid loyalty to the Soviet Union, British policies towards the three satellites, from 1941 on, were mainly improvised and very loosely co-ordinated. Until the collapse of Italy in the summer of 1943, there was very little the British could do except through propaganda and rare secret contacts with anti-German elements. Their main effort was put into pressure – by B.B.C. broadcasts and other propaganda channels – on the Hungarians and Rumanians to send as few troops as possible to fight with the Germans against Russia, and on the Bulgarians not to send troops to Russia, at the same time warning them that by occupying Greek and Yugoslav territory they were releasing German troops to fight against Russia.

Since the Rumanians and Hungarians had always been mutually jealous and suspicious, and since neither had accepted the 1940 Vienna Award dividing Transylvania as just – though the Rumanians were naturally far more bitter – British propaganda had a chance of exploiting these suspicions and fears, with the aim of limiting both countries' war effort against Russia.[2] The difficulty was that while the British wanted on principle to keep the ultimate fate of Transylvania open until the peace settlement, which made it possible to dangle it before both Rumanians and Hungarians as a possible reward for good behaviour, Stalin had already made up his mind in 1941 that Rumania should have all Transylvania and perhaps more (presumably as compensation for the loss of Bessarabia and northern Bukovina to Russia). But until the spring of 1944 this difference did not hamper British propaganda, which had some success. When Italy collapsed in 1943 Hungary initiated negotiations with Rumania – a reasonable move since both countries were thinking of turning against Germany – but these failed;[3] and by the end of the year both countries were concentrating troops in Transylvania; there were some clashes with loss of life.[4] This obviously did not suit the Germans.

Tentative peace feelers began to come from the Hungarians from the time of Stalingrad onwards, and there were visible stirrings in Rumania. The standard British reply to the Hungarians was that so long as Hungary continued to fight against Britain's allies and to help the Axis it could expect neither sympathy nor consideration.[5] But on 11 February 1943 Cadogan minuted:

I begin to wonder . . . whether we are right in always turning down flat any approach from the satellite states. I suppose we are afraid of appearing to 'appease' them. It seems to me that in the present critical phase for Germany, anything that we can do to make the satellite states more of an embarrassment to Germany would be all to the good. Of course there are two dangers (1) of rousing the suspicions of our Allies and (2) of having to give commitments that would be embarrassing later . . . I only hope our minds are not rigidly closed . . . [6]

On this Eden commented: 'there may be a case for modifying our attitude slightly but if we do so we can only do it in agreement with the U.S. and Soviet governments.'[7] Sargent held a meeting on 24 February; the main result was agreement that Rumania was in a different position from the other two satellites, being claimed by the Russians as part of their sphere. In the case of Hungary, 'there would be advantage from the propaganda point of view as well as from that of policy in adopting a less negative attitude and, if a suitable opportunity arises, in regard also to Bulgaria. Neither of these countries have a direct conflict of interest with Russia.' The propaganda line for Hungary should be that 'we have no desire to see Hungary torn to pieces or to penalize the Hungarian people for the follies of their government . . . It is our intention that the future of Hungary should be guided by the Atlantic Charter . . . Our attitude will be influenced by the practical steps taken by the Hungarians themselves.'[8] For Bulgaria, a similar line could be followed. As for the Rumanians, the Southern Department thought it would be impossible to encourage any peace feelers or hold out any inducement to them to throw in their hand without prior consultation with the Soviet government, which had its 'territorial desiderata'.[9]

On 10 March Eden embodied these views, together with details of the latest Hungarian feelers, in despatches to Moscow and Washington proposing the slightly softened line towards Hungary and Bulgaria, but adding that if Britain received any approach from Rumania, it 'would take the line that the Soviet Union is primarily concerned as bearing the main burden of the war being waged by Rumania . . . and should be approached in the first place'. H.M.G. considered that 'the Soviet government are in a better position than they are themselves to hold out inducements to the Rumanians to abandon the Axis'.[10]

Molotov did not reply until 7 June – and then, in the first place, to complain about remarks made by a prominent British trades unionist favourable to exiled Hungarian Social Democrats. On the main matter, he said that he considered it possible for the Allies to have informal contacts and to enter into conversations – keeping each other previously informed – with opposition elements in Hungary; but in relations with all the satellites they should follow the principles of unconditional surrender, return of occupied territories, indemnity for war damage, and the punishment of war criminals. Molotov then made two important points: the Soviet government 'stand for the preservation of the satellite states and harbour no designs on the independence of these states', and it did not recognise the Vienna Award on Transylvania.[11]

In the Foreign Office, Roberts minuted cautiously that Molotov's reference to the independence of satellite states 'may imply that the Soviet government would not favour affiliation into the U.S.S.R.'; this at least was something gained.[12]

But no immediate reply went to Moscow. The Italian collapse and a peace feeler from Franz von Papen (then German ambassador in Turkey) prompted Churchill to telegraph from Quebec, where he was to meet Roosevelt, that he thought there was no need to go on 'continually uttering the slogan "unconditional surrender"'; 'we certainly do not want, if we can help it, to get them all fused together into a solid block for whom there is no hope'.[13] The same presumably applied to the satellites. So when Eden finally replied to Molotov on 6 September he said he wanted to follow 'a common line' over the satellites and accepted Molotov's four principles, but added that the unconditional surrender formula should not be so presented as completely to discourage groups who might help the Allies.[14]

By this time the collapse of Italy had caused great stirrings in the satellite countries, raising visions of Allied landings in the Balkans and opening up the practical possibility of Anglo-American bombing of South-East Europe. When approaches came from the Rumanians, Eden was willing to defer completely to the Russians. Hungary was a different matter. A Hungarian peace feeler in August (see also pp. 251 ff. below), opened up a difference between the British and Russians over timing and strategy in responding to satellite moves towards surrender. Churchill was against undue hurry, telegraphing from Quebec on 7 September: 'their desertion of Germany would be of the utmost value provided it took place at the right moment. On the other hand, it would be improvident of us to squander the Hungarian volte-face and merely produce a premature outbreak followed by a German Gauleiter or super-quisling government installed by force. The timing is everything . . . I should myself like to see the Balkans much riper than they are now, and . . . to let impending events in Italy, if they turn out well, play their part.'[15]

But Molotov was all for speed and turning on the heat. He told Clark Kerr on 20 September that he believed it would be to the advantage of the allies to act 'quickly and resolutely, not allowing either Germans or pro-German Hungarian circles to recover from confusion connected with Italy's surrender'. Immediate surrender would create more favourable conditions both on the Eastern front and in Italy; postponement would allow Germany to recover from confusion and strengthen her position in South-East Europe.

Churchill presumably wanted to wait till the Italian campaign had reached the point where the British would have forces available for some sort of action in South-East Europe. Molotov wanted immediate gains, and presumably did not mind if satellite surrender attempts ended in no more than a German occupation, which, from the Soviet standpoint, would remove from the scene satellite political leaders whom they disliked. But both arguments turned out to be irrelevant, because the Western allies came up against unexpectedly strong German resistance in Italy, the Germans re-established control of South-East Europe, and in any case the Hungarians were not ready to act. Churchill, in the House of Commons on 21 September, coined a phrase as a substitute for unconditional surrender: 'satellite states, suborned or overawed, may perhaps, if they can help to shorten the war, be allowed to work their passage home'.

At the Moscow conference of Foreign Ministers in October, the Russians continued to press for speed and talked on the assumption that it would be possible to end the war by the end of the year if only the Anglo-Americans would really try. As for the satellites, Anglo-Soviet differences over Hungary were left unsolved (see p. 254 below), and discussions on Rumania ended so vaguely that later misunderstandings were almost inevitable. (See p. 228 below.) Bulgaria was hardly discussed. (See p. 216 below.) All that was agreed was a formula, proposed by Eden, that the three governments 'agree to inform each other immediately of any peace feelers . . . to consult together with a view to concerting their action in regard to such approaches'.[16]

Thereafter the British continued to report religiously the most feeble of feelers, till finally Eden minuted: 'we don't want these gossipy feelers. It is embarrassing to have to keep reporting them to our allies, and may be dangerous if we don't.'[17] British correctness was not matched by the Russians.

The Teheran conference, with its public forecast of operations 'from the south' as well as the east and west, produced mixed feelings in the satellites, which included the hope of Allied landings in the Balkans. At the very least, Rumanians and Hungarians hoped for Anglo-American airborne forces which would descend from heaven to save them from Soviet occupation or at least hold Russian anger in check. Yet this was a practical impossibility. The War Office said in February 1944 that a force of 1,000–2,000 paratroops would represent a 'very high proportion indeed of all the paratroops we have available in the Mediterranean theatre and could only be sent to Rumania at the expense of the battle in Italy'.[18] Five months later the American military authorities thought the provision of American airborne troops to be 'impracticable'.[19]

During the winter of 1943-4, therefore, the British turned their thoughts more and more to bombing the satellites as a way of getting them out of the war, or at least forcing the Germans to occupy them. With Overlord looming ahead, this became more and more important. At first the bombing priorities recommended by the Chiefs of Staff were: first, Bulgaria, next Budapest and then Bucharest; the reasons were largely practical.[20] Up till late January, only Bulgaria had been bombed: there had been two raids on Sofia in December, and one raid on Sofia and two small raids on smaller towns in January.[21] Some officials in the Foreign Office thought that bombing would go far to bring about the defection of the satellites, but Cadogan was totally sceptical. 'The Hungarians are not going to defect,' he minuted in late February; 'bombing of Budapest is going to have no political effect. I do wish Departments would understand that no satellite is going to "surrender unconditionally" until it has got assurance of much better protection by the Allies than Italy has got.'[22]

But in the spring of 1944, the bombing of Sofia seemed to be having real repercussions in Bulgaria, and the first British contacts with the Bulgarian Partisans created hopes – which proved mistaken – that they could do great things, especially if they were provided with cover by Allied air attacks. But there was still a serious problem of priorities: it was the Americans who had the necessary long-range heavy bombers and who had to be persuaded that bombing the satellites was worth while. Churchill intervened powerfully from time to time, but the overall priority for South-East European targets remained relatively low.

In early March this frustrating situation provoked discussion in the Foreign Office about the possibility of following a single policy towards all three satellites and getting them to turn against Germany simultaneously. As the Southern Department put it: 'we can either continue to deal with them piecemeal, to carry on desultory and inconclusive contacts and to bomb them when we happen to have a few planes to spare; or we can consider the Balkan problem as a whole, in relation to our general strategy, and make a determined effort by coordinating our policy towards all three countries with a military plan for bombing and possible invasion to get all three countries out of the war.'[23]

The discussion had been sparked off by Christopher Steel,[24] then attached to the Minister of State in Cairo. He wrote that all three satellites were squeezed between the dominant fears of Russia and Germany, and 'while Bulgaria is in some ways on the Russian side, they all see their principal hope of survival as independent states in some kind of relations with the Anglo-Saxon powers'. Their problem, he added, was 'how and when to fall into Anglo-Saxon arms . . . and even whether the Anglo-Saxon arms are good enough anyway'. In this situation, Steel suggested, 'the theoretical best objective . . . would be to use bombing threats on Rumania, Hungary and Bulgaria so as to produce a planned volte face of all three at the same time in conjunction with an Allied landing'. This might be an altogether outside chance, but that was no reason for not having a shot at it.[25]

In theory, the British Chiefs of Staff were bound to be sympathetic to any major effort at detaching the satellites from Germany, if only because they wanted the maximum possible diversion of German forces from North-West Europe in preparation for Overlord. For purposes of strategic deception alone, the Controlling Officers in London thought that the development of a threat to Germany from Bulgaria was important.[26] Early in March General Maitland Wilson, the Supreme Allied Commander Mediterranean, urging the British Chiefs of Staff to get the U.S. 15th Air Force to give higher bombing priority to Bulgaria, so as to get Bulgaria out of the war, spoke of 'the extreme importance of this possibility to our whole European strategy . . . in containing enemy forces away from OVERLORD'.[27]

But there were very grave practical difficulties in the way of any concerted attempt to bring about the defection of the satellites. These were set out by Cavendish-Bentinck,[28] the Foreign Office representative on the Joint Intelligence Committee, in comment on Steel's proposal: '1. we have not forces available to carry out operations in the Balkans in the face of any organised German opposition. 2. Our bombing in the Balkans has to be carried out by agreement with the Americans. There is no hope of persuading the U.S. Chiefs of Staff to agree to a large "pre-arranged plan" for bombing Balkan targets.' He concluded: 'I do not think it is much good asking for an "overall military policy for the Balkans" if there is not the wherewithal to carry it out.'[29] Cadogan was even more concise: 'Mr. Steel seems to share the delusion of some of the satellites that we can stage a "Balkan Expedition". We can't. We could tell Mr. Steel this. We can't tell the Satellites, but while they remain in ignorance of the truth we can discount . . . the value of their "peace feelers".'[30] Sargent, however, renewed Steel's plea for 'a consistent and persistent policy'. Cadogan replied: 'it isn't so much a policy we want as an expeditionary force, and I'm afraid that's not forthcoming.'[31]

The ban on letting the satellite leaders know that there could be no Anglo-American expeditionary force, imposed for reasons of strategic deception, obviously added to the difficulties in the way of a coherent policy. But it was taken very seriously. In late March a message was drafted for General Maitland Wilson to send urgently to Marshal Antonescu, which contained the words: 'no land assistance can be given you from this theatre'; these had to be deleted 'on security grounds'.[32]

Even if the Western allies had no expeditionary force, more might have been achieved, at an earlier stage, in detaching the satellites from Germany, if the Soviet Union had been willing to work closely with the British in the political field and to forge a truly joint policy towards the satellites. In the spring of 1944 Eden made various efforts in this direction. Molotov responded with one constructive move – an assurance to Rumania about its post-war frontiers and independence. But in general the Russians remained intensely suspicious and anxious to handle the satellites independently of the British, except in so far as they could make use of British contacts for their own purposes. It was soon clear that the Russians were not interested in a simultaneous 'jump out' by the three satellites. They preferred to deal with each satellite separately, bringing about political changes inside each country until a suitably pro-Soviet government was ready to take power at the moment of the 'jump out', which was to be delayed until the Red Army could march in. If in September 1943 the Russians had been in a hurry and Churchill had wanted to wait for things to ripen, these positions were now reversed.

In the middle of March 1944 British hopes of a Hungarian jump out were shattered when German troops marched in to prevent one. A Rumanian delegate had arrived in Cairo but was then kept kicking his heels throughout the summer until the time came for the Red Army to advance into Rumania; and no Bulgarian delegate turned up until August.

However, once Overlord was successfully launched, the British stopped worrying seriously about the satellites. In a discussion with Sargent in London in July, Steel 'questioned whether we had any interest' in trying to speed up negotiations with the Rumanians: in the spring it was important, because armistice negotiations and the threat of Rumania coming out of the war locked German troops which might otherwise have been used for Overlord.[33] Militarily, if not politically, the British felt they could now afford to wash their hands of the satellites.

By the end of September 1944 the Soviet Union had won military control of the satellites, and with it, the political initiative. The British–Soviet arguments over the satellites in the autumn and winter of 1944 were the opening of a political struggle for post-war power, with the British yielding ground at every step.

Britain and Bulgaria,
        1941–4

When the British left Bulgaria in March 1941, they had no political
commitments to any person or group. They were finished with King
Boris. Their only ties were S.O.E.'s contacts with the Left Agrarians
and Velchev's Military League. The Left Agrarian leader, Dr G. M.
Dimitrov, a strong and attractive personality, had been brought out by
S.O.E. to the Middle East, after a brief stay in Yugoslavia from where
he had hoped to send a small 'expedition' into Bulgaria – a project
killed by the German invasion of Yugoslavia.[1] Another Left Agrarian,
Dimitri Matsankiev, was also brought out with S.O.E. help. Both from
then on did propaganda work for the British, G. M. Dimitrov broadcasting from the Middle East and Matsankiev from the B.B.C. in
London. The text of an anti-German, anti-Boris declaration by Dimitrov
was broadcast from London in February 1942. But the Foreign Office
refused any form of political recognition for the exiled Bulgarians.[2]

Dimitrov also tried to help S.O.E. to establish W/T contact or other
links with fellow Left Agrarians inside Bulgaria, including Nikola
Petkov and Asen Pavlov. These efforts were persistently dogged by bad
luck; so also were attempts to send in W/T sets from Istanbul. S.O.E.
had also hoped to establish contact through G. M. Dimitrov with the
Military League; and Velchev in turn was believed to have links with
Mihajlović, who had earlier been Yugoslav Military Attaché in Sofia.
During 1942 S.O.E. considered sending Dimitrov to Mihajlović's H.Q.,
so that he could work from there into Bulgaria. But British relations
with Mihajlović were not good enough, and Mihajlović's own position
not strong enough, for S.O.E. to put this plan into practice. So by the
end of 1942 S.O.E. was not hopeful about early results in Bulgaria.[3]
Mihajlović was reported in November 1942 to have had contact through
one of his commanders with Velchev;[4] but nothing came of this. In
January 1943 Mihajlović told Col. Bailey, who had just arrived, that
he was very favourable to Dimitrov and wanted him to speak on the
radio, but did not think the time was ripe for him to come to his own
H.Q.[5]

At this time the British had no contact with the Bulgarian Communists – though the former Minister, Rendel, always thought them
the strongest political force and was sceptical of S.O.E.'s efforts to base

their activity on the Agrarians and Velchev.[6] During 1942 the Communists were very active politically, working under the tight control of Georgi Dimitrov, their exiled leader in the Soviet Union. Directly after Hitler's attack on Russia – by their own account – they decided to 'start preparations for armed struggle against the Hitlerite occupiers and Bulgarian monarcho-fascists' and to work in the Bulgarian army with the slogans 'not one soldier to the Eastern front' and 'fraternize with the Yugoslav Partisans'. They claimed to have formed partisan detachments as early as 1941 (if so, these cannot have been very effective) and, more convincingly, to have formed 'combat groups' for sabotage and diversion, mainly in the towns.[7] In all this they were backed by the radio station *Hristo Botev* broadcasting from the Soviet Union under Georgi Dimitrov's control. By the end of the year the police were uncovering Communist groups inside the Bulgarian army.[8]

In April 1942 the Bulgarian Communists suffered a heavy blow. Groups of Bulgarian exiles had been sent in from the Soviet Union by submarine or dropped from aircraft, but were caught; the result was the arrest of a number of prominent Party members. Following this 'affair of the parachutists' 18 Communists were executed in July 1942.[9] Perhaps the disastrous end to this enterprise – the only one of its kind recorded – caused the Russians to steer clear of this kind of activity in South-East Europe and to use British help to get a mission to Tito. In the case of Bulgaria they had a special reason for caution; they did not want to risk losing their Legation in Sofia as a listening post and channel for political pressure.

In the summer of 1942 the Communist Party launched a larger political project, on Georgi Dimitrov's orders – the formation of the Fatherland Front, or Otechestven Front (O.F.). Its programme, drawn up by Georgi Dimitrov, was broadcast on 17 July by *Hristo Botev*, calling for a break with Germany, conversion of the army into a 'people's army' which would fight under Soviet leadership for the destruction of Germany, and formation of a people's democratic government.[10] The Communists sought the co-operation of the Agrarians, the small Social Democrat party, and various other 'democratic' groups.[11] In August 1943 a National Committee of the O.F. was formed, in which these parties, together with Velchev's Military League, also known as Zveno, took part. One member of it was Nikola Petkov,[12] one of the leading Left Agrarians and a man of great courage and distinction, who four years later was denounced and executed by the Communist government. The Communists later accused Petkov of having prevented the Agrarians, during the war, from joining the O.F. committees in the towns and villages;[13] this may or may not have been true, but there may well have been friction between the two parties which had been at loggerheads off and on since the early 1920s.

BRITISH LACK OF CONTACT

In all this the British had no part, though they were aware of the existence of the O.F. from August 1942.[14] When Bailey was sent in to Mihajlović at the end of 1942, he had instructions to ask Mihajlović for help in establishing contact with the O.F.; but Mihajlović must have known the Communist role in it and did his best to prevent any contact.[15] Since he controlled the area of eastern Serbia bordering Bulgaria, little could be done; it was for that reason that in the summer of 1943 S.O.E. decided to try to contact the O.F. with the help of the Yugoslav Partisans. (See p. 193 above.)

During 1942 and 1943, almost the only means of communicating with Bulgaria – apart from radio propaganda – was through the former Bulgarian Minister in London, Nikola Momchilov, who had resigned when Bulgaria joined the Tripartite Pact and was strongly pro-British. In July 1942 he suggested to the Foreign Office that he should send letters to personal friends in influential positions in Bulgaria. As a result letters from him were sent through the S.I.S. in August to three senior officers in the Bulgarian army, serving in occupied Yugoslavia, urging them to join in driving out the Germans.[16] Towards the end of 1942, Momchilov suggested sending a letter to the Minister of War, Nikola Mihov; the Foreign Office submitted a draft of the letter to the Chiefs of Staff, who wanted it toned down so as to make it clear that he was not advising immediate open defiance of the Axis but only non-co-operation.[17] Momchilov agreed.

While these consultations were going on, there was a curious intervention by the Soviet ambassador, Maisky, who told Eden on 2 December that he had heard rumours that the British had recently sent a message to King Boris through Momchilov. Sargent minuted: 'somebody has evidently leaked – inaccurately'; Eden was alarmed and minuted that Maisky must be 'told fully what we have been doing, or we shall have the old revival of suspicions'. On 21 December Eden explained what was going on to Maisky, who asked to be told 'what type of officers' Momchilov had communicated with, as it would be of interest to him.[18] There does not seem to have been any enquiry on the source of the leak. The letter was sent off in January 1943.[19] There is no available evidence whether it arrived.

Momchilov's interest in the Bulgarian army was shared by the exiled Left Agrarian, Matsankiev, now in London. He wrote a paper in January 1943 – passed to the Foreign Office – suggesting that contact should be made with the Military League/Zveno which could give 'proper guidance' to the army on the most effective way of co-operating with the allies.[20] In the following four months there was a series of assassinations of army officers or senior police officials,[21] and in May

Matsankiev wrote a second paper suggesting that these had been the work of a resistance centre within the army and that the British should try to make contact.[22] S.O.E. consulted Cairo and replied on 16 June that 'the only real elements capable of bringing about a revolution are, either the Communists or the Military League, possibly assisted by the Agrarians under Dimitrov'. S.O.E. were doing their best, from Istanbul, to contact 'friendly elements' and were hoping to send an officer to their sub-mission in Serbia nearest to Bulgaria 'with the whole task of working into the country'.[23] (This was the first indication of the proposed Mostyn Davies mission.) The Foreign Office answered that they were not thinking of a revolt, but of establishing firm and reliable contacts with the Bulgarian army, since, whatever the popular backing of the Communists and Agrarians, 'it is the Bulgarian army which has been entrusted with the job of defending the Balkans and to the army therefore we should address our greatest efforts'.[24] (The Foreign Office therefore had much the same view as the Bulgarian Communists on the importance of infiltrating the army.)

In August 1943, after the collapse of Italy, King Boris visited Hitler, and died in mysterious circumstances soon after his return home. This produced a crisis atmosphere in Sofia and revived Foreign Office interest in Bulgaria. But there was a painful lack of information. In September Sargent scrawled a pathetic note: 'have we any idea what is happening in Bulgaria? Can nobody tell us anything . . . C.? S.O.E.? Middle East Intelligence?' The Southern Department replied that there was nothing from S.O.E. whose Bulgarian contacts were 'rotten'; there had been a little from C. but 'nothing very illuminating'.[25] A telegram went to Moscow in the hope of obtaining information there; and a brief drawn up for Eden's coming visit to Moscow for the Foreign Ministers' conference suggested that the Russians, who still had a Legation in Sofia, would be able to provide an 'up-to-date picture' of the situation.

According to the brief, the 'opposition of the extreme Left, Left Wing Agrarians and Communists' were most likely to take over when the existing régime collapsed; the Communists were by far the most efficiently organised and most active party. British policy, as stated in the brief, was to see that Bulgaria restored Greek and Yugoslav territory after the war, and to see Bulgaria a member of a future Balkan confederation; whether joining the confederation or not, Bulgaria 'should retain her sovereign independence'[26] – which presumably meant that it should *not* become part of the Soviet Union.

BOMBING BULGARIA OUT OF THE WAR

Just before the Moscow conference, Churchill and the Chiefs of Staff became interested in bombing Sofia as a means of political pressure. There was an argument whether or not there should be advance warning, threatening bombing if the Bulgarians failed to withdraw from Greece and Yugoslavia. Churchill told the Chiefs of Staff on 19 October that he was against this: 'he had known the Bulgarians for 30 years . . . They were a peccant people to whom a sharp lesson should be administered . . . It was the first blow that counted and he felt that a heavy bombing attack should be made on Sofia as soon as possible.' The Chief of Air Staff however argued that the mere threat might work without an actual attack. Churchill got his way: the British recommended to the Combined Chiefs of Staff in Washington a heavy attack as soon as possible; leaflets should be dropped explaining that the attack was being made because the Bulgarians were supplying eight divisions in support of Germany and 'to oppress our allies'. Since the Russians were not at war with Bulgaria, they need not be consulted.[27] The Combined Chiefs of Staff agreed – with a condition which meant serious delay: 'provided the Air Forces can be made available without detriment to the more important operations'.[28] Eden, now in Moscow, was kept informed and telegraphed to Churchill, 'I presume I may now tell U.J. [Uncle Joe] what is intended?'[29] Churchill agreed; Eden told Stalin, who answered, 'Yes, Sofia should certainly be bombed – Bulgaria was a province of Germany.'[30]

That was the furthest Stalin went towards co-operating with Britain over Bulgaria. In response to Eden's plea for information about the internal situation, Molotov produced a vague general statement of little interest.[31] He showed no sign of helping the British to bring pressure to bear on Bulgaria.[32]

The first air attack, in November, did not produce any startling results in Bulgaria.[33] In the interval between the Moscow conference and the Teheran conference, the Foreign Office therefore turned to the idea of persuading the Soviet Union to join in a three-power warning 'demanding from Bulgaria the withdrawal of her divisions from Greece and Yugoslavia under pain of further bombing and the breaking off of diplomatic relations by Russia.[34] Advancing beyond this, they suggested to Eden, now in Cairo: 'if the Soviet government were now to follow up the bombing of Sofia by formally threatening to declare war on Bulgaria unless she surrenders it is possible that this might decide Bulgaria to take the plunge.'[35]

The idea was not unreasonable: two years earlier the British had, against their better judgment, declared war on Rumania and Hungary to please the Russians, so why should not the Russians now reciprocate? But when the British delegation in Teheran discussed it, it was argued that 'it could not possibly be to the Russians' interest to cause the . . . surrender of the Bulgarians in order that the Turks should forestall them in occupying Bulgaria'. But it was thought possible that the Russians might agree to break off diplomatic relations with Bulgaria to get Turkey into the war; the reverse of this argument was, as Cadogan put it, that 'the main point of getting Turkey into the war is to bring about (possibly) a Bulgarian surrender'.[36] (See also pp. 137–8 above.)

At Teheran, Stalin cast doubts on the practicality of getting Bulgaria out of the war by claiming that there were three German divisions in Bulgaria. (The British thought the figure much smaller.) His aim was clearly to show that it was not possible for the Bulgarians to act.[37] The furthest Stalin went was to say that if Turkey came into the war and was then attacked by Bulgaria, the Soviet government would declare war on Bulgaria.[38] – a doubly hypothetical proposition, with both hypotheses unlikely to be realised. Although Churchill did not give up the hope of persuading Stalin to declare war,[39] the idea of Soviet political action to back up Anglo-American bombing faded from sight. However, on 27 December the Moscow *Pravda* published an article by Georgi Dimitrov calling for Bulgaria to break with Germany quickly.[40]

The British were left to try to persuade the Americans to step up bombing priority for Bulgarian targets. This was not easy. But Churchill was persistent, even when convalescing in Casablanca.[41] A heavy attack by 141 Fortresses was made on 10 January, on which Churchill for the first time commented 'Good'.[42]

THE KUYUMDJISKI AFFAIR

At the beginning of February, the British learnt that the Americans had a different finger in the Bulgarian pie. Already in November 1943 S.O.E. had told the Foreign Office about difficulties with the O.S.S. representatives in Istanbul, who seemed to be allowing the Bulgarians to exploit Anglo-American differences.[43] On 9 February Roosevelt told Churchill he had received an 'unconfirmed report' that the Bulgarian government wanted to send a mission to Istanbul to discuss 'conditions under which Bulgarian army would join the Allies'. Roosevelt suggested that if this were true bombing attacks should be suspended for a limited period.[44] Reading this, Churchill wrote in the margin: 'why?'[45]

This was the start of a non-event which did credit neither to the Americans nor the British. Donovan, the head of O.S.S., had, after over-riding the objections of the British in Cairo, sent a special mission under Col. Jadwin to Istanbul, where it was free from any British control. (See p. 119 above.) A member of this mission described as a 'financier', an American of Bulgarian origin called Kuyumdjiski,[46] contacted the Bulgarian Minister in Turkey, Ivan Balabanov. From this contact emerged the proposal that the Bulgarian government should send a delegation to Istanbul, for the purpose set out by Roosevelt, and that there should be a ten days' suspension of bombing.[47]

All this was obviously unwelcome to S.O.E. who felt that O.S.S.

were poaching in their own preserves; Eden also reacted with suspicion
and some resentment. He told Churchill that the British had stipulated
that the Jadwin mission should not negotiate with the Bulgarians and
that Kuyumdjiski should make no commitments; he felt that they had
gone beyond their terms of reference and that Kuyumdjiski was
'entirely unsuitable'. Eden said there were two reasons why he was
suspicious – the 'untrustworthiness of Kuyumdjiski' and 'the fact that
the Bulgarian government prefer to deal with an American mission
rather than with the Russians'. 'one would have thought that if the
Bulgarian government really wished to surrender to the Amercans and
ourselves they would have asked the Soviet government to mediate on
their behalf'. (Eden did not worry about this when a few months later
the Bulgarians approached the British.) But in spite of his suspicions
Eden thought the Bulgarian government should be told to send out a
mission to meet representatives of the three Allies, perhaps in Cairo;
but there should be no suspension of bombing.[48]

Accepting Eden's view, Churchill got Roosevelt to agree that bombing should not be suspended and that they should make a joint
approach to the Soviet government.[49] A few days later the Russians
agreed that Bulgaria should be asked to send a mission to confer with
American, British and Soviet representatives but said it was the business
of Britain and America to decide the bombing question.[50] The Foreign
Office imagined that things would now go ahead and a Bulgarian
delegation would soon arrive.[51] Preparations were discussed; the
Foreign Office were determined to keep O.S.S. out of any negotiations.[52]

But nothing whatever happened. On 8 March Jadwin's superior
officer in O.S.S., Col. Macfarland, confided in Steel in Cairo that he
himself had refused to believe Kuyumdjiski's report and had insisted
that the whole thing should be repeated before a 'real American
officer'; he also had doubts of Balabanov, and had therefore not passed
on to him the agreement of the three allied governments that a Bulgarian delegation should come to Cairo.[53] This provoked in the Foreign
Office the smug comment: 'this shows that our suspicions of the Jadwin
mission were fully justified'.[54] Churchill's comment was more practical:
' "bomb with high priority *now*" [underlined three times] should be
our maxim'.[55]

BRITISH BOMBING AND RUSSIAN PROPAGANDA?

This was not only Churchill's view but also the view of the Bulgarian
Partisans with whom Mostyn Davies was now in contact. They had
reported that the Allied air raid on Sofia on 10 January was of great
help to them; the underground organisation in Sofia had taken full
advantage of the dislocation of police control caused by the bombing,

and were now making good use of a statement made in parliament by Petko Stainov (a respected non-Communist politician and ex-diplomat) and an open letter by the former Prime Minister, Kimon Georgiev (linked with Velchev and the Military League), both attacking the Bulgarian government. The Partisans wanted more air attacks, if possible with advance warning to themselves.[56] Learning this, the Foreign Office told Cairo that 'we are all agreed here about the promising potentialities of the Bulgarian situation'; but whether it could be exploited depended on whether they could secure the necessary priority for bombing Bulgaria and for S.O.E. work there, and 'whether we can get the Russians to play'.[57]

Eden had already told the Moscow Embassy he was convinced Bulgaria was 'one of the weakest spots in the German defences' and the Russians must play their part: there should be 'a combination of British bombing and Russian propaganda either to bring about a coup d'état . . . or else batter the present Bulgarian government into suing for peace'.[58] Churchill approved Eden's approach but did not want to intervene himself with a personal message to Stalin: relations were strained over Poland.[59]

No definite approach was made to the Russians, however, because fresh developments in Rumania and Hungary put fresh demands on the British and American Air Forces, which made it impossible to tell the Russians that bombing of Bulgaria would be intensified.[60] But there were fairly heavy raids in March which caused a good deal of chaos; and perhaps partly stimulated by these, the Soviet government carried out fairly intensive propaganda against the Bulgarian government in April. In May they sent a stiff note complaining of the facilities which the Bulgarian government were giving the Germans in ports and air-fields, and later demanded, as a proof of good faith, that Soviet consulates in the Black Sea ports should be re-established. The result of Soviet pressure was that the Bozhilov government fell and a more moderate Bagrianov government was formed; no action was taken about the Soviet consulates.[61] The Russians did not keep up their pressure; they had presumably decided to wait until they were ready to advance militarily into South-East Europe.

During May, there were signs of stirrings inside the Bulgarian army. The head of the British mission in eastern Serbia, Henniker-Major, reported that two complete companies of Bulgarian troops totalling 225 men and ten officers had deserted to the Yugoslav Partisans with full equipment; he had been impressed by their discipline and smartness.[62] These Bulgarians were formed into the Partisan brigade 'Georgi Dimitrov'.[63] Henniker-Major also reported a clash between Bulgarian and German troops in the Serbian town of Niš in which 30 Germans were killed.[64] The Bulgarian Partisans with whom the British were in contact did not achieve much but managed to destroy a bridge. S.O.E.

told the Foreign Office that General Wilson seemed anxious to increase the flow of supplies to the Partisans.[65]

RUSSIAN MOVES TO TAKE OVER BULGARIA

By the end of July, the Bulgarian situation looked sufficiently hopeful for the British and Americans to table draft proposals for an armistice in the European Advisory Commission in London. The Russian representative was at first without instructions, so nothing could be done. On 24 August however he was authorised to discuss the armistice; he accepted nine out of 12 clauses in an agreed Anglo-American draft,[66] but then received fresh instructions from Moscow and on 29 August withdrew from the discussions.[67]

This was a clear signal that the Soviet Union had taken control of Bulgarian affairs and from then on would handle them independently, allowing Anglo-American participation on sufferance only. This position had been reached by a complex series of events during August. On 14 August Stoicho Moshanov, a former speaker of the Bulgarian parliament, approached Sterndale-Bennett,[68] the Counsellor at the British Embassy in Turkey, in the train between Istanbul and Ankara, saying that he had been charged with a mission to see the Ambassador, Knatchbull-Hugessen, and give him an official memorandum. Two days later, the ambassador received Moshanov, who said he had an official message from his government, that they wanted to get out of the war and asked what conditions would satisfy the Allies.[69] On 23 August Moshanov again saw the ambassador, saying he was authorised to treat with the Allies as quickly as possible. On 24 August the British Embassy in Moscow was informed by Molotov that he had no objection to the Bulgarians being told that the procedure agreed in February [at the time of the Kuyumdjiski-Balabanov affair] was still open to them.[70] On 25 August Knatchbull-Hugessen was instructed to tell Moshanov to go to Cairo to meet the British and American representatives, and the Anglo-American draft armistice terms were sent to Cairo; since Russia was not at war with Bulgaria, it was not thought necessary to wait for Soviet concurrence.[71] None the less, Eden told the War Cabinet on 28 August that it was still hoped that three-power agreement could be reached 'almost immediately'.[72]

Eden had failed to see that there had clearly been a switch in Soviet policy, almost certainly caused by the unexpected coup carried out by King Michael of Rumania on 23 August. This opened up new vistas for the Russians, making it possible for them to reach the Bulgarian frontier earlier than foreseen. On 26 August Molotov told the British and American ambassadors that the Bulgarian government had decided to adopt 'an attitude of complete neutrality' and to disarm any German troops who tried to withdraw from Rumania through Bulgaria. It had also on 25 August asked the German government to withdraw German troops already in Bulgaria; if not they too would be disarmed.[73]

For the moment the Russians seemed satisfied; but on or before 29 August the Soviet chargé d'affaires left Sofia without explanation, leaving no one with whom the Bagrianov government could deal. Soviet-based radio broadcasts to Bulgaria were calling on the masses to rise against the 'Bagrianov Fascists' and impose a Fatherland Front government.[74]

This was the position when Moshanov finally arrived in Cairo on 30 August. The Bagrianov government was on the verge of being forced out of office, so nothing was achieved at his first meeting with the British and American representatives on 1 September. On 2 September a new government under a Right-Wing Agrarian, Konstantin Muraviev, was formed in Sofia; but Moshanov refused to act for it, on the grounds that it did not contain 'certain left wing opposition elements' and so could not have full Soviet support.[75] Moshanov's mission petered out. On 5 September the Muraviev government decided to declare a state of war with Germany, but then heard over the radio that the Soviet Union had declared war on Bulgaria. Before midnight the Bulgarian Minister in Ankara had asked the Soviet ambassador for an armistice, while in Sofia the government told the German Minister that there was war between the two countries.[76] In the Foreign Office, the Southern Department minuted: 'so the Bulgarians now find themselves at war with the Germans and Russians simultaneously. No wonder after $5\frac{1}{2}$ hours of Bulgarian–Russian war they asked for an armistice. It is all very Balkan.'[77] But it was the Russians, not the Balkan Bulgarians, who dictated events.

The Russians had decided to get rid of the Muraviev government. The Fatherland Front, or rather the Bulgarian Communists, acted. They 'revolutionized' the army; on 7 September the Soviet forces crossed into Bulgaria from Rumania. The next day the Politburo of the Communist Party met the Partisan General Staff and ordered a general uprising. That night army and partisan units seized the War Ministry, the Ministry of the Interior, the radio and other key points in Sofia.[78] They carried out the strategy which they had chosen in preference to the all-out partisan war advocated by the Yugoslavs: they seized power with the direct support of the Soviet armies.

On 9 September the Muraviev government collapsed and a Fatherland Front government took power with Kimon Georgiev as a non-Communist figurehead. The exiled Left Agrarian leader, G. M. Dimitrov, was allowed to return on 16 September, to a tumultuous welcome. But the British missions sent in by S.O.E. had to leave Bulgaria, ordered out by the Russians, on 27 September.[79]

The armistice negotiations took place in Moscow, not Cairo. On 6

October Eden told Churchill that deadlock had been reached; the Russians were insisting on certain conditions which would have the effect of ensuring Russia's predominant position in Bulgaria 'now and after the war'. They wanted the Allied Control Commission to be like the one in Rumania 'which would in effect mean that it would be entirely under Russian control'. They used the precedent of the A.C.C. in Italy in resisting British demands for an equal share of power and responsibility.[80] (See also pp. 143–5 above.)

In the end the British gave way. Their minds were fixed on Greece, not Bulgaria. They did at least get the Russians to order the Bulgarians to release the British officers whom they had put under house arrest in Greek Thrace, and they made sure that all Bulgarian troops left Greek soil.[81] But when the Left Agrarian, G. M. Dimitrov, was put under house arrest by the Communist Interior Minister in the spring of 1945, the British could not help him; he found refuge with the American Minister who got him out of the country. That marked the end of British influence in Bulgaria.

The British had better contacts in influential places in Rumania than anywhere else in South-East Europe, except perhaps Greece. Yet, because Rumania was geographically inaccessible and because Stalin made it clear from the start that he intended to secure a dominant position, their contacts could never be properly used.

As well as their link with Maniu, undoubtedly the most respected political leader in the country, and with the Liberal leader, Dinu Bratianu, who had strong influence in business and banking circles, the British had personal contacts in the Foreign Ministry, where there was an important pro-British group centred round Grigore Niculescu-Buzesti, a clever, determined and single-minded man. This group was linked both with Maniu and with the King, and both Maniu and the King had contacts in the senior ranks of army. The British also had ties with members of the governing élite, the oil industry and the banking world. A prominent Jewish industrialist and financier, Max Auşnit, was strongly pro-British and was in touch with Maniu.

One uncertain factor was Maniu's relationship with the head of the government, Marshal Ion Antonescu, who, though passionately anti-Soviet, was sympathetic to the British. Maniu, in company with Bratianu, made a series of long semi-public protests to Antonescu against his pro-German war policy; yet until the end he seemed quite ready to leave it to Antonescu to carry out a switch-over to the Allied side, though he assumed that thereafter he himself would take power. Antonescu on his side clearly respected Maniu and made it possible for him, though dogged by Rumanian and German security agents,[1] to move freely about the country, publish broadsheets and weekly bulletins, and keep up political contacts under the guise of attending christenings and religious festivals.[2] Ion Antonescu's close associate and deputy, Mihai Antonescu, was generally despised by pro-British Rumanians who regarded him as a time-server; but there were fairly frequent contacts between him and Maniu.

From the start S.O.E. had difficulties in keeping contact with Maniu. The W/T set left with him in February 1941 was discovered by the authorities in August 1941; by the spring of 1942 S.O.E. had supplied a new set and a new cipher, through the services of a Turk acting as honorary consul for Finland.[3] This was the first of a series of W/T sets sent into Rumania by S.O.E.; but owing to lack of efficient operators, not more than one ever seemed to be functioning at any one time, if that.[4]

S.O.E. therefore had to use other slower and less certain methods of keeping in touch with Maniu.

When in June 1941 the Rumanians found themselves, under Antonescu's leadership, fighting alongside the Germans against Russia, there was at first great enthusiasm. This soon faded when Rumanian troops, after reconquering Bessarabia, went on fighting across the old 1939 frontier deep into Russia. In a petition to Antonescu of 18 July Maniu declared this to be aggression; and thereafter he consistently demanded that Rumanian troops should be withdrawn to the 1939 frontiers and that the army's strength should be preserved and used for the recovery of Transylvania from Hungary. Copies of Maniu's protests reached London and were used in B.B.C. broadcasts to Rumania.[5]

Antonescu did not seem to resent these protests, but took the stand that in fighting Russia, Rumania was fighting for Europe. When Britain declared war on Rumania in December 1941, he issued a proclamation that this act had 'no foundation': 'Rumania receives this provocation knowing that in struggling against Communism she is serving not only the nation's cause, but is defending equally ... the whole of civilisation.'[6]

But by the beginning of 1942 some of Rumania's diplomats were trying to make contact with Britain. In Lisbon the newly-appointed Minister tried to approach the British Minister to explain 'Rumania's unhappy position',[7] and the former Minister told the Legation that Maniu was looking forward to the day when the Antonescu government would be overthrown as a result of Axis reverses and he himself could return to the scene.[8]

During January 1942 the Foreign Office and S.O.E. reviewed policy towards Maniu, in particular whether or not he should be encouraged to leave Rumania. They agreed that 'Maniu is our best hope of starting an anti-Axis movement' and that 'a coup d'état would be the goal to aim at'; he should therefore stay in Rumania. S.O.E. said they were offering Maniu a 'War Chest' which should 'prove very handy'. They also reported that Maniu wanted 'some guarantee' from Russia; the Foreign Office replied that if this meant a promise to restore Bessarabia and Bukovina, it would not be worth while even approaching the Russians.[9] Later in January, it seemed that Maniu had made up his mind to leave Rumania for 'British territory', and the Foreign Office asked Cairo to issue travel documents for the party under English names.[10] But once again Maniu changed his mind. In March the Foreign Office told Washington that it seemed 'he will prefer to stay where he is'.[11]

THE BRITISH APPROACH TO RUSSIA ON MANIU

In spite of doubts about Maniu's capacity to make up his mind, the Foreign Office thought it right, during the negotiations for an Anglo-Soviet treaty in the spring of 1942, to approach the Russians on Maniu. On 21 March Eden gave Maisky an aide mémoire suggesting that the increasing opposition in Rumania 'might be turned to advantage by persuading Rumania to drop out of the war', adding that the only person with whom negotiations could be conducted was Maniu. If the Russians wished, the British would put the Soviet representative in Istanbul in touch with Maniu's agents. If Rumania 'dropped out', Hungary, because of the quarrel over Transylvania, would probably follow suit. On 27 March Eden sent Maisky a further aide mémoire,[12] and on 29 April wrote again asking whether Maisky had yet received his government's views.[13] On 15 May he drew Maisky's attention to 'the vital importance of any revolutionary movement ... from the point of view of its probable effect on German oil supplies'.[14]

On the same day Maisky told Eden that the Soviet government 'did not for the moment want to take any action with M. Maniu'.[15]

By mid-summer 1942 things were unpleasant enough for Rumania for Mihai Antonescu to send a letter to the Rumanian Legation in Lisbon, destined for the British, saying that Rumania only wanted Bessarabia; if Rumanians were engaged in 'more extensive operations in Russia' this was because they were not free agents; they had no feelings of hostility to Britain and hoped to regain 'autonomy of action'.[16] Eden agreed with the view that this was 'an interesting symptom'.[17]

In September S.O.E. received a communication from Maniu which high-lighted the main stumbling-block to any Rumanian action: 'so long as we do not know positively ... that the allied nations are willing to exclude a Russian invasion of Rumania once the German front collapses ... it is practically impossible for our Opposition ... to come out against the Axis and organise anything with concrete effect'.[18] On this the Southern Department minuted: 'we are quite unable to give Maniu ... satisfactory assurances about Russian intentions'. The Foreign Office did not want to take the matter up with the Russians; they had managed to exclude frontier questions from the Anglo-Soviet treaty and did not want to give the Russians 'an opportunity to press their claim, probably with embarrassing results'.[19]

Towards the end of 1942, Maniu again seemed to want to leave Rumania, and S.O.E. favoured the idea, partly because they thought that the Russians might agree to talk to him.[20] At this point Maniu's view was that sabotage inside Rumania was inadvisable because it would only lead to German reprisals and a tighter German economic grip; a revolt in the army would only invite a Hungarian attack. Maniu also mooted the idea of landings by Allied (not Soviet) para-troopers[21] – an idea which, mirage-like, haunted all Rumanians up to their surrender to the Russians in 1944.

The Foreign Office, seeing dangerous water ahead, decided to raise the Rumanian question again with the Russians. 'Our own view is that we can take no action with regard to Rumania, except in concert with the Soviet government', they told Washington in January 1943.[22] Meanwhile they thought Maniu had better stay put. This worried Maniu; in February S.O.E. learned that he was 'surprised' at this decision and had asked whether he could send a group of Rumanians to London and whether they would be 'accorded treatment at least equal to that enjoyed by Hungarians'.[23] (Maniu's obsessive dislike and jealousy of the Hungarians tended to cloud his judgment.)

The Foreign Office remained unwilling to respond to Maniu until they had got some sort of opinion out of the Russians. On 20 February they told S.O.E. that Clark Kerr was taking the question up in Moscow.[24] In March the Russians at last reacted, saying that they themselves did not want to contact Maniu, but they thought British contacts should be maintained, since the influence of the Maniu group would grow in the event of Allied military successes: 'it is possible that in the course of negotiations a basis may be found for collaboration between this group and the British and Soviet governments'.[25] The Foreign Office cautiously decided, in March, that if any peace feelers were received from Rumania they would 'take the line that the Soviet Union is primarily concerned as bearing the main burden of the war being waged by Rumania . . . and should be approached in the first place'.[26] This ruling however presumably did not apply to contacts with Maniu.

In April the Foreign Office heard through the Turks that King Michael and his mother 'made no secret of their view that the only hope for Rumania . . . was an Anglo-Saxon victory', on which Sargent commented rather tritely: 'he is trying to reinsure like every other Rumanian quisling'.[27] In June Mihai Antonescu visited Rome, saw Mussolini, the King and the Pope, and spoke publicly of 'Latinity' as the basis of the future organisation of Europe. Foreign Office experts commented that in plain English this meant the formation of a Latin bloc and the conclusion of a separate peace with the Anglo-Saxon democracies.[28] But Mussolini did not encourage him.

Soon after, Mussolini fell. Mihai Antonescu turned to the Turks, telling them that, since 'the end of the war with Italy has come', he wished to know what the British wanted Rumanians to do; the B.B.C. had said that Rumania must make unconditional surrender, but 'if we accept that, to whom, where and how must we make it?' Mihai Antonescu said he had also appealed to the Hungarian and Bulgarian

Ministers to forget private quarrels in the joint interest of all three countries. Finally, 'if a British force showed itself near Rumania', it would not be opposed but would meet immediate collaboration.[29] The Foreign Office at once reported this move to Moscow saying it was for the Russians to decide on the reply. Fairly promptly, Molotov said it was not a serious peace feeler and not important; no reply should be returned. The Foreign Office duly told the Turks they would not reply to Mihai Antonescu.[30]

In September yet another feeler came through the ex-Minister in Lisbon, again from Mihai Antonescu: should the King and some members of the government leave the country for Allied territory and then denounce the Germans, leaving Marshal Antonescu behind 'to keep order until the arrival of Allied troops' (which clearly meant Anglo-American troops)?[31] The newly-arrived Rumanian minister in Ankara, Alexandre Creţianu, a Maniu man and well known to S.O.E., was anxious to get in touch with the British Embassy.[32] But the Foreign Office gave instructions that neither the Ambassador nor S.O.E. were to contact Creţianu.

On 30 September the Rumanian Military Attaché in Ankara, Col. Theodorescu, told the British Military Attaché, General A. C. Arnold, that Marshal Antonescu had instructed him to say that above all the Rumanians did not want Russia to occupy their country; they were ready to 'cooperate with any Anglo-American force entering the Balkans before the Russians, and would place at its disposal 22 divisions, pilots, gold, wheat and maize'. They believed Bulgaria would co-operate with an Anglo-American force: 'the sooner the Allies landed in the Balkans the better'.[33] A rival plan for an anti-Antonescu military rising reached S.O.E. in Istanbul in mid-October.[34]

Early in October, Maniu once again suggested that he should fly out of Rumania to the Middle East.[35] He also sent a fresh protest to Antonescu demanding immediate withdrawal from the war.[36] The Foreign Office reaction to Maniu's suggestion was utmost alarm and embarrassment. The Moscow conference of Foreign Ministers was about to begin: 'we do not want Maniu to come out at present. He could scarcely have chosen a more inopportune moment ... We are ... proposing to ... try to work out some common policy with the Russians and Americans. If ... we were suddenly to produce Maniu like a rabbit from a hat, the Russians would probably think we were double-crossing them, and any chance of reaching an agreement would be correspondingly reduced.'[37] However, the news was sent to Eden in Moscow.

There, Maniu was one of many matters which Eden hoped to discuss with Molotov. His brief from the Foreign Office contained the suggestion that Maniu should be asked to send an envoy to Istanbul, where he could be put in touch with a Soviet agent [presumably the

N.K.V.D.]; he should work to overthrow the pro-German regime and withdraw Rumania from the war even if this meant a full-scale German occupation.[38]

At first, little news reached the Foreign Office from Moscow; the Northern Department noted that the Soviet attitude on Rumania was 'rather unsatisfactory.'[39] The full conference record showed however that it was entirely negative. When on 25 October Eden asked for views on Rumanian approaches, Molotov said, first, that Rumania should surrender unconditionally, and next, that 'as to Maniu's group, he thought that it was inadvisable to establish contact with him now. There was nothing to discuss with him and it was useless, in any case, as he could not give anything to the Allies.' Eden, according to the record, accepted this verdict without question: 'the question of Maniu and his group was one for the Soviet government to decide, and in the light of what M. Molotov had said, they would see that action was taken, so far as lay within their power, in that sense'. The U.S. Secretary of State, Cordell Hull, said he had nothing to add.[40]

What Eden understood Molotov to mean, or wanted to imply himself, is not clear. From the record it looks as though Molotov, stepping back from his position in March 1943, was now against *all* contacts with Maniu, including British contacts, and that Eden accepted his view. But probably this was not what Eden meant, and there may have been a genuine misunderstanding. In any case, almost immediately after the conference things happened which caused fresh Soviet suspicions and had bigger consequences than could have been foreseen.

THE 'AUTONOMOUS' PARTY

From the spring of 1943 onwards, S.O.E. had been training teams to go into Rumania to contact Maniu; in June, with Mihajlović's help, Captain David Russell and a Rumanian W/T operator named Turceanu had entered Rumania from Yugoslavia. But Russell had been murdered and robbed, possibly by their Serbian guide; Turceanu was eventually captured by the Rumanians. During the summer months, S.O.E. was sending code messages to Maniu over the B.B.C. German Service, and by this means was able to fix a landing place for a fresh party, formed by the former oil executive, de Chastelain, Major Ivor Porter,[41] formerly a lecturer at Bucharest University, and a Rumanian. The party was given the code-name 'Autonomous'.[42]

Its purpose, as originally planned, was to organise disruption of enemy communications, perhaps also to organise 'some sort of coup d'état'.[43] But while planning was going on and the mission was waiting to go in, various things happened: S.O.E. learned that Maniu wanted to send a special emissary to the Middle East; the Foreign Office agreed; and on 19 November, rather surprisingly in view of Molotov's attitude at the Moscow conference, the Russians also agreed to 'take part in negotiations with Maniu's emissary'.[44]

At this point S.O.E. suggested to the F.O. that the instructions to the 'Autonomous' party should be widened: they should contact Maniu and give him advice on the need for unconditional surrender. The Foreign Office agreed, adding that it must be stressed that all approaches must be addressed to the Russians and Americans as well as the British.[45]

The Russians were in fact beginning to show signs of wanting to set up their own contacts with Rumanians – whether Antonescu or Maniu – independently of the British. One approach from Maniu to the British, during November, was through the Rumanian Legation in Stockholm, where there was an official in close contact with his group.[46] The Foreign Office told the Soviet government about this channel on 20 November,[47] and at the beginning of December the Minister in Stockholm, Victor Mallet,[48] also told the Soviet Minister, Madame Alexandra Kollontay, a veteran revolutionary of some independence of mind; she then revealed that she herself had had an indirect approach from the Rumanian Legation which had aroused her interest; she told Mallet she thought there were considerable opportunities for detaching the Axis satellites if the psychological moment were chosen.[49] However, Mme Kollontay failed to get authorisation from her government to make contact. But a Legation official named Spitchkine called unannounced on the Rumanian Minister – who was unaware of the contacts with the Allies passing through his Legation – and was snubbed and left hastily. This annoyed Mme Kollontay who told Mallet that Spitchkine was merely a 'little boy'.[50] S.O.E. surmised that Spitchkine might well be a N.K.V.D. representative acting independently of his Minister.[51]

The Autonomous party was finally dropped, after various delays, on 22 December 1943. The signals for the landing place had been arranged with Maniu's people, but there was thick mist so that nothing could be seen, and the party dropped blind. Within 24 hours they were picked up by the Rumanian gendarmerie and taken to Bucharest where they were kept under arrest and interrogated thoroughly by the Rumanian State Security organisation, and also for some days by a German intelligence officer. With the Rumanians, de Chastelain at first used his cover story, which was that he had come to contact Antonescu, but then told the true story, that he had come to contact Maniu. The Marshal accepted this and sent word that although the party had come as his enemies, he did not want them to fall into the hands of the Germans: statements would therefore have to be prepared which would satisfy the Germans while not telling them the truth or giving them a pretext for demanding to take over the prisoners. He got Mihai Antonescu, as an international lawyer, to draw up the statements which the prisoners then signed.[52] Thereafter de Chastelain urged Antonescu himself, in writing and face to face, to sue for peace. Antonescu refused repeated German requests – some said to come from Hitler himself[53] – that the party should be sent to Germany. He presumably thought that they, their W/T set and their ciphers might come in useful later on.

Once they had been captured, news of their arrival in Rumania was certain to leak to the outside world. This was very awkward, since the Russians had not been told about Autonomous. S.O.E. had suggested that they should be told, but the Foreign Office felt it would be better to wait until the party had safely arrived, since there had already been so many delays over its despatch.[54] The British in Cairo were worried about this, commenting on 28 December that the enemy might put out some tendentious story about the British Secret Service trying to arrange an anti-Soviet front with Rumania.[55] At the beginning of January therefore the Soviet representative in Cairo, Novikov, was told about Autonomous.[56]

There seems to have been no immediate Soviet reaction. But on 16 January the Turkish press carried a story, said to originate in Budapest, about the Autonomous party, saying that they had asked to see Antonescu and had brought with them a facsimile of an alleged German peace offer to Russia[57] (which was not true). The next day the Moscow *Pravda* carried a story, said to come from Cairo, about a supposed meeting in the Iberian Peninsula between 'two British leading personalities' and Ribbentrop to 'elucidate the terms of a separate peace with Germany'. If this was a Soviet riposte to the story about Antonescu who by then had gone to Hitler.)
considered by Eden and by Clark Kerr in Moscow.[58]

But the Russians did not formally raise objections with the British, even when the S.O.E. representative, on instructions, told his Soviet opposite number at the end of January.[59]

THE STIRBEY MISSION

It looked as though that was the end of the matter. The Foreign Office concentrated on trying to get Maniu's emissary – who turned out to be Prince Barbu Stirbey, a distinguished elder statesman, connected through his daughter's first marriage with an officer of S.O.E., and also the uncle of Creţianu, the recently-appointed Rumanian ambassador in Turkey – to Cairo, and into contact with the Russians. Meanwhile, Maniu was trying to find out through the British more about Soviet intentions towards Rumania, also whether the Allies were thinking of by-passing him and doing a deal with Antonescu. He also asked whether the British wanted him to co-operate with the small and weak Rumanian Communist Party.[60] Two Communist representatives had approached him late in 1943 with a ten-point programme for a united front; Maniu had repelled them because they seemed to accept Soviet acquisition of Bessarabia and Bukovina, but was now thinking again.[61] But the Foreign Office, to put pressure on Maniu, decided that none of his questions should be answered until his emissary had actually arrived.[62] Maniu was therefore left with no British guidance about the Communists – who were popularly regarded in Rumania as of no importance, a tiny group of foreigners, Jews, Bulgarians, or Ukrainians; this was not entirely accurate.

The Chiefs of Staff were also anxious to put pressure on Maniu, at least to get negotiations started, so as to divert German attention away from western Europe; and the 'Controlling Officers' had the same interest.[63]

Stirbey finally arrived in Istanbul at the end of February and, after much unwanted publicity, in Cairo, where he first met the British, Soviet and American representatives on 17 March. The Foreign Office had wished to exclude S.O.E. altogether from the proceedings, but Col. E. C. Masterson was eventually allowed to attend as an observer. In fact, Masterson coached Stirbey so well on what would be expected of him that the Foreign Office comment to Moscow was that Stirbey's attitude had been 'sensible and more encouraging than might have been expected'.[64] Stirbey had gone well beyond what Maniu would have liked in suggesting that a plebiscite should be held in Bessarabia and Bukovina 'the result of which would be a foregone conclusion' – that is, it would leave the Russians in possession – and in implying that the Rumanians would welcome a Soviet landing on the Black Sea coast. But Stirbey was in line with Maniu's own views when he said that Antonescu could carry out an anti-German coup more effectively than Maniu could, since Maniu would first have to carry out an anti-Antonescu coup; Stirbey added that he personally thought an Antonescu coup would 'last longer'.[65]

In spite of Stirbey's efforts to sweeten them, the Russians remained unimpressed. Molotov told Clark Kerr that Maniu could not be expected to oppose Antonescu, but was rather his instrument; Stirbey's statement was unimportant and it was doubtful whether the Cairo talks could lead to results.[66]

In any case, attention switched during March from Maniu and Stirbey to Antonescu. The move of German troops into Hungary in mid-March made similar action in Rumania seem likely; the Russians advanced into Bessarabia, and this caused panic in Rumania. On 22 March the British in Cairo received a message through Ankara from Mihai Antonescu saying that the Marshal had been summoned to Hitler who was expected to ask for more Rumanian troops for the front. Mihai put the question: 'I must know at once what is the impression made by recent events in Hungary . . . it is necessary to know upon what eventual political and military help we can count.'[67] The British in Cairo then decided, without first consulting the Russians, that General Maitland Wilson, as Supreme Commander Mediterranean, should send a personal message to Antonescu, bidding him not to visit Hitler but to surrender at once to the three great Powers and order Rumanian troops to put up no resistance to the Russians. 'We shall judge by results', the message ended menacingly.[68] The Soviet Minister, Novikov, was told after the message had gone, and thereupon complained to the Americans, though not the British.

The message did not in fact reach Antonescu until he had come back from his visit to Hitler. He then asked de Chastelain to send an answer to Wilson on the W/T set he had brought with him. De Chastelain found that the crystals had been stolen, so revealed that Maniu had a set, which he might be able to use. On this pretext he was allowed to see Maniu, whom he urged to rise against Antonescu; Maniu seemed to agree.[69] (Maitland Wilson followed up his message to Antonescu with a message to Maniu, urging him to act against Antonescu who by then had gone to Hitler).

In Moscow, meanwhile, Molotov, informed of the Wilson message to Antonescu, said that he was willing to establish contact with Antonescu, and suggested that the Rumanian Supreme Command should contact the Soviet Command 'for the settlement of practical problems'; and he later agreed to follow up Wilson's message to Maniu.[70]

Although Molotov expressed scepticism about the success of these various moves, there is no doubt that he took the chances of an immediate switch by Rumania really seriously. On 2 April he told the British that he was about to issue a declaration when the Red Army crossed the 1940 frontier of Rumania, stating that the Soviet government 'has no intention of taking possession of any portion of Rumanian territory or of changing the existing social order of Rumania and that the entry of Soviet troops into Rumanian territory is dictated exclusively by military necessity'.[71] This declaration seemed remarkably reassuring and on 4 April Churchill expressed 'admiration' for it. There was also good progress on armistice terms. In early March Eden had suggested that the Russians should submit their draft terms to the European Advisory Commission,[72] and on 11 April Churchill told the War Cabinet that the Soviet Union had presented its terms. These seemed very reasonable: Russia would retain Bessarabia and northern Bukovina but Rumania would get back Transylvania 'or the greater part thereof'. Churchill said he had asked Molotov, on this point, to add a reservation that this was 'subject to confirmation at the peace settlement', and Molotov had agreed. The Russians were not asking to occupy Rumania but only for free movement of troops as demanded by the military situation.[73]

On 12 April the Russians asked Stirbey in Cairo to convey these

terms to both Antonescu and Maniu. S.O.E. sent them to de Chastelain for transmission to both. This meant that Antonescu received
the terms through Maniu. At this point a breach between the two
seemed to open up. According to a letter written by Maniu in mid-
April, the Marshal 'wished to continue the war at the side of the
Germans', while Maniu believed Molotov's assurances; as soon as he
was certain that Antonescu could not be moved, he himself would act
in conjunction with the King.[74]

MAP 7. The Red Army Entry into Rumania, April 1944

On 21 April there was a heavy Anglo-American air attack on
Bucharest. On 22 April Molotov sent Churchill a friendly message:
'we consider that on the question of Rumania we have agreed with
regard to the main urgent questions ... Now it is for us to increase
from all sides the pressure on the Rumanians so that they shall abandon their hopeless and criminal position.' Churchill replied the next
day: 'I entirely agree ... Please telegraph freely if there is anything
you want done. Meanwhile we are keeping up the bombing; but we
regard you as our leaders in Rumanian affairs'.[75]

MOLOTOV'S LITTLE BOMBSHELL

At this point the climate of Anglo-Soviet relations over Rumania seemed set fair. But trouble was brewing. The Anglo-American bombing of Bucharest had caused great resentment among Rumanians – who saw it as totally indiscriminate – and made things difficult for the Autonomous party. De Chastelain, though a prisoner, was now being allowed to send out occasional messages, clearly because it suited the Antonescus that he should. A message dated 19 April was received in Cairo three days later; de Chastelain said that among 'officials with whom we are in contact' there was lack of faith in the Russians; they thought it impossible to collaborate with the Red Army and were convinced that Rumania had been 'abandoned' to Russia and that the British had lost the initiative and supremacy, hinting that their attitude would be different if Anglo-American troops approached Rumanian territory.[76] This message was shown to the Russians in spite of its unflattering character, as all messages from Rumania always were, to prove British good faith. It was certain to rankle.

Then on 26 April the S.O.E. representative in Moscow, Brigadier George Hill, told his N.K.V.D. opposite number, General Ossipov, that there was a plan to send joint S.O.E./O.S.S. parties to Rumania, and suggested that the Russians might 'in principle' like to participate. (S.O.E. and the Foreign Office were arguing whether – as the Foreign Office wanted – a Russian could be included in the first party; S.O.E. thought this would mean a danger of 'betrayal and even murder'.) At first, Ossipov's reaction was 'warm appreciation'; but the next day he had changed, saying that the N.K.V.D. did not wish to participate and could not supply Soviet credentials for S.O.E./O.S.S. personnel.[77]

Late on 30 April the storm broke over the head of the unsuspecting Churchill – a 'personal and secret' message from Molotov declaring that the de Chastelain party were in fact a 'semi-official British mission with the Antonescu government', using their own radio station and ciphers, which must mean that there was a 'definite' British–Rumanian agreement of which he had not been informed. Molotov demanded 'an explanation'.[78] (See also p. 140 above.)

This, coming little over a month after a similar row with Molotov over alleged British–German peace talks in Berne,[79] stung Churchill into drafting a highly emotional midnight reply:

> I expect you and Stalin to believe me when I say I know nothing at all about this business and I can only suppose you have got hold of a mare's nest ... In all this Rumanian business I am working with you and Stalin ... I am prepared to cooperate with you in every way. I am prepared to dismiss anyone who stands in the path

... You are absolutely mad if you suppose we are in any intrigue with Rumania or anybody in Rumania ... Tell me what you want, trust me and have no misgivings ... Of course, if you do not believe a single word we say, it really would be better to leave things to run out as they will ...[80]

The next day Eden sent Churchill a long and slightly inaccurate explanation of the Autonomous story, and agreed that Molotov's message was 'couched in such offensive terms' and was 'such a deliberate misrepresentation of facts' that Churchill should send a sharp reply. A slightly watered-down version of his original draft went to Moscow.[81]

When Clark Kerr gave it to Molotov there was an argument about the meaning of 'mare's nest' but no softening of Molotov's attitude and no apology. Churchill was determined to get both. There followed a series of exchanges and lengthy British explanations, which made Eden and the Foreign Office more and more uncomfortable.[82] On 28 May Churchill lashed out at the unfortunate Clark Kerr: 'the ambassador knows quite well that this is a false accusation, yet he cringes before Molotov ... Believe me this is not the way to get on with the Russians.' Against this, Eden wrote in the margin: 'yet no one is more effusive to the Russians than P.M.'[83] In mid-June, Churchill's mind was at last diverted to bigger things. Molotov never retracted.

There seems to have been little effort in London to analyse Molotov's motives. If several months earlier Molotov had accused the British of bad faith in sending a mission to Maniu so soon after Eden had apparently promised, at the Moscow conference, to drop Maniu, this might have been understandable. Eden himself seemed to forget just what had happened at Moscow: he told the War Cabinet on 11 May that Molotov had then 'encouraged him to keep in touch with Maniu'.[84] Three days later, in a minute to Churchill, he corrected this, saying that the 'encouragement' had been in March 1943, and that in October Molotov, though he 'showed no desire that the Russians should be put in contact with Maniu ... did not object to our maintaining contact'.[85] Even this did not tally well with the official record. (See p. 228 above.) Yet it would have been hard for Molotov to press a charge of bad faith on this count, since even before the Autonomous party had been sent, the Russians themselves had agreed to meet an emissary from Maniu,[86] and had been dealing with Stirbey in Cairo since March. Perhaps for this reason, Molotov accused the British, not of sending a party to Maniu, but of sending one to Antonescu; yet even then they had been using the de Chastelain channel to send their armistice terms to Antonescu.

One possibility was that Molotov simply wanted to stop S.O.E. sending fresh parties into Rumania, together with O.S.S.; he must have learnt of this project shortly before sending the message. Possibly, too, he did not want the N.K.V.D. interfering in Rumanian affairs: there could have been private rivalries between the Soviet Foreign Ministry and the N.K.V.D., such as were suggested by the Kollontay–Spitchkine incident a few months earlier.

One theory held in the Foreign Office was that Molotov's message was a reaction to the de Chastelain message of 19 April reporting anti-Soviet feeling in Bucharest. If so, it seemed excessive, even for the hyper-sensitive Russians. Another theory, suggested by Eden to the War Cabinet, was that Molotov wanted to 'establish a case for sending a Soviet mission to Greece'.[87] Yet when the Russians did this, they did not use the Autonomous mission as a pretext.

There was still another possibility. Molotov may have wished to provide himself in advance with a defence against any charge of ill faith which the British might make when they found out that the Russians, without telling their allies, had themselves contacted the Antonescu government through Madame Kollontay in Stockholm, who had at last got permission from Moscow to act.[88] The British did not find this out until the end of May, when Maniu sent a second envoy, the former diplomat, Constantin Vişoianu, to join Stirbey in Cairo.[89] The Southern Department suggested that Clark Kerr might find this useful in his duel with Molotov,[90] but there is no sign that it was so used.

One direct result of the Molotov message was to push the British one step further towards washing their hands of Rumania by trading Rumania against Greece. On 5 May Clark Kerr suggested that possibly the Russians' suspicions of British behaviour in Rumania 'are encouraging them in their apparent nascent tendency to play independent hand in relation to Greece'.[91] Following up this pointer, Eden saw Gusev three days later and launched the negotiations which ended in the percentage agreement five months later; there was also an inconclusive discussion of the Molotov message,[92] which could therefore be seen as an immediate cause of Eden's proposing the kind of deal on spheres of influence which he had been evading since his first meeting with Stalin in 1941.

In the operational field Eden's first reaction was, as he told Gusev, to impose a blanket ban on all parties going to Rumania; his failure to consult S.O.E. beforehand led to Selborne's warning against 'appeasing' the Russians which so infuriated Eden. (See p. 140 above.) But it soon emerged that not only S.O.E., but also S.I.S. and M.I.9, the body concerned with helping Allied airmen and war prisoners to escape from enemy territory, were planning to send parties into Rumania; two, in fact, had parachuted in early in May, and Clark Kerr had to tell Molotov this on 19 May.[93] Eden was compelled to lift the ban to the extent of allowing S.I.S. and M.I.9 plans to go ahead, and Molotov was told on 29 May that four parties were to be sent in to 'rescue some 300 British and American airmen'.[94]

Inside the Foreign Office, it emerged that Sargent believed that S.O.E. was responsible for this rescue work: 'the whole thing looks to me like a S.O.E. ramp in order to give jobs to their redundant staff.'[95] Molotov may well have been equally confused; as the Southern Department minuted, it was doubtful 'whether the Russians would draw a fine distinction between S.O.E., S.I.S. and M.I.9, even if they knew that there were three such distinct bodies'.[96]

So Eden's reaction, or over-reaction, to the Molotov message was probably pointless.

In the same anxious effort to placate the Russians, Eden also put a ban on de Chastelain's using his ciphers or sending radio messages to Cairo. Selborne protested that this would rob de Chastelain of his value to the Rumanians and so would remove their main reason for keeping him and his companions out of German hands.[97] Eden took no notice. In later stages of the attempts to negotiate with Maniu through Cairo, the lack of reliable communications was a constant complaint. In Bucharest, the Autonomous party were at this time seriously afraid of being sent to Berlin. So far they had been reasonably well treated, but were put under stricter control on 23 May.[98]

KING MICHAEL'S COUP

The Cairo talks were not helped by the arrival of Vişoianu on 25 May since Maniu, while accepting the Soviet armistice terms in principle, still thought he could bargain about them – all the more because it was apparently common knowledge in Bucharest that 'better terms' had been offered to Antonescu through Stockholm.[99] Vişoianu therefore told the allied representatives that Maniu hoped to put through a plan for a military switch-over which would have to be most carefully concerted with the Allies; but he also hoped that the 'great advantage to be anticipated from services which Rumania would be rendering to the Allies would influence them favourably in considering his observations on the armistice terms'.[100]

Vişoianu also saw Steel separately and asked for 'some private assurance to Maniu that Great Britain had not disinterested herself in the Balkans'.[101] This provoked Eden to comment: 'I should have preferred this interview not to have taken place'; it was not to be repeated, and Vişoianu should be told that the British and Soviet governments were acting in concert over Rumania so that there was no use in his trying to obtain assurances about British policy 'as distinct from that of the Soviet government'. If he wanted to say anything, he should say it to Steel and Novikov jointly.[102]

But Steel was not reproved for the answer he gave to a further question from Vişoianu – first put to the British by Maniu in January, but left unanswered – whether Maniu should form 'a democratic coalition embracing the Rumanian Communist Party'. To this Steel replied that while the British government could make no official pronouncement, in his own view a broad national union of this kind would be 'warmly welcomed by allied public opinion'.[103]

Perhaps as a result of this cautious advice, Maniu agreed in June to the formation of a National Democratic Bloc (or Patriotic Bloc) in which his own National Peasant Party and the Liberals joined with the Communists and the Social Democrats, who had already set up a 'United Workers' Front' of their own in April. The Bloc was linked with the King and the Generals close to him. In the words of an official Rumanian Communist history, 'a contact and collaboration were . . . established between the Communist Party and the Royal Palace; the latter was seeking to dissociate itself – through the King's participation in the anti-Hitlerite action – from the disaster which awaited the Nazis, to avoid sharing the responsibility with the fascist government'.[104] Not surprisingly, the Communist history did not mention the services which the rich industrialist, Max Auşnit, claimed to have rendered in organising the Bloc, in financing the Communist Party, and in organising the 15,000 workers of the Reşiţa steel works for resistance.[105]

On 11 June Maniu sent a message to Cairo announcing the formation of the Bloc and saying that he agreed to conclude an armistice on the conditions presented by the Allies – adding yet again, 'we are convinced we shall obtain amelioration of these conditions when they are applied'.[106] The Soviet reply, given to Vişoianu, was that there could be no question of any further discussion whatever of the armistice terms; what was required was positive action.[107]

Finally on 27 June a message arrived in Cairo explaining Maniu's plan to get Rumania out of the war, drawn up under the King's supervision and backed by the National Democratic Bloc. Action by the King was to be synchronised with Allied action – a massive Soviet offensive, heavy bombing of communications with neighbouring countries, and 'three airborne brigades with if possible an additional 2,000 parachute troops to be landed in the interior of the country'; these could be either Anglo-American or Soviet.[108]

Maniu's apparent willingness to accept Soviet airborne troops was regarded by the British in Cairo as 'a definite step forward'.[109] The sending of an Anglo-American force was a practical impossibility. (See p. 208 above.) What is unclear is why this fact still had to be veiled in such deep secrecy, even after Overlord was well launched. But what was clear was that, the original job of strategic deception once done, the British were no longer in such a hurry to get Rumania out of the war.

They sat and waited, quite patiently, for the Soviet reply to the Maniu plan. But Moscow was silent – Maniu referred in a rather desperate message of 5 August to the 'allies' impenetrable silence', which, he said, confused 'factions favourable to the allies'; 'nobody can understand how such a definite offer of collaboration can remain unanswered for five weeks'.[110] The British in spite of their waning interest, prodded Moscow gently, but without result.[111]

The Russians had other ideas. They certainly wanted to wait until they were quite ready to strike militarily. They had perhaps also grown tired of Maniu – who was in any case likely to prove an embarrassment to them as a future political leader – and hoped for better things from Antonescu through the Kollontay channel. That was presumably why Kollontay was able to offer better armistice terms. These, as the British learnt in July, were – in addition to an unconditional promise to return Transylvania – promises to allow 'free areas' where the Rumanian government would be completely free to administer its own affairs, and where no foreign troops would enter; to show leniency over reparations; and to allow 15 days between the signing of an armistice and a Rumanian declaration of war on Germany.[112]

Soviet hopes of Antonescu were knocked on the head when Antonescu saw Hitler at the beginning of August. He intended to tell Hitler that Rumania was going to get out of the war, but to give him due notice. But Hitler struck first; his opening question was whether Rumania intended to fight on. Antonescu lacked the courage to say no, and temporised by saying the question itself was insulting. The Rumanian Minister in Berlin, Ion Gheorghe, who was present, believed Antonescu's real aim was to win time in the hope of persuading the western allies to prevent the occupation of Rumania by the Russians.[113] He returned home in deep depression and did nothing. He thought Hitler capable of bringing everything down in a general blood-bath and this paralysed him.[114]

Maniu was still hesitating to move without an answer from Moscow. But on 5 August Stirbey and Vişoianu sent a message to him and to Buzeşti, who was working very closely with the King, that it would be in Rumania's interest that the Opposition should act, even without any help from abroad.[115] Yet it was not until 20 August, when the Red Army was already launching the long-waited offensive on the Rumanian front, that Maniu sent a message saying 'we have decided to take action'; even then he added 'let us know what you can give us'. On the morning of 23 August a further message arrived in Cairo: 'the Opposition . . . is completely in the dark as to what they should do.'[116]

The King knew what to do. He had planned the coup for 26 August and had told Creţianu to tell Stirbey.[117] But he was afraid the Germans would find out. On the night of 22 August he got on a tram and secretly visited a member of the National Democratic Bloc, and made it clear that he was going to get rid of the Antonescus. On the morning of 23 August Antonescu held a cabinet meeting, accused the Opposition of treating for peace over his head and declared that the decision lay with him alone: he would give the Germans warning, and since they would refuse to discuss the matter, he would go on leading Rumania right to the end, until the 'final victory of the Axis'.[118] He was clearly

MAP 8. The Red Army Advance into Rumania, Bulgaria, Eastern
Yugoslavia, August–September 1944

a man at his wit's end. Meanwhile Mihai Antonescu was planning to fly to Turkey, taking de Chastelain with him.[119]

The King then summoned Antonescu who at first refused to obey, but went to the Palace with Mihai in the afternoon. The young King asserted his royal authority sharply and demanded that the Marshal should send a telegram announcing the cessation of hostilities. Antonescu refused and said it was unthinkable that the Marshal – like

General de Gaulle, he usually referred to himself in the third person – should betray his German allies. The King accused him of usurping his royal rights: 'you I know, consider me to be a stupid stammering child; my Rumanians will judge that.' He said that as Chief of the Army he had already given his orders; he called in the guards and the two Antonescus were arrested.[120]

The Autonomous party were freed and driven to the Palace; outside it they were mobbed by crowds cheering and kissing them and carried shoulder high. They escaped and entered the Palace, where the King was trying to contact Istanbul on a W/T station which for some time he had been trying to use for contact with the Allies. It was decided that de Chastelain should fly to Istanbul to help maintain the contact, while Porter was to remain in Bucharest to handle that end.[121] With the help of Turceanu, David Russell's W/T operator,[122] who was released from prison, and working in the vaults of the National Bank because of the heavy German bombing of Bucharest which followed the coup, Porter established contact with Cairo and was able to give information on German positions and pass requests for allied air support.[123]

THE AFTERMATH OF THE KING'S COUP

The Russians were taken by surprise by the King's coup[124] but Molotov reacted smartly and on 25 August issued a conciliatory and reassuring declaration on the lines of the earlier Soviet declaration in the spring; this, he told the British and American ambassadors, was intended to 'influence Rumanian opinion, especially that of the army'.[125] But he was determined to keep the situation under exclusive Soviet control. The violent German onslaught on Bucharest following the coup resulted in an urgent message from Maniu on 25 August asking for 200 allied fighter aircraft.[126] This and later appeals for help led Maitland Wilson to propose sending a small liaison mission to Rumania to see what could best be done.[127] Eden said that no mission should fly in until the Russians had agreed;[128] the Chiefs of Staff strongly favoured sending a mission.[129] The Soviet reply was that 'the matter should be raised after the Rumanian armistice was signed';[130] in effect, they said no. Meanwhile an O.S.S. party had flown in: there were 1,000 American prisoners of war in Bucharest, so they had a good reason. There were only 30 British prisoners. On 4 September the Foreign Office said that 'pending further instructions no member of any secret organisation should be sent to Rumania and Bulgaria.[131] De Chastelain was not allowed to return to Bucharest, as he had promised the King.[132] Oddly, Porter was allowed to stay in Bucharest, and with the help of a staff of Rumanian collaborators, was able to send out military and political information.

One reason which the Foreign Office gave for this deference to the Russians was that the British had just been complaining to Moscow about the despatch of a Soviet mission to Greece without their knowledge: 'it would not help our case if we promptly did the same in Rumania.'[133] The ghost of Greece haunted British dealings with Rumania from then on. After the armistice had been signed in Moscow on 12 September, a British Mission arrived in Bucharest. By the beginning of November the British were already at loggerheads with the Soviet mission because of its intervention in Rumanian affairs, acting in the name of the Allied Control Commission but without consulting its British and Amercan members. This provoked Churchill to the comment that the British mission evidently did not understand that 'we have only a 10 per cent interest in Rumania and are little more than spectators'. He minuted to Eden: 'you had better be careful about this or we shall get retaliation in Greece'.[134]

On 1st December the British mission reported that Maniu had said that if the British government wanted Rumania, if necessary, to cast in her lot with Russia rather than the Anglo-Saxon powers, he would quite understand the position but would be grateful to receive a word from them to this effect. Churchill wrote on the telegram reporting this: 'Foreign Secretary – surely we are not called upon to make such admission. W.S.C.'[135] A few days later it was learned that the Russians were preparing to station three divisions in Rumania – or, as they put it, to 'rest three tired divisions from the line'.[136] Eden and the Chiefs of Staff agreed that though this might be part of a Soviet plan to install Communist rule, it would be difficult to sustain a charge that the Russians were contravening the armistice terms.[137]

Churchill clearly felt the consequences of his percentage agreement with Stalin to be decidedly irksome, but believed it must be preserved. While the civil war was on in Greece, he minuted to Eden that considering the way the Russians had 'backed up' the British in Greece, 'we really must not press our hand too far in Rumania. Remember the percentages we wrote out on paper . . . It is an awful thing that one cannot have it both ways, but you and I took great responsibility and we cannot overplay our hand in Rumania, least of all at a time like this. Without letting it appear in telegrams, you ought to make your will felt.'[138]

After the Greek civil war had been won, Churchill's anxieties eased, and he was willing in February 1945 to allow Eden to ask Molotov to take urgent measures 'to prevent the situation occurring in which a minority rule will have been established over the Rumanian people by force of arms'. 'Whilst we fully admit the Soviet predominating interest in Rumania as agreed at the Moscow conference,' Eden added, 'there is an Inter-Allied Control Commission in that country . . . We should be placed in an impossible position if we had to condone decisions or action taken in the name of that Commission but to which we had the strongest objection.' But the only threat Eden could use was to publish Anglo-Soviet differences.[139]

By then it was too late. The Russians were in the full flush of victory. They were in physical control of Rumania and could determine its political future – which had no place for King Michael, Maniu or other pro-British Rumanians.

19 Britain and Hungary, 1941-4

Hungary was drawn into war against Russia as Germany's ally by what many Hungarians believed to be a German trick – the bombing of Kassa (Košice), a town close to the north-eastern frontier, by aircraft said to have Russian markings.[1] From the first day, there were powerful pro-British elements at work. The Regent Horthy himself, 73 years old in 1941, was not a man of great intelligence and in complex and fluctuating situations found it hard to take firm decisions; but he was devoted to his country and, according to his own rather uncertain lights, honourable, he despised and detested Hitler and looked on the Nazi leaders as gangsters, but admired the British and, as a former Austro-Hungarian admiral, respected British sea-power. In the gentry, who formed the governing élite and the higher ranks of the bureaucracy, there was also a pro-British tradition which was shared in varying degrees by liberal intellectuals, would-be social reformers and Social Democrats.

But the army was a different matter. From the days of the Habsburg empire the army had had a tradition of brotherhood-in-arms with the Germans which was not easily broken. During the Second World War, however, the manners and behaviour of some of the Nazi-style senior officers disillusioned and even disgusted some Hungarian officers;[2] and certain Hungarian Generals played a difficult and courageous role in trying to break with Germany. But there always remained strong pro-German elements in military high places.

The main problem for the British was that in almost all cases pro-British feelings were much less powerful than fear of Russia, based on historical memories of Russia's role in Hungary a century earlier and of the brief Communist régime of Béla Kun in 1919. Given the course of Allied strategy, it was very hard for the British to counter this fear.

Among the pro-British politicians an important aim, from 1941 on, was to convince the British that Hungary was not really at war with the western allies at all (which, in a limited sense, was true) and to cultivate kindly feelings towards Hungary in Britain and America. This had been the aim of the plan for sending Bethlen, Eckhardt and other politicians to the West in the spring of 1941. Eckhardt actually left for the United States in January 1941, with funds provided by the pro-British Governor of the National Bank, Lipót Baranyai.[3] Bethlen stayed in Hungary.

Eckhardt's efforts to start up a big free Hungarian movement in the West, working for Hungary's cause, came up against many difficulties (including his own lack of political sense and Habsburg efforts to take him over) and eventually collapsed. Efforts in London to start up a much more modest movement had a certain very limited success, but there was no outstanding figure apart from Count Gyula Károlyi, the former Prime Minister, discredited in the eyes of all nationalist Hungarians as having prepared the way for the Béla Kun dictatorship.

In any case the British government had not the slightest idea of recognising any Hungarian freedom movement. It was one of the misfortunes of the Hungarians that Lord Rothermere had launched his big press campaign in the late 1920s for 'Justice for Hungary' and territorial revision. This had aroused false hopes in Hungary and the deepest resentment and suspicion among Hungary's neighbours, who became convinced that the British were suckers for the Hungarian feudal aristocracy and, unless very firmly restrained, would betray the vital interests of their allies for the sake of Hungary's bogus charms. the Czechs felt this particularly strongly and during the Second World War did their utmost to turn the British against Hungary and expose every Hungarian peace feeler as a hollow sham. Since President Beneš and his colleagues in London were extremely active and persistent, they had some success.

The Hungarians were their own worst enemies, in that they harped perpetually on their claim for frontier revision, not only against Rumania, which might seem reasonable since Rumania was fighting Britain's Russian allies a good deal harder than Hungary was, but also against Britain's smaller allies, Czechoslovakia and Yugoslavia; and the Hungarian march into Yugoslavia in April 1941 had left a particularly bad impression on the British. The Hungarians thereby provided the Czechs with plenty of ammunition.

Partly perhaps for this reason, Eden showed a marked dislike for Hungary, at least in the early years of the war, and a marked reluctance to believe that any anti-German move by Hungary could be sincere and genuine. In this he was encouraged by Sir Robert Bruce-Lockhart, first ambassador to the exiled Czechoslovak government and later Director-General of the Political Warfare Executive. It was left mainly to the Central Department of the Foreign Office, which was responsible for Hungary, and especially to Frank Roberts,[4] to argue the case for giving the Hungarians some small encouragement to work against Germany. This he did with persistence and sober logic.

It was uphill work, at least until 1943. László Bárdossy, who had succeeded Teleki as Prime Minister in April 1941, followed a policy which at least outwardly was whole-heartedly pro-German. In January 1942 Hungarian occupying troops in Yugoslavia, repressing disturbances, carried out a slaughter of civilians in Novi Sad. The news of this reached the outside world and shocked the British among others (also some Hungarians). In the spring, following German pressure, the Hungarian Second Army was sent to the Russian front.

Thereafter Horthy got rid of Bárdossy, replacing him by Miklós Kállay, a single-minded and courageous man of one of the oldest Hungarian families; he had his political blinkers but his patriotism was strong. Horthy also got his son István elected deputy Regent; since István was widely known to be strongly pro-British, this annoyed the Germans considerably. In the summer István was killed when – quite unnecessarily – piloting an aircraft; there were rumours – which the British helped to spread – that the Gestapo had arranged the accident.

The appointment of Kállay was in fact the beginning of a serious Hungarian movement to detach the country from Germany and return to quasi-neutrality – all under the cloak of outwardly pro-German pronouncements – while preserving a degree of political liberty unknown else in Hitler-dominated Europe. However, this movement was not clearly visible to the outside world and could easily be presented as a rather despicable attempt to 'reinsure' with the allies, an interpretation in which there was of course some truth. On 1st July Hubert Ripka, Information Minister in the exiled Czechoslovak government, presented a long document to the Foreign Office accusing British propaganda to Hungary of appealing to revisionist and anti-democratic circles and even 'exculpating them in advance of all guilt'; in particular it attacked C. A. Macartney,[5] a distinguished historian and expert on Hungary who broadcast regularly in the B.B.C. Hungarian service.[6]

The aim of British propaganda, as set out in a 'draft plan for political warfare in Hungary' in February 1942, was to build up a political opposition based on 'anti-German Catholics, intellectuals favouring land reform, Social Democrats and progressive aristocrats',[7] which sounded a hotch-potch but later became a reality. Macartney addressed his highly personal broadcasts mainly to the governing élite, but with the clear purpose of needling or goading them into resistance to German demands. In the Foreign Office, Roberts defended him; Lockhart, now head of P.W.E., took an opposite line, minuting that 'of all European countries Hungary provides the poorest field for British propaganda . . . We have . . . nothing to expect from Hungary during the war . . . we can achieve nothing except at the expense of our smaller Allies. That is why I have always urged that Hungary should be our lowest priority . . . Mr Macartney should be given a rest from broadcasting . . . To the Hungarians he is a symbol of British softness towards Hungary. He is a reminder of the era of the late Lord Rothermere.'[8]

Lockhart had Eden's private ear, and in the end Macartney was 'rested', though not until the following year.

The British were probably better informed about Hungary than any other South-East European country. The Hungarian press, in spite of lip-service to the German allies, was remarkably free and was carefully read in London. In Stockholm Vilmós Böhm, a Hungarian Social Democrat who had briefly been War Minister in Károlyi's government in 1919 and had lived in exile ever since, had been recruited to work in the Press Reading Bureau attached to the British Legation in Stockholm. Pro-British contacts in the Hungarian Legation fed him regularly with diplomatic and other reports on the internal situation not only of Hungary but of other South-East European countries too.

A senior official of the Hungarian Foreign Ministry, Aladár Szegedy-Maszák, who was to play a key role in efforts to get Hungary out of the war, found opportunities to visit Stockholm and had private talks there with Böhm about the future. Not surprisingly, Böhm's reports were regarded in the Foreign Office as 'excellent and reliable' and were moreover 'substantially confirmed in intercepts from the Italian Minister at Budapest'.[9]

FIRST HUNGARIAN PEACE FEELERS

During the winter of 1942–3, the Hungarian Second Army was involved in heavy fighting around Voronezh and suffered disastrous losses in January. This turned Hungarian public opinion against the war. Böhm had talks in Stockholm with a Hungarian in close touch with Szegedy-Maszák and his group in the Foreign Ministry, A. Gellért, and early in 1943 evolved a four point plan: no more troops for the Eastern front; this to be announced publicly at an agreed moment; in the case of invasion of South-East Europe, Hungary to offer no resistance and open its frontiers to British, American and perhaps Polish troops; Hungary to provide the British with information. Gellért agreed to 'father these proposals and transmit them to Budapest'.[10] Soon after, Szegedy-Maszák himself visited Stockholm and told Böhm: 'if England and America were to come we would welcome them. If Russia came the whole country would be afraid, not only the government but the peasants too, yes, even the workers.' He added that he was 'an enthusiastic supporter of a democratic regime based on a union of Social Democrats, peasants and intelligentsia'.[11] About the same time, an almost identical message was passed to 'an allied diplomat' in Istanbul by the diplomatic correspondent of the outspokenly liberal *Magyar Nemzet*, Dr. A. Frey.[12]

The internal evolution in Hungary was described by Roberts early in February as 'satisfactory': 'a relatively strong democratic opposition composed of the Peasant and Socialist parties and representing workers and intellectuals has grown up. As Hungary has preserved a much greater degree of liberty than any other satellite or occupied country, these people have been very vocal and made speeches in and outside the Hungarian parliament condemning the present orientation of Hungarian policy.' There was also a right-wing opposition around Bethlen; the Primate, Cardinal Serédi, had made a speech which could only be interpreted as an attack on Nazi philosophy; 'there has been a strong movement . . . to moderate any persecution of the Jews and the Jewish organisations here are sympathetic towards Hungary'. It was this minute by Roberts which inspired Cadogan to suggest a reconsideration of British policy towards the satellites. (See pp. 205–6 above.)

Parallel with Böhm's contacts in Stockholm, and ultimately more important, were a number of Hungarian approaches to the British or Americans in Istanbul. Professor Albert Szentgyörgy, a distinguished scientist and discoverer of Vitamin C, winner of the Nobel Prize for medicine in 1937, arrived in Istanbul to give some lectures on 7 February. He contacted S.O.E. and claimed to represent the Social Democrats, Károly Peyer and Arpad Szakasits, the Peasant Party leader, Imre Kovács, the deputy leader of the Smallholders Party which Eckhardt had once led, Béla Varga, the Legitimist leader, Count A. H. Sigray, and the deputy editor of the Social Democrat newspaper *Népszava*, C. Kállai (who was actually a Communist, though this was not clear until later[13]). This looked like the hoped for 'union of workers, peasants and intellectuals'.[14] Szentgyörgy said all these had promised their full support to any action he might undertake in agreement with the allies; the Prime Minister, Kállay and the head of the Foreign Ministry Press Department, Antal Ullein-Reviczky, also knew of the project. He claimed that all would accept himself as Prime Minister of a government to be formed at the time of the German collapse; he would then help the allies – once he had cleaned up the General Staff – with a potential Hungarian army of one million, though he wanted an allied occupation 'to afford time for the establishment of a democratic regime'.[15]

Eden informed Washington and Moscow and asked for their views on a reply.[16] But before any action could be agreed, the Gestapo found out what was going on, and the story got out; and President Beneš – as reported by Reuter and then widely reproduced – declared in a broadcast from London in mid-March that two Hungarian professors, with the knowledge of the Hungarian authorities, had recently negotiated with Anglo-Saxon representatives in a neutral country.[17] The Hungarian authorities denied the story, but the cat was out of the bag. In S.O.E. terms Szentgyörgy was 'blown' and no longer useful as an intermediary.

In April Horthy was summoned to Hitler who told him that the

Germans had irrefutable proof that the Kállay government had been in contact with the Anglo-Saxons both in Turkey and elsewhere; this bordered on 'treason'. So long as Kállay was Prime Minister, Hitler said, he could have no confidence in Hungary.[18] He also demanded strong measures against what he called the 'popular front', but the Hungarians called the union of workers, peasants and intellectuals.[19] Hitler added that the Hungarians were over-indulgent to the Jews.[20]

Finally, Hitler accused the Hungarians of fighting badly on the Eastern front, virtually sabotaging the German Army's efforts. (One of the Hungarian Generals commanding troops on the front at this time later remarked that it was very difficult and complicated to give orders of such a kind as to result in the troops fighting badly.)[21] Horthy rejected Hitler's accusations and demands angrily.[22] There was also some discussion of a German demand that Hungarian troops should be sent to Yugoslavia, to the Belgrade area. This also Horthy rejected.[23]

In the hope of backing up German pressures, right-wing Hungarians tried to stage a political coup on Horthy's return home. They were foiled by the vigilance of Kállay and in particular of Ferenc Keresztes-Fischer, the Minister of the Interior and a firm supporter of the group which was working for a break with Germany. But to prevent more political agitation by the right-wing groups, parliament was prorogued – a move which the British at first interpreted wrongly as a concession to Hitler.[24] On 29 May Kállay made a speech which the Foreign Office described cuttingly as 'a good example of the equivocal policy which Kállay has tried consistently to maintain' – 'resistance to German and Italian demands consistent with the maintenance of correct relations and the safeguarding of his own position inside Hungary, accompanied by friendly gestures towards the Americans and ourselves ... the whole governed by the one aim of preserving ... as much as possible of Hungary's existing economic resources, social structure, political system and territorial gains'.[25]

While the British at this time favoured – but did not demand – some change in Hungary's social structure, they did not think of embracing elements further to the left than the Social Democrats – a party of some strength, in the most industrialised of all the South-East European countries, even if it was still predominantly a land of poor peasants or agricultural workers – or the mildly revolutionary Peasant's Union and the young intellectuals known as 'village explorers'. In the summer of 1943, however, it struck them that this formula might not satisfy the Russians.

This was because of the Soviet reaction to a story in the *Daily Telegraph* of 4 June about a 'secret' visit by George Gibson of the T.U.C. General Council to Stockholm, where he met exiled politicians from South-East Europe and gave them good advice in the name of the British Labour movement, in particular that the Hungarians should attach themselves to any future federation in the area. The Foreign Office was immediately nervous about the effect this story would have in Hungary and even more in the Soviet Union. A telegram was sent to Moscow explaining that Gibson had been in contact with Böhm (who belonged to a group of Socialist exiles which included Willy Brandt as its secretary).[26] The Foreign Office stressed that Gibson was speaking only for himself and that there was 'no question of secret conversations between this country and the satellites'.[27]

This provoked Molotov into sending an answer to Eden's proposals of the previous March for a modification of policy towards the satellites (see p. 206 above) – but he got in first with the tart comment: 'the Soviet government consider Mr. Gibson's statement to be unjustified and regard his remarks and suggestions as not calculated to please Soviet public opinion and the Soviet government. The Soviet government consider that ... the responsibility must be borne not only by the Hungarian government but to a greater or less extent by the Hungarian people.'[28] Molotov added that the Soviet government did not think Hungary should be included in any federation in the area – to which in any case they were unwilling to commit themselves. And they did not consider the Vienna Award on Transylvania 'fully justified'.[29]

One of various things conveyed by Mototov's letter was that he did not like Böhm. His dislike grew when after long hesitation the Foreign Office allowed Böhm to visit London in late August; because of various hitches he stayed longer than intended, till late October. The Foreign Office conscientiously informed Moscow and Washington of Böhm's unofficial status and aims, but Molotov sent a letter to Clark Kerr alleging that Böhm was holding many meetings of a political nature and 'conducting negotiations to assist the Hungarian government to evade responsibility which awaits them for their participation in the war'.[30] The British denial that Böhm was carrying on negotiations was not accepted in Moscow, where Vyshinski repeated the charge.[31] On 1 December *Soviet War News* carried a sharp criticism of the 'alliance' of the Hungarian Social Democrats with the Smallholders and 'certain small groups', which had 'interfered little with the government's foreign policy and behaved very conservatively'. This 'opposition', *Soviet War News* added, 'very inadequately reflects the growing dissatisfaction in the country'.

This looked like a clear warning that Moscow would not be satisfied until the 'alliance' embraced the Communist Party, which was now trying to come to life again after long years of repression, and was working under the name of the 'Peace Party'. Roberts minuted: 'the main difference I foresee arising between our own and Soviet policy towards Hungary is in our respective attitudes towards the left-wing Hungarian opposition. The general ideas of this opposition are such as we should normally welcome and on which we should desire the countries of central Europe to base their policies after the war. The Soviet government, however, are strongly opposed to Social Democratic forces everywhere.'[32]

THE SURRENDER GROUP'S 'UNCONDITIONAL SURRENDER'

In the summer of 1943, the immediate problem was how to deal with the more serious peace feelers produced by Mussolini's fall. In mid-August a young Hungarian, László Veress, who had joined the Foreign Ministry just before the war and knew and loved England, arrived in Istanbul acting on behalf of Szegedy-Maszák's Foreign Ministry group and the wider group which had recently received unwanted publicity in the *New York Times* and had become known as the 'surrender group'.

Early in 1943, on behalf of the Foreign Ministry group, Veress had visited Lisbon to establish contact with the Western allies, and then – having decided Lisbon was too insecure – went in March to Istanbul. There he made contact with S.O.E., who suggested setting up W/T communication; Veress, though lacking explicit authority, accepted. His tactics throughout his activities was to move slightly ahead of the group in the hope of involving them in action. Kállay was at first alarmed at the idea of W/T contact and unwilling to risk provoking the Germans. It was also awkward for Veress that his original S.O.E. contact was György Palóczy-Horváth, a left-wing writer who had left Hungary in 1935, and who did not conceal his Communist sympathies and was regarded by the Hungarian government as a full party member, which naturally worried them. However Bethlen, with whom Veress was in contact, favoured establishing contact with the British.[33]

At the beginning of August 1943, after Mussolini's fall and on the advice of the Foreign Ministry and Keresztes-Fischer, Kállay agreed that a staff officer should be appointed for talks with the British on military matters. The plan was that the officer selected should be appointed Military Attaché in Turkey, as cover, but the Germans managed to get another man appointed to the job, so this fell through. But the other part of the plan was that Veress should go to Istanbul and establish lasting and firm relations with the British.[34] This went ahead: the Hungarian Foreign Ministry knew of the Badoglio government's efforts to negotiate Italy's surrender and hoped to act in parallel.

When in mid-August Veress got to Istanbul and made contact, he soon decided that the only thing to do was to say firmly that Hungary accepted unconditional surrender, was anxious to have this realised as soon as possible, would defend the country's frontiers against the Germans, and would give the allies full access to Hungarian airfields

and military installations. This statement was communicated to the
British Embassy on 7 August.[35] Veress also said that the group on
whose behalf he was speaking included the Chief of General Staff,
General Ferencz Szombathelyi: he had been explicitly authorised to
do this by a top secret telegram from Budapest giving a prearranged
signal: 'buy missing copies of *The Times*.' Other military supporters
were General V. Nagy, Defence Minister until June 1943; General H.
Náday, Commander of the First Army; and Col. Kádár, Head of the
Intelligence Section of the General Staff.[36]

The British accepted the Veress statement as genuine and reliable.
At this moment Churchill and the Chiefs of Staff were in Quebec for
the Quadrant meeting with Roosevelt. The Vice Chiefs of Staff in
London were therefore asked for their views. They replied on 23
August that 'militarily and politically Hungarian capitulation would
gravely embarrass Germany and if, as we consider possible, Rumania
followed suit, Germany would be faced with critical situation to
restore which she must almost certainly invade Hungary . . . Con-
sequent weakening of her position in other theatres would be greatly
to our interest.' They added that the best time for Hungarian capitulation would be if it was synchronised with that of Italy. The most
important British requirement was the denial of Hungarian transport
facilities to Germany, which would cause loss of Rumanian oil and
affect German power to send reinforcements to the Eastern front and
the Balkans. The Vice Chiefs of Staff concluded that 'Hungary should
be told to give evidence of her good intention to assist Allies by ceas-
ing all cooperation with Germans, by obstruction, delaying action, and
even possibly minor sabotage'.[37]

The British duly informed the Russians and Americans of the Veress
statement. Molotov's first reaction was that he had no objection to the
British hearing what Veress had to say, but he believed the possibility
of Hungary's surrender was remote at present and the approach should
be regarded as only a feeler.[38] But when Molotov was consulted about
the reply which the British wanted to give Veress, which included the
Vice Chiefs of Staff's recommendation about non-co-operation,
obstruction and minor sabotage, he replied tersely that he had no
objection to a message based on the principle of unconditional surrender, but it would be tactically inexpedient to include these other
points.[39]

Churchill on the other hand was for patience and allowing the situation to ripen. (See p. 207 above.) Roberts minuted that the two were
difficult to reconcile: 'the P.M. wants to make our approach more
attractive, and the Russians restrict it purely to unconditional surrender, removing all the jam.'[40] Eden produced a reply which conceded
something to Churchill but nothing to Molotov. Roosevelt's only contribution to the argument, according to Churchill, was that it was 'all

very interesting'.[41] Eden telegraphed to Molotov that his suggestion had not been adopted because 'we think it most improbable that the Hungarian government can be expected at this stage of the war to announce their acceptance of unconditional surrender, but there is certain action of a less obvious kind . . . which they could take now and which would obviously benefit the United Nations war effort'. He hoped the Soviet government would not see 'any grave objection'.[42]

The British reply delivered to Veress by the Ambassador, Knatchbull-Hugessen,[43] on a British launch in the Bosphorus on the night of 9/10 September was a sort of acceptance of Hungary's surrender: 'H.M.G. will expect the Hungarian government to make at a suitable moment a public announcement of their acceptance of unconditional surrender and to take at the earliest moment the action originally suggested by the Hungarian government . . .' (This presumably meant military talks with a Hungarian staff officer.) The British reply included the demand for ending co-operation with the Germans, obstruction, delaying action and minor sabotage, to which Molotov had objected, and proposed British–Hungarian military talks in Istanbul for this purpose.[44] Finally, the reply requested that Veress' credentials should be transmitted to the British in a neutral capital.[45]

The Americans fully approved the British line 'particularly as regards the danger of provoking an untimely outbreak'.[46] But Molotov stuck to his guns, maintaining his disapproval of any demand for any action short of unconditional surrender, which should be immediate.[47]

On 10 September Veress went back to Budapest taking two heavy suitcase W/T transmitters and, with the approval of Horthy and Keresztes-Fischer's permission, and at considerable risk to himself, procured the services of two detectives employed by the Chief of Political Police to operate them.[48] The contact worked.[49] But the messages which Veress sent did not live up to S.O.E.'s hopes. This was because the Hungarians themselves were seriously discouraged by the setbacks to the allied advance in Italy. There was also a great deal of muddle. On 29 September Veress said the credentials would be presented in Lisbon. But Antal Ullein-Reviczky, one of the pro-British activists in the Foreign Ministry, arrived in Stockholm as Minister in late September, apparently intending to act as the main contact with the British. Then there was a rumour in Lisbon that some Americans had said that Eisenhower's H.Q. was the only place where unconditional surrender could be discussed.[50] Yet more confusion was created by reports, which came to Hungary through Eckhardt, that the Americans were planning to put Otto Habsburg on the throne of Hungary.[51] (Otto had also seen Churchill in September and claimed to have been given the 'greatest encouragement' by him.)[52]

These various red herrings were cleared away, and the Veress channel confirmed as the main channel, at least for the British; and in early

November the Hungarian Minister in Lisbon confirmed to the British Ambassador the authenticity of the communications made in Istanbul, thereby meeting the British demand of 9 September for the transmission of credentials. During the autumn, the exchanges with Veress through S.O.E. were mainly concerned with establishing military contact and scaling down Hungary's military effort for Germany. Veress had to report on 9 October that although the Hungarian government agreed to military contact in principle, 'the Hungarian army has not kept in step with the political evolution of public opinion. The purge of key positions in the army is systematically going on . . . these measures are not yet complete, consequently there are obstacles to the establishment of military contact.' This meant that the surrender group could not arrange for a staff officer to go to Istanbul nor for a S.O.E. party to be received in Hungary: 'the Hungarian government cannot at present guarantee the safe existence . . . of a British military mission in Hungary, nor that its stay could be kept secret'.[53] But Veress reported that though the Germans had constantly pressed Hungary to send troops to the Balkans, this had been refused.[54] Given the bad relations then existing between Kállay and the General Staff, it was probably hard for him to guarantee fulfilment of such an undertaking, but with one minor infringement it seems to have been fulfilled.

The Hungarians also consistently refrained from firing at British or American aircraft over-flying Hungarian territory, a practice confirmed at the Veress talks in Istanbul. In late August 1943 the Germans were reported to have asked the Hungarian government to be allowed to establish German anti-aircraft batteries inside Hungary. The Hungarians refused. In early October two trains of German anti-aircraft personnel and guns arrived in western Hungary and set up two bases; the Hungarians protested but the Germans replied that it was necessary because experience showed that Hungarian batteries never fired on allied aircraft. The Hungarians continued to try to get them out, meanwhile warning the British of the position, through Stockholm, so that their aircraft could take account of it.[55]

At the end of October S.O.E. began to press the surrender group to accept a S.O.E. party, telling them that it would consist of uniformed British officers and would 'advise on reduction of Hungary's help to Germany by sabotage and other means'.[56]

But the Moscow Foreign Ministers' conference made Eden nervous and unhappy about this project. Molotov repeated his objections to 'negotiations being conducted with the Hungarian government as regards sabotage'. Nobody, he said, was more interested than the Soviet government in striking heavy blows against the Germans wherever it might be; they sympathised with anyone who harmed Germans, 'but they thought that this was not a subject for negotiations. They objected to negotiations about half-measures; in any case it was impossible to make sure that they were being carried out.' Eden promised to look into the matter, discuss it with the Chiefs of Staff and speak to Molotov outside the conference, 'when he thought it would be possible to reach agreement'. He assured Molotov that he thought that the Soviet government 'should have the deciding voice' in such matters which concerned countries with which they were actively engaged in fighting.[57]

On this Geoffrey Harrison[58] of the Central Department minuted that although Eden had said before that Russia should have a deciding voice over Rumania, this was the first time he had said it over Hungary.[59] Eden was briefed to re-state the case for going slow over Hungary to Molotov. In the event he did not find time to do so.[60] Roberts suggested that in the circumstances British policy over Hungary's surrender should go on as before – that a Hungarian switch-over should be timed at the moment most convenient to allied war requirements; meanwhile Hungary's war effort should be reduced as far as possible. But Eden minuted: 'I am not happy about this. Russians have maintained that Hungary must surrender unconditionally and must be told so. We cannot, so it seems to me, take any other line . . . Russians are fighting Hungarians and we are not. Russians therefore have cause to think that they should have strongest voice in deciding allied policy . . .'[61]

Presumably unaware of this argument, S.O.E. were stepping up pressure on the Hungarians to accept a British party. In late November they sent a message; 'British Foreign Office dissatisfied with your recent messages. Cannot accept present position and if Hungarian government really means business, it must make a better offer.'[62] Later S.O.E. said they found it hard to believe that a group as influential as Veress' claimed to be should not be able to receive and keep a party of only two people. If they really could not do this, S.O.E. did not see much point in continuing negotiations.[63] S.O.E. told the Foreign Office that if the reply to this was unsatisfactory, they thought they should break off contact completely.[64]

This would have suited the Foreign Office, in view of Eden's nervousness about Russian feelings. However, the Hungarians were stung by S.O.E.'s taunt about so 'powerful' a group being unable to receive a mission,[65] and during December agreed to receive one,[66] also suggesting that they should send a mission to Tito's forces in northern Yugoslavia.[67]

Both for S.O.E. and for Veress himself, Kállay's readiness to accept a S.O.E. mission seemed a real achievement. Eden thought otherwise. Roberts minuted that acceptance of the mission might just be a sop to the British, but 'we can accept it as such and get out of it what we can in the form of increased sabotage etc'. But Eden wrote: 'does not this conflict with what I told the Russians at Moscow?' Roberts suggested informing the Russians about the proposed mission, presenting

it as 'a useful minor test of the Hungarian government's future intentions'. Against this Eden wrote: 'I think this pretty dangerous and
likely to arouse Russian suspicions.' He concluded: 'I can see little
advantage in this S.O.E. mission and would prefer to drop it.'[68]

(There is no evidence whether Eden knew of S.O.E.'s project to make
contact with resistance elements in Hungary through Yugoslavia, for
which purpose Basil Davidson had been dropped into Bosnia in August
1943, and during the winter was making – or fighting – his way with
the Partisans towards Hungarian-occupied territory. His later efforts
to get left-wing groups going inside Hungary failed.)[69]

Because of Eden's ban, when at the end of December 1943 Veress
reported that he was 'most eagerly' awaiting the arrival of the British
party,[70] S.O.E. could send him no answer. Veress was left waiting. He
said later that this was a bitter disappointment to the Hungarian
government; they attributed the delay (correctly) to 'the Russian
factor' and thought it confirmed German propaganda that Hungary
had been placed in the exclusively Russian sphere of influence (in this
they were premature).[71] But they kept up their preparations; the mission was to be received at a landing ground on the estate of Count
Mihály Andrássy near the Yugoslav frontier, and the Chief of Police
was to take care of the party – though the arrival of a party of escaped
British prisoners of war on this estate caused a change of plan in early
March to another landing ground in south Hungary.[72]

The Hungarian government was trying hard, but vainly, to detach
Hungary from Germany and get the troops home. On 26 January 1944
the Chief of Staff, Szombathelyi, visited Hitler's H.Q. and repeated
earlier demands for the withdrawal of Hungarian troops still on the
Russian front. The Germans refused.[73] On 12 February Horthy wrote
a letter to Hitler asking that the Hungarian forces should be brought
home so that they could defend the Carpathians without German
help.[74] Hitler did not even answer.

In the spring of 1944 the British were planning to bomb Budapest,
or at least to threaten to bomb it; there was some division of opinion
which course was wiser. Roberts put forward an unorthodox argument
for bombing as a political act: 'our main difficulty in carrying out a
realistic Hungarian policy is that the Russians suspect us of undue
tenderness towards Hungary. The best and indeed only practicable
way to dispose of such suspicions is to carry out acts of war against
Hungary, which could only be air raids . . . Having shown to the
Russians that we mean business, it will then be very much easier to
secure their agreement for any further conversations with the Hungarians.'[75] But targets in Italy and Bulgaria still had higher priority,
so there were seldom aircraft available. Allied bombing did not in fact
begin until after the Germans occupied Hungary in March.

Before then, the surrender group had decided that they must make a desperate effort to break out of the deadlock in which they were caught. At the end of February, Veress went again to Istanbul and told S.O.E. that the group had come to the conclusion that they ought to make contact with the Russians, in the hope that arrangements could be made for the Hungarian divisions still on the Eastern front to go over to the Russians, in such a way that their surrender would appear natural and the outcome of a hopeless military situation. The group wanted British advice on how to do this. They were also ready to supply Tito's forces with food and other necessities over the frontier in the Muraköz district.[76]

On this Roberts minuted:

> We know from secret sources that the Hungarian government have received the impression that (a) the Americans are likely to disinterest themselves in European affairs and (b) that Europe has been divided up into English and Russian spheres of influence and that Hungary falls into the Russian sphere. The Budapest authorities are pretty realistic and, although their information is incorrect, they seem to have reached a conclusion which we can only welcome.

Roberts suggested that the British might as well get as much kudos as they could, and should suggest to the Russians joint talks with the Hungarians. Tito should be asked about the offer of supplies; and the despatch of a S.O.E. mission to Hungary should be cleared with the Russians.[77]

Eden approved Roberts's proposal for joint Anglo-Soviet talks with the Hungarians and even relented about the S.O.E. mission, agreeing with Selborne that it should go in during the April moon period; the Russians were to be so informed.[78] The Chiefs of Staff met and approved this course of action, saying that 'there would be considerable diplomatic advantages, if the surrender of the Hungarian divisions to the Russians could be arranged under the aegis of H.M.G'. Supplies to Tito would be 'an earnest of Hungarian good intentions'.[79]

THE GERMAN OCCUPATION

All this came just too late. On 15 March German troops started concentrating on the Hungarian border. On 17 March Hitler summoned Horthy to meet him; against the advice of some of his closest counsellors, he decided to go. Hitler told him that he had all of the proofs of the Hungarian government's treacherous activities (he only specifically mentioned the Szentgyörgi affair, however);[80] he said the presence of German troops in Hungary was essential and he wanted Horthy to sign an invitation. Horthy refused; Hitler told him the troops had already crossed the frontier and Horthy could consider himself a prisoner of war. Later he agreed to let Horthy go home if he promised there would be no resistance to the Germans. Horthy went home without promising, and held out for three days before agreeing to a German demand that he should appoint a new government. He finally gave way when the Germans threatened that Rumanian, Croatian and Slovak troops would take part in the occupation of Hungary – which was intended as the ultimate humiliation – and that the lives of Horthy's family 'could not be guaranteed'. Horthy then appointed the man Hitler wanted, Döme Sztojay, the Minister in Berlin.

Kállay took refuge in the Turkish Legation. Keresztes-Fischer was arrested and taken to a German concentration camp, where he was killed. One of the more prominent and wilder members of the opposition, Endre Bajcsy-Zsilinszky, was also arrested and finally executed on Christmas Day 1944.[81] The two detectives who had operated Veress's W/T sets were arrested and one of the sets found and seized. Veress himself escaped to Transylvania, crossed the frontier into Rumania at a place where there was no German control, went to Bucharest, thence to Sofia, and finally reached Zagreb, from where he made his way to the Croatian Army Corps H.Q. of Tito's forces; he was flown out to Bari in an American aircraft on 10 June.[82] Other more senior members of the Hungarian Foreign Ministry, including Szegedy-Maszák, were arrested.

The worst sufferers from the German occupation were inevitably the Jews, for whom Hungary had been a relatively safe haven. In October 1943 Professor Lewis Namier of the Jewish Agency had told the Foreign Office that his people were most seriously concerned about the consequences to 'the 800,000 Jews, who now enjoy comparative security in Hungary' of any Hungarian break with Germany which might result in a German occupation. The only hope for them, he said, was that the Hungarians would not move until it was practically certain that the Germans could not react. The Foreign Office promised to bear this in mind.[83] In mid-February 1944 the Foreign Office minuted, about Hungary: 'there is much greater freedom of thought and expression than elsewhere in Nazi Europe, trade unions continue to function and the Jews are treated humanely.'[84] With the German occupation in March, the Hungarians lost control to the Germans. Deportations of Jews started on 20 April.[85] As Horthy himself wrote later: 'they collected the Jews of the country and transported them under most inhuman conditions to Germany.'[86] It was not until mid-July that Horthy managed to recover any control and stop the deportations – for a brief time.[87]

The German occupation meant the end of the surrender group as the British had originally known it, with Kállay, Keresztes-Fischer, Szegedy-Maszák and his collaborators removed from the scene of action. Szombathelyi was removed from his post as Chief of Staff: he was a well-wisher of the surrender group, though he was always sceptical about the practical possibility of British-American military help, foreseeing that it would be the Russians who would arrive first in Hungary.[88] Once the group had been destroyed the Foreign Office tended to think that it had never been worth much anyway. Broad, in Bari, wrote of the group's 'obvious weakness'.[89] In London a member of the Central Department wrote of its 'ineffectiveness and hesitancy'.[90] This was after Veress had arrived in Bari and given a full report, which was inevitably tinged by the deep depression he felt over the failure of the whole undertaking.[91]

One comment in the Foreign Office was that Veress only seemed 'to have brought the group along as far and as fast as he did by dint of constantly exceeding his authority'; there was even doubt as to what authority he had for communicating the surrender offer in August 1943.[92] This was true, though it must also be said that S.O.E., when transmitting Veress's statements to London telegraphically, sometimes considerably hardened what Veress had actually said, in so far as this later emerged from fuller accounts, so that his statements appeared more firm and categorical than they had in fact been.

Nevertheless, the group had moved forward and its members had taken very real personal risks; a genuine effort had been made to get Hungarian troops home and detach Hungary gradually from Germany. The biggest problem for the British was the group's desire to get Anglo-American protection against the Russians; but this had been eased by the group's decision to approach the Russians, though if possible with British help.

Perhaps the best proof that the group had real potential value to the allies was that the Germans thought it necessary to destroy it, at the cost of using up troops to occupy Hungary.

With the surrender group dispersed, there remained Horthy. It was clearly a hard decision for him to stay at his post, accepting the humiliation of German dictation, but he seems to have taken it without much hesitation. The South African, Col. C. T. Howie, who after escaping from a German prison camp spent some months in Hungary in 1944, and for a week or so lived in the Regent's Palace and used the Palace communications, commented that the Regent was 'apt to adopt the view of the last person who spoke to him, with the result that there was much shilly-shally in the conduct of affairs'. Howie also said that Horthy was 'a gentleman and an officer' and so felt that to hit the Germans in the back when they were running away would not be sporting.[93] Then, too, Horthy had the tendency, almost inevitable in representatives of small weak countries, to be somewhat chameleon-like in his efforts to please. Writing to Stalin in the crisis of October 1944 he appealed to him to spare Hungary 'the people of which has so many affinities with the Russian people'.[94] Writing to King George VI from exile in Belgium in 1945, he made a different appeal: 'as we always say, only English and Hungarian are lasting a race of Gentlemen. Your Majesty also has hungarian blood . . .'[95] But his letters to Hitler were seldom so effusive.

The fact remained that Horthy was the king on the Hungarian chess-board, with little power but great importance, and his authority over the army remained strong. That was why Hitler did not finally remove him in March 1944. If Horthy could not help the Jews, his presence somehow saved many of the political opposition from deportation or death. Of the Social Democrats, Peyer went into hiding, Anna Kéthly was imprisoned but survived.[96] 'My remaining made the keeping of parliamentary form possible,' Horthy himself wrote.[97] Szombathelyi, though no longer Chief of Staff, remained active trying to plan a military conspiracy.

In spite of the German occupation, S.O.E. continued efforts to contact resistance groups.[98] Between April and June, three parties were sent into Hungary, two were captured, one had to withdraw to Yugoslavia.[99] In early July a mission led by Col. Peter Boughey – who had originally been destined to contact the surrender group – was parachuted blind into Hungary without any pre-arranged contact, against the advice of S.O.E. Cairo, near Lake Balaton. They were almost immediately captured by the Hungarian police but managed to convince them that they were escaped prisoners of war.[100] Two further parties were dropped during September, one to the Pecs area, the other to Slovakia, as a way of reaching Hungary. Both ended disastrously.[101]

When the Foreign Office was considering Soviet policy in Europe in the summer of 1944, a cabinet paper of 7 July sponsored by Eden defined policy towards Hungary. The general aim, as in the Balkans, would be to 'avoid any direct challenge to Russian influence in . . . countries adjacent to the Soviet Union' but to 'avail ourselves of every opportunity to spread British influence, profiting from . . . the moral authority and esteem which we may reasonably expect to enjoy in Hungary'. More precisely, 'in so far as Soviet policy stops short at restoring their lost territories to Czechoslovakia and Yugoslavia, at promoting a more equitable territorial settlement in Transylvania; at insisting upon far-reaching measures of land reform and the substitution of a more genuinely democratic régime for the present oligarchical structure of society and government, British and Soviet policy can go hand in hand, since we should also wish to promote all these objectives'. There was the danger that the Soviet Union 'might find it difficult to refrain from supporting the more extreme elements of the left'. But the paper concluded: 'in so far as Hungary is a country with a western outlook . . . the desired reforms can probably be promoted more effectively by British than by Soviet precepts. Without therefore attempting to displace Soviet influence, which must be great in central Europe, we should not hesitate to make our voice heard in Hungary and to show that we expect to be fully consulted regarding developments.'[102]

If the voice had been Eden's, it would not have sounded very friendly. In late July the Foreign Office heard through Madrid that 'all Hungarian parties from extreme left to Christian Socialists have reached a complete understanding and signed an agreement' with the purpose of resisting the Germans; the group asked for broadcast messages of moral support.[103] In the Foreign Office, Roberts thought this a genuine development even if the 'united front' was not yet ready for overt action.[104] Eden however ruled against any message, or propaganda support, minuting rather savagely: 'Hungary is much disliked by Russians, Czechs, and others. She is likely to have a poor time.'[105]

King Michael's coup of 23 August in Rumania, combined with the Red Army advance westwards, inevitably produced turmoil in Budapest. Horthy managed to get rid of the Sztojay government and replace it by one under General Geza Lakatos, who had distinguished himself by an anti-German order of the day in 1942.[106] At this time it seems that Horthy was most influenced by his surviving son, Miklós, who, as Col. Howie remarked, 'was not nearly so stupid as he appeared to be'.[107] His son's wife, Ilona, was certainly not stupid and was well able to sway her father-in-law.[108]

On 26 August György Bakach-Bessenyey, who had been Minister in Berne until, with other Hungarian diplomats in neutral countries, he resigned at the time of the German occupation, sent a message to Budapest offering to act as intermediary with the allies. Two days later he got back a message: 'conversations can begin, supreme authority charges Bessenyey to intervene . . . There are no Hungarian forces outside the frontiers. Troops of occupation are being recalled. Do not yet discuss territorial questions. Most important is independence with democratic régime,[109] which obviously meant independence of the Soviet Union and a non-Communist régime. Informed of this, Eden proposed to the Russians and Americans, unenthusiastically, that they should reply that the three major allies would communicate surrender terms to any plenipotentiary named by Horthy. The Americans agreed in principle.[110] The Russians showed no interest in this or other Hungarian approaches in other neutral capitals. On 4 September the British proposed that the European Advisory Commission should discuss armistice terms for Hungary, and submitted a British draft.[111] This also remained without response.

On 22 September General H. Náday, former commander of the Hungarian First Army, accompanied by Col. Howie and a Hungarian crew, crash-landed in Italy near Termoli and was taken to Caserta, where he told the British that Horthy and the government realised the desperate straits of Hungary; they were 'now prepared to do what they could to help shorten the war' and wanted to know if Allied forces could give some help. They realised that a Russian occupation was inevitable, but if they could be assured that Anglo-American troops would participate in the occupation, they would do everything possible to take action against the Germans. Almost as an afterthought, Náday said he was authorised by the Regent and government to ask for an armistice.[112] The British at once informed the Russians and Americans, both in the E.A.C.[113] in London and in Moscow and Washington. Washington replied promptly that Náday would be a suitable channel for the presentation of armistice terms.[114] In Moscow, Vyshinski said on 2 October that Náday did not possess authority to receive armistice terms. As for help from allied forces, the Soviet government did not consider it expedient to say anything to him.[115] Roberts minuted that this was disappointing but not surprising: 'the Russians are probably not yet ready to launch an all-out attack on Hungary and wish to keep their hands free.'[116]

THE SOVIET TAKE-OVER

Vyshinski's reply marked the end of British influence on Hungarian events. From then on, it was the Russians who played the hand. Already they held higher cards. On 6 October Molotov told the British and American ambassadors that a few days before a Hungarian peace mission, composed of minor notables, had been allowed to pass through Red Army lines and had been brought to Moscow.[117] (A few days later he informed them that the mission had come bearing letters from a certain Col. Makarov, whom they had taken to be an authorised Soviet representative, inviting them to Moscow and promising not only complete independence but also the territorial integrity of Hungary within its existing frontiers, adding that the present Hungarian administration would continue to function in all areas free of Germans. Makarov's letters contained the statement that 'they were written at Marshal Stalin's orders'. Now, however, Molotov said that Makarov was 'a partisan in Slovakia whose connexion with this affair was confined to helping Hungarian ministers to cross the front line', who 'obviously' had no authority to act on behalf of the Soviet authorities.)[118]

Before they knew of the Makarov affair, the British had already said that they thought this a much more promising development than the Náday approach, and had agreed to a Soviet proposal for a reply to Budapest demanding immediate evacuation of all Czechoslovak, Yugoslav and Rumanian territory – that is, a return to the Trianon frontiers – and an immediate declaration of war on Germany. They also agreed to Molotov's request that the three powers should negotiate the armistice terms, not in the E.A.C. in London, but in Moscow.[119]

By this time Churchill and Eden were in Moscow, and on 11 October Molotov was trying to beat down Eden over the 50–50 deal on Hungary just agreed between Churchill and Stalin (see pp. 144-5 above), pressing for 75-25 instead. In Budapest, Horthy made his last desperate bid to turn against the Germans, and on 11 October the Hungarian mission in Moscow, accepting the Soviet conditions, asked that the Red Army should hold up its advance on Budapest to make it possible to transfer Hungarian troops to the interior for defence against the Germans. The Russians agreed.[120]

An essential part of Horthy's plan was that the two Army Commanders facing the Russians in Transylvania, General Béla Miklós and General L. Veress, should make contact with the Soviet commanders and arrange for the switch-over. But the Germans were too well informed. Hitler had told Antonescu in August that he had put up with a good deal of *Schweinerei* from some sections of the Hungarians and at the slightest sign of a recurrence he would teach Hungary a lesson it would not forget for generations.[121] There was also muddle and indecision on the Hungarian side. Horthy was not in the habit of giving clear-cut or exact instructions; instead he would let his subordinates know the way his mind was working. This applied even to such close collaborators as General Veress, whom he had appointed to be his *homo regius* or deputy in the event of his own arrest by the Germans, which he thought certain.[122]

So 15 October, the day planned for Hungary's switch-over, both militarily in Transylvania and politically in Budapest, was a day on which the courage and devotion of individuals were nullified by indecision and muddle, so that the Germans could step in. Horthy's order to his army and to the people, broadcast after a good deal of dithering soon after midday, was in effect countermanded by another order broadcast a few hours later by the Chief of Staff who had succeeded Szombathelyi in April, General Janos Vörös, a man of uncertain loyalties, though later acceptable to the Russians. In consequence the armies of Transylvania went on fighting – but with the Germans, not against them. General Veress was caught on his way back to the front from Budapest, where he had been briefly to see Horthy, and became a prisoner of the Germans. General Miklós made his way to the Russians, but without effecting the planned military switch-over.[123]

Horthy later gave his own account in his own English to King George VI: 'seeing the total annihilation of my country inevitable, I asked for the German Minister and told him my decision to request armistice . . . I was convinced that this action meant my arrest sooner or later. The Germans were too ready to act and got immediately hold of the radio and telephone central, so that I was incapable of giving further orders. The Germans had about 600 tanks in town and so resistance was hopeless. The Royal Castle was occupied and plundered. I was taken to Bavaria where I was in captivity, until the American troops came . . .'[124]

The king had been removed from the Hungarian chess-board. The Germans replaced him by a pawn, the erratic and irresponsible fascist leader, Ferencz Szálasi; some Hungarian troops went on fighting with the Germans, eventually retreating with them to Austria, later still forcibly repatriated by the British to Russian-occupied Hungary.

When Horthy's coup failed, the Russians resumed their advance into Hungary. Early in November the ambivalent General Vörös arrived in Moscow and broadcast an appeal – in Horthy's name – to all Hungarians to come over to the Russians.[125] On 14 November Molotov told Clark Kerr that the Hungarian delegates and Generals were forming a democratic 'centre' to rally other like-minded elements.[126] On this Roberts minuted ironically: 'the Russians seem less prejudiced than we are about the Hungarians. They are very ready to use Horthy's Generals and to make propaganda in his name.'[127] Just before Christmas

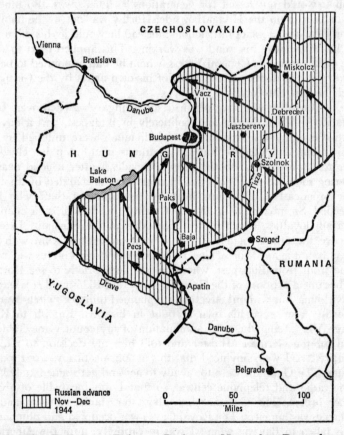

MAP 9. The Red Army Drive on Budapest, November–December 1944

the Soviet embassy in London told the Foreign Office that Miklós, Vörös and other Hungarians had left Moscow at the beginning of December for Hungary, and that there was now a Provisional National Assembly which was about to meet and elect a provisional national government under Miklós.[128] The British told enquiring Hungarian diplomats that they 'naturally' welcomed the formation of a government 'representative of progressive elements in Hungary'.[129]

The British had no cause to complain of its composition, which was undistinguished and heterogeneous but certainly not Communist. The fact remained that they had not been consulted and had played no part in events leading to its formation. So much for Stalin's 50 per cent or even Molotov's 25 per cent for the British share in decision-making about Hungary. The influence which the British could subsequently exercise through membership of the Allied Control Commission was as small in Hungary as in Rumania or Bulgaria.

20   Postscript

'Expense of spirit in a waste of shame' – these words were written about another form of activity, but it is tempting to use them of any large and strenuous undertaking which fizzles out unheroically, such as the British effort in South-East Europe between 1939 and 1945.

But even if the outcome was unheroic muddle, there was not much cause for shame. It was true that in 1941 the British bullied the Yugoslavs unmercifully to go to war. But they had also bullied the Turks, and they, being united on this, resisted without difficulty. It was the disunity of the Yugoslavs which gave British bullying an opening; and even then, it was the Serbian conspirators, not the British, who planned and carried out the coup of 27 March. It was Hitler, not the British, who finally plunged Yugoslavia into war. And even if he had originally intended to leave the Yugoslavs alone in the spring of 1941, the British were probably right in thinking that in the long term he would have found some means of dragging them into the German war effort.

The British did not create civil war in Greece, Yugoslavia or Albania. They helped the Communists, but the Communist-led resistance movements would have existed – and would almost certainly have wiped out all rival movements – without British help. Greece is the most controversial case; but there, Woodhouse, who is in the best position to know, has written that if the British had never gone to Greece at all during the occupation, this would only have been another way of conceding victory to the Greek Communist Party.[1]

It was true that the leaders of the Axis satellites were, for reasons of strategic deception, allowed to believe that Anglo-American military operations in South-East Europe were possible when they were not; for these countries, it might have been better if they had been told earlier and more plainly that they must make their own peace with Russia and that Britain could do very little to help them. On the other hand, the British themselves did not realise quite how powerless they were in the face of the Red Army's advance westwards and Stalin's determination to establish total political monopoly in all areas conquered by the Red Army. In this failure to understand Stalin the British can be charged with naiveté, blindness, even arrogance. But the pressing needs of war-time alliance and lingering fears of a second Soviet–German deal were powerful impulses to wishful thinking and to the ignoring of danger signals.

The British hoped that, while the Soviet Union's security requirements would prevail in countries near its borders, there could be some kind of Anglo-Soviet influence-sharing, matched by power-sharing inside those countries between liberals and the Left, between peasant parties, social democrats and communists. This idea turned out to be a pipe-dream, but it was not shameful.

Nor were British aims entirely negative – first to defeat Germany and then to hold back Soviet power. Positive and constructive policies were also discussed at length by back-room experts and propagandists and at times by politicians too, though the politicians usually wanted above all to keep their hands free. Detailed recommendations were drawn up for post-war frontiers which would be more just than those drawn after the 1914–18 war, including autonomy for Transylvania and minor revisions of the Trianon Treaty. The plans for confederations, though partly aimed at creating a bulwark against the Russians, had also a genuinely constructive aim, to overcome destructive national rivalries and the harmful economic consequences of splitting up East and South-East Europe into small non-viable states.

In the social field, the British did not simply stand for the preservation of the existing order. Serious thought was given in back rooms to the needs of the poor, under-employed and under-skilled mass of peasants in South-East Europe and to the need for land reforms backed by adequate credit, training in new agricultural methods and gradual industrialisation. In 1942 a small unofficial 'peasant conference' was held in London under the auspices of Professor R. W. Seton-Watson, authorised rather nervously by the Foreign Office. Exiled members of peasant parties of South-East Europe took part; the aim was to start planning for a better post-war world in which these parties would play a more effective and useful role than in the past. The project petered out because the Russians let some of the participants know that they did not like it: they saw the peasant parties – the natural representatives of the majority, given the stage of economic development in South-East Europe – as probably their greatest enemies, a more serious menace to the establishment of Soviet control than the numerically weak Social Democrats.

British political and economic planning for the post-war world had no effect on South-East Europe, except Greece. All that the British could claim was that they had made a contribution which could not be accurately weighed or measured to the defeat of Hitler's Germany. In terms of military cost-effectiveness it seems clear that – even if at the time the British considerably over-estimated the number of German divisions held down in South-East Europe – a useful diversion of German manpower and resources was achieved, at low cost (to the British). The B.L.O.s and other ranks who went into the area between 1941 and 1945 faced great risks and suffered relatively heavy casualties; but the total number, in terms of the overall military picture, was very small indeed. In materials, by far the biggest effort went into supplying Tito's forces, and the total of arms and all materials supplied to them by sea and air between the summer of 1943 and 1945 was under 80,000 tons.[2] As for the charge that the British ruthlessly sacrificed the lives of others, it is true that the death roll in Yugoslavia was appallingly high. But far more deaths were attributable to internal strife than to German reprisals; and the Partisans would have gone on fighting Germans in any case, whether the British helped them or not.

The British therefore did not have much cause for shame and more for modest content that in South-East Europe they had done a little to help win the Second World War – even if they got nothing out of it themselves.

Notes

NOTE ON SOURCES

The main source material for this book has been the Foreign Office, Cabinet and Chief of Staff papers, together with some S.O.E. reports and correspondence, now available in the Public Record Office. The bulk of the source references therefore refer to these. I have also made use of the official war histories and the published records of individuals who took part in events, from Churchill and Field-Marshal Lord Wilson to the British Liaison Officers in the field or Yugoslav Partisans such as Milovan Djilas, Svetozar Vukmanović-Tempo and Vladimir Dedijer; and to try to get a view from the other side I have dipped into official Communist histories of the countries concerned, where these have been available to me.

What I have found especially valuable has been the help given to me personally by individuals who were involved in one way or another in South-East Europe during the Second World War. George Taylor and Bickham Sweet-Escott, who held central executive positions in S.O.E. from the days when it was Section D, have been particularly generous in giving me their personal memories, and George Taylor also made available to me papers in his possession, including the Pirie Report on Greece; in the source references these are referred to as 'G.T. papers'; other information given to me by him appears as 'G.T. to E.B.'. I also had invaluable help on Rumania from Ivor Porter, and he appears in the source references as 'I.P.' Professor W. J. M. Mackenzie, the author of the official but unpublished history of the S.O.E., was extremely kind in helping to clear up obscure points and sort out difficulties; he appears in the source references as 'W.J.M.M.'. I should also make particular mention of Dr László Veress, who was most generous in giving me first-hand information about Hungary and his own experiences, in 1943–4; he appears simply as 'Veress' (not to be confused with General L. Veress de Dalnok, who also very kindly gave me some pointers from his personal memories, and whom I have also quoted).

Where other people have given me information from their own personal memories, their names appear in full in the source references. I have mentioned them and thanked them in the foreword.

I have to thank the Rt. Hon. Anthony Crossland, M.P., for permission to use material from the Dalton Papers, now in the London

School of Economics Library. These I have referred to as 'Dalton Papers'.

CHAPTER I

1 Documents of British Foreign Policy, Third Series v 197.
2 *Ibid.*, p. 1.
3 *Ibid.*, pp. 1 ff.
4 *Ibid.*, pp. 84 ff.
5 *Ibid.*, p. 183.
6 David Dilkes, *The Diaries of Sir Alexander Cadogan 1938–1945*, p. 173.
7 DBFP, loc. cit., p. 207.
8 *Cadogan Diaries*, p. 119.
9 *Ibid.*, p. 117.
10 FO 371/23752 F.P. 36/879 8.5.39.
11 Lord Lloyd, Secretary of State for Colonies, 1940–1.
12 *Cadogan Diaries*, p. 121.
13 Eden, *Facing the Dictators*, pp. 513 ff.
14 DBFP Third Series VI 294.
15 FO 371/24885 Note on Hungarian-Rumanian relations in Aug. 1939 22.1.40.
16 FO 371/24984 Hoare letter to Nichols 23.1.40.
17 DBFP, loc. cit., p. 267.
18 DBFP, loc. cit., p. 437.
19 DBFP Third Series v 197.
20 Cripps was ambassador in Moscow, 1940–2.
21 FO 371/24845 Cripps letter to Collier 16.7.40.
22 PREM 3/374/13A Churchill minute 25.10.44.

CHAPTER 2

1 DBFP Third Series v 107.
2 DBFP Third Series VI 294.
3 CAB 65/1 W.M. (39) 8 8.9.39, W.M. (39) 15 14.9.39.
4 FO 371/29750 Rendel to Eden R 4411/1041/7 27.3.41.
5 CAB 65/1 W.M. (39) 61 26.10.39.
6 FO 371/24950 Bucharest 17 8.1.40, FO 371/24427 O'Malley memorandum 12.1.40.
7 FO 371/24991 Hoare despatches 11 and 25.3.40.
8 FO 371/24887 Hoare despatch 20.3.40.
9 FO 371/24886 Halifax letter to Chatfield 16.2.40 Annex III.
10 FO 371/24887 Athens 175 2.4.40.
11 FO 371/24869 Politika 25.4.40, *The Times* 30.4.40.
12 FO 371/24889 M.P. (40) 140 29.4.40.
13 Sir Ronald Campbell, P.C., G.C.M.G., C.B., Ambassador in Cairo, 1946–50. FO 371/24890 Belgrade 368 18.6.40.
14 François Fonvieille-Alquier, *The French and the Phoney War 1939–40*, p. 67.
15 CAB 65/1 W.M. (39) 8 8.9.39.

16 CAB 65/1 W.M. (39) 12 11.9.39.

17 CAB 65/1 W.M. (39) 15 14.9.39.

18 CAB 65/1 W.M. (39) 21 20.9.39.

19 CAB 65/1 W.M. (39) 23 22.9.39.

20 CAB 65/1 W.M. (39) 39 6.10.39.

21 CAB 65/1 W.M. (39) 95 26.11.39.

22 CAB 65/2 W.M. (39) 107 7.12.39, W.P. (39) 149.

23 CAB 65/1 W.M. (39) 99 30.11.39.

24 CAB 65/2 W.M. (39) 107 7.12.39.

25 CAB 65/2 W.M. (39) 115 14.12.39.

26 CAB 65/2 W.M. (39) 120 20.12.39, W.M. (39) 115 14.12.39.

27 CAB 65/2 W.M. (39) 123 27.12.39.

28 FO 371/24884 Rome 32 10.1.40.

29 FO 371/24884 Campbell letter to Nichols 1.1.40 R 222/G/54.

30 FO 371/24884 Minute by Lt-Col. C. S. Clarke to H.M. Minister Belgrade 1.1.40.

31 FO 371/24884 Campbell letter to Nichols 1.1.40 R222/G/54.

32 *Ibid.* Belgrade 4 3.1.40.

33 FO 371/24879 Rendel letter to Halifax 10.2.40.

34 Later Sir George Rendel, K.C.M.G., H.M. Ambassador to Belgium 1947–50.

35 FO 371/29750 Rendel despatch to Eden 27.3.41 R/4411/1041/7.

36 FO 371/24884 monitoring report.

37 FO 371/24884 Note by Military Attaché Athens 8.1.40.

38 C.O.S. (40) 186 8.1.40.

39 FO 371/24888 Gen. Marshall Cornwall letter to Nichols 6.4.40.

40 FO 371/24885 C.O.S. M.R. (40) 4.

41 FO 371/24888 C.O.S. (40) 282 (S) 8.4.40.

42 FO 371/24886 Allied Military Committee M.R. (40) 32nd meeting 4.2.40.

43 FO 371/24886 Allied Military Committee M.R. (40) 10 5.2.40.

44 FO 371/24886 Halifax letter to Chatfield 16.2.40 R2173/G/112.

45 FO 371/24887 Halifax memorandum on S. E. Europe W.P. (40) 110 26.3.40.

46 FO 371/24888 Forbes memorandum 28.3.40.

47 FO 371/24888 Col. Rozoy letter 3.5.40.

48 FO 371/24888 Allied Military Committee D. F. 110 6.4.40 R4346/G/24.

49 FO 371/24888 C.O.S. draft paper M.R. (J) (40) 6.4.40.

50 FO 371/24889 Extract from War Cabinet Conclusions 105 (40) S.

51 Sir Pierson Dixon, G.C.M.G., C.B., H.M. Ambassador to France, 1960–4.

52 FO 371/24889 Dixon minute 6.5.40, Nicholls minute 13.5.40.

53 FO 371/29782 Angora 670 28.3.41.

54 FO 371/24890 J.P. (40) 216 4.6.40.

55 FO 371/24890 Sofia 276 DIPP 11.6.40, Belgrade 283 DIPP 1.6.40.

56 FO 371/24890 Nicholls minute 15.6.40.

57 FO 371/24890 C.O.S. (40) 525 3.7.40.

58 FO 371/24890 FO circular telegram 128 5.7.40.

CHAPTER 3

1 CAB 65/1 W.M. (39) 19 18.9.39.
2 CAB 65/1 W.M. (39) 20 19.9.39.
3 CAB 65/1 W.M. (39) 22 21.9.39.
4 CAB 65/1 W.M. (39) 24 23.9.39.
5 CAB 65/1 W.M. (39) 31 29.9.39.
6 CAB 65/1 W.M. (39) 36 4.10.39.
7 CAB 65/1 W.M. (39) 39 6.10.39.
8 CAB 65/1 W.M. (39) 51 18.10.39.
9 *Ibid.*
10 FO 371/24845 Moscow no. 1 1.1.40.
11 CAB 65/2 W.M. (39) 107 7.12.39.
12 FO 371/24884 Hoare letter 8.12.39 R/421/1021.
13 Sir Fitzroy Maclean, Bt, later Head of British Mission to Marshal Tito.
14 FO 371/24884 Maclean minute 24.12.39 R/421/100.
15 FO 371/24884 Collier minute 26.12.39.
16 FO 371/24835 Maclean paper 2.2.40 N2736/G.
17 FO 371/24886 Halifax despatch to Knatchbull-Hugessen 14.2.40.
18 FO 371/24887 Knatchbull-Hugessen letter to Nichols 7.3.40.
19 CAB 65 W.M. 76 (40) 27.3.40.
20 FO 371/24887 Cadogan minute 26.3.40.
21 CAB 65 W.M. 76 (40) 27.3.40.
22 *Ibid.*
23 FO 371/24888 Meeting of Heads of Missions (South-East Europe) 8.4.40 R/3367/G/93.
24 FO 371/42845 Moscow 865 13.10.40.
25 *Nazi-Soviet Relations*, pp. 209–10.
26 FO 371/24844 Moscow 312 DIPP 14.6.40, Moscow 334 DIPP 15.6.40.
27 FO 371/24844 Tass statement.
28 FO 371/24844 Moscow 335 DIPP 17.6.40.
29 FO 371/24844 Maclean minute 19.6.40.
30 FO 371/24844 FO 165 DIPP to Moscow 24.6.40, 166 DIPP to Moscow 25.6.40.
31 *Ibid.*
32 FO 371/24845 Cripps letter to Collier 16.7.40.
33 FO 371/24845 Nichols minute 6.9.40.
34 FO 371/24845 Cripps despatch to Halifax 16.8.40.
35 FO 371/24845 FO 641 to Moscow 15.10.40.
36 *Nazi-Soviet Relations*, p. 216.
37 *Ibid.*, p. 167.
38 *Ibid.*, pp. 222–59.
39 FO 371/24845 N 9046/G 8.11.40.
40 *Ibid.*
41 *Nazi-Soviet Relations*, p. 330.

CHAPTER 4

1 FO 371/24886 Knatchbull-Hugessen letter to Halifax 12.2.40 R1864/56.

2 FO 371/24888 Forbes memorandum 28.3.40.

3 Hugh Dalton, *The Fateful Years*, p. 296.

4 Dalton Papers, record of meeting held in Foreign Secretary's Room, 1.7.40.

5 *The Times* 11.4.40.

6 FO 371/24985 Chatfield letter to Hore-Belisha 5.1.40.

7 FO 371/24985 Hoare letter to Sargent 11.1.40.

8 FO 371/24992 Lockhart letter 11.5.40, Cadogan minute 12.5.40.

9 FO 371/24978 Wing Cdr A. H. H. Macdonald to Rendel 9.1.40.

10 Sir Eric Berthoud, K.C.M.G., associated with the Anglo-Iranian Oil Company and appointed oil expert attached to the British Legation on the outbreak of war. Ambassador to Poland 1956–60.

11 FO 371/30001 Berthoud report 2.3.41 R5342/G.

12 See Chapter 2, note 13.

13 FO 371/24886 Campbell letter to Halifax 12.2.40, Nichols minute 28.2.40 R2142/5/67.

14 Roskill, *Hankey: Man of Secrets*, p. 433.

15 W. N. Medlicott, *The Economic Blockade* 1 246.

16 FO 371/24893 E.P. (E.W.) (40) 3.

17 FO 371/24887.

18 Later Sir Ronald Cross, Bt, K.C.M.G., K.C.V.O., High Commissioner in Australia, 1941–5.

19 Later Sir Evelyn Shuckburgh, G.C.M.G., C.B., Ambassador to Italy, 1966–9.

20 FO 371/24893 Cross letter to Simon 1.4.40, Shuckburgh minute 10.4.40.

21 Medlicott, p. 264.

22 G.T. to E.B.

23 FO 371/24893 Kahn letter to Lee 4.4.40, Lee to Kahn, 5.4.40.

24 FO 371/24883 Dunn letter to A. Chester Beatty 5.4.40.

25 Later Sir Charles Hambro, K.B.E., Chairman, Hambros Bank.

26 Later Sir Frank Nixon of the Export Credits Guarantee Department.

27 Later Sir George Rendel, K.C.M.G., H.M. Ambassador to Belgium, 1947–50.

28 FO 371/24875 Sofia to FO 20.5.40.

29 FO 371/24893 FO 1584 ARFAR to Washington 4.9.40.

30 FO 371/24875 Ad Hoc Committee on Balkan Purchases 6.8.40.

31 FO 371/29778.

32 DBFP Third Series v 1ff.

33 FO 371/30001 Berthoud report 2.3.41 R 5342/G.

34 CAB 65/1 W.M. 1 (39) 16.9.39.

35 CAB 65/2 W.M. (39) 108 8.12.39.

36 FO 371/30001 Berthoud report 2.3.41 R5342/G.

37 FO 371/24968 Hoare letter to Halifax 29.12.39.

38 FO 371/24968 Halifax despatch to Hoare 2.1.40.

39 FO 371/24985 Broad minute 10.1.40.

40 FO 371/24985 W.M. 22 (40) 24.1.40, W.M. 28 (40) 31.1.40.

41 FO 371/24982 Bucharest 28 Saving 28.3.40.

42 FO 371/24982 Hoare minute 2.4.40.

43 FO 371/24887 W.M. 70 (40) 16.3.40.

44 FO 371/30001 Berthoud report 17.1.41 R 4360.

45 *Ibid.*

46 Later Sir Maurice Bridgeman, K.B.E., Chairman of B.P., 1960–9.

47 G.T. to E.B.; Medlicott, p. 255.

48 CAB 65/1 W.M. 16 (39) 15.9.39.

49 Medlicott, p. 254.

50 *Ibid.*, p. 256.

51 FO 371/23752 Broad letter to Turner 19.12.39.

52 'Goeland' = the French word for sea-gull or sea-mew = Society for Energetic Action by the Ministry of Economic Warfare – a name invented by Maurice Bridgeman. Sweet-Escott to E.B.

53 Medlicott, p. 255.

54 FO 371/29774 Rose minute 7.8.41, FO 371/29775 letter to Perkins 24.10.41.

55 Medlicott, p. 258.

56 FO 371/24992 Bucharest 546 DIPP 21.6.40.

57 FO 371/29975 Hoare letter to Eden 21.2.41 R2962/2/37.

58 FO 371/24992 Broad minute 26.11.40.

59 Medlicott, p. 258.

60 FO 371/29775 M.E.W. 2124 to Ankara 27.9.41.

61 FO 371/29990 Macrae letter to D. J. Scott 4.11.40.

62 B. S.-W to E.B.

63 FO 371/30001 Berthoud report 2.3.41.

64 G.T. to E.B.

65 Roskill, p. 435.

66 Medlicott, p. 255.

67 W. J. M. Mackenzie to E.B.

68 FO 371/24992 FO 70 to Bucharest 18.1.40, Bucharest 75 26.1.40.

69 FO 371/24888 Notes for meeting of H.M.R.R. from S.E. Europe 10.4.40.

70 FO 371/24888 Forbes report 13.5.40.

71 FO 371/30001 Dixon minute 27.11.41.

72 G.T. to E.B. This was presumably rather different from the scheme for 'demolition raids on oil refineries supplying the German Army' mentioned by Christopher Sykes in his *Orde Wingate*, p. 224, since he seems to be referring to the period *after* the war started.

73 Sweet-Escott, *Baker Street Irregular*, p. 22; Dalton Papers, Report from A/D and D/HY on Certain S.O.2 Activities in Yugoslavia 24.6.41; W.J.M.M. to E.B.

74 FO 371/24996 Broad minute 21.6.40.

75 FO 371/23752 Hoare letter to Halifax 20.12.39 and attached report.

76 FO 371/23752 Godfrey letter to Jebb 29.12.39.

77 FO 371/29990 Macrae report 4.11.40.

78 *Ibid.*

79 G.T. to E.B.

80 *The Times* 9.4.40.

81 *Ibid.*

82 Later Sir Peter Garran, K.C.M.G., Ambassador at The Hague, 1964–70.

83 FO 371/24888 Campbell letter to Cadogan and attached report.

84 FO 371/24430 Belgrade 83 to FO 23.3.40.
85 Later Sir Owen O'Malley, K.C.M.G., Ambassador at Lisbon, 1945–7.
86 FO 371/24888 minutes of meeting of Chiefs of Staff with H.M.R.R. from S.E. Europe 15.4.40.
87 FO 371/24427 O'Malley despatch to Halifax 23.4.40.
88 FO 371/24889 Knatchbull-Hugessen to Halifax 27.4.40.
89 Keesing's Contemporary Archives.
90 FO 371/24996 Broad minute 21.6.40.
91 C.O.S. (40) 344, 11.5.40.
92 Dalton Papers, Report from A/D and D/HY 24.6.41.
93 Dalton Papers, Misc. 1941–2 Tel. 3025 A.D. from C.D. 3.4.41.
94 *Ibid.*, Tel. 3027 C.D. to A.D. 5.4.41.
95 Sir Eric Berthoud to E.B.
96 FO 371/30020 Macnab report.
97 FO 371/24899 W.P. (40) 200 11.6.40.
98 Sweet-Escott, *Baker Street Irregular*, p. 35.
99 FO 371/29975 Hoare despatch to Eden 21.2.41 R2969/2/37.
100 FO 371/29975 Hoare despatch to Eden 21.2.41.
101 FO 371/24993 Hankey letter to Nichols 23.9.40.
102 W.J.M.M. to E.B.
103 FO 371/29990 S.O.2 report 'General Situation in Rumania' 18.12.40.
104 FO 371/29975 Hoare despatch to Eden 13.2.41.
105 FO 371/29990 Dixon minute 23.1.40.
106 *Ibid.*
107 *Cadogan Diaries*, p. 351.
108 FO 371/29990 Bucharest 159 25.1.41.
109 FO 371/29991 FO 17 to Bucharest 28.1.41.
110 FO 371/30000 Bucharest 173 28.1.41.
111 W.J.M.M. to E.B.
112 PREM 3 374/13A Cairo 387 25.2.41.
113 FO 371/30000 W.O. 52925 to C.-in-C. M.E. 21.2.41.
114 PREM 3 374/13A Istanbul unnumbered to Cairo 22.2.41.
115 PREM 3 374/13A Cairo 387 25.2.41.
116 CAB 66 W.M. (40) 287 27.11.40.
117 PREM 3 374/13A P.M. to C.A.S. 27.11.40.
118 FO 371/24921 Hardinge letter to Cadogan with enclosure 2.12.40.
119 FO 371/24921 Athens 1349 16.12.40, A.O.C.-in-Chief M.E. to Air Ministry A. 483 16.12.40.
120 PREM 3 374/205 P.M. Personal Minute M. 446 22.12.40.
121 CAB 66 W.P. (41) 39 (Revise).
122 PREM 3 374/13A Cairo 378, 389 25.2.41.
123 PREM 3 374/13A FO to Cairo, P.M. for S. of S. 27.2.41.
124 FO 371/29782 Anglo-Greek Conversations Record 2.3.41.
125 FO 371/29782 Anglo-Greek conversations: meeting at British Legation Athens 4.3.41.
126 FO 371/30001 Ismay letter to Jebb 9.4.41.
127 Air Chief Marshal Sir Arthur Longmore, G.C.B., D.S.O., A.O.C. in C. M.E. 1940–1
128 G.T. to E.B.

129 FO 371/30001 Berthoud letter to Kisch 28.4.41.

130 FO 371/30001 Sir M. Stewart letter to Eden 26.5.41; Dixon minute 27.11.41.

131 FO 371/25033 report of Shea mission, W.J.M.M. to E.B.

132 Sweet-Escott, pp. 28–9, G.T. to E.B.

133 FO 371/35033 Campbell despatch to Halifax 16.7.40.

134 W.J.M.M. to E.B.

135 FO 371/24888 Meeting of H.M.R.R. in London April 1940.

136 Sir George Rendel, *The Sword and the Olive*, pp. 175–8 (Rendel calls Dimitrov 'Ivanov' for the sake of discretion).

137 W. S. Bailey to E.B.

138 W.J.M.M. to E.B.

139 Dalton Papers, Report from A/D and DH/Y 24.6.41.

140 FO 371/24892 Record of meeting between FO and S.O.E. 9.12.40.

141 *Ibid.*

142 FO 371/24892 Broad minute 16.12.40.

143 FO 371/29803 German White Book 6.4.41 R7844/3552/67.

CHAPTER 5

1. FO 371/24866 Grafftey-Smith (later Sir Laurence Grafftey-Smith, K.C.M.G., High Commissioner Karachi, 1947–51), reports Jan.–Apr. 1940.

2 DBFP Third Series VI 437; Hoptner, *Yugoslavia in Crisis 1934–1941*, pp. 124–7.

3. FO 371/24866 Rome to FO 24.5.40.

4 CAB 65/1 W.M. (39) 39 6.10.39.

5 FO 371/29719 S.O.2 memorandum 25.2.41, FO 371/24866 Capt. Thomas Davies letter to Broad 8.4.40, *Ibid.*, Section D paper 25.8.40.

6 FO 371/25033 Belgrade 308 DIPP 5.6.40.

7 FO 371/24868 Record of meeting at FO 2.7.40.

8 FO 371/24868 Sir Andrew Ryan's report on interview with Zog 3.7.40, Sargent minute 19.7.40.

9 See Julian Amery, *Approach March*, p. 162, for Djonović's role in this.

10 FO 371/24866 Section D paper 25.8.40.

11 FO 371/24866 FO to Cairo 7.9.40.

12 FO 371/24866 Dixon minute 18.9.40.

13 FO 371/24867 Reply to PQ and FO minute thereon 19.6.40.

14 FO 371/24867 Dixon minute 15.9.40.

15 FO 371/29715 W. C. Knight minute 7.7.41.

16 FO 371/24868 Ryan report 8.11.40.

17 FO 371/24868 S.O.E. to Istanbul 20.11.40.

18 Later Sir Michael Palairet, K.C.M.G., Ambassador to exiled Greek government, 1942–3.

19 FO 371/24868 Athens to FO 23.11.40.

20 FO 371/24868 FO to Athens 26.11.40.

21 FO 371/24868 Athens to FO 29.11.40.

22 Later Sir Pierson Dixon, G.C.M.G., C.B., Ambassador to France, 1960–4.

23 FO 371/24866 Dixon minutes of 28.11.40, 23.11.40.
24 FO 371/24867 Meeting held by Sargent 2.12.40.
25 FO 371/24892 Meeting held at FO 9.12.40.
26 FO 371/24867 FO to Athens 8.12.40.
27 FO 371/24868 Athens to FO 9.12.40, 14.12.40.
28 FO 371/24867 Belgrade to FO 31.1.41.
29 FO 371/29712 Nicholls minute 24.1.40.
30 FO 371/24868 Belgrade to FO 3.12.40.
31 FO 371/24866 Belgrade to FO 1.12.40, 10.12.40.
32 FO 371/24892 Record of meeting between FO and S.O.2 R8860/5/67.
33 FO 371/24867 S.O.E. Belgrade to London 18.12.40.
34 FO 371/24868 Athens to FO 18.12.40.
35 FO 371/24867 S.O.E. Athens to Belgrade 19.12.40.
36 FO 371/24867 FO to Athens 20.12.40.
37 FO 371/24867 FO to Athens 21.12.40.
38 FO 371/24867 War Office to C.-in-C. Middle East 20.12.40, Air Ministry to A.O.C. Middle East 21.12.40.
39 FO 371/24867 Athens to FO 21.12.40.
40 *Ibid.*
41 FO 371/24867 Dixon minute 26.12.40, Broad letter to Hopkinson 27.12.40.
42 FO 371/24867 S.O.E. London to S.O.E. Belgrade 27.12.40.
43 FO 371/24867 Eden minute 28.12.40.
44 FO 371/29719 Broad letter to Hopkinson 28.2.41.
45 *Ibid.*, W. C. Knight minute 8.3.41.
46 Sweet-Escott, p. 64; W.J.M.M. to E.B.

CHAPTER 6

1 FO 371/29750 Rendel despatch to Eden 27.3.41 R4411/104/7.
2 FO 371/24880 Clutton minute 26.11.41.
3 FO 371/29750 Rendel despatch 27.3.41.
4 FO 371/24881 Campbell despatch 1.2.40.
5 FO 371/25032 Campbell letter to Cadogan 14.5.40, Nichols letter to Campbell 27.5.40.
6 FO 371/24870 Bowker minute 2.12.40.
7 FO 371/24881 Sofia 847 DALLY 23.11.40.
8 FO 371/24869 Sofia Legation report 26.1.40.
9 FO 371/24881 Annual Report 1939.
10 FO 371/24869 Rendel report on audiences with King Boris 23.4.40.
11 FO 371/24878 FO to Sofia 16.7.40.
12 FO 371/24878 Sofia to FO 19.7.40.
13 FO 371/24985.
14 CAB 65/1 W.M. (39) 15 14.9.39.
15 FO 371/24878 Sofia 433 11.10.40.
16 FO 371/24878 Sofia 697 15.1.40, Sofia 702 16.10.40, Sofia 731, 23.10.40.
17 FO 371/24870 FO to Sofia 28.10.40, Sofia to FO 29.10.40.
18 FO 371/24891 Moscow 972 7.11.40.
19 FO 371/24872 Bulgarian Communist Party appeal.

20 FO 371/24877 Communist Manifesto (B.C.P.) received by H.M. Legation 8.8.40.

21 FO 371/24877 Sofia to FO 7.8.40.

22 FO 371/24872 Sofia to FO 18.10.40.

23 *Nazi-Soviet Relations*, pp. 244–6; see also p. 26 above.

24 *Ibid.*, p. 259.

25 FO 371/24880 Sofia 387 21.11.40.

26 FO 371/24880 Sofia to FO 2.12.40.

27 FO 371/30068 Angora 1407 8.6.41.

28 Bulgarska Komunisticheska Partia, *Istoria* (Moscow, 1960), pp. 351–2.

27 *The Times* 11.12.40.

30 FO 371/24880 draft telegram initialled Halifax 1.12.40.

31 FO 371/24870 Sofia to FO 3.12.40.

32 FO 371/24880 Sargent minute 28.11.40.

33 FO 371/24870 Sofia to FO 27.11.40.

34 CAB 65/17 W.M. (41) 3 7.1.41.

35 FO 371/29777 Moscow 68 25.1.41.

36 FO 371/29777 Eden despatch to Cripps 29.1.41 R700/113/67.

37 FO 371/29777 Moscow 151 20.2.41.

38 FO 371/29750 Rendel despatch to Eden 27.3.41 R4411/1041/7.

39 FO 371/248777 Sargent minute 12.2.41.

40 FO 371/29747 Sofia 386 3.3.41.

41 FO 371/29750 Rendel despatch to Eden 27.3.41 R4411/1041/7.

42 FO 371/29748 Sofia 406 5.3.41.

43 FO 371/29764 Record of meeting held at G.H.Q. M.E. 31.3.41.

CHAPTER 7

1 FO 371/22428 Makins minute 7.11.40.

2 FO 371/24431 Draft annual report enclosed in Chancery letter to FO 11.6.40.

3 FO 371/24427 Sargent minute 22.2.40.

4 FO 371/24426 O'Malley letter to Strang 5.1.40.

5 FO 371/24431 Draft annual report 11.6.40.

6 FO 371/24427 Sargent minute 22.2.40.

7 FO 371/24431 draft annual report 11.6.40.

8 FO 371/24426 O'Malley letter to Strang 5.1.40.

9 FO 371/24427 O'Malley memorandum 12.1.40, FO 371/24429 Budapest 51 14.2.40.

10 FO 371/24425 Makins letter to Leith-Ross 19.4.40.

11 FO 371/24427 Note by Hungarian Minister 9.2.40, Sargent minute 22.2.40.

12 FO 371/24426 Budapest 62 20.2.40.

13 FO 371/24427 O'Malley despatch to Halifax 1.3.40.

14 FO 371/24427 O'Malley despatch to Halifax 9.3.40.

15 FO 371/24427 O'Malley despatch to Halifax 26.4.40.

16 FO 371/24427 Sargent and Cadogan minutes 9.5.40, FO 122 to Budapest 10.5.40.

17 FO 371/24984 Budapest 291 12.7.40.

18 FO 371/24890 Budapest 279 8.7.40.
19 FO 371/24890 FO 203 to Budapest 11.7.40.
20 FO 371/24985 FO 287 to Budapest 30.8.40. FO 371/22428 Hungary and Rumania Contact Meeting 9.9.40.
21 FO 371/22428 Budapest 323 7.8.40.
22 FO 371/24985.
23 FO 371/22428 Budapest 444 9.10.40.
24 FO 371/22428 M.A. Budapest to War Office 1114 cipher 15.10.40.
25 Later Lord Strang; Permanent Under-Secretary FO, 1949–53.
26 FO 371/22928 FO 363 to Budapest 23.10.40.
27 FO 371/22428 Budapest 465 19.10.40.
28 FO 371/24429 Budapest 311 29.7.40.
29 FO 371/22428 Budapest 323 7.8.40.
30 *Nazi-Soviet Relations*, pp. 180, 187, 252.
31 FO 371/24931 Moscow 1027 23.11.40.
32 FO 371/24431 Budapest 531 21.11.40, FO 433 to Budapest 2.12.40.
33 FO 371/22428 Budapest 565 8.12.40.
34 FO 371/24426 FO 235 to Budapest 7.12.40.
35 FO 371/22428 Budapest 594 22.12.40.
36 FO 371/24430 Budapest 547 23.12.40.
37 FO 371/24430 M.A. Budapest to W.O. 04400 cipher 7.12.40.
38 FO 371/22428 Budapest 565 8.12.40.
39 FO 371/25034 Belgrade 1001 26.11.40, 1024 30.11.40.
40 FO 371/309660 O'Malley letter to Zimmern 26.1.43.
41 FO 371/26602 Budapest 51 23.1.41.
42 FO 371/26602 Budapest 53 26.1.41.
43 FO 371 26602 FO 79 to Budapest 11.2.41.
44 *Ibid.*
45 FO 371/26602 M.A. Budapest to War Office 08924 cipher 24.3.41.
46 FO 371/26602 Budapest 208 3.4.41.
47 *Ibid.*
48 Szinai and Szucs, *Confidential Papers of Admiral Horthy*, p. 175.
49 FO 371/26602 Budapest 221 6.4.41.
50 FO 371/26630 D.O. to Dominions P.M.s 188 7.4.40.
51 Later Sir Frank Roberts, G.C.M.G., G.C.V.O., Ambassador at Bonn, 1965–8.
52 FO 371/26602 Roberts minute 7.7.41.
53 FO 371/29779 Belgrade 381 10.3.41.
54 See e.g. Dalton Papers, Dalton minute to Leeper, 26.4.41.

CHAPTER 8

1 FO 371/24991 Hoare despatches to Halifax 26.1.40, 8.2.40.
2 FO 371/24888 Hoare letter to Nichols 16.5.40.
3 FO 371/29975 Hoare despatch to Eden 21.2.41 R4962/2/37.
4 FO 371/24958 Bucharest 623 1.7.40, M.A. Bucharest 282/R/40 8.8.40.
5 Philip Broad, C.M.G., later Political Adviser at A.F.H.Q. Italy.
6 FO 371/24968 Broad minute 27.6.40.
7 Later Lord Butler, K.G., C.H.

8 FO 371/24968 Butler minute 28.6.40.

9 See p. 26 above.

10 FO 371/24968 Bucharest 662 7.7.40.

11 Professor Hugh Seton-Watson of the School of Slavonic and East European Studies.

12 Later Lord Hankey, K.C.M.G., K.C.V.O., U.K. delegate to O.E.E.C., O.E.C.D., 1960–5.

13 FO 371/24992 Hankey despatch to Halifax R7352/475/37 22.7.40 (enclosing Seton-Watson report), 371/24993 Bucharest 791 26.7.40.

14 FO 371/24992 Hankey despatch to Halifax 22.7.40, Bucharest 860 7.8.40.

15 FO 371/24984 FO 712 to Bucharest 6.8.40.

16 FO 371/24992 Seton-Watson minute 5.8.40, Bucharest 88 9.8.40.

17 FO 371/24992 Seton-Watson memorandum 11.8.40.

18 FO 371/24992 report by British Consul Cluj 3.8.40.

19 FO 371/24985 Budapest 380 31.8.40, Bucharest 1031 30.8.40.

20 E.g. FO 371/24968 Rose and Nichols minutes 3.9.40, Bucharest 1002 27.8.40.

21 *Nazi-Soviet Relations*, p. 178–81.

22 FO 371/24968 Bucharest 1045 3.9.40.

23 *Ibid.*, Bucharest 1052 3.9.40.

24 FO 371/29975 Hoare despatch to Eden 21.2.41 R4962/2/37.

25 FO 371/24992 M.A. Bucharest to W.O. 00232 cipher 6.9.40.

26 FO 371/24992 Bucharest 1112 9.9.40.

27 FO 371/24992 Bucharest 1124 11.9.40.

28 FO 371/24992 Dixon minute 16.9.40.

29 FO 371/24989 Dixon minute 3.10.40.

30 FO 371/24990 Record of meeting 24.10.40 R8044/G.

31 FO 371/29990 Dixon minute 11.2.41.

32 FO 371/29977 Hoare despatch to Eden R1052/937/G 13.2.41.

33 FO 371/29976 Record of meeting at FO 20.2.41 R1493/G.

34 FO 371/29991 Broad letter to Hopkinson 20.4.41. From then on, V. C. Georgescu, in Bucharest, was largely responsible for keeping W/T contact with S.O.E. Cairo.

35 Sweet-Escott, p. 51; A.M.A. Istanbul to C.-in-C. M.E. 1/347 cypher 10.5.40.

CHAPTER 9

1 FO 371/24889 Extract from War Cabinet Conclusions 105 (40) S 27.4.40.

2 FO 371/25031 Halifax minute 17.5.40.

3 FO 371/24890 Joint Planning Committee Preliminary Draft J.P. (40)216 2.6.40, pencilled unsigned Sargent minute.

4 FO 371/25033 Belgrade 342 DIPP 12.6.40.

5 FO 371/25031 Campbell letter to Halifax 6.7.40.

6 FO 371/25031 Campbell despatch to Halifax 27.4.40.

7 FO 371/25037 Moscow 210 11.5.40.

8 FO 371/24800 Rapp, Zagreb, letter to Belgrade Legation 4.6.40.

9 FO 371/25033 Belgrade 457 15.7.40.

10 FO 371/25033 Belgrade 572 16.8.40.

11 FO 371/25033 Belgrade 542 10.8.40.

12 FO 371/25033 FO 310 to Belgrade 1.7.40.

13 FO 371/25033 FO 315 to Belgrade 3.7.40.

14 FO 371/25033 Belgrade 542 10.8.40.

15 FO 371/25033 M.A. Belgrade to W.O. 00178 cipher 28.10.40.

16 FO 371/25033 Dixon minute 31.10.40.

17 FO 371/25034 Letter from King George VI to Prince Paul 15.11.40.

18 FO 371/25034 Nichols minute 8.11.40, Dixon minute 19.11.40.

19 FO 371/25034 M.A. Belgrade to W.O. 00257 cipher 28.11.40.

20 FO 371/25031 Belgrade 979 23.11.40.

21 FO 371/25031 P.M.'s Personal Minute no. 340 24.11.40.

22 FO 371/25031 COS (40) 978, W.P. (40) 461 24.11.40.

23 FO 371/25031 FO 754 to Belgrade 24.11.40.

24 FO 371/25034 Belgrade 1003 DEDIP 26.11.40.

25 FO 371/25034 Belgrade 995 26.11.40.

26 FO 371/25034 FO 764 to Belgrade 27.11.40.

27 FO 371/25034 Belgrade 1076 8.12.40, Nichols minute 12.12.40.

28 FO 371/25034 Belgrade 1078 9.12.40.

29 FO 371/25034 Dixon minute 13.12.40.

30 See also Hoptner, *Yugoslavia in Crisis 1934–1941*, pp. 197–8.

31 FO 371/25034 Belgrade 1065 7.12.40.

32 Maček, *In the Struggle for Freedom*, p. 207.

33 Later Sir Thomas Rapp, K.B.E., Head of British Middle East Office Cairo 1950–3.

34 E.g. FO 371/25032 Campbell letter to Halifax 10.2.40.

35 FO 371/30259 Military Attaché's report on Yugoslav army 30.12.40.

36 FO 371/25034 M.A. Belgrade to W.O. 0020 cipher 12/11 13.11.40, 00223 13/11 14.11.40.

37 FO 371/25034 Belgrade 1010 28.11.40.

38 FO 371/25034 Dixon minute 30.11.40.

39 FO 371/25034 N.A. to D.N.I. 1845/21 Nov 22.11.40.

40 FO 371/25034 Dixon minute 23.11.40.

41 FO 371/24886 Sargent letter to Campbell 26.3.40.

42 Julian Amery, *Approach March*, pp. 146–57; Dalton Papers, A.D. and D/HY Report 24.6.41.

43 FO 371/25033 Belgrade 482 25.7.40.

44 Amery, pp. 174–6.

45 *Ibid.*, p. 175.

46 FO 371/25033 Nichols minute 27.7.40.

47 Amery, p. 178.

48 FO 371/25033 Nichols minute 27.7.40.

49 FO 371/25033 FO 383 to Belgrade 3.8.40.

50 FO 371/25033 Belgrade 761 15.10.40.

51 FO 371/25033 FO 534 to Belgrade 24.10.40.

52 G.T. to E.B.

53 Dalton Diaries 8.1.41.

54 FO 371/30089 Belgrade 61 of 12.1.41, 64 and 67 of 13.1.41.

55 FO 371/30089 P.M. Personal Minute Serial no. M.55/1 14.1.41.

56 FO 371/29777 Eden despatch to Palairet 21.1.41 R513/113/67.

57 See e.g. FO 371/39777 Dixon letter to J. G. Stavridi 7.2.41.

58 FO 371/33145 Memo by Field-Marshal Sir John Dill 21.4.41.

59 FO 371/29802 Sargent minute 24.2.41, CAB 66 W.P. (41) 45 1.3.41.

60 CAB 65 (18) 22 (41) 3.3.41.

61 FO 371/29802 Text of message from H.M. to Prince Regent (no date), CAB 66 W.P. (41) 45 1.3.41.

62 FO 371/29782 Anglo-Greek Conversations Record no. 4 22.2.41.

63 FO 371/33145 Report on Mission of the S. of S. to the Eastern Mediterrean, Feb–Apr 1941 by P. Dixon 21.4.41.

64 *Ibid.*

65 FO 371/29779 Belgrade 355 7.3.41.

66 FO 371/29779 Campbell letters to Prince Regent of 2.3.41, 8.3.41; Campbell letters to Cvetković of 18.3.41, 20.3.41; Belgrade, 384 10.3.41; Nichols minute 11.3.41.

67 Wilson, *Eight Years Overseas*, p. 75.

68 FO 371/29782 Anglo-Greek Conversations. Record of meeting at H.M. Legation Athens 8.3.41.

69 FO 371/30285 Cunningham letter to Eden 8.3.41.

70 FO 371/29780 Belgrade 144 to Cairo 16.3.41.

71 FO 371/29781 Belgrade 442 17.3.41.

72 See FO 371/29780 Athens 274 13.3.41.

73 FO 371/29779 Campbell letters to Cvetković 18.3.41, 20.3.41.

74 FO 371/29781 Belgrade 441 16.3.41.

75 FO 371/29779 Belgrade 380 10.3.41.

76 FO 371/29780 Belgrade 429 15.3.41.

77 FO 371/29780 Cairo 588 16.3.41.

78 FO 371/29781 Belgrade 444 17.3.41.

79 Later Sir Terence Shone, K.C.M.G., Deputy Permanent Representative, U.N., 1948.

80 FO 371/33145 Report on Mission of the S. of S. to the Eastern Mediterranean by Dixon 21.4.41.

81 Dalton Papers Report from A/D and D/HY 24.6.41.

82 *Ibid.*

83 *Ibid.*; FO 371/29779 Belgrade 352 7.3.41.

84 *Ibid.*; *Ibid.*, Belgrade 381 10.3.41.

85 FO 371/29680 Belgrade 433 16.3.41.

86 Dalton Papers Report from A/D and D/HY 24.6.41.

87 FO 371/30253 Belgrade to Cairo 22.3.41, P.M. to Cairo (Eden) 835 22.3.41.

88 Gladwyn Jebb, later Lord Gladwyn; at that time detached from the Foreign Office to serve as Chief Executive Officer under Dalton.

89 Dalton Diaries 21.3.41.

90 FO 371/30253 Belgrade to Cairo 24.3.41.

91 Dalton Papers Report from A/D and D/HY 24.6.41.

92 FO 371/30253 Belgrade to Cairo for Eden 27.3.41.

93 FO 371/33490 Campbell (Washington) letter of June 1942.

94 Milovan Djilas, *Memoir of a Revolutionary*, pp. 367 ff.

95 CAB 65 (18) 32 (41) 27.3.41.

96 FO 371/30255 H.M. Consul General Zagreb 14 27.3.41.

97 King Peter of Yugoslavia, *A King's Heritage*, p. 82.

98 FO 371/29782 Athens 502 24.3.41.

99 FO 371/29782 Cairo 728 25.3.41.

100 FO 371/29782 Athens 514 26.3.41, FO 407 and 409 to Belgrade 27.3.41.

101 FO 371/30243 Sargent minute 25.3.41.

102 King Peter, *A King's Heritage*, loc. cit.

103 FO 371/30255 Athens 589 1.4.41.

104 FO 371/30255 Belgrade 298 to S. of S. Athens 4.4.41.

105 FO 371/30255 Athens 673 9.4.41.

106 FO 371/30255 Dixon minute 13.10.41 on conversation with Tsouderos.

107 FO 371/30255 Belgrade 298 4.4.41, Eden minute 11.7.41.

108 FO 371/30255 Extract from letter of 18.8.41 to Duke of Kent from Prince Paul of Yugoslavia R10412/G.

109 FO 371/30255 Dixon minute 11.12.41, Sargent minute 12.12.41.

110 See Dalton Papers, Dalton minute to Leeper 26.4.41; Dalton Diaries 18.4.41.

CHAPTER 10

1 FO 371/24909 Palairet despatch to Halifax 20.2.40 enclosing memorandum by military attaché 19.2.40.

2 FO 371/24909 Sargent minute 15.3.41.

3 FO 371/24892 Record of meeting between FO and S.O.2 9.12.40 R8860/5/67.

4 FO 371/24919 Nichols letter to Hollins 16.10.40.

5 PREM 3 374/13A Dill to P.M. 23.11.40.

6 FO 371/24921 H.Q. R.A.F. to Air Ministry A.483 16.12.40.

7 FO 371/24921 Athens 1357 18.12.40.

8 FO 371/24921 Athens 1419 24.12.40.

9 FO 371/24921 Nichols minute 27.12.40.

10 FO 371/29776 Angora 73 11.1.41.

11 FO 371/29778 Air Attaché Athens to Air Ministry 1103 19/2 19.2.41.

12 FO 371/29789 Palairet memorandum enclosed in letter to Eden 13.2.41.

13 FO 371/29782 Anglo-Greek Conversations Record no. 1 Appendix v(i) 22.2.41.

14 FO 371/29778 FO to H.M.R.R. in various capitals 28.2.40.

15 FO 371/29779 FO 852 to Cairo for S. of S. Athens 8.3.41.

16 FO 371/29779 reports communicated to FO by Greek Counsellor 11.3.41.

17 Documents of German Foreign Policy Series D xi, pp. 1018 ff.

18 FO 371/29777 Angora 200 27.1.40.

19 FO 371/30125 Text (French) of Hitler's letter to Inönü 28.2.41.

20 FO 371/29803 German White Book 6.4.41. For different assessment Hitler's intentions see Martin van Creveld, *Hitler's Strategy 1940–1 The Balkan Clue*, pp. 88-91.

21 FO 371/29770 M.A. Athens to W.O. 10 cipher 5.1.41.

22 FO 371/24892 R. A. Butler minute 5.12.40.

23 FO 371/24919 Athens 916 1.10.40.

24 Cf. CAB 66 W.P. (40) 431 Chiefs of Staff report 8.10.40.

25 FO 371/24926 Athens 966 18.10.40.

26 FO 371/24926 Istanbul 30 14.10.40.

27 FO 371/24926 COS (40) 255 21.10.40.

28 FO 371/24919 FO 777 (R) and 774 (R) 28.10.40.

29 FO 371/24919 FO 782 to Athens 20.10.40.

30 FO 371/24919 British Military Mission Athens no.   2.11.40.

31 CAB 65/13 W.M. (4) 282 4.11.40.

32 FO 371/24921 Hardinge letter to Cadogan 2.12.40 enclosing letter from George II to George VI 17.11.40.

33 FO 371/24892 Amery letter to Halifax 14.12.40, Belgrade 1074 8.12.40.

34 FO 371/29778 Cairo 345 20.2.41; FO 371/29782 Donovan report 20.2.41.

35 Sir Eric Berthoud to E.B.

36 FO 371/29776 Eden minute to P.M. R/113/G 6.1.41.

37 Wilson, *Eight Years Overseas*, p. 69.

38 FO 371/29777 Eden despatch to Palairet R513/113/67 21.1.41.

39 CAB 65/17 W.M. (41) 10.2.41.

40 FO 371/33145 F.M. Sir John Dill memorandum on the Decision to send British Forces to Greece in 1941, 21.4.41.

41 CAB 66/15 W.P. (41) 40 24.2.41 and attached telegram from W.O. to C.-in-C. M.E. 51265 12.2.41.

42 W.O. 193 964 X/K 284. Despatch of a Force to Greece. Points put to the P.M. by D.M.O. & P. 16.2.41.

43 CAB 66 W.P. (41) 38 24.2.41 Personal and Secret telegram from P.M. to Mr Eden 467, Cairo 358 S. of S. to P.M. no 14 21.2.41.

44 CAB 66/15 W.P. (41) 39 (Revised) 24.2.41.

45 FO 371/29782 Anglo-Greek Conversations Record 22.2.41.

46 FO 371/29782 Anglo-Greek Conversations in Athens 27.2.41.

47 FO 371/29782 Anglo-Greek Conversations in Athens 2–4.3.41.

48 *Ibid.*

49 FO 371/29782 Former Naval Person to President Washington 9.3.41.

50 FO 371/29782 Record of meeting at Athens 28.3.41.

51 FO 371/30124 Nichols minute 29.3.41.

52 CAB 65/2 W.M. (39) 115 14.12.39.

53 CAB 65/18 W.M. (41) 33 31.3.41 Tel. to U.K. H.C. in Australia 162 30.3.41.

54 FO 371/30226 Cairo 1231 5.5.41.

55 FO 371/29779 Belgrade 394 11.3.41.

56 FO 371/30225 Air Attaché Belgrade to Air Ministry Y.204 3.4.41.

57 FO 371/29782 Anglo-Yugoslav Discussions 31.3.41–1.4.41.

58 FO 371/29782 Anglo-Greek–Yugoslav Discussion at Florina 3.4.41.

59 Wilson, p. 71.

60 FO 371/30269 Campbell Vrnjačka Banja to FO 11.4.41.

61 FO 371/30269 Churchill to Campbell Vrnjačka Banja 13.4.41.

62 FO 371/30226, Shone, Cairo, letter to Nichols 25.5.41 enclosing account by Stojan Gavrilović of his personal experience 6–16.4.41 R6394/297/92, CAB 65/18 W.M. (41) 44 28.4.41.

63 CAB 66 W.P. (41) 77 26.4.41.

64 CAB 65/18 W.M. 45 (41) 1.5.41.

CHAPTER II

1 CAB 65/19 W.M. (41) 93 15.9.41.
2 CAB 65/19 W.M. (41) 94 18.9.41.
3 FO 371/29655 Moscow 25 and 26 HECTIC 18.12.41.
4 *History of the Second World War*, IV: Michael Howard, *Grand Strategy*, p. 599.
5 FO 371/32876 W. N. Ewer's memorandum 27.2.42, FO minutes thereon.
6 Howard, loc cit., pp. 600–1, C.O.S. (42) 90 (O) Annex 1 14.8.42.
7 Howard, pp. 617–20, Paper by P.M. for Casablanca Conference 17.11.42.
8 Howard, pp. 602–12, C.O.S. (42) 466 (O) FINAL 31.12.42.
9 Howard, pp. 614–16, Memorandum by the Joint Chiefs of Staff C.O.S. 135 26.12.42.
10 Howard, p. 621, Memorandum by Combined Chiefs of Staff, C.O.S. 155/1 19.1.43.
11 Howard, p. 624, C.O.S. 170/2 23.1.43.
12 FO 371/37579 C.O.S. (43) 44 11.2.43.
13 G.T. papers, Keble to Eddie 26.2.43; Auty and Clogg, ed., *British Policy towards Wartime Resistance in Yugoslavia and Greece*, p. 121.
14 See e.g. FO 371/37584 Howard minute 23.4.43.
15 Howard, pp. 643–7, C.O.S. 234 17.5.43.
16 Howard, pp. 660–4, C.O.S. 242–6 25.5.43.
17 Auty and Clogg, ed., p. 26.
18 Churchill, *Second World War*, V: *Closing the Ring*, p. 410.
19 CAB 66/40 W.P. (43) 353 31.7.43.
20 PREM 3 66/2 H. L. Ismay minute 4.10.43.
21 PREM 3 66/4 Hollis minute to P.M. 12.10.43.
22 PREM 3 66/4 Hollis minute to P.M. 16.10.43.
23 *History of the Second World War*, V: J. Ehrman, *Grand Strategy*, p. 554, C.O.S. meeting 19.10.43.
24 Ehrman, pp. 554 ff., P.M.'s paper 'Future Operations in Eur. and Med. Theatre' 20.11.43.
25 FO 371/37031 Proceedings of Foreign Ministers Conference 19–30.10.43 N/6921/5412/G.
26 FO 371/37031 Record of Proceedings of the Foreign Ministers Conference 5th meeting 23.10.43.
27 PREM 3 310/13 President to P.M. T.1699/3 22.10.43.
28 FO 371/29782 Former Naval Person to President, Washington 9.3.41.
29 W.J.M.M. to E.B.
30 PREM 3 310/13 P.M. to President T. 1705/3 no. 470 23.10.43.
31 FO 371/37162 Washington 5802 24.12.43, PREM 3 79/1 Eden minute to P.M. P.M./44/60 10.2.44.
32 Churchill, v 305.
33 PREM 3 79/1 MEDCOS 44 26.2.44.
34 *Ibid.*
35 PREM 3 79/1 C.O.S. (44) (65) (O) 28.2.44.
36 PREM 3 79/3 Sargent minute 7.10.44, Moscow 3026 17.10.44.
37 See e.g. FO 371/37185 Cairo 1957 25.8.43.
38 FO 371/43646 Clutton minute 25.5.44.

39 FO 371/43646 Sargent letter to Knatchbull-Hugessen 2.6.44.

40 FO 371/39253 B.A.F. to A.F.H.Q. 14.8.44.

41 Churchill, loc. cit., pp. 356 ff.

42 Auty and Clogg, ed., p. 125.

43 'Trotsky' Davies, *Illyrian Adventure*, pp. 77–8.

44 See FO 371/43588 Cadogan minute 11.3.44, FO 371/43992 Sargent letter to Hollis 21.2.44.

45 FO 371/43993.

46 FO 371/43551 Earle letter to Sargent 8.6.44.

47 FO 371/43555 C.O.S. (44) 187 (O) 8.6.44.

48 FO 371/43636 P.M.'s Personal Minutes M.487/4 and 498/4 4.5.44.

49 Churchill, vi 53.

50 *Ibid.*, p. 56.

51 *Ibid.*, p. 57.

52 *Ibid.*, pp. 108–9.

53 *Ibid.*, pp. 133–7.

54 Howard, *The Mediterranean Strategy in the Second World War*, pp. 65–6.

55 Churchill, vi, 304.

56 *Grand Strategy*, iv, v; Howard, *The Mediterranean Strategy in the Second World War*, *passim*.

CHAPTER 12

1 FO 371/30125 – text.

2 FO 371/30125 FO memorandum 23.4.41.

3 FO 371/30125 Angora 1226 18.5.41.

4 FO 371/30125 Angora 1242 20.5.41.

5 FO 371/33311 Knatchbull-Hugessen despatch to Eden 5.3.42.

6 FO 371/33311 Knatchbull-Hugessen despatch to Eden 5.3.42.

7 FO 371/33311 Angora 219 28.1.42, Eden minute 2.2.42.

8 CAB 65/19 W.M. (41) 67 9.7.41, Moscow 655 27.6.41.

9 FO 371/29780 FO to H.M.R.R. in various capitals 14.3.41.

10 CAB 66/19 W.P. (41) 248 26.10.41.

11 CAB 66/19 W.P. (41) 272 FO 78 to Kuibyshev 4.11.41.

12 CAB 66/19 W.P. (41) 272 FO 136 to Kuibyshev 12.11.41.

13 CAB 66/19 W.P. (41) 272 FO 139 to Kuibyshev 13.11.41.

14 CAB 66/20 W.P. (41) 287 25.11.41, FO 188 to Kuibyshev 21.11.41.

15 FO 371/32874 W.P. (42) 8 5.1.42 Record of Interview between Foreign Secretary and Stalin 16.12.41.

16 FO 371/32874 W.P. (42) 8 5.1.42 Record of Meeting between Foreign Secretary and Stalin 17.12.41.

17 CAB 66/20 W.P. (41) 288 29.11.41.

18 FO 371/32874 390 TAUT to P.M. 5.1.42.

19 FO 371/32874 HUSH – MOST SECRET GREY 261 8.1.41.

20 FO 371/32876 Dominions Office to Dominions P.M.s 18.3.42.

21 FO 371/32875 FO 932 to Washington 10.2.42, W.P (42) 48 28.1.42.

22 FO 371/32879 Dixon memorandum 30.3.42.

23 *Ibid.*

24 *Ibid.*

25 FO 371/32880 N2182/G meeting held 21.4.42.

26 E.g. FO 371/33133 FO 287 to Cairo 17.1.42.

27 FO 371/33133.

28 FO 371/33133 Rendel letter to Eden 1.1.42.

29 FO 371/33142 Rendel letter to Eden 3.1.42, Rendel despatch to Eden 11.1.42.

30 FO 371/33133 Sargent minute 11.1.42.

31 FO 371/33133 R472/43/67.

32 FO 371/33133 Rendel letter to Howard 28.1.42.

33 FO 371/33133 Dixon minute 20.1.42, Eden despatch to Palairet R979/43/67 10.2.42.

34 FO 371/32879 FO draft telegram to Kuibyshev 16.4.42.

35 FO 371/32880 Cadogan minute 23.4.42, Eden minute 24.4.42.

36 FO 371/32882 Record of Second Meeting with Soviet delegation 21.5.42 N2902/G.

37 FO 371/32881 FO 3339 to Washington 25.5.42.

38 FO 371/32881 Sargent minute 26.5.42.

39 FO 371/32881 Cadogan minute 26.5.42.

40 FO 371/33134 Sargent paper 1.6.42.

41 FO 371/32882 Record of Seventh Meeting with Soviet delegation 9.6.42 N/3000/G.

42 FO 371/36955 Warner minute 9.7.43.

43 FO 371/32918 G. M. Wilson minute 23.9.42.

44 FO 371/33154 Sargent minute 8.1.43.

45 Later Sir Douglas Howard, K.C.M.G., M.C., Minister at Holy See, 1954–7.

46 Later Sir Christopher Warner, K.C.M.G., Ambassador at Brussels, 1951–5.

47 FO 371/33154 Howard minute 1.1.43, Warner minute 2.1.43, Sargent minute 11.1.43.

48 Later Lord Inverchapel, G.C.M.G., Ambassador at Washington, 1946–8.

49 FO 371/37179 FO 426 to Angora 23.3.43.

50 FO 371/37179 Brief for Eden 8.3.43.

51 FO 371/37179 Clutton minute 19.3.43.

52 FO 371/37179 Knatchbull-Hugessen letter to Sargent 7.6.43.

53 FO 371/37179 Angora 67 Saving 20.6.43.

54 FO 371/34449 Molotov letter 7.6.43.

55 CAB 66/38 W.P. (43) 292 1.7.43.

56 FO 371/36956 Eden despatch to Clark Kerr 31.8.43 N4977/66/G.

57 *Ibid.*

58 FO 371/36955 FO 1019 to Moscow 2.8.43.

59 Later Lord Harvey, G.C.M.G., G.C.V.O., C.B., Ambassador to France, 1948–54.

60 FO 371/36956 Harvey minute 15.9.43, Eden minute 15.9.43.

61 Dalton Papers, Notes of a Conversation with Maisky 14.9.43.

62 FO 371/36957 Min. of State Cairo 2239 30.9.43.

63 FO 371/37162 Moscow 56 SPACE 22.10.43, PREM 73/79/1 Moscow 108 SPACE 29.10.43.

64 FO 371/37614 Moscow to FO 31.10.43.
65 FO 371/37031 Record of proceedings of Foreign Ministers' Conference 19.10.43, 30.10.43 N6921/5412/G.
66 FO 371/37031 Warner minute 20.10.43.
67 FO 371/37162 FO 1753 to Angora 21.12.43.
68 FO 371/37476 Anglo-Turkish Conversations in Cairo Nov 1943 R12407/55/G.
69 PREM 3 66/4 C.O.S. (43) 626 (O) 14.10.43.
70 FO 371/43999 FO 1309 to Moscow 30.4.44.
71 FO 371/43999 FO 1310 to Moscow 30.4.44.
72 FO/43999 FO 1311 to Moscow 30.4.44, FO 1464 to Moscow 15.5.44, Minutes of 29th meeting of FO–S.O.E. committee 9.5.44.
73 FO 371/44000 Churchill minute serial no. M.5134 7.5.44.
74 A number of Soviet missions were dropped by S.O.E. to France, Belgium, Holland, Austria and Germany between 1942 and 1944. The Foreign Office did not know about the first parties but reached agreement with S.O.E. (intended to safeguard the exiled governments) in December 1942. There were many complaints from the Russians over delays in sending in Soviet parties – though such delays were common with British missions, too. W.J.M.M. to E.B., G.T. to E.B.
75 FO 371/44000 Selborne letter to Eden 19.5.44.
76 FO 371/44000 note by Eden on Rose minute 25.5.44.
77 FO 371/43636 P.M.'s Personal Minute M.498/4 4.5.44.
78 FO 371/44000 Eden despatch to Clark Kerr R7214/9/G 5.5.44.
79 FO 371/43636 FO 1560 to Moscow 25.5.44.
80 FO 371/43636 W.P. (44) 304 7.6.44.
81 FO 371/43636 Extract from War Cabinet Conclusions 13.6.44.
82 FO 371/43636 Stalin to P.M. serial no. T 1453/4.
83 FO 371/43636 Washington 4028 25.7.44.
84 Djilas, *Conversations with Stalin*, pp. 70–1.
85 FO 371/43772 Cadogan minute 1.8.44, Eden minute 3.8.44.
86 FO 371/43772 C.O.S. (44) 257 (O) 3.8.44, Ismay minute to P.M. 3.8.44.
87 FO 371/43772 FO 2529 to Moscow 15.8.44.
88 FO 371/43551 AMSSO to A.H.F.Q. Italy GUARD CLASP 58 15.8.44.
89 FO 371/43772 Moscow 2206 21.8.44.
90 Woodhouse, *Apple of Discord*, p. 199.
91 FO 371/43772 Bari 478 23.8.44.
92 PREM 3 79/1 OCTAGON to AMSSO GUNFIRE 247 17.9.44.
93 PREM 3 79/1 AMSSO to OCTAGON CORDITE 365 19.9.44.
94 PREM 3 79/2 Eden minute to P.M. P.M./44/645 6.10.44.
95 FO 371/43772 Southern Dept memorandum 5.10.44 R7903/9/G.
96 PREM 3 79/3 Moscow 2769 10.10.44.
97 Churchill, VI 198.
98 *Ibid.*, p. 202.
99 *Ibid.*, p. 203.
100 PREM 3 79/3 Moscow 2774 HEARTY no. 2 11.10.44.
101 PREM 3 79/3 FO 3560 to Moscow 11.10.44.
102 PREM 3 79/3 Moscow 3013 17.10.44.
103 Churchill, VI 432.

104 FO 371/44292 FO 989 to Bari 3.12.44, FO 4555 to Moscow 3.12.44, Belgrade 75 21.12.44.

105 FO 371/44363 C.O.S. (44) 382 28.11.44, FO 371/44292 Dew minute 23.12.44.

106 Churchill, vi 388.

107 Churchill, vi 250.

108 FO 371/43697 FO 10307 to Washington 6.12.44.

109 FO 371/43698 Athens 593 13.12.44.

110 FO 371/43698 Washington 6688 15.12.44.

111 FO 371/43772 Athens 560 11.12.44.

112 FO 371/43772 Athens 292 21.11.44.

113 FO 371/43699 Salonika 34 to FO 23.12.44.

114 FO 371/43699 FO 4735 to Moscow 16.12.44.

115 Churchill, vi 432.

CHAPTER 13

1 For Chiefs of Staffs' views, see C.O.S. (40) 39, W.P. (40) 168 25.5.40, C.O.S. (40) 883 4.9.40.

2 Churchill minute of Mar 1943 quoted in Howard minute of 23.4.43, FO 371/37584.

3 PREM 3 510/7 C.O.S. (43) 336 (O) 23.6.43.

4 FO 371/30221 Jebb letter to Howard 2.12.41.

5 PREM 3 510/7 C.O.S. (43) 336 (O) 23.6.43.

6 G.T. to E.B.

7 FO 371/43992 Cadogan minute 7.2.44.

8 FO 371/44000 Eden minute 29.5.44.

9 Dalton Papers, Dalton letter to Hankey 3.6.40, paper on meeting held in Secretary of State for Foreign Affairs' office 1.7.41.

10 W.J.M.M. to E.B.

11 Dalton Papers, Diary 27.3.41.

12 General Sir Hastings Ismay (later Lord Ismay), then P.M.'s Chief Staff Officer.

13 Dalton Papers, Ismay letter to Dalton 28.3.41.

14 G.T. papers, D.H.Z. letter to A.D. 28.3.41.

15 Dalton Papers, Diary, 8.5.41.

16 Dalton Papers, Diary 9.7.41.

17 Dalton Papers, Diary 11.7.41, A.D. report 24.6.41.

18 Dalton Papers, Selborne letter to Dalton 21.5.42.

19 Dalton Papers, Dalton minute 5.11.41.

20 FO 371/37586 Maclagan report of 21.5.43, which gives evidence of this.

21 Sweet-Escott to E.B.

22 E.g. FO 371/33443, Sargent minute 12.11.42, FO 371/33134 Sargent paper 1.6.42 R3793/43/67.

23 See F. W. Deakin, *The Embattled Mountain*, p. 127.

24 Amery, *Approach March*, p. 179; G.T. to E.B.; Glen to E.B.

25 FO 371/29789 Palairet letter to Secretary of State 13.2.41.

26 FO 371/43699 King George II letter to Churchill 14.12.44, sent by Churchill to Roosevelt T2359/4 no. 852 14.12.44.

27 FO 371/29789 Palairet to Eden 13.2.41.
28 FO 371/33164 Cairo 119 9.1.42.
29 FO 371/33164 Cavendish-Bentinck minute 9.3.42, H. Caccia minute 30.3.42.
30 FO 371/33164 Warner minute 10.3.42.
31 FO 371/33164 Tsouderos letter to Eden 3.3.42.
32 Pirie Report (G.T. papers).
33 *Ibid.*
34 *Ibid.*
35 *Ibid.*
36 *Ibid.*
37 FO 371/33187 Dixon letter to Warner 31.8.42.
38 Pirie Report.
39 Brigadier Edmund Myers, C.B.E., D.S.O.
40 The Hon. C. M. Woodhouse, D.S.O., O.B.E., later Commander of the Allied Military Mission in Greece.
41 G.T. papers, Keble letter to G.H.Q. 5.12.42.
42 FO 371/30226 Palestine 605 to Colonial Office 6.5.41.
43 FO 371/30219 Rose minute 14.8.41.
44 FO 371/30215 Dixon minute 22.8.41.
45 FO 371/30219 Simović letter to Churchill 14.8.41.
46 Deakin, p. 207.
47 Deakin, p. 126.
48 CAB 65 (19) W.M. (41) 91 8.9.41.
49 Deakin, pp. 127–8.
50 E.g. FO 371/33470 Eden to Selborne 26.9.42, Selborne to Eden 24.9.42, Eden to Selborne 2.10.42, FO 371/33471 Rendel minute 29.9.42.
51 FO 371/33469 Rendel letter to Howard 17.9.42.
52 FO 371/33469 Brief for Rendel 21.8.42.
53 Vladimir Dedijer, *With Tito through the War*, p. 40.
54 FO 371/44244 Stevenson letter to Eden 30.12.43.
55 PREM 3 510/4 C.O.S. 2206A to Cs. in C.M.E. 15.10.41.
56 CAB 65 (19) W.M. (41) 107 30.10.41.
57 FO 371/30220 Dixon minute 29.10.41.
58 Dalton Papers, Diary 4.11.41.
59 FO 371/30220 FO minute 28.10.41.
60 PREM 3 510/1 Extract from letter from Minister of Economic Warfare to P.M. 11.12.41.
61 W.J.M.M. to E.B.
62 FO 371/30220 Simović letter to Eden 13.11.41 R9873/162/92.
63 Hoptner, p. 186.
64 FO 371/30220 Simović letter 13.11.41.
65 Deakin, p. 142.
66 FO 371/30220 Cadogan letter to Simović 18.11.41.
67 FO 371/30220 FO 155 to Kuibyshev 16.11.41.
68 FO 371/30221 Simović letter to Eden 26.11.41 R10199/G.
69 FO 371/30221 FO 233 to Kuibyshev 29.11.41.
70 CAB 65 (19) W.M. (41) 120 27.11.41.
71 CAB 65 (19) W.M. (41) 122 1.12.41.

72 PREM 3 510/1 C.O.S. (42) 139 26.2.42; FO 371/33465 Rose minute 8.2.42.

73 CAB 65 (25) W.M. (42) 4 12.1.42; Rendel, *The Sword and the Olive*, p. 213.

74 FO 371/30215 P.W.E. directive 14.11.41.

75 FO 371/30215 P.W.E. directive 19.12.41.

76 FO 371/33135A FO 1041 to Cairo 4.4.42, FO 1306 to Cairo 8.5.42, FO 1402 to Cairo 22.5.42.

77 FO 371/33456 Krek to Lockhart 24.2.42.

78 Later Sir Douglas Howard K.C.M.G., M.C., Minister at Holy See, 1954–7.

79 FO 371/33134 Howard letter to Toynbee 13.4.42.

80 FO 371/33473 Boughey letter to Dew 27.11.42, enclosing telegram from Hudson of 15.11.42.

81 FO 371/33470 Rendel letter to Jovanović 10.10.42.

82 FO 371/33472 Boughey to Southern Department.

83 W.J.M.M. to E.B.

84 FO 371/37578 Eden minute 3.1.43.

85 W.J.M.M. to E.B.

86 FO 371/37580 Moscow 97 22.2.43, FO 125 to Moscow 24.2.43.

87 FO 371/37582 Sargent letter to Hambro 24.3.43.

88 FO 371/37583 Clark Kerr letter to Sargent 3.4.43.

89 FO 371/37584 Howard minute 23.4.43.

90 *Ibid.*, Eden minute 30.4.43.

91 W.J.M.M. to E.B.

92 CAB 65 (40) W.M. (43) 172 20.12.43.

93 G.T. papers, Keble to Eddie 26.2.43.

94 'Trotsky' Davies, *Illyrian Adventure*, p. 42.

95 Later Lord Casey; Minister of State M.E. and member of War Cabinet, 1942–3.

96 PREM 3 66/2 Mideast to Air Ministry N.O.S./90 3.10.43.

97 *Ibid.*, Churchill minute 4.10.43.

98 *Ibid.*, Ismay minute to P.M. 4.10.43, Churchill initials 6.10.43.

99 *Ibid.*, Eden minute to P.M. P.M./43/297 9.10.43, Churchill minute 17.10.43.

100 *Ibid.*, Cairo 1917 13.10.43.

101 PREM 3 66/4 Report by Joint Intelligence Sub-Committee 14.7.43.

102 *Ibid.*, C.O.S. (43) 626 (O) 14.10.43.

103 *Ibid.*

104 Svetozar Vukmanović-Tempo, *Revolucija koja Teče*, pp. 347–52.

105 Vladimir Dedijer, *Jugoslovensko-Albanski Odnosi 1939–1948*, pp. 127–8.

106 Davies, p. 79. See also *Histoire du Parti Travail d'Albanie*, p. 193.

107 FO 371/43646 W.P. (44) 304 7.6.44.

108 For useful summary see FO 371/43699 FO 10577 to Washington 15.12.44.

109 FO 371/43697 P.M.'s Personal Minute Serial no. M.1161/4 28.11.44.

110 Report by SACMED to C.C.S., *Greece 1944–45* (H.M.S.O., 1949).

111 See exchanges between Churchill and Eden, Dec 1943–Feb 1944, FO 371/44243–7.

112 CAB 66 (48) W.P. (44) 17.4.44. Maclean letter to P.M. 18.3.44.

113 FO 371/43587 Last letter to Rose 14.3.44.
114 Djilas, *Conversations with Stalin*, pp. 70–2.
115 FO 371/44292 MEDCOS 208 7.11.44.
116 FO 371/44291 Howard to Earle 9.11.44.
117 See King Peter II, *A King's Heritage*, p. 252.

CHAPTER 14

1 Denis Laskey, C.M.G., Ambassador to Austria 1972–.
2 FO 371/43564 Laskey minute 16.11.44.
3 FO 371/43566 Dew minute 3.8.44.
4 FO 371/43551 Aghnides letter to Eden 21.8.44.
5 FO 371/29715 Dixon minute 8.7.41.
6 FO 371/33107 Eden despatch to Cripps R332/332/G 13.1.42.
7 FO 371/33113 Dixon minute 30.3.42 R2125/2125/90.
8 FO 371/33112 Dixon letter to Glenconner 10.6.42.
9 *Ibid.*, Glenconner letter to Dixon 4.6.42.
10 FO 371/33110 Sargent minute 11.7.42, Eden minute 12.7.42.
11 Dedijer, *Jugoslovensko-Albanski Odnosi 1939–1948*, pp. 15–20.
12 *Ibid.*, p. 58. See also *Histoire du Parti du Travail d'Albanie*, pp. 91 ff.,
p. 235.
13 FO 371/33116 Istanbul to M. of I. 519 EMPAX 3.8.42.
14 FO 371/33116 Message from Yugoslav P.M. to Gen. Mihajlović
R5899/G 3.9.42.
15 Dedijer, pp. 87–9. *Histoire du Parti du Travail*, pp. 129 ff.
16 FO 371/33107 Sargent minute 18.11.42.
17 FO 371/33107 Extract from War Cabinet Conclusions 164 (42) 3.12.42.
18 FO 371/33108 Aghnides to Eden 14.12.42.
19 FO 371/33108 Min. of State Cairo 2218 18.12.42.
20 FO 371/33108 Dixon minute 12.12.42, Sargent minute 14.12.12.
21 FO 371/33108 Kuibyshev 1586 19.12.42.
22 FO 371/33107 D.O. to Dominion governments D. no. 543 14.12.44.
23 G.T. papers, Keble to Eddie 26.2.43.
24 Lt-Col. Neil McLean, D.S.O., M.P. for Inverness 1954–64.
25 FO 371/37144 Boughey letter to Laskey 30.5.43.
26 FO 371/37144 Pearson letter to Nichols 14.10.43.
27 FO 371/37144 Boughey to Laskey 30.5.44, Pearson to Dixon 16.7.44.
28 FO 371/37138 Harrison minute 6.7.43, Harrison to A. G. Brotman 15.7.43.
29 Dedijer, pp. 91–3; Vukmanović-Tempo, pp. 366–7. *Histoire du Parti du Travail*, pp. 173–9, 236.
30 FO 371/37144 Pearson to Dixon 18.8.43.
31 FO 371/37144 Pearson to Howard 2.10.43, weekly progress report no.
60 by S.O.E., Pearson to Nichols 14.10.43.
32 FO 371/37144 Extract from Provisional minutes of FO–S.O.E. Committee 19.10.43 R10626/G.
33 PREM 3 66/2 C.O.S. (43) 626 (O) 14.10.43.
34 'Trotsky' Davies, *Illyrian Adventure*, p. 54.
35 Davies, p. 81.
36 Davies, pp. 79–80.

37 Davies, pp. 84, 171
38 Davies, pp. 90–1.
39 FO 371/37145 Boxshall to Howard 20.11.43.
40 FO 371/37145 S.O.E. Sitrep 19.11.43.
41 FO 371/37145 Min. of State Cairo 282 13.12.43.
42 FO 371/37145 Boxshall letter to Dew 27.12.43.
43 Davies, p. 147.
44 FO 371/43550 Force 133 weekly review 17.2.44, FO 371/43563 Talbot Rice to Howard 8.2.44, FO 371/43566 Bari 416 to Caserta 7.11.44.
45 FO 371/43555 C.O.S. (44) 49 (O) 3.6.44.
46 FO 371/43563 Talbot Rice to Howard 8.2.44.
47 FO 371/43550 Talbot Rice to Howard 24.4.44.
48 FO 371/43550 Boxshall to Howard 14.3.44.
49 FO 371/43563 Bari 133 to Algiers 10.6.44.
50 FO 371/43551 Talbot Rice to Dew 9.6.44 and enclosures.
51 FO 371/43563 Broad to Macmillan 28.6.44.
52 FO 371/43563 MEDCOS 130 16.6.44.
53 FO 371/43563 C.O.S. (44) 20 (O) 22.6.44.
54 FO 371/43550 Rose minute 15.4.44.
55 FO 371/43563 Dew minute 28.6.44.
56 FO 371/43563 Laskey minute 27.6.44.
57 FO 371/43563 Broad to Macmillan 17.7.44.
58 FO 371/43551 Bari 200 to Algiers 28.6.44, FO 371/43566 Oakley Hill to Laskey 24.7.44.
59 FO 371/43551 Bari 257 to Algiers 7.7.44.
60 Dedijer, p. 132.
61 FO 371/43551 Bari 300 to Algiers 18.7.44.
62 FO 371/43551 P.M.'s Personal Minute M.882/4 19.7.44.
63 *Ibid.*, Eden minute P.M./44/551 23.7.44.
64 FO 371/43551 Bari 7 to Caserta 13.7.44.
65 Amery, *Approach March*, p. 403.
66 FO 371/43563 Minutes of 21st meeting of Political Committee Caserta 9.8.44.
67 FO 371/43551 Bari 48 2.8.44.
68 FO 371/43551 Bari 80 to Casserta 12.8.44, A.M.S.S.O. to A.F.H.Q. Italy GUARD CLASP 58 15.8.44, Dixon (Rome) letter to Dew 28.8.44. See p. 142 above.
69 FO 371/43552 Bari 138, 139 to Caserta 26.8.44.
70 FO 371/43552 Bari 177 to Caserta 2.9.44.
71 FO 371/43563 S.O.E. Bari telegram 8.9.44.
72 FO 371/43564 Broad despatch to Macmillan 13.10.44.
73 FO 371/43566 Bari 216 to Caserta 14.9.44.
74 FO 371/43566 Bari 215 to Caserta 14.9.44.
75 Amery, *Approach March*, pp. 378–83.
76 FO 371/43566 Bari 304 to Caserta 10.10.44.
77 FO 371/43566 Rome 758 31.10.44.
78 FO 371/43566 Bari 416 to Caserta 7.11.44.
79 FO 371/43564 Bari 359 to Caserta 24.10.44.
80 FO 371/43556 Palmer letter to Eden 3.12.44.

81 *Ibid.*, Eden letter to Palmer 25.12.44.
82 FO 371/43564 Caserta 184 to Bari 19.12.44.
83 W.J.M.M. to E.B.

CHAPTER 15

1 FO 371/24872 Rendel letter to FO 10.7.40.
2 FO 371/24880 Sofia to FO 13.12.40.
3 FO 371/24880 Rendel letter to Halifax 5.1.40, F. D. W. Brown minute 17.1.40.
4 FO 371/24877 B.C.P. Manifesto on the Macedonian Question.
5 FO 371/29785 Sofia Chancery letter to Belgrade Chancery 9.12.40.
6 FO 371/29785 Campbell despatch to Halifax R145/145/67 6.1.41.
7 *Ibid.*
8 Vukmanović-Tempo, p. 138.
9 Vukmanović-Tempo, pp. 308–9 418.
10 Elisabeth Barker, *Macedonia, Its Place in Balkan Power Politics*, p. 88.
11 FO 371/32879 Dixon memorandum 30.3.42.
12 FO 371/33134 Sargent paper 1.6.42 R3793/43/67.
13 Vukmanović-Tempo, p. 294.
14 *Ibid.*, p. 436.
15 *Ibid.*
16 *Ibid.*, pp. 315–320.
17 *Ibid.*, pp. 363–7.
18 *Ibid.*, pp. 356–61.
19 *Ibid.*, p. 317.
20 FO 371/43579 Last to Rose 29.2.44, enclosing Report by B.L.O. on Yugoslav–Bulgarian border.
21 Vukmanović-Tempo, pp. 358–9.
22 *Ibid.*, p. 347.
23 *Ibid.*, pp. 353–5.
24 *Ibid.*, p. 360.
25 Palmer and King, *Jugoslav Communism and the Macedonian Question*, p. 96. But see also *Histoire du Parti du Travail d'Albanie*, p. 236.
26 *Ibid.*, p. 99.
27 Dino Kiosev, *Borbite na Makedonskija Narod za Osvobozhdenie* (Sofia, 1950), p. 149.
28 Vukmanović-Tempo, pp. 359–61; Palmer and King, p. 99.
29 Vukmanović-Tempo, pp. 349–52.
30 *Ibid.*, p. 352.
31 *Ibid.*, pp. 374–5.
32 Woodhouse to E.B. 23.8.74.
33 'Trotsky' Davies, pp. 229–30.
34 FO 371/43556 Pink minute 21.12.44.
35 W.J.M.M. to E.B.
36 Maclean to E.B. 28.8.74.
37 Sir John Henniker-Major, K.C.M.G., Director of British Council, 1968–72.
38 Henniker-Major to E.B. (Aug 1974).

39 For this reason they are treated here rather than in Chapter 17 below, q.v.

40 FO 371/37613 Yugoslav Sitrep week ending 13.10.43.

41 *Ibid.*

42 FO 371/37613 Last letter to Rose 22.10.43.

43 FO 371/37618 Yugoslav Sitrep week ending 3.12.43.

44 FO 371/37616 Yugoslav Sitrep week ending 19.11.43.

45 FO 371/37618 Appreciation regarding the Military Situation in Serbia so as to determine what in the Future should be our Military Policy 19.11.43.

46 FO 371/37619 Last to Rose 20.12.43, enclosing Yugoslav Sitrep for Week ending 17.12.43.

47 FO 371/43579 Last to Rose 29.2.44.

48 Vukmanović-Tempo, pp. 397–9.

49 FO 371/43579 Steel to Howard 24.2.44, enclosing two papers on Bulgarian resistance.

50 Vukmanović-Tempo, p. 399.

51 Sweet-Escott, p. 305, W.J.M.M. to E.B.

52 Sweet-Escott, p. 211, W.J.M.M. to E.B.

53 W.J.M.M. to E.B.

54 Vukmanović-Tempo, pp. 353–5.

55 *Ibid.*, pp. 359–61.

56 *Ibid.*, pp. 378–80.

57 *Ibid.*, pp. 388–9.

58 For detailed documentation of Slav Macedonian complaints against E.A.M./E.L.A.S. see *Egejska Makedonija vo N.O.B. 1944–1945* (Skopje, 1971).

59 Vukmanović-Tempo, pp. 426–8.

60 Hristo Andonovski, *Vistinata na Egejska Makedonija*, pp. 122–3.

61 *Ibid.*, p. 122.

62 B. Cvetkoski, A. Apostolov, F. Gligorov, *Istoria za IV Klas Gimnazija*, pp. 227–8.

63 FO 371/43639 Captain P. H. Evans report 1.12.44, sent by Athens Embassy to FO 12.12.44.

64 FO 371/43579 Last to Rose 29.2.44, enclosing report by B.L.O. on Yugoslav–Bulgarian frontier.

65 FO 381/43579 Steel to Howard 24.2.44.

66 PREM 3 66/8 Churchill Minute Serial no. M. 495/5 to FO 4.5.44.

67 *Ibid.*, Churchill Minute Serial no. 502/4 5.5.44.

68 *Ibid.*, Eden Minute PM/44/336 12.5.44.

69 PREM 3 79/2 Eden minute to P.M. PM/44/585 10.8.44.

70 *Ibid.*, [?] J.M.M. letter to Lawford 18.8.44.

71 FO 371/43649 Houstoun-Boswall despatch to Eden 10.11.44.

72 *Ibid.*, Bari 1042 16.11.44.

73 Vangia Cašule, *From Recognition to Repudiation* (Skopje, 1972), pp. 39–40.

74 Vukmanović-Tempo, pp. 420 ff.

75 FO 371/43649 Eden note on Bari 473 to Caserta 23.11.44.

76 FO 371/43649, Maclean Belgrade 21 10.12.44.

77 FO 371/44395 Bari 1059 19.11.44.

78 FO 371/44395 Bari 442 to Caserta 13.11.44.
79 *Ibid.*, Dominions Office to Dominion P.M.s 27.11.44.
80 FO 371/44395 FO 882 to Bari 17.11.44.
81 *Ibid.*, FO 4316 to Moscow 17.11.44.
82 *Ibid.*, Bari 1059 19.11.44.
83 FO 371/43649 FO 137 to Sofia 21.11.44.
84 FO 371/43649 Sofia 141 22.11.44.
85 PREM 3 66/8 W.P. (44) 707 5.12.44.
86 PREM 3 66/8 Extract from W.M. (44) 164 11.12.44.
87 FO 371/43649 Athens 427 2.12.44.
88 *Ibid.*, Bari to Caserta 13.12.44.
89 *Ibid.*, Maclean Belgrade 54 16.12.44.
90 *Ibid.*, Belgrade 21 10.12.44.
91 *Ibid.*, FO 4886 to Moscow, 10823 to Washington 27.12.44.
92 PREM 3 66/8 A.M.S.S.O. to ARGONAUT FLEECE 89 2.2.45.
93 *Ibid.*, A.M.S.S.O. to ARGONAUT FLEECE 212 6.2.45.
94 *Ibid.*, Extract from Protocol of Crimea Conference 11.2.45.
95 Barker, *Macedonia*, pp. 100–1, quoting Pijade article in *Borba* 6.3.49
and Ranković speech 19.1.49.

CHAPTER 16

1 Dedijer, *Tito Speaks*, p. 235.
2 See e.g. FO 371/30965 P.W.E. Directive 3, 9.5.42.
3 FO 371/34507 P.R.B. Stockholm, Hungary no. 67 6.8.43.
4 FO 371/34507 Stockholm 1027 12.12.43.
5 FO 371/34505 FO 66 Saving to Lisbon 13.2.43.
6 FO 371/34504 Cadogan minute 11.2.43.
7 *Ibid.*, 12.2.43.
8 FO 371/34447 Roberts minute 26.2.43.
9 *Ibid.*, Howard minute 24.2.43.
10 *Ibid.*, Eden despatch to Washington and Moscow 10.3.44 C2652/155/G.
11 FO 371/34449 Molotov letter to Mr A. C. Kerr 7.6.43.
12 FO 371/34495 Roberts minute 16.6.43.
13 FO 371/34450 P.M.'s minute to F.S. 14.8.43.
14 FO 371/34449 FO 1274 to Moscow 6.9.43.
15 FO 371/34451 WELFARE 639 7.9.43.
16 FO 371/34452 Moscow conference record, item 13 C13324/155/G.
17 FO 371/34453 Eden minute 2.1.44.
18 FO 371/43992 Calthorpe letter to Howard (Feb 1944).
19 FO 371/44004 Washington 197 Saving 24.7.44.
20 FO 371/39252 A. W. Noble minute 16.2.44.
21 *Ibid.*, Cavendish-Bentinck minute 31.1.44.
22 FO 371/39252 Allen minute 18.2.44, Cadogan minute 21.2.44.
23 FO 371/43588 Rose minute 8.3.44.
24 Later Sir Christopher Steel, G.C.M.G., M.V.O., H.M. ambassador at
Bonn, 1957–63.
25 FO 371/43588 Cairo 417 4.3.44.
26 PREM 3 79/1 Eden minute to P.M. 3.3.44.

27 PREM 3 27/1 MEDCOS 61 4.3.44.
28 Victor Cavendish-Bentinck, C.M.G., Ambassador to Poland 1945–7.
29 FO 371/43588 Cavendish-Bentinck minute 10.3.44.
30 *Ibid.*, Cadogan minute 11.3.44.
31 *Ibid.*, Sargent minute 22.3.44, Cadogan minute 23.3.44.
32 FO 371/43995 Algiers 58 to Cairo 26.3.44, FO 875 to Moscow 27.3.44.
33 FO 371/44003 Clutton minute 12.7.44.

CHAPTER 17

1 W.J.M.M. to E.B.
2 FO 371/33124 Howard minute 18.2.42.
3 G.T. papers, record of meeting held by A/D on Bulgarian affairs 23.12.42.
4 G.T. papers, Sitrep no. 1 on Yugoslavia 28.11.42; FO 371/33473 Rendel to Dixon 3.12.42.
5 FO 371/37579 Pearson to Howard 2.2.43.
6 FO 371/33473 Rendel to Dixon 3.12.42.
7 Bulgarska Komunisticheska Partia, *Istoria* (Moscow, 1960), pp. 357–9.
8 *Ibid.*, p. 361.
9 *Ibid.*, p. 361.
10 *Ibid.*, pp. 362–3.
11 *Ibid.*, p. 364.
12 *Ibid.*
13 *Ibid.*, p. 366.
14 FO 371/33119 P.W.E. Directive 1–7.8.42.
15 W.J.M.M. to E.B.
16 FO 371/33119 Dixon minutes of 23.7.42 and 31.8.42.
17 *Ibid.*, Sargent letter to Hollis 11.12.42.
18 FO 371/33119 FO minutes 2.12.42, 23.12.42 R8411/G.
19 FO 371/37155 Rose and Howard minutes of 29.1.43.
20 *Ibid.*, Matsankiev paper 12.1.43.
21 *Ibid.*, Matsankiev paper, 4.5.43.
22 *Ibid.*, Howard to Pearson 17.5.43.
23 *Ibid.*, Boughey to Howard 16.6.43.
24 FO 371/37153 Howard to Boughey 21.6.43.
25 *Ibid.*, Sargent note 11.9.43, Rose minute 13.9.43.
26 FO 371/37153 FO Draft Brief on Bulgaria 27.9.43.
27 PREM 3 79/1 C.O.S. (43) 638 (O) 19.10.43, Air Ministry OZ3572 to Britman Washington 20.10.43.
28 *Ibid.*, AGWAR to ETOUSA FAN 256 24.10.43.
29 *Ibid.*, Moscow 85 SPACE 24.10.43.
30 *Ibid.*, Moscow 108 SPACE 29.10.43.
31 FO 371/37153 Molotov minute 27.10.43.
32 *Ibid.*, Rose minute 10.11.43, Howard minute 17.11.43.
33 FO 371/37161 Rose minute 1.12.43.
34 FO 371/37162 Nichols minute 23.11.43.
35 FO 371/37162 Air Ministry GRAND 254 to Mideast 26.11.43.
36 FO 371/37162 Minutes written at Teheran on GRAND 254.

37 *Ibid.*, Clutton minute 16.12.43.
38 FO 371/37162 FO 1753 to Angora 21.12.43.
39 FO 371/37162 FROZEN 460 P.M. to F.S. 11.12.43.
40 FO 371/37157 Moscow 1641 29.12.43.
41 PREM 3 79/1 FROZEN 283 29.12.43, FROZEN 992 30.12.43, FROZEN 1195 9.1.44.
42 PREM 3 17/1 H.Q. M.A.A.F. ADVANCED A.119 10.1.44.
43 FO 371/37162 Pearson to Nichols 7.11.43 R11675/G.
44 PREM 3 79/1 President to P.M. 463 9.2.44.
45 *Ibid.*
46 *Ibid.*, Eden minute to P.M. P.M./44/60 10.2.44.
47 *Ibid.*, Resident Minister Algiers 230 9.2.44, A.F.H.Q. 49441 to Air Ministry 9.2.44, FO 381/43587 Jadwin to Donovan 7.2.44.
48 *Ibid.*, Eden minute P.M./44/60 10.2.44.
49 FO 371/43587 President to P.M. 465 12.2.44.
50 FO 371/43587 Moscow 475 21.2.44, PREM 3 79/1 President to P.M. 482 26.2.44.
51 FO 371/43587 FO 1664 to Washington 25.2.44.
52 PREM 3 79/1 C.O.S. (W) 1190 4.3.44.
53 *Ibid.*, Cairo 461 9.3.44.
54 FO 371/43588 Howard minute 10.3.44.
55 *Ibid.*, written on telegram by Churchill.
56 PREM 3 79/1 Cairo 349 24.2.44.
57 FO 371/43588 FO 298 to Cairo 1.3.44.
58 *Ibid.*, FO 531 to Moscow 25.2.44.
59 PREM 3 79/1 Eden minute to P.M. P.M./44/117 3.3.44, Churchill minute N 227/4 4.3.44.
60 FO 371/43588 FO 953 to Moscow 31.3.44.
61 FO 371/43589 Angora 790 to FO 23.5.44.
62 FO 371/43289 Broad letters to Macmillan 23.5.44, 25.5.44.
63 Bulgarska Komunisticheska Partia, *Istoria*, p. 370.
64 FO 371/43589 Broad letter to Macmillan 3.6.44.
65 *Ibid.*, Provisional Minutes of 30th FO–S.O.E. meeting 13.6.44.
66 PREM 3 79/2 W.P. (44) 475 27.8.44, C.O.S. (44) 287 (O) 25.8.44, Eden minute P.M./44/598 30.8.44.
67 FO 371/43597 FO 7663 to Washington 29.8.44, PREM 3 79/2 memorandum on Bulgarian armistice 6.10.44.
68 Later Sir John Sterndale-Bennett, K.C.M.G., Head of British M.E. office, Cairo, 1953–5.
69 FO 371/43590 British Embassy aide memoire to U.S. State Dept. 20.8.44.
70 FO 371/43597 Moscow 2225 24.8.44.
71 PREM 3 79/2 W.P. (44) 475 27.8.44.
72 *Ibid.*, W.M. (44) 111 28.8.44.
73 FO 371/43590 Moscow 2259 26.8.44.
74 FO 371/43579 Cairo 2032 30.8.44.
75 PREM 3 79/3 Minister Resident Cairo no. 5 CITIZEN 3.9.44.
76 FO 371/43579 Angora 1509 6.9.44.
77 *Ibid.*, Howard minute 7.9.44.

87 Bulgarska Komunisticheska Partia, *Istoria*, p. 382.
79 FO 371/43581 Last letter to McDermott 27.9.44.
80 PREM 3 79/2 Eden minute to P.M. P.M./44/645 6.10.44.
81 PREM 3 79/4 FO 3585 to Moscow 12.10.44, FO 3650 to Moscow 14.10.44.

CHAPTER 18

1 FO 371/29991 Report on situation in Rumania 9.8.41, FO 371/44002 Masterson report 5.6.44.
2 FO 371/44002 Masterson report 5.6.44.
3 FO 371/33256 Glenconner to Dixon 20.3.42, W.J.M.M. to E.B.
4 See e.g. FO 371/33257 Pearson to Dixon 3.12.42.
5 See e.g. FO 371/33259 P.W.E. Directive 14–21.3.42.
6 FO 371/29995 Reuter, Vichy 7.12.41.
7 FO 371/37386 Draft Brief for S. of S. (Oct 1943).
8 FO 371/33252 Lisbon 5 Saving 5.1.42.
9 FO 371/33256 Glenconner to Dixon 7.1.42, Dixon to Glenconner 16.1.42.
10 FO 371/33261 Dixon minute 22.1.42 FO 406 to Cairo 22.1.42.
11 FO 371/33261 FO 1674 to Washington 14.3.42.
12 FO 371/33256 Aide Memoire 5.6.42.
13 FO 371/33261 Eden letter to Maisky 29.4.42.
14 FO 371/33256 Aide Memoire 5.6.42.
15 *Ibid.*
16 FO 371/33257 Lisbon 23 Saving 4.7.42.
17 *Ibid.*, Eden minute 12.7.42.
18 FO 371/33257 Pearson to Dixon 23.9.42 and 10.10.42.
19 FO 371/33257 Dixon minute 21.10.42, G. M. Wilson minute 22.10.42.
20 FO 371/33257 Pearson to Dixon 28.11.42.
21 *Ibid.*, Pearson to Dixon 3.12.42.
22 FO 371/33262 Southern Dept. letter to Washington Chancery 3.1.43.
23 FO 371/37386 Boxshall to Rose 14.2.43.
24 FO 371/37386 Rose to Boxshall 20.2.43.
25 FO 371/37386 Draft Brief for S. of S. on Rumanian Peace Feelers 28.9.43.
26 FO 371/37386 Howard minute 11.8.43.
27 FO 371/37386 Angora 728 13.4.43, Sargent minute 20.4.43.
28 F.O.R.D. memorandum on Axis-Controlled Europe. Rumanian Peace Moves 10.8.43.
29 FO 371/37386 Angora 1448 9.8.43.
30 FO 371/37386 FO 1109 to Moscow 15.7.43, Moscow 796 23.8.43, FO 1236 to Angora 27.8.43.
31 FO 371/37386 Boxshall to Rose 20.10.43, Draft Brief for S. or S. 28.9.43.
32 *Ibid.*, Howard minute 6.10.43.
33 *Ibid.*, Angora 1786 2.10.43.
34 *Ibid.*, Pearson to Nichols 15.10.43.
35 *Ibid.*, Pearson to Nichols 13.10.43, enclosing Istanbul tel. 12.10.43.
36 *Ibid.*, Pearson to Nichols 14.10.43.

37 FO 371/37396 Nichols to Pearson 16.10.43.
38 *Ibid.*, FO Brief on Rumania 6.10.43.
39 FO 371/37031 Warner minute 29.10.43.
40 FO 371/37031 Record of Moscow Conference 7th meeting 25.10.43.
41 Later Ivor Porter, C.M.G., O.B.E., H.M. Ambassador to Senegal, Guinea, Mali and Mauritania, 1971–3.
42 I.P. to E.B., W.J.M.M. to E.B.
43 FO 371/44000 Talbot Rice to Howard 9.5.44.
44 *Ibid.* See also FO 371/37387 Nichols minute 11.11.43, FO 371/37387 Moscow 1362 19.11.43.
45 FO 371/37387 Pearson letter to Howard 19.11.43, Howard to Pearson 22.11.43.
46 FO 371/37398 Pearson to Howard 19.11.43.
47 FO 371/37387 FO 1981 to Moscow 20.11.43.
48 Later Sir Victor Mallet, G.C.M.G., C.V.O., Ambassador at Rome, 1947–53.
49 FO 371/37387 Stockholm 1010 6.12.43.
50 FO 371/37388 Stockholm 194 Saving 28.12.43.
51 *Ibid.*, Boxshall to Rose 3.1.44.
52 I.P. to E.B.
53 *Ibid.*
54 FO 371/44000 Talbot Rice to Howard 9.5.44, Eden minute P.M./44/341 14.5.44.
55 FO 371/43992 Steel to Nichols 28.12.43.
56 *Ibid.*, Cairo 18 4.1.44, Rose minute 7.1.44, FO 371/44000 Eden minute P.M./44/341 14.5.44.
57 FO 371/43992 FO 266 to Moscow.
58 FO 371/43999 Eden minute P.M./44/301, FO 371/43992 Clark Kerr letter to C.D. 6.2.44.
59 FO 371/43992 Clark Kerr letter to C.D. 6.2.44.
60 FO 371/43992 Boxshall to Howard 22.1.44.
61 *Ibid.*, Boxshall letters to FO of 18.1.44 and 27.1.44 and enclosed reports.
62 *Ibid.*, Cairo 185 of 30.1.44 FO 188 to Cairo 9.2.44.
63 *Ibid.*, C.O.S. (44) 59 (O) 24.2.44, FO 371/43993 W.C.O. to Clutton 2.3.44.
64 FO 371/43993 FO 756 to Moscow 18.3.44.
65 FO 371/43993 Cairo 614 17.3.44.
66 FO 371/43994 Moscow 790 23.3.44.
67 *Ibid.*, Cairo 566 22.3.44.
68 *Ibid.*
69 W.J.M.M. to E.B.
70 FO 371/43999 Molotov letters to Clark Kerr 25.3.44, 27.3.44.
71 FO 371/43984 Millard to Colville 2.4.44, FO 1067 to Cairo 2.4.44.
72 PREM 3 374/13A Eden minute P.M./44/148 13.3.44.
73 PREM 3 374/13A W.M. (44) 47 Confidential Annex 11.4.44.
74 FO 371/43999 Boxshall to Rose 5.5.44.
75 *Ibid.*, Extracts from messages Molotov to Churchill 22.4.44, Churchill to Molotov 23.4.44.
76 FO 371/43999 Cairo 1036 22.4.44.

77 FO 371/43999 Moscow 1072 26.4.44, Boxshall to Sargent 29.4.44, Cairo 1108 29.4.44.
78 *Ibid.*, FO 1310 to Moscow 30.4.44.
79 Churchill, *The Second World War*, VI 388.
80 FO 371/43999 Churchill draft message 1.5.44.
81 *Ibid.*, Eden minute P.M./44/301 1.5.44, FO 1328 to Moscow 2.5.44.
82 FO 371/44002 Cadogan minute 29.6.44 Eden minute 1.7.44.
83 FO 371/44001 P.M.'s Personal Minute no. M 647/4 28.5.44.
84 CAB 65 (46) W.M. (44) 63 11.5.44.
85 FO 371/44000 Eden minute P.M./44/341 14.5.44.
86 FO 371/37387 Moscow 1362 19.11.43 FO 371/43992 Rose minute 6.1.44.
87 CAB 65/46 W.M. (41) 63 11.5.44.
88 Ion Gheorghe, *Rumäniens Weg zum Satelliten-Staat*, p. 431. See also Ghiţa Ionescu, *Communism in Rumania*, pp. 74–5.
89 FO 371/44000 Cairo 1334 26.5.44.
90 *Ibid.*, Rose minute 28.5.44.
91 FO 371/43999 Moscow 1142 2.5.44.
92 FO 371/44000 Eden despatch to Clark Kerr R7214/9/G 5.5.44.
93 FO 371/44001 Clark Kerr letter to Molotov 19.5.44.
94 FO 371/44001 Clark Kerr letter to Molotov 29.5.44.
95 FO 371/44000 Sargent minute 28.5.44.
96 FO 371/44002 Reed minute 19.6.44.
97 FO 371/44000 Selborne letter to Eden 19.5.44.
98 I.P. to E.B., W.J.M.M. to E.B.
99 FO 371/44002 Boxshall to Dew, Reed minute 5.7.44.
100 FO 371/44000 Cairo 1333 26.5.44.
101 FO 371/44000 Cairo 1341 26.5.44.
102 FO 371/44000 FO 1896 to Cairo 2.6.44.
103 FO 371/44000 Cairo 1341 26.5.44.
104 Anescu, Bantea, Cupşa, *Participation of the Romanian Army in the Anti-Hitlerite War*, p. 155.
105 FO 371/44002 Steel to Dew 24.6.44.
106 FO 371/44001 Boxshall to Reed 12.6.44.
107 FO 371/44001 14.6.44.
108 FO 371/44002 Cairo 1542 27.6.44.
109 *Ibid.*
110 FO 371/44005 Boxshall to Reed 9.8.44.
111 E.g. FO 371/44004 Moscow 2049 5.8.44.
112 FO 371/44003 Cairo 1614 8.7.44.
113 Gheorghe, pp. 398–9.
114 FO 371/44005 Angora 1372 21.8.44.
115 FO 371/44004 Boxshall to Reed 5.8.44.
116 FO 371/44005 Cairo 1947 23.8.44.
117 *Ibid.*, Cairo 67 to Caserta 24.8.44.
118 I.P. to E.B.
119 *Ibid.*
120 Transcript of tape recording in possession of I.P.
121 FO 371/44005 Boxshall to Reed 27.8.44, I.P. to E.B.

122 See p. 228 above.
123 I.P. to E.B.
124 FO 371/44005 Moscow 2234 24.8.44.
125 FO 371/44005 Moscow 2235 25.8.44.
126 PREM 3 374/13A Cairo to Caserta 25.8.44.
127 *Ibid.*, A.F.H.Q. to ETOUSA AGWAR NAF 766 27.8.44.
128 *Ibid.*, C.A.S. to P.M. 31.8.44
129 *Ibid.*, Hollis to P.M. 2.9.44.
130 *Ibid.*, A.M.S.S.O. to J.S.M. Washington 4.9.44.
131 FO 371/44006 F.O. 3110 to Cairo 4.9.44.
132 *Ibid.*, FO 732 to Caserta 6.9.44.
133 *Ibid.*, Howard minute 29.8.44.
134 PREM 3 374/13A P.M.'s Personal Minute M.1070/4.
135 *Ibid.*, Bucharest 247 1.12.44.
136 *Ibid.*, Eden minute P.M./44/754 9.12.44.
137 *Ibid.*, Hollis minute 18.1.45.
138 *Ibid.*, P.M.'s Personal Minute no. M.1207/4 11.12.44.
139 *Ibid.*, Draft tel. to H.M. Ambassador Moscow, initialled W.S.C. 23.2.45.

CHAPTER 19

1 FO 371/39624 Broad despatch for Macmillan 17.9.44.
2 General L. Veress de Dalnok to E.B.
3 FO 371/30966 O'Malley to Sir Alfred Zimmern 26.1.43.
4 Later Sir Frank Roberts, G.C.M.G., G.C.V.O., H.M. Ambassador in Bonn, 1963–8.
5 Dr C. A. Macartney, Professor of International Relations, Edinburgh, 1951–7.
6 FO 371/30965 Ripka letter to Nichols 1.7.42, R. Murray minute 25.7.42.
7 FO 371/30965 Draft Plan for Hungary 3.2.42.
8 FO 371/30965 Lockhart minute 3.8.42.
9 FO 371/34505 Roberts minute 5.6.43.
10 FO 371/34502 P.R.B. Stockholm Hungary no. 12 8.2.43.
11 FO 371/34496 P.R.B. Stockholm Hungary no. 18 9.3.43.
12 C. A. Macartney, *October the Fifteenth*, II 141; FO 371/34495 Chancery Washington to Central Department 19.3.43.
13 Macartney, p. 48.
14 FO 371/34497 P.R.B. Stockholm Hungary no. 47 18.5.43.
15 FO 371/34447 Eden despatch to Washington and Moscow 10.3.43.
16 FO 371/34447 FO 223 to Moscow 13.3.43.
17 FO 371/34448 Angora Chancery to Central Department 20.3.43.
18 FO 371/34497 P.R.B. Stockholm Hungary no. 44 13.5.44.
19 FO 371/34497 P.R.B. Stockholm Hungary no. 42 6.5.44.
20 *Ibid.*, P.R.B. Stockholm no. 43 9.5.43.
21 General L. Veress to E.B.
22 FO 371/34505 W.P. (43) 240 12.6.43.
23 FO 371/34497 P.R.B. Stockholm Hungary no. 44 13.5.44.
24 FO 371/34505 W.P. (43) 240 12.6.43.

25 *Ibid.*
26 FO 371/34495 Böhm letter 27.5.43.
27 FO 371/34495 FO 657 to Moscow 4.6.43.
28 FO 371/34449 Molotov letter 7.6.43.
29 *Ibid.*
30 FO 371/34506 Moscow 1084 8.10.43.
31 *Ibid.*, Moscow 1262 7.12.43.
32 FO 371/34499 Roberts minute 12.12.43.
33 FO 371/39264 Broad letter 15.7.44 and enclosed report.
34 *Ibid.*
35 FO 371/34451 Cadogan letter to Sir R. Campbell Lisbon 6.10.43.
36 Veress to E.B., FO 371/39264 Broad letter and enclosure 15.7.44.
37 FO 371/34450 WELFARE 261 20.8.43, CONCRETE 507 23.8.43.
38 FO 371/34450 Moscow 855 1.9.43.
39 FO 371/34495 Moscow 905 7.9.43.
40 FO 371/34451 Roberts minute 7.9.43.
41 FO 371/34451 WELFARE 666 8.9.43.
42 *Ibid.*, FO 1295 to Moscow 9.9.43.
43 From the available official papers it is not clear whether it was Knatchbull-Hugessen or Sterndale-Bennett who presented the British reply, but Veress himself is quite clear that it was Knatchbull-Hugessen, whom he subsequently met again in London [E.B.].
44 FO 371/34451 CONCRETE 781 7.9.43 WELFARE 66 8.9.43 CONCRETE 805 9.9.43.
45 *Ibid.*, Perkins letter to Roberts 10.9.43 enclosing telegram from Y.P. to Cadogan.
46 *Ibid.*, Washington 4144 15.9.43.
47 *Ibid.*, Moscow 982 20.9.43.
48 Veress to E.B.
49 FO 371/34451 Perkins to Roberts 30.9.43.
50 FO 371/34452 Perkins to Roberts 27.10.43.
51 FO 371/34452 Threlfall to Roberts 23.11.43.
52 *Ibid.*, Wheeler Bennett minute 1.10.43.
53 FO 371/34452 Perkins to Roberts 27.10.43, enclosing Veress letter, 9.10.43.
54 FO 371/34452 Perkins to Roberts 29.10.43.
55 Macartney, p. 185; FO 371/34499 Stockholm 894 25.10.43.
56 FO 371/34452 Roberts minute 30.10.43.
57 *Ibid.*, Moscow Foreign Ministers' Conference Item 13C 13324/155/G.
58 Later Sir Geoffrey Harrison, K.C.M.G., Ambassador at Moscow, 1965-8.
59 FO 371/34452 Harrison minute to Strang 27.10.43.
60 *Ibid.*, Harrison minute 13.11.43.
61 *Ibid.*, Roberts minute 16.11.43, Eden minute 20.11.43.
62 FO 371/34453 Threlfall to Roberts 26.11.43.
63 *Ibid.*, Threlfall to Roberts 2.12.43.
64 *Ibid.*
65 FO 371/39264 Broad letter 15.7.44 and enclosed report.
66 FO 371/39251 Roberts minute 26.12.43.

67 *Ibid.*, Allen minute 23.12.43.
68 *Ibid.*, Roberts minute 26.12.43, Eden minute 28.12.43.
69 W.J.M.M. to E.B., Basil Davidson, *Partisan Picture, passim.*
70 FO 371/39251 Threlfall to Roberts 31.12.43.
71 FO 371/39264 Broad letter 15.7.44.
72 *Ibid.*
73 FO 371/39264 P.R.B. Stockholm Hungary no. 55.2.7.44.
74 FO 371/39252 Threlfall to Roberts 3.3.44, Miklos Szinai and Laszlo Szucs, *The Confidential Papers of Admiral Horthy*, pp. 267-9.
75 FO 371/39252 Roberts minute 15.2.44.
76 *Ibid.*, Threlfall to Roberts 18.2.44, 3.3.44.
77 *Ibid.*, Roberts minute 4.3.44.
78 *Ibid.*, Harvey letter to C.O.S. 13.3.44.
79 *Ibid.*, C.O.S. (44) 252 (O) 15.3.44.
80 Szinai and Szucs, p. 285.
81 Szinai and Szucs, p. 408.
82 FO 371/39264 Broad letter 15.7.44 and enclosed report.
83 FO 371/34498 A. W. G. Randell minute 14.10.43, Allen minute 28.10.43.
84 FO 371/39252 FO minute 16.2.44.
85 Szinai and Szucs, p. 296.
86 PREM 3 226/3 Millard letter to Martin with enclosure 14.6.45
87 Macartney, pp. 306-7, FO 371/39253 Madrid 1290 30.8.44.
88 Veress to E.B.
89 FO 371/39264 Broad letter 15.7.44.
90 *Ibid.*, Allen minute 29.7.44.
91 Veress to E.B.
92 FO 371/39264 Allen minute 29.7.44.
93 FO 371/39254 Makins to Roberts and enclosure 25.9.44, record of conversation with S.A.C. Caserta 23.9.44.
94 PREM 3 226/2 Moscow 2706 6.10.44.
95 *Ibid.*, Millard to Martin and enclosure 14.6.45.
96 FO 371/39264 Berne 3610 2.8.44.
97 PREM 3 226/2 Millard to Martin and enclosure 14.6.45.
98 FO 371/39264 Bari 295 to Algiers 17.7.44.
99 W.J.M.M. to E.B.
100 Sweet-Escott, pp. 203-4, W.J.M.M. to E.B.
101 W.J.M.M. to E.B.
102 FO 371/39051 Draft Cabinet paper by S. of S. 7.7.44 W.P. (44) 436 9.8.44.
103 FO 371/39264 Madrid 1142 27.7.44.
104 *Ibid.*, Roberts minute 1.8.44.
105 FO 371/39264 Harvey minute 2.8.44, Eden minute 6.8.44.
106 FO 371/39253 Perkins to Roberts 2.9.44.
107 FO 371/39254 Makins to Roberts 25.9.44.
108 See e.g. Macartney, p. 404.
109 FO 371/39253 Berne 4094 29.8.44.
110 *Ibid.*, Eden minute 30.8.44, FO 2602 to Moscow 1.9.44, FO 525 to Bari 9.9.44.

111 PREM 3 226/2 W.P. (44) 499 4.9.44.

112 PREM 3 226/2 Caserta 393 23.9.44.

113 FO 371/39254 Hood minute 25.9.44, FO 3172 to Moscow, 8453 to Washington 24.9.44.

114 *Ibid.*, Washington 5232 25.9.44.

115 *Ibid.*, Moscow 2639 2.10.44.

116 *Ibid.*, Roberts minute 5.10.44.

117 PREM 3 226/2 Moscow 2705 6.10.44.

118 FO 371/39254 Moscow 163 CITIZEN 11.10.44.

119 PREM 3 226/2 FO 3434 to Moscow 7.10.44.

120 *Ibid.*, Moscow 165 CITIZEN 11.10.44.

121 FO 371/43590 S.O.E. Istanbul 23.8.44.

122 General Veress to E.B.

123 For a detailed and fascinating account of the events of this day, see Macartney, pp. 391–443.

124 PREM 3 226/3 Millard letter to Martin and enclosure 14.6.45.

125 FO 371/39267 Soviet Monitor 10.11.44.

126 *Ibid.*, Moscow 3393 14.11.44.

127 *Ibid.*, Roberts minute 16.11.44.

128 *Ibid.*, Memorandum from Soviet Ambassador 21.12.44.

129 *Ibid.*, FO 1416 to Madrid 31.12.44.

CHAPTER 20

1 Auty and Clogg, ed., *British Policy Towards Wartime Resistance in Yugoslavia and Greece*, p. 144.

2 W.J.M.M. to E.B.

Select Bibliography

GENERAL

Auty, Phyllis, and Richard Clogg (eds), *British Policy towards Wartime Resistance in Yugoslavia and Greece* (Macmillan, 1975).

Churchill, Winston S., *The Second World War*, vols III, V, VI (Cassell, 1948–54).

Dalton, Hugh, *The Fateful Years* (Frederick Muller, 1957).

Dalton Papers (held by the Library of the London School of Economics).

Dilkes, David, *The Diaries of Sir Alexander Cadogan 1938–1945* (Cassell, 1971).

Documents of German Foreign Policy, Series D, vol. XI (H.M.S.O., 1956–).

Eden, Anthony (Earl of Avon), *Memoirs: The Reckoning* (Cassell, 1965).

History of the Second World War: Sir Llewellyn Woodward, *British Foreign Policy in the Second World War*, vols II and III (H.M.S.O., 1971).

——, Howard, Michael, *Grand Strategy*, vol. IV (H.M.S.O., 1972).

——, Ehrman, John, *Grand Strategy*, vol. V (H.M.S.O., 1956).

——, Medlicott, W. N., *The Economic Blockade* (H.M.S.O., 1952).

Howard, Michael, *The Mediterranean Strategy in the Second World War* (Weidenfeld and Nicolson, 1968).

Nazi–Soviet Relations (Washington: Department of State, 1948).

Seton-Watson, Hugh, *The East European Revolution* (Methuen, 1955, rev. ed., 1957).

Sweet-Escott, Bickham, *Baker Street Irregular* (Methuen, 1965).

Van Creveld, Martin, *Hitler's Strategy 1940–1941 – The Balkan Clue* (Cambridge University Press, 1973).

ALBANIA

Amery, Julian, *Approach March* (Hutchinson, 1973).

——, *Sons of the Eagle* (Macmillan, 1948).

Davies, 'Trotsky', *Illyrian Adventure* (Bodley Head, 1952).

Dedijer, Vladimir, *Jugoslovensko-Albanski Odnosi (1939–1948)* (Belgrade: Borba, 1949).

Histoire du Parti du Travail d'Albanie (Tirana: Institut des Etudes Marxistes–Leninistes, 1971).

Vukmanović-Tempo, Svetozar, *Revolucija koja Teče–Memoari* (Belgrade: Kommunist, 1971).

BULGARIA

Bulgarska Komunisticheska Partia, *Istoria Bulgarskoi Komunistich-eskoi Partii* (Moscow: Gosudarstvennoe Izdatelstvo Politicheskoi Literatury, 1960) [Russian translation of Bulgarian edition of 1959].
Kiosev, Dino G., *Borbite na Makedonskija Narod za Osvobozhdenie* (Sofia: Narodna Prosveta, 1950).
Rendel, Sir George, *The Sword and the Olive* (John Murray, 1957).

GREECE

Hamson, Denys, *We fell among Greeks* (Cape, 1946).
Kousoulas, D. George, *Revolution and Defeat, the Story of the Greek Communist Party* (Oxford University Press, 1965).
Leeper, Sir Reginald, *When Greek meets Greek* (Chatto & Windus, 1950).
McNeill, William H., *The Greek Dilemma* (Gollancz, 1947).
Myers, E. C. W., *Greek Entanglement* (Rupert Hart-Davis, 1955).
Woodhouse, C. M., *Apple of Discord* (Hutchinson, 1948).

HUNGARY

Macartney, C. A., *October Fifteenth*, vols i and ii (Edinburgh, 1961).
Szinai, Miklós, and László Szúcs (prepared by), *The Confidential Papers of Admiral Horthy* (Budapest: Corvina Press, 1965).

MACEDONIA

Andonovki, Hristo, *Vistinata za Egejska Makedonia* (Skopje: Misla, 1971).
Arhiv na Makedonja, *Dokument za Uchestvoto na Makedonskiot Narod od Egejskiot Del na Makedonja vo Antifashistichkata Vojna 1941–1945 Godina* (Skopje, 1971).
Barker, Elisabeth, *Macedonia – its Place in Balkan Power Politics* (Royal Institute of International Affairs, 1950).
Cašule, Vangia (ed.), *From Recognition to Repudiation [Bulgarian Attitudes on the Macedonian Question]* (Skopje: Kultura, 1972).
Kiosev, Dino G., *Borbite na Makedonskija Narod za Osvobozhdenie* (Sofia: Narodna Prosveta, 1950).
Kofos, Evangelos, *Nationalism and Communism in Macedonia* (Salonika: Institute for Balkan Studies, 1964).
Palmer, Stephen E., Jr, and Robert R. King, *Yugoslav Communism and the Macedonian Question* (Archon Books, 1971).
Vukmanović-Tempo, Svetozar, *Revolucija koja Teče–Memoari* (Belgrade: Kommunist, 1974).
Mitrev, Dimitar, *La Macédoine Pirine* (Skopje: Kultura, 1962).

RUMANIA

Anescu, Col. Vasile, Col. Eugen Bantea and Col. Ion Cupşa, *Partici-*

pation of the Romanian Army in the Anti-Hitlerite War (Bucharest: Military Publishing House, 1966).

Gheorghe, Ion, *Rumäniens Weg zum Satelliten-Staat* (Heidelberg: Kurt Vowinckel Verlag, 1952).

Ionescu, Ghiţa, *Communism in Rumania 1944–1962* (Oxford University Press, 1964).

YUGOSLAVIA

Auty, Phyllis, *Tito* (Longman, 1970).

Clissold, Stephen, *Whirlwind* (Cresset Press, 1949).

Davidson, Basil, *Partisan Picture* (Bedford Books, 1946).

Deakin, F. W., *The Embattled Mountain* (Oxford University Press, 1971).

Dedijer, Vladimir, *Tito Speaks* (Weidenfeld and Nicolson, 1953).

——, *With Tito through the War* (Alexander Hamilton, 1951).

Djilas, Milovan, *Conversations with Stalin* (Rupert Hart-Davis, 1962).

——, *Memoir of a Revolutionary* (New York: Harcourt Brace Jovanovich, 1973).

Hoptner, J. B., *Yugoslavia in Crisis, 1934–1941* (Columbia University Press, 1962).

Maček, Vladko, *In the Struggle for Freedom* (New York: Robert Spellman and Sons, 1957).

Maclean, Fitzroy, *Eastern Approaches* (Cape, 1949).

——, *Disputed Barricade* (Cape, 1957).

Pavlowitch, Stevan K., *Yugoslavia* (Benn, 1971).

Peter II, King, *A King's Heritage* (Cassell, 1955).

Pribitchévitch, Svetozar, *La Dictature du Roi Alexandre* (Pierre Bossuet, 1933).

Roberts, Walter R., *Tito, Mihailović and the Allies 1941–1945* (Rutgers University Press, 1973).

Rootham, Jasper, *Miss Fire* (Chatto, 1946).

Vukmanović-Tempo, Svetozar, *Revolucija koja Teče–Memoari* (Belgrade: Kommunist, 1971).

Index